Public Sector Accounting and Control

N. W. Marsland, FCA, IPFA

LONGMAN
London and New York

First published 1981
Second impression 1985

All rights reserved; no part of this publication may be reproduced, stored in a retrieval system, or transmitted in any form or by any means, electronic, mechanical, photocopying, recording or otherwise, without the prior written permission of the Publishers.

© 1981 Copyright Polytech Publishers Ltd.

Set in 10 pt Times series
Produced by Longman Group (FE) Ltd
Printed in Hong Kong

Foreword

I have attempted in this book to give an outline, in as simple a manner as possible, of the legal provisions, financial arrangements, auditing practices, accounting procedures and costing methods applicable to public authorities. For reasons of time and space, there are omissions and abbreviations in regard to many topics, and, I am sure, ambiguities arising mainly from the need to simplify. I apologise for these beforehand.

The fullest treatment has, for various reasons, been given to local authorities, but the reader is asked to remember that the text dealing with local government contains many topics of a nature common to all public bodies — one thinks of auditing techniques as an obvious example.

Notwithstanding the limits imposed upon my coverage of aspects of the subject, it is my hope that students will derive benefit from this work in an area where study is not assisted by the content being continually affected by Government action in changing the underlying law.

This book is intended for students preparing for the Business Education Council (BEC) option modules for Accounting Technicians "Public Sector Accounting and Audit" and "Public Sector Organisation and Financial Practice" at the National Award level. It can also be of use to students seeking to pass the examinations of the Chartered Institute of Public Finance and Accountancy, and, indeed, to anyone making a study of local administrations and central departments generally.

Contents

Chapter

1	The Organisations of the Public Sector	1
2	A Brief History of Local Government	13
3	The Legal Basis of Local Government	20
4	Internal Structure and Organisation of Local Authorities	49
5	Sources of Income of Local Authorities	67
6	Financial Control of Local Authorities	90
7	The External Audit of Local Authorities in England and Wales	131
8	Internal Auditing in Local Authorities	143
9	Water Authorities	178
10	Passenger Transport Executives	188
11	Development Corporations for New Towns	196
12	Health Authorities	203
13	The Gas Supply Industry	222
14	The Electricity Supply Industry	229
15	The Central Departments of the State	238
16	Public Corporations	254

Appendix

I	Examples of Internal Control Procedures	276
II	Examples of Costing Methods applicable to Public Authorities	281
III	Examples of Audit Programmes applicable to Public Authorities	288
IV	Examples of Internal Control Questionnaires	304
V	Examples of Flow Charts of Internal Control Procedures	311

Suggestions for Further Study and Reading 321
Index 322

Chapter 1

The Organisations of the Public Sector

Introduction

The acceptance of a need for some sort of central authority, wielded by what is nowadays generally described as "the State", grew in the beginning out of the desire of the inhabitants of a locality or tribal area, and eventually, of a region or country, for a measure of protection for themselves and their goods and property. The exercise of this authority was intended to give them a reasonable prospect of living ordered, and possibly happy, lives, and, at the same time, create conditions under which commerce and trade would be encouraged and prosperity enjoyed. The protection received from the rudimentary State derived its strength from the saying that "unity is strength", and each individual who enjoyed its benefits also accepted restrictions upon his or her time, actions and wealth in return. One can, however, envisage that a single family or small tribe was often eager to exchange an uncertain life of freedom spent in fighting a savage land and savager men for membership of a sheltered community despite the duties which such a relationship entailed.

The initial form taken by the State was a matter of personal leadership and was embodied in a local chief or king. It was designed to provide the minimum level of service needed to safeguard its citizens against unrest and violence arising within its borders and attacks coming from outside. It carried out these duties by providing a framework for making and enforcing law, together with a system for raising and maintaining an army or militia composed of those able-bodied men who were capable of bearing arms. Security was thus provided against internal and external enemies, and the atmosphere under which commerce could flourish was preserved in return for money, goods and services provided by the populace. It was traditional in the system for the leader, chief or king to be advised by a council of elders whose age and experience implied a measure of acquired wisdom in statecraft.

In the course of the centuries since those distant times, however, there has been a world-wide development of society whose needs, particularly when one considers the present position in this country, have created a demand for services which involves the State to an extent which goes far beyond its original purposes. The way in which this demand has expanded and diversified has been gradual, each step appearing to lead inevitably and logically to the next, as society became more complex — roads began by being of a military nature so that the army could move quickly across the country, later they were built for trade and communications, the enforcement of law finally required a full-time police force, the formation of towns led to the observation of minimum sanitary rules for the avoidance of disease and its damage to the health of the people. In addition, the expansion of demand for services has been affected by new inventions and advances in technology which were, of course, unknown in more primitive times — electricity and gas are obvious examples.

The extent to which the central Government (i.e. the State) is now involved in providing services and undertaking activities of an industrial or commercial nature has caused it to adopt administrative arrangements which are much more elaborate than those which were found to be adequate in the days when it merely maintained law and order. The State now acts through a highly developed system of central departments which are accompanied by a wide assortment of public sector organisations operating at local, regional and national levels.

One sees that needs which, at the start, were catered for, more or less adequately, according to the attitudes and standards then ruling, by charities and similar organisations (because rendering the service was unlikely to bring a profit except of a spiritual nature) and, in other cases, by private enterprise (because a profit was possible and the person carrying out the service could make a living), have become areas considered appropriate for governmental action. The modern State thus acts via an array of public bodies whose functions include local government, personal health, water, gas and electricity supply, passenger transport, the building of new towns, etc. — all of which are in themselves collections of various services. The government also acts, of course, through its central departments which are responsible for such matters as the keeping of the Queen's Peace, defence, foreign relations, and the general supervision of the public sector bodies. Finally, one must mention the more individualistic organisations which operate such services as the post and telephones, coal mining, railways, canals, radio and television broadcasting, each of which having followed its own particular path of development under varying degrees of central control.

The remainder of this introductory chapter is now to be devoted to a general indication of the principal areas of control which are of interest to a student of law and finance in relation to the public sector bodies.

Legal Status and Administrative Arrangements
Parliament has developed a legal institution or device known as a "public or statutory corporation" which is used as a general format for the public sector bodies, whilst allowing for a great degree of variation in individual cases. Each body is termed a "creature of statute" which means, in effect that its powers and duties (as a public corporation) are restricted to those which Parliament has seen fit to give to it, and, furthermore, each is given the status of a legal person, distinct from the members and officers composing it, with the power to contract and otherwise carry out its allotted

duties. (As a matter of interest, the central government departments are taken together under the legal entity of the Crown.)

The precise nature of the powers, duties and internal structure of each public body and central department is the result of many inter-acting factors. These factors include the nature and history of the service (whether it is social or commercial), the sources of income and the basis on which charges are made (whether customers pay for work done or goods or services received, users pay a compulsory levy, or subsidies come from the government), the presence or absence of monopoly (whether it is illegal for a private person to carry on the activity or provide the service), the need to plan or finance on a national scale (whether economies of scale are realisable in respect of operation and management), the intentions, attitudes and political doctrines of the government in power at the time the body was first formed or re-organised (whether it is to be a central department, statutory corporation, charter corporation or, on occasion, a limited company), and the degree of public participation considered appropriate (whether members of the body are elected or appointed, whether user or consumer councils are formed, whether financial accounts and documents are open to inspection, etc.). An important element in central control is the power of the Minister who has been made responsible to Parliament for supervising the organisation's activities, to issue directions on its general policies or to interfere in its everyday activities – this power varies with regard to the different bodies, and has its effect upon the individual structures.

It would be a matter of general truth to say that the effect of the points made in the preceding paragraph together with the measure of individual discretion given to bodies regarding the detail of their administrative set-up means that every public sector organisation has its own unique pattern of procedures which, nevertheless, observe the requirements of the laws which govern their operations. But matters of detail apart, one can discern a number of measures which are common to most kinds of public authority and nationalised undertaking, the most important of which being the sovereignty of Parliament which has the power to create, dissolve and alter the role of any of its subordinate institutions.

Financial Control

Financial control, which might be called, when it comes down to essentials, the proper use of money and moneysworth, is a vital ingredient to the successful operation of every kind of enterprise. The managers of any undertaking are involved in a continuous attempt to convert the funds at their disposal into a mix of resources – salaries and wages for labour, materials for stock in trade, machinery and vehicles for fixed assets, rent for accommodation, gas, electricity and oil for fuel and power – which will enable them to realise the undertaking's objectives in the best possible way as they see it. A commercial firm is regarded as having a measure of its efficiency always ready to hand and this is expressed directly in terms of money as the firm can try to maximise profits or, at least, minimise losses where trading conditions are adverse. But it must be remembered that the lack of return on the resources invested ultimately means the disappearance of the business in question. In the same way, the more commercially-orientated public authorities (e.g. gas, electricity, transport, etc.) have that same monetary test of efficiency, though the results of failure are less drastic and inevitable than in commerce, but they are nevertheless affected by the need to have regard to social, political and national economic factors in their decision-making to a greater extent than is the case with a private firm, and this reduces the role played by the profit motive. Non-commercial public sector bodies have even greater difficulties in assessing their level of success in performance. This is because, in addition to the cash flows involved, their activities also affect the happiness, welfare and life style of people and it is thus well nigh impossible to evaluate them in terms of money. Nevertheless, attempts are made to develop techniques of "cost-benefit analysis" which are used to arrive at some conclusions on the values of the costs incurred and the benefits arising from individual schemes.

Because of the difficulty of assessing results in most parts of the public sector, the public nature of the funds being used, the scale of the operations and the probable absence of competition, it is felt that the need for effective financial control is of the greatest importance in assuring the optimal use of resources. It is also well to remember, particularly in relation to public bodies, that one cannot regard financial control as originating only from within an organisation. Controls also operate from outside — the external audit is one example, as is the impact of public opinion in the form of complaints and protests.

Internal Control

A system of internal control can be defined as those measures which the managers take in order to carry out their duty of providing an orderly framework within which the organisation can function smoothly.

These measures should include rules to ensure that: —
(a) the assets belonging to the body are adequately protected from being lost, stolen, damaged wilfully or mis-used,
(b) reliable financial information is given by the records kept so that there is a basis of accurate facts for correct decision-taking,
(c) decisions are only arrived at after there has been proper discussion, without the organisation being committed prematurely to any line of action,
(d) once a decision has been taken and action authorised, it must be carried out without unnecessary delay.

To implement the above measures, there needs to be an internal control system with at least the following features: —
(a) a plan of the organisation showing the line of command from the top rank to the lowest levels, and for each post on the ladder, its title or

designation, the name of the officer who occupies it, the duties and area of responsibility involved, the superior (or superiors) from whom orders are taken and to whom reports are made, and the subordinates to whom instructions are given. The plan is supported by detailed job descriptions and provisions aimed at maintaining an effectual management, e.g. procedures for the recruitment, training, promotion, retirement or dismissal of staff. Each employee must know his role in the organisation and be able to fulfil it.

(b) detailed procedures for initiating, authorising, carrying through and recording transactions, and for the safe custody of assets acquired in the course of business. These procedures must comply with the principles of internal check which call for these responsibilities to be divided among the staff in respect of any one transaction.

(c) systems for converting the records of transactions into data which is usable as a basis for enlightened decision-making, together with arrangements for providing standards or targets against which to measure the actual results and highlight areas of concern.

(d) mechanisms for the investigation of errors and weaknesses which are revealed in operating the above systems. These investigations should be, as far as possible, an integral and automatic part of the scheme, so that slackness does not lead to any possible improvement being overlooked.

External Control

Public sector authorities are, as a general rule, much more susceptible than commercial firms to pressure from factors which operate from outside their own organisation. This in no way denies the need of a business to satisfy its customers in order to ensure its continued existence, but public authorities are subject to intervention from the general public on a far greater variety of subjects. Public opinion in the form of complaints by individuals or groups can influence the decisions, actions and management procedures of both appointed and elected bodies. Changes in the voters' electoral preferences, both in central and local government, can alter the political balance of the membership and lead to changes in policies. There are officials appointed by the central government (such as Commissioners for Local Administration or Ombudsmen) or by individual organisations (such as public relations officers) whose duties are to receive complaints and to undertake enquiries as to their validity.

Statutes, regulations and orders passed by Parliament, and the case law which is the result of the courts' interpretation of their effect forces all the organisations in the land to observe legal requirements in their actions, but, here again, the public sector is subjected to a more stringent control than private businesses because public money is involved and for other reasons already mentioned.

Linked with the legal requirements, there are financial factors which affect the decisions and actions of organisations. For instance, public bodies have to present their accounts duly audited in a statutory or recommended form in order to obtain government subsidies, recharge the costs of joint schemes, etc. and, of course the audit itself is one form of external control.

External Audit Arrangements

Every public sector organisation is required by law to submit its financial accounts to an external auditor. The auditor is a person qualified in accountancy and trained in auditing who is independent of the body whose accounts he audits and who can therefore be relied upon to act professionally and express opinions which are both informed and impartial.

Though the detailed legal provisions vary for the different forms of publicly-owned enterprise, the external auditor has a general duty to protect the interests of the public against the mis-use or mis-appropriation of public funds. The wide range of organisational types encountered in the public sector means that by "the public" one can denote taxpayers, ratepayers, local government electors, consumers of gas, electricity and water, and users in the case of other services.

The auditor carries out his commission by an examination and assessment of the accounts and financial position of the organisation, followed by a report containing his findings which is published in the manner prescribed by the applicable ruling statute. He is assisted throughout by being given such statutory powers as are necessary for the adequate completion of his task.

In addition to defending the public interest, the external audit also gives a release to the management of the public body in respect of the period to which the accounts relate. A favourable report indicates that the large sums usually involved have been properly handled and the matter is now closed.

Comparison with the arrangements for the external audit of commercial firms shows that the legal provisions controlling public sector external audits call for increasing stringency as the nature of the organisation varies from rendering a service which is paid for by the users, to the provision of services supported by compulsory levies on a section of the public. Parliament reasons that an undertaking linked directly with its customers is under greater pressure to operate efficiently and to control costs more than one where payment for the service and its enjoyment are divorced.

The Nature and Objectives of Internal Audit

Any business which has developed beyond the one-man self-employed stage faces the problem of reduction in control because the owner is required to rely on his staff instead of doing everything himself. The larger the business grows, the smaller becomes the involvement of the man or men at the top in the actual operations. Delegation of duties is unavoidable and the owner is forced to introduce ways of making sure that his employees carry out their duties in the way he wants. In other words, a large-scale organisation needs an internal control system to regulate its operations, but more importantly, in the present context, it needs a method of ensuring that the internal control is operating as it should, and even of improving it by reviewing procedures and removing weaknesses.

This arrangement for the review of internal control usually takes the form of internal audit. Internal audit duties can be carried out by administrative staff as part of their duties or, more efficiently in the long run, be allotted to a staff who are completely involved in review work. These members of staff are therefore employed solely to see that the administrative control procedures fulfil their purposes adequately, are being constantly tested for possible improvement, and, very importantly, being applied properly so as to create ordered work conditions and to provide accurate records for enlightened decision-taking.

Unlike the external auditor, the internal auditors are a part of management and have the responsibility of reporting to it. They must, however, have a measure of independence to enable them to enquire, assess and report effectively and objectively – the higher the level of management they report to, the better. Ideally, they should be dissociated from actual operation of the controls they review, but complete disentanglement from executive functions is difficult in real situations.

Thus, as the scale of operations of an undertaking grows larger, so does the need for, and the occurrence of internal audit. Public sector organisations, because of their size and their use of public funds, almost invariably employ internal auditors, (in many cases, they are required by law to do so), whose duty it is to promote measures for the security of assets, for the operation, review and improvement of sound financial control and, with increasing emphasis, for the best use of resources in the public interest.

Directors of limited companies are under no statutory duty to employ an internal audit staff, but failure to do so might lead to criticism by the shareholders in the event of a large-scale fraud being discovered.

The Inter-relationship between External and Internal Audit

Internal audit is, by nature, a continuous audit, where the staff check current activities and records in a planned manner throughout the year. The external audit was traditionally a completed audit which meant that the examination was concentrated into a relatively short period beginning at, or after, the end of the financial period involved. In recent years, however, the external auditor has come to recognise the advantages of continuous auditing and to adopt it to an increasing extent. Therefore, the present external audit usually consists of an element of continuous nature in the form of periodical visits during the year with a closing stage made up of a completed audit. Advantages accruing from adopting continuous checks include the earlier discovery of errors and fraud, pressure on the staff to keep records up to date, the possibility of more detailed work and the shortening of the time taken after the year end. Against that, figures may be altered after being audited and there may be a loss of direction and concentration between visits.

Differences are also observable between the two types of auditors in their attitude to their work because of the dissimilarity of their aims. The external auditor contracts to supply his services and has to take his statutory duties seriously. He is the guardian of other people's interests, which makes him more legalistic in approach.

The internal auditor, on the whole, has somewhat less concern for legalities. The finer points of Balance Sheet presentation mean little to him, though ultra vires matters (e.g. illegal payments) do concern him. He is mainly concentrating on the day-to-day operational and financial efficiency of the business and its systems and the accuracy of its records. His loyalty is to the management, or rather, to the firm. Another difference between the auditors is in the scope of their duties. The external auditor's duties as laid down under the ruling legislation cannot be reduced, though it can be agreed for more work to be done, whereas the internal auditor's duties are those allotted by management.

On the other hand, one can point to similarities. The two auditors are allies in a common campaign for the good of the organisation and its owners. Both are interested in obtaining a high level of internal control and the accurate recording of transactions, one for efficient management information, the other for the reliability and fair presentation of the figures in the final accounts. They also use the same techniques in their everyday work – both proceed in much the same manner to vouch transactions, verify assets, and otherwise obtain and evaluate evidence to test the records before them.

The compatibility in aims and the ability of each to understand what the other is doing leads almost spontaneously to a degree of co-operation in expediting work and reducing areas of apparent overlap. Although the external auditor cannot evade or delegate his legal responsibilities, he must have regard to the existence (and potential usefulness) of the internal auditor who is often checking the same ground and has a more detailed knowledge of many areas than he himself has. The external auditor thus becomes the senior partner in an arrangement to pool resources, though he has to be in a position to enforce his ideas when necessary and must retain the quality of unpredictability in his actions because, after all, the internal auditor is also being audited.

These remarks on the relationship between the external and internal audits have purposely been kept wide in application. They refer equally to commerce and the public sector, with the provisos that internal audit is statutory in some classes of public organisation and that co-operation is officially encouraged between them in many parts of the public sector.

Public Sector Accountancy

A student of accountancy normally studies commercial book-keeping before being introduced to public sector accounting. The transition should, however, cause little trouble to the student as the principles involved are the same for both areas. In a similar way, anyone who has learned accountancy from first principles in a public or local authority has no real difficulty in understanding the methods used in private business. Items debited in commercial books are also debited in public sector books, and the same can be said of credit entries. The rule of double entry and of the equality of debit and credit entries is of universal application.

In view of the fact that the study of public sector accounting usually starts after the student has spent some time on commercial aspects, it would appear to be time ill-spent to begin again from scratch, as it were. For example, a petty cash imprest account is in the same form and governed by the same rules in both areas of study. Furthermore, a public sector accountant needs a knowledge of commercial application of the common principles in order to be able, for instance, to interpret balance sheets of firms for investment and other purposes.

Despite the basic book-keeping being identical in both private and public sectors, there are differences in the approach to, and the reasons for record keeping, in the words and descriptions used, and the form in which the accounts are presented. Many of these variations can be attributed to the need to observe differing statutory codes, in the case of public bodies, by obeying various public general and private Acts, or in the case of limited companies, by observing the Companies Acts. Other divergences also arise from the recommendations issued by professional accountancy bodies which may have different degrees of relevance according to the nature and activities of an organisation.

Public sector accounts and accounting systems are intended to show how the managements of public bodies have carried out their stewardship of the public funds under their control. The report on them is made to the public, but another use for the accounts is to supply reliable financial information to the managers (i.e. the members and officials) for decision-taking and policy-making, as well as for negotiating with central government and other public sector organisations on national resource allocations, levels of charges, etc.

The range of services provided in the public sector is extremely wide. At one end, there are non-trading services, at the other, trading undertakings, whilst in between are many state and local authority-operated enterprises of intermediate nature. One might give as examples, road cleansing as a non-trading service which it is hard to imagine making a profit, electricity supply as a trading undertaking of profit-making nature, and housing as a service capable of either method of approach. The position is made no clearer by the existence, side by side, of ad-hoc bodies (created to supply one service only) and multi-purpose authorities (which operate many services of differing nature).

The form and content of the final accounts and the underlying financial administration of each class of public organisation is affected by the attitude of the government, past and present, to the degree of commercialism in the service provided. The less commercially-inclined bodies, e.g. those which can make compulsory levies upon the citizens, are subject to more regulation than those which charge customers for services or goods supplied. Indeed, this latter class is treated more in line with limited companies, being put under the duty of operating according to the best commercial principles. As has been mentioned, directives and recommendations of accountancy bodies help to explain and apply the best practices, particularly in respect of the form of the accounts and the treatment of the items they contain.

Different classes of organisation have, under the influence of their own peculiar history and framework, arrived at dissimilar solutions to problems of universal nature, in their attempts to produce reliable, informative accounts and honest reports. The treatment of capital assets is an example of a difficulty common to all organisations which is solved in a variety of ways with varying degrees of success.

Another source of variation is the wording used in the governing Acts and regulations. This has introduced differences in terminology between commercial and public sector undertakings. Besides such obvious differences as revenue and net revenue account instead of trading, profit and loss and appropriation account, and surplus/deficit in place of profit/loss, there are expressions such as abstract of accounts, consolidated loans fund, debt charges, capital provision, etc. which may sound strange to an accountant in commerce, when first heard.

Finally, an attempt to explain and give examples of the accounting methods and systems of public authorities requires the adoption of simple manual ledger postings where the double entry is clearly shown. It must be remembered, however, that these authorities operate on a large scale, using computers and other machinery, and that, in real life, the double entry is not immediately apparent, although it is nevertheless still present.

Costing in the Public Sector

Costing methods used in the public sector organisations are affected by the nature and objectives of the particular organisation involved. Trading undertakings, especially those producing a product in competition with the private sector, can use and develop costing to its greatest extent and variety. On the other hand, those bodies which provide a service for which no charge is made, i.e. which are financed out of a compulsory levy, have difficulty in discovering means of comparing costs and measurements of performance and quality of service. House refuse collection is a service of this nature where costs are influenced by the geography of the area, the density of the housing, the nature and volume of the refuse, the nature of the receptacles, the distances to tips, besides such immeasurable items as the cleanness of the pick-up.

This means that in most public authorities the role of costing is relegated to the providing of reliable cost information on which to base expenditure control aimed at securing economy of operation. Weakness in methods can be pinpointed to permit them to be improved in respect of value for money, or be discontinued. Even so, a high unit cost may not necessarily be the result of inefficient operation, as more expense in one area of service may give greater savings elsewhere. The fixing of boarding-out allowances for children in care who are living with foster parents is affected by the scales paid by neighbouring authorities but, also, by the fact that the cost of keeping a child in a community home is much greater. Somewhat similarly, in the case of a central purchasing department, for instance, an increase in the percentage on cost of purchases which is charged to recover administrative costs does not necessarily indicate a more expensive service. Efficient purchasing policies may reduce the cost of a maintained throughput of paper so that the recovery of the overheads requires an increased percentage on cost, although the total charge to the other departments served is reduced. (For instance, if the department costs £120,000 to run and purchases amounted to £2,400,000, the oncost, put simply, would be 5%. If, however, good buying brought purchases of equal volume down to £2,000,000, then the oncost needed would now be 6%, even though overall costs are £400,000 less.)

The emphasis on expenditure means that costing usually takes the form of a detailed analysis of the authority's outgoings and tries to relate them to some suitable unit of service or standard job, (e.g. cost per 1,000 dustbins emptied, cost of replacement of a bath in a council dwelling). Sometimes, costs need to be as accurate and fair as possible as in cases of rechargeable work carried out for the public (as individuals) or other authorities, but non-trading income is usually influenced by factors other than the cost of service e.g. the social function and role of the service, the income levels of the users, the danger of frightening away potential users by scaling charges for a socially-desirable service at too high a level.

Other factors which are having an increasing influence upon the adoption of improved costing methods by local authorities are the requirements of the audit code of practice under the Local Government Act 1972, and the accounting code of practice for direct labour organisations under the Local Government Planning and Land Act 1980. The audit code places a duty upon the external auditor to direct his attention to such matters as the receipt of value for money, the fairness of apportionments of establishment expenses, unexplained high labour costs, and failures to review scales of charges. The second code requires D.L.O.s to be treated as separate trading undertakings with their own financial and management accounts, and places them in competition with private firms for local authority contracts.

Questions
1.1 What are the objectives of an internal control system for an organisation?
1.2 Why is a public corporation called a "creature of statute"?

1.3 What factors do you think affect the internal structure of a public authority?
1.4 How can the success or failure of a public body be measured in the carrying out of its functions?
1.5 Discuss the use of costing as it is applied in local and public authorities.
1.6 Describe the role of the external auditor in respect of the finances and accounts of public sector organisations.
1.7 Compare and contrast the duties of the internal and external auditors.
1.8 In what ways and how far can internal and external auditors work together?
1.9 Indicate some ways in which the nature of a public organisation affects its accounting arrangements.
1.10 Draw up the organisation chart for a firm or department of an authority with which you are familiar.

Chapter 2

A Brief History of Local Government

Although there is evidence that local government existed in this country in Roman times, the origins of our present system are to be found in the institutions brought and set up here by the Anglo-Saxons who invaded the British Isles and destroyed the settled order. These institutions must, at the start, have been linked to tribes and localities, but as the small Saxon kingdoms formed and united into a national State, the unit of government covering the country became the shire, in which the freemen held meetings at which local matters affecting government, finance, etc. were decided. The shires were divided into hundreds, whose inhabitants sent representatives to the shire meetings and also held their own meetings to discuss matters affecting the hundred. The name for the sub-division of the shire varied from hundred on occasion – some shires which had a large influx of Danes in later Anglo-Saxon times were divided into wapentakes. Finally, the hundred was divided into townships or boroughs (groups of farms with a nucleus of houses) which also had their own meetings of freemen. It is from this period that local government in this country derived its tradition of being local "self" government, although the range of powers delegated by the King was narrow, and the services were rudimentary, and, in any case, the degree of democracy then present was limited.

After the Norman Conquest, government became more centralised and restrictive, and the feudal system was introduced to this country. The shire meetings were replaced by manorial courts which were presided over by officials responsible to the lord of the manor. Town or borough meetings were similarly presided over by an official – a "major", later mayor – but the boroughs began to gain freedom from the manor by buying charters of self-government, trading rights, etc. from the King or the lord of the manor. It must be said that these borough corporations, as they were called, had little to do with local government as we know it, except for some charity work for the needy, but applied themselves mainly to looking after corporation property and the interests of their members.

The officer who presided over the meetings of the shire freemen and was responsible to the King was called the sheriff. He continued in office under the Normans – the shire became the county – but the shire meetings had gone. He gradually lost his powers, however, as time passed, partly because of a tendency by office-holders to commit oppressive actions. He was, in effect, superseded by newly-created officers called "Justices of the Peace" who were (and still are) "worthy people" in the county, and who were given the task of governing the shires during the chaos left by the Black Death. There is an implication that the office was actually created because of the effects of the Black Death. In any case, the J.P.s gradually took charge of such local government as existed in their counties, and continued these duties up to the last years of the nineteenth century.

In Tudor times, the dissolution of the monasteries and the wars with Spain caused an increase in poverty. The government decided to introduce an ordered form of public assistance, but although the justices were available to supervise the new system, there was the problem of who should actually carry it out. The manorial system had decayed, the sheriff was archaic, and the boroughs were venal and suspect and, in any case, did not cover the country. The choice was in fact an inspired one. The government chose the ecclesiastical parish to carry out the Poor Relief Act 1601. This was the unit of church organisation which had continued to operate over the centuries of change. It had begun as a purely religious organisation by the appointment of churchwardens from among the parishioners at meetings which were later called vestry meetings. During the Middle Ages, it became the practice to appoint or elect additional parish officers whose duties were not religious – the constable (who was appointed by the J.P.s), the surveyor of highways, and the overseer of the poor – the last mentioned of these collecting and paying out funds to help the needy people in the parish. Charitable work is an obvious area of operation for a religious body, and it seems that this aspect of the church's work decided the government's choice of the parish as the vehicle of its new poor relief and rating system. At the time of the passing of the 1601 Act and for two centuries later, the members of the vestry were local people of substance and standing (and they had to be members of the Church of England) and, as has been said, the justices, who on occasion were the same people, had a supervisory role. The eighteenth century saw the heyday of local government, it is said, because State interference was for a time at a low ebb between the high tides of the early Stuarts and the Commonwealth and the formation of central departments to intervene in local government matters in the nineteenth century.

The 1700's also saw the beginning of the flood of single-purpose bodies (ad hoc organisations) which were formed, as and when required, in a piece-meal manner, to provide the inhabitants with services which they began to need as the Industrial Revolution developed. There were boards for building roads (usually toll), paving, lighting, watching, street cleaning, sewers and all kinds of improvements. The members of such boards were called commissioners and were elected on various differing qualification bases. In addition, areas over-lapped, voting rights varied, functions conflicted, and, as time went by, confusion could reign in an area on these matters.

The social and political changes resulting from the Industrial Revolution – the increase and movement of population, the creation of large congested towns, the development of industrial areas and the effects of their processes – laid bare the inadequacies of the local government of the time. The hungry thirties of the nineteenth century saw the passing of the Poor Law

Amendment Act 1834 under which a central department (the Poor Law Commissioners) was created to supervise locally-elected boards of guardians who were to administer the poor law in areas now composed of united parishes. The Municipal Corporations Act 1835 reformed the borough corporations and, although they were only given power at that time to form police forces, it prepared them for their future role as multi-purpose local authorities.

The occurrence of epidemics in urban areas brought about the formation of local health boards in 1849 (with a central department — The General Board of Health — to control them) with duties aimed at preventing disease and safeguarding water supplies. About this time, Parliament passed the Clauses Acts. These were, in effect, codes of operation applicable to railways, water supply, gas supply, land development, town improvements, cemeteries, etc. (Gas was dealt with in 1870). This was in response to the boom in such services and meant that these clauses could be incorporated into new legislation — which was usually a Private Act — without ado.

The drive to create ad hoc bodies was now beginning to peter out and the last example of importance was the formation of school boards in 1870 to provide universal education.

The move now began towards the abolition of these single-purpose boards and bodies and the transfer of their duties to multi-purpose bodies. In 1871, the boroughs took over the local health board functions in their areas, and urban and rural sanitary authorities were formed a little later to take over health duties in the rest of the country. This meant that there was now a tier of health bodies — boroughs, urban and rural sanitary districts — covering the whole country and available for additional burdens. 1871 also saw the creation of the Local Government Board to supervise health and poor law matters. The Local Government Act 1888 introduced county and county borough councils and put an end to the J.P.s' long reign in county government. It was intended that there would only be counties but pressure by the larger towns resulted in them becoming counties themselves, i.e. county boroughs. Within the counties, the sanitary districts were given a more dignified title of urban and rural district councils, and the rural parish system was brought back to a full and ordered existence. These new authorities received the powers and duties of the ad hoc boards in their areas with the exception of education (which they received in 1902) and poor law (which came over in 1929). During all this time, London had remained a welter of parishes, improvement areas, etc., although the formation of the Metropolitan Board of Works in 1855 had improved certain services. Under the 1888 Act, the Metropolitan Board of Works became the London County Council but it was only in 1899 that 28 Metropolitan Boroughs were formed to take over the duties of the former district boards and parishes.

The first half of the twentieth century witnessed a dramatic growth in local authority activities, both in variety and scale of operations. Education expanded, especially higher and technical. Health and hospital services improved and moved into new areas of maternity and child welfare. Police, fire and highways all responded to increased needs of modern life. Housing became a major activity and town and country planning essential. In the area of trading, authorities became involved in many activities – gas, electricity, water, markets, crematoria, industrial estates, airports, tramways and buses and other more unusual examples, such as municipal banks.

The years before the start of the second World War in 1939, were a period of consolidation of the law. The law of local government was codified in a series of statutes which included the Local Government Act 1933, the Housing Act 1936, the Public Health Act 1936, the Food and Drugs Act 1938, and others. These Acts also increased the powers of the central departments to influence and interfere in the way in which local authorities provided their services. Over the years of the twentieth century, the Ministries had grown in number and in their range of duties, so that in the 1930's, the central departments involved in supervising local government included the Ministry of Health (formed from the Local Government Board in 1919), the Board of Education (formed in 1899 out of a committee of the Privy Council), the Home Office, the Treasury, the Ministry of Agriculture and Fisheries, and the Ministry of Transport.

At the start of the thirties, the grant system was revised. Government grants had been related mainly to specific services but now a block grant was introduced which was intended to aid all services.

The period 1939-45 was taken up by the war, and local government was depleted of personnel and resources, house building stopped and the general level of services fell. It is impossible to guess what impact this had upon local government, except, perhaps, to accelerate the changes which did take place in the post-war period.

The position in 1945 was that the structure of local government was, in essence, the same as was laid down in 1894 (in the provinces) and 1899 (in London) and in the interim, people had moved into the towns and the suburbs, the population had also increased, while the motor car eliminated distance so that the separation between town and country (inherent in the urban, rural district split) was becoming irrelevant. A person could work in the city and live in the country – in other words, local authorities were providing services to inhabitants of adjacent areas without any recompense. Thus the solution was seen as enlarging local authority areas so as to bring cities and dormitory areas together. Another aspect of the controversy was the idea that there was an optimal size of population for each function or service and that large-scale operations should give economies. This gave further strength to the move for larger areas which would have the resources to provide the best standard of service, as a divisional set-up could be adopted where the service needed a relatively small optimal population. A third area of criticism was that, outside the county boroughs, many people were confused as to which authority did which services, and whom they should approach in case of complaint or need. It was argued that there should be a logical, understandable division of duties among authorities in any one area. (It is debatable whether the post-1974 system has answered this criticism).

The move towards larger areas started in 1945 with the re-emergence of the concept of the ad hoc organisation together with a preference for counties and county boroughs for new services and the transfer of existing services from the boroughs and districts to the counties.

The ad hoc approach was adopted for electricity, gas, hospitals, out-door relief of the poor, certain transport undertakings, prevention of pollution of rivers and valuation for rating which were removed from local government and made the responsibility of specialised organisations. New powers which were allocated to counties and county boroughs included personal health services, welfare of the aged, children, etc., and additional planning powers. Transfers from boroughs and districts to counties occurred in education, police and fire and some planning functions. In 1946, development corporations began to build new towns to alleviate local authority difficulties regarding overspill. In 1974 (to go forward a little), water, sewerage and sewage disposal, and river functions were passed to regional water authorities. Outside the local government sector, coal mining and railways were nationalised in the later forties.

During the post-war period until 1959, the government paid a block grant aimed to assist all services, and specific grants, usually as a percentage of net expenditure, on several services such as education, children in care, personal health, police, etc. After 1959, most of the specific grants were brought within the block grant system, though police grants and housing subsidies remained specific in nature.

In addition to the transfer of services within the public sector, the actual organisations were under review, particularly the local authorities. A Boundary Commission was formed in 1945 but soon complained that it needed to consider the allocation of functions besides boundaries. It was dissolved in 1949. In 1958, the government set up two Local Government Commissions, one for England and one for Wales, which were to review the organisation of local government. The Commission for England was empowered to review the pattern of authorities and the distribution of functions in the five main conurbations (Merseyside, South East Lancashire, Tyneside, West Midlands and West Yorkshire), London being excluded from the terms of reference. The commission for Wales reported with some measure of success but an Act of 1967 dissolved both bodies. As the English re-organisation was still in need of a solution, a Royal Commission under Lord Redcliffe-Maud was now appointed to consider the whole country outside London. This Commission reported in 1969 but the final version for re-organisation was prepared by the government who rejected the Commission's proposals. The new system came into operation on 1st April 1974 after a period of overlap of old and new authorities from 1972.

In the meantime, the London Government Act 1963 had re-organised local government in Greater London, forming the Greater London Council and 32 London boroughs. It is apparent that the experience obtained in London as to the division of functions between boroughs and county (e.g. refuse collection and disposal) and the overlapping of old and new authorities, and other matters were borne in mind when the rest of the country was reorganised under the Local Government Act 1972.

The system under the Local Government Act 1972 consists of two main tiers, counties and, below them, districts or boroughs. There are six metropolitan counties in the main conurbations, and these contain metropolitan districts or boroughs. Metropolitan districts or boroughs have more functions than non-metropolitan districts or boroughs, whilst metropolitan counties have less than their counterparts. Parishes also exist in the rural areas of both types of county and carry out a number of minor functions.

An indication of the main division of functions is as follows: –

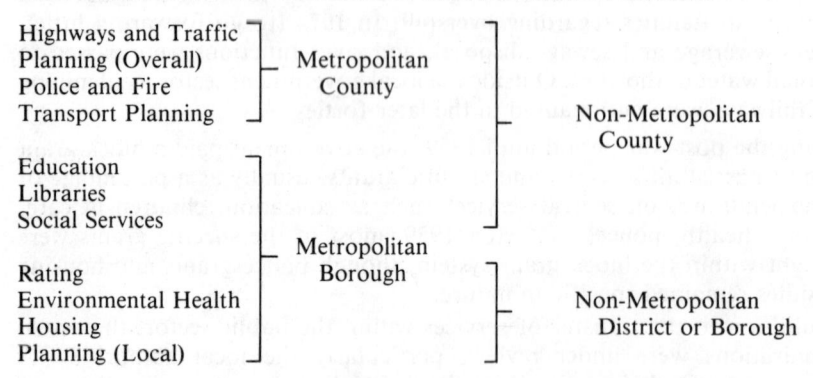

Highways and Traffic Planning (Overall) Police and Fire Transport Planning	Metropolitan County	
		Non-Metropolitan County
Education Libraries Social Services		
	Metropolitan Borough	
Rating Environmental Health Housing Planning (Local)		Non-Metropolitan District or Borough

The position regarding water supply has not altered since 1974, the authorities created then being concerned with developing the services allotted to them. Passenger transport is operated by "executives" in the metropolitan counties, and the shire counties co-ordinate privately- and publicly-owned bus undertakings in their areas. New town development corporations now number some thirty new communities but emphasis has moved to the inner city areas in respect of what is called urban renewal. The National Health Service was re-organised from the 1st April 1974 when regional and area health authorities were formed and added personal health services and family practitioner services to the hospitals they already operated. The gas industry has become centralised into a corporation in order to administer North Sea gas on a national basis, whilst the electricity supply industry is de-centralised for distribution and centralised for generation in the same way as when it was first nationalised. The central departments still carry out their statutory duties of supervising the public sector authorities, though names have changed and functions have been passed round. The main department dealing with local government is now entitled the Department of the Environment.

Pressure for change is never absent in the public sector. Debate has always existed on the need for a further re-organisation of local government since that of the 1972 Act but the consensus appears to be that it is too soon for another such traumatic experience, at least for those members of staff who were in service in 1972/4 and the few months following. At the present, health authorities are under discussion as a subject of possible streamlining and other measures of re-organisation. The law is also being changed relating to the systems of block grant and the control of the capital expenditure of local authorities. Changes in the district audit are under consideration including the possible amalgamation with the Exchequer and Audit Department.

Questions
2.1 Outline the form of local government which developed under the Saxons.
2.2 Give a brief description of the changes in the local government system of the time which occurred after the Norman Conquest.
2.3 Outline the way in which the parish has developed in English local government.
2.4 How did the Industrial Revolution affect local government in the 18th and 19th centuries?
2.5 What is an "ad hoc" organisation? Give an example.
2.6 Discuss some of the reasons for the pressure for local government re-organisation in the post-war period.
2.7 What changes took place in local government under the London Government Act 1963?
2.8 Indicate a number of effects of the invention of the internal combustion engine upon local government in the present century.
2.9 Outline the main changes which took place in the local government and allied sectors on the 1st April 1974.
2.10 What changes do you perceive as possible in the near future in local government and public authorities?

Chapter 3
The Legal Basis of Local Government

Introduction

Local government in the United Kingdom is traditionally taken to mean the running of services and the provision of amenities in an area for the benefit of the people living there by a number of local inhabitants who have been elected for that purpose by the remainder. These elected persons (who are given the designation of "councillor"), taken as a body, form a local authority which has the power to engage the staff and to acquire the resources (e.g. plant, materials, buildings) it needs to carry out its tasks. To pay for all this, the local authority has the power to levy a rate upon the inhabitants of its area (or to precept for its needs, i.e. demand money, from the local authority entitled to levy the rate in the particular locality).

It is also traditional here that local government means local self-government, and, although it is true under the present system that local authorities receive all their powers from Parliament, they are not merely agents carrying out the orders of the central government. They enjoy a wide measure of discretion in their actions and decision-making, and in their interpretation of their role in government so that they can take account of local circumstances and use their local knowledge. They supply an element of stability and continuity to government as their membership is not changed by reversals of the central government at the national elections. Their own elections, nevertheless, enable them to react to changes in local conditions, needs and opinions. Another way in which they serve the country is by acting as a training ground for future M.P.s.

In the eyes of the law, a local authority is a separate legal person from the members, i.e. the councillors, who compose it, and the officers who act for it. This is known as corporate status, and such bodies are called "corporations". (The same idea exists in commerce, where limited liability companies are also separate legal entities from their directors and shareholders). Unlike a human being, a local authority enjoys a perpetual existence and a seal is used as a signature on important documents. It is subject to the courts and the law of the land in the same way as an ordinary individual, though there are some minor variations arising mainly from its lack of a physical body — it cannot be imprisoned for instance.

Corporations (of which local authorities, water authorities, transport, electricity, gas undertakings and limited companies, are examples) are also particularly subject to the operation of the doctrine of "ultra vires" (i.e. the latin for "beyond the powers"). Unlike a human being, who has a general power to do what he pleases so long as he does not violate the rights of others or commit illegal acts, a local authority has no such inborn rights but only the powers given to it by the law. These powers are usually kept to the minimum needed for the authority to carry out its duties adequately, and any actions which overstep the limits, i.e. go beyond the given powers, are discouraged by the courts who declare the actions as void and having no legal effect. Thus if a contract is made for a purpose outside the authority's powers, the court may declare it void and the position would be as if it had not been made. The court may stop the authority from continuing, and any payments it has made may be charged on those persons responsible for them being made. One can imagine cases where the other party to the contract suffers loss but he is supposed to know the law. It is of interest that the failure of a local authority to follow its own procedures does not make a contract void, if nothing else is wrong.

The Local Government Act 1972 was designed to reduce the limiting effects of the doctrine upon local authorities in two ways. Firstly, they now have the power to do anything calculated to facilitate, is conducive to, or incidental to the carrying out of their functions. Secondly, they have power to spend up to a 2p. rate on any purpose which is not illegal but which they think will benefit the area or its inhabitants. Notwithstanding these added powers, the doctrine of ultra vires is ever present as a check on a local authority's acts, bringing with it the threat of court action by a private individual, a district auditor or the Attorney-General.

Local authorities have two main roles under the law – they provide services and amenities to the population in their area but they also have a duty to regulate activities there under powers granted to them by various statutes.

When a local or public authority is given the duty to provide a service in its area of operation, the Act which creates the duty usually arms the authority with powers to over-ride the legal rights of individuals in its pursuit of the common good of its inhabitants. In effect, an authority can do things which would be a civil wrong or tort, if a private person did them. However, so long as an authority acts within its legal powers and, most important, in a way according to the law, it has a measure of protection against action at law by persons who feel aggrieved by what an authority has done, or indeed, what it has not done. Even where a person has a claim against a public body, there is a limitation to the period in which he can bring the case, usually seven years, and an authority cannot be made to operate a service which is only of a discretionary nature. (It can only be made to give consideration whether it should carry out the service or not). In recent years, there have been signs that the degree of protection enjoyed by local and other authorities against claims by the public is being reduced, as the rights of individuals have received more attention in their relation to those of government and its funds.

One aspect of local and public authority power is that of the compulsory purchase of land and property without which it would often be impossible to run a service.

Thus, when an Act of Parliament requires or empowers an authority to carry on a service, it is the practice for the body to be able to buy land by compulsion from a reluctant private owner who has refused to agree to sell. For the protection of owners and other people with interests in the land, there is a set procedure to be followed in arranging for compulsory purchase. The authority must prepare plans, publicise them, approach those who have interests in the land, and notify the appropriate central department. On receipt of the application, the department, in most cases arranges for a public enquiry or provides in some other way for objections from the public to be heard. The department confirms the compulsory purchase order (varied where necessary) or refuses it. The final step is for the authority to advertise the confirmation (where this has been given) and proceed to buy the land in return for compensation based on the District Valuer's valuation.

The second duty mentioned above is fulfilled by the making of bye-laws (from the Danish word "by" meaning "town") for such matters as "good rule and government", the prevention of nuisances, etc. whereby people are protected from annoyance caused by the anti-social actions of their neighbours. Most bye-laws are made under the Local Government Act 1972 which contains the procedure for their making, publication, confirmation and cancellation. Confirmation is needed before the bye-law can come into effect and this is the responsibility of a central department, usually the Department of the Environment. The courts may, on occasion, consider the legality of disputed by-laws − whether they are consistent with the general law, indicate with certainty who is required to comply with them, and are a proper and reasonable use of the enabling Act. It often occurs that the central departments draw up model bye-laws for local authorities to copy and confirmation often depends on keeping in essence to the model form, as this may have been already tested in the courts.

To have the right to vote in the election of a member of a local authority a person must reside in the area involved, be a British subject or a citizen of Eire, be 18 years of age or over, have no legal incapacity (for instance, not be an idiot nor have been convicted for corrupt practices at an election), and, most important, must appear in the current register of electors.

To be a candidate for election as a councillor, a person must be at least 21 years of age, be British or Irish, and must satisfy one of the following conditions: − he or she must be a registered elector for the area, or have resided, occupied premises or worked there for the 12 months previous to the election date. (There is a concession in respect of parishes − a candidate can live within three miles of the parish). Candidates may be selected by local branches of political parties from among their members, or be members of local pressure groups such as ratepayers' associations, or independent persons who have a record of interest and action in local affairs which they hope will persuade their neighbours to vote for them. To prevent injustice to those without substantial financial backing, there is a maximum limit to the amount which a candidate is allowed to spend on an election.

Persons may be disqualified from being candidates for such reasons as being a paid employee of the council, an undischarged bankrupt (or having made a composition with his creditors because of difficulty in paying his debts), having been convicted of corruption in respect of an election, or sentenced to at least three months' imprisonment without the option of a fine during the previous five years.

An existing councillor may become disqualified from office by a court order for a specified period (decided by the court) where he is found to be responsible in a case of a local authority having spent more than £2,000 on an illegal matter. He can be similarly disqualified, usually for five years, by having a district auditor's certificate issued against him for a loss or deficiency of £2,000. A further ground for disqualification arises when a councillor fails to attend meetings for a period of six months – if the local authority does not approve his absence, it may declare that the office is vacant and he ceases to be a councillor.

The ban on councillors being employees of the local authority is extended for a further twelve months after they have ceased to be councillors and this still applies apparently even in cases where they work for no pay.

Elections are controlled by returning officers and are only held when the number of candidates exceeds the number of vacancies for councillors, otherwise the candidates are declared to be elected automatically. Voting is in secret and usually in person at a polling booth, though proxy and postal votes can be arranged. Rules exist to prevent anyone voting more than once for a candidate or more than once in the same class of election.

The Structure of the Local Government System

The present local government system was established by the London Government Act, 1963, for Greater London, and by the Local Government Act, 1972 for the remainder of England and Wales. Both Acts were attempts to increase the administrative areas of services so as to obtain economies of scale without reducing local democracy by making the council too remote from the voters.

An illustration of the pattern is as follows: –

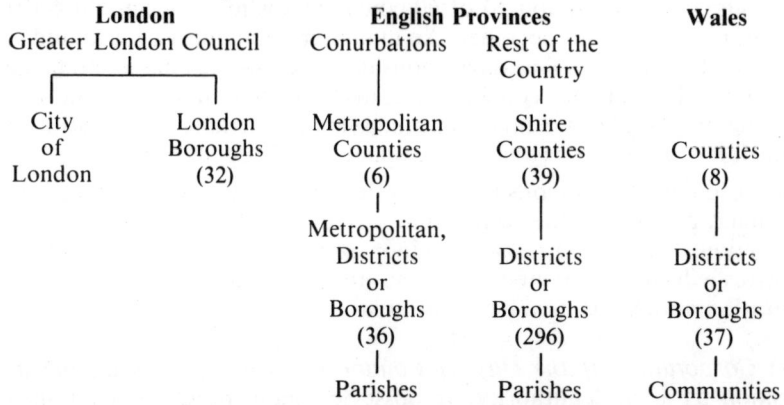

London	**English Provinces**		**Wales**
Greater London Council	Conurbations	Rest of the Country	
City of London / London Boroughs (32)	Metropolitan Counties (6)	Shire Counties (39)	Counties (8)
	Metropolitan, Districts or Boroughs (36)	Districts or Boroughs (296)	Districts or Boroughs (37)
	Parishes	Parishes	Communities

Notes:

The Metropolitan Counties are Greater Manchester, Merseyside, South Yorkshire, Tyne and Wear, West Midlands and West Yorkshire.

A District Council can apply for the granting of a charter to become a Borough. All the Districts in the Metropolitan Counties have become Boroughs (or are Cities).

The Greater London Council administers the area of "Greater London" as created by the London Government Act 1963. This includes (a) the "inner London boroughs" which occupy the area of the former London County Council, and (b) the "outer London boroughs" which were added to bring the county boundaries to the limits of the conurbation.

The council consists of 92 councillors who are elected for a four year term and all retire together. It must hold an annual meeting and such other meetings as it thinks necessary. At the annual meeting, the councillors elect a chairman, vice-chairman and deputy chairman from among their members to preside over council meetings and to carry out civic duties. The council may pay each a reasonable allowance for the expenses incurred in office.

The G.L.C. is responsible for the fire services, principal (metropolitan) roads, overall planning, housing (new accommodation inside or outside the county – though to a diminishing extent – and strategy for the county), traffic control and transport planning, some parks, and refuse disposal.

The Metropolitan Police Authority is responsible for policing the area and education in inner London is under the Inner London Education Authority (the I.L.E.A.) which is an independent committee of the county council whose members are from the G.L.C., the City of London and the inner London boroughs.

The country precepts for its needs upon the London boroughs and the City of London – they are the rating authorities.

The London Boroughs consist of 12 inner and 20 outer London boroughs which occupy the lower tier of local government in the capital. Each borough council is composed of 60 councillors who are elected for a four year term and all retire together. An annual meeting must be held and such additional meetings as the council considers necessary. A mayor and deputy mayor are elected by the councillors from among their number at the annual meeting to preside at council meetings and undertake civic duties. The council has power to pay each a reasonable expense allowance.

The boroughs are responsible for rating, housing, social services, local planning, environmental health, minor roads, refuse collection, consumer protection, parks and various minor services. Although the I.L.E.A. controls education in inner London, the outer boroughs are the local education authorities for their own areas.

The Corporation of the City of London or "the City" is unique in its position as a local authority. It possesses many privileges contained in charters granted by various monarchs and these have helped it to ensure that its constitution and powers have not been adversely affected by legislation. Indeed, the London Government Act, 1963, increased the City's powers, specifically in respect of social services and minor roads.

The local government powers of the City are vested in three assemblies (known as courts).

1. *The Court of Common Hall* consists of the Lord Mayor, the sheriffs, the aldermen (26, including the Lord Mayor, and elected for life by the voters) and those liverymen who are freemen of the City. Each year, it elects two City sheriffs, and nominates two aldermen from among the ex-sheriffs as candidates for election as the next Lord Mayor.

2. *The Court of Aldermen* which is the assembly of the 26 aldermen, elects the new Lord Mayor from the two candidates nominated.

3. *The Court of Common Council* is the actual executive body which carries out the local government and other functions of the City. It consists of the Lord Mayor, the aldermen and the common councilmen (who are gradually being reduced in number to 130). The councilmen are elected annually.

The Common Council is responsible for broadly the same range of services as a London borough – rating, housing, social services, environmental health (it is the port health authority), minor roads, libraries, etc. It also controls the Corporation's properties and maintains some of the main Thames bridges. The City is also within the I.L.E.A. area.

The Metropolitan Counties are six in number and are the main provincial conurbations of England – Greater Manchester, Merseyside, South Yorkshire, Tyne and Wear, West Midlands and West Yorkshire. Following the example of the Act of 1963 for London, the Act of 1972 made one local authority responsible for each of the most densely populated areas of the rest of the country. The county council consists of between 60 and 100 councillors elected for four years and all retiring together. There must be an annual meeting of the council and such other meetings as it considers necessary. A chairman and vice-chairman are appointed at the annual meeting to preside over council meetings and carry out civic duties. Both may be paid a reasonable allowance.

The main functions of the council are overall planning, country and national parks, transport planning, highways, public transport, consumer protection, refuse disposal, police and fire services (subject to any amalgamation schemes), museums and art galleries (concurrent powers with the districts), etc.

The county precepts upon its districts, these being the rating authorities.

The Metropolitan Districts (or Boroughs) occupy the second tier in the metropolitan counties. They are densely populated areas of urban character with enough financial resources to support main services such as education, social services, etc. The council comprises 50 to 80 councillors who are elected for a four year term. One third of them retire each year for three consecutive years, and in the fourth year, the county council elections are held. There must be an annual meeting and such other meetings as the council thinks to be necessary. A chairman and vice-chairman are appointed by the councillors at the annual meeting and the council may pay them a reasonable expense allowance each. Where the district has been given borough status, the chairman and vice-chairman become the mayor and deputy mayor. Their duties are the same – to preside over council meetings and to carry out civic duties.

The council is responsible for rating, education, social services, environmental health, local planning, housing, libraries, museums and art galleries (concurrent powers with the county), refuse collection, etc.

The Non-metropolitan (or Shire) Counties occupy Wales and the less built-up remainder of England outside London and the six other conurbations. The council is composed of 60 to 80 councillors who are elected for a four year term and all retire together. There must be an annual meeting and other meetings may be held as the council consider necessary. A chairman and vice-chairman are elected by the councillors from among themselves at the annual meeting to preside over the council and to carry out civic duties. The council may resolve to pay them reasonable expense allowances.

The council's main functions include overall planning, transport planning, education, social services, fire and police services (subject to any amalgamation schemes), consumer protection, refuse disposal, libraries, museums and art galleries (concurrent powers with the districts), etc.

The county precepts for its needs upon its districts as they are the rating authorities.

The Non-metropolitan (or Shire) Districts (or Boroughs) are the second tier local authorities in the shire counties. They do not have the population and financial resources of the metropolitan boroughs so the main services, such as education, are operated by the county council. The council comprises between 30 and 60 councillors elected for four years. This class of local authority has a choice as to the manner in which elections are held – the members may all retire together or one third of them may retire in three consecutive years (the fourth being used for the county council elections). The council must hold an annual meeting and such others as it thinks fit. A chairman and vice-chairman (or if it is of borough status, a mayor and deputy mayor) are elected at the annual meeting to preside at council meetings and to carry out civic duties. Each may receive a reasonable allowance in respect of the expenses of office.

The councils are responsible for rating, local planning, environmental health, housing, museums and art galleries (concurrent powers with the county), refuse collection, etc.

Parishes (in England) or Communities (in Wales) are the lowest tier of local government under the Local Government Act, 1972. In England, parishes are found only in rural areas, though they occur in both types of county (but obviously much more frequently in the non-metropolitan). In Wales, however, communities cover the whole country.

In the more populous parishes or communities, there are elected councils with parish or community meetings. In the less populous, there are meetings only. There has to be an annual meeting, and if there is no actual council, there must be at least one other meeting in the year. Councillors are elected for four years and retire together. A chairman and vice-chairman are elected annually by the council members to preside at meetings. The chairman may be paid an allowance but not the vice-chairman. If there is no council, a chairman is elected at the parish or community meeting to preside over it. In some cases, parishes or communities have been allowed to call themselves towns.

Functions can include minor services such as allotments, footpaths, community or village halls, bus shelters, cemeteries and crematoria, swimming pools, etc. Parish or community councils precept on the district.

Local Authority Services

Art Galleries and Museums. County and district councils have the power to establish and maintain museums and art galleries which may be situated within or outside the local authority's area. The relevant Act is the Public Libraries and Museums Act 1964, and it permits admission charges to be made and bye-laws to be drawn up to control the behaviour of visitors to the museum or gallery. A local authority can also contribute towards the expenses of anyone, including another local authority, providing or helping to provide a museum or art gallery. An "Art Fund" can be built up and exhibits can be purchased out of it. A parish or community council has the power to give support to arts and crafts and thus can pay towards the costs of a museum or art gallery in the locality.

Cemeteries and Crematoria. The modern legal position may sometimes be made a little complicated by the existence of a somewhat out-of-date (but still effective) code under the Burial Acts which deals with "burial grounds" which may date back for centuries. Having made this point, however, this book deals with the law as it applies to cemeteries (an offshoot of the Public Health Acts) and their most recent development, crematoria.

London boroughs, districts or boroughs, parish and community councils, and also parish meetings, can provide and manage cemeteries within their own areas or in the areas of other local authorities under the Local Government Act 1972. Land intended for use as a cemetery may be bought by agreement from a willing owner or it may be purchased compulsorily where this is shown to be necessary. The local authority can provide funeral chapels there for services to be held, and mortuaries for keeping dead bodies. In addition, it has a wide discretion in how it runs the cemetery, and can provide such roads as are needed as well as laying out the plots and carrying out landscaping to improve its appearance of peace and beauty, so as to attract potential occupants of grave spaces.

Crematoria may be provided under the Cremation Acts by London boroughs, district, parish and community councils (but not parish meetings). The post-war years have seen an appreciable growth in local authority crematoria because of the increase in acceptance of cremation, the possibility of a new type of undertaking which might prove viable at a time when local authorities are losing such opportunities, and a certain element of prestige in providing a local service against competition from outside.

The authority providing the cemetery or crematorium may make such charges as it decides and the scale of charges must be available to the public.

The Secretary of State for the Environment has the power to regulate the way in which cemeteries and crematoria are managed, and, furthermore, a crematorium needs his approval before it can start to operate. The regulations require, for instance, that registers of burials and cremations must be kept in a prescribed form.

There is power under the Local Government Act 1972 for a district or a parish to charge the cost of a cemetery or crematorium to a part only of its area. This departure from the usual practice of rating the whole of the area as a general expense permits flexibility where the area served is somewhat localised, especially in rural surroundings.

Among the income received by cemeteries are lump sums for the maintenance of graves in perpetuity. Such amounts are invested and the annual income is brought into the revenue account to meet the cost of the work carried out.

Another possible source of income to crematoria which raises some legal points as to ownership and is the subject of public outrage and controversy, is the fact that valuable metals (usually gold and silver from rings, jewellery, etc.) remain in a fused state in the ashes in many cases. Such items might be sold and the income either brought to the credit of the rates or used for charitable aims. On the other hand, they might be buried in a secret place at a depth which would prevent their discovery by electronic metal detectors in unauthorised hands — this is the method which is favoured officially.

Civil Defence

Under the Civil Defence Act 1948, local authorities (for all practical purposes, the county councils) can carry out certain functions such as administrative arrangements, the provision of sirens, the auxiliary fire service, the emergency ambulance service, temporary accommodation for the homeless, emergency feeding, evacuation, billeting and rehousing, demolition of damaged buildings, and emergency water supplies for domestic use.

The central control of these services is allotted to various government departments, including the Home Office, the Department of the Environment, the Ministry of Agriculture, Fisheries and Food, and the Department of Health and Social Security. Grants are payable by the government towards the expenditure of local authorities on these services.

The Local Government Act 1972 gives a discretion to a county, district or London borough to spend, grant or lend money as it thinks necessary where an emergency or disaster threatening life or property has occurred or is likely to occur in its area. The council must notify the Secretary of State as soon as it can and he has the power to make it stop its actions or limit them in respect of further expenditure.

The Community Land Act 1975

Labour governments have made several attempts since the last war to either nationalise land or to divert to the public purse a portion of the profits arising from the increase in the value of land as it undergoes development. It is argued that the actions of the State in providing the infrastructure in an area (e.g. roads, housing, schools, amenities, etc.) and in carrying out its own schemes of industrial and other types of aid raise the selling price of land in that area, and that it is unjust for the private landowner to keep the whole of the increase in the sale price for his land. The latest attempt, which is being, in effect, terminated by the Conservative administration, took place under the Community Land Act 1975 and the Development Land Tax Act 1976. It was intended that local planning authorities (counties and districts) would in due course be empowered to control land development by acquiring all the land in their areas suitable for development and selling or leasing it as required to private developers. The land would be bought at a price net of Development Land Tax but disposals would be at market value, so that a profit would accrue to the local authority. The land would be released in accordance with the structure plan and each authority drew up Land Acquisition and Management Schemes which had to be co-ordinated between county and districts. Land for residential development was to be sold freehold, but for other purposes (i.e. industrial or commercial building schemes), the land could only be leased out. Separate Community Land accounts had to be kept, to which all costs had to be charged — land acquisition, salaries of staff involved, interest on monies tied up — as though they were all capital in nature. (The interest would arise as a charge upon the total debit on the account and be credited to the authority's main funds which were in effect maintaining the burden until the land was disposed of). It was envisaged that the early years' transactions would result in deficits which would be carried forward. Ultimately, the account should go into surplus, and when this occurred, the profit was to be shared by the local authority (30%), the central government (40%), and the remaining 30% was to be divided among those local authorities with accounts still in deficit. The money arising from the surplus would only be used to repay outstanding debt or reduce the need to borrow for capital purposes.

In the event, the government has (via the 1980 Act) effectively removed the Community Land Act from the statute book. The accounts were ordered to be closed on the 31st March 1980, all balances were to be transferred to other accounts within the authority, no further consents to acquire land would be given, and there were no longer any restrictions upon the way in which any existing land was disposed of.

Consumer Protection

Local government has been involved in consumer protection for many years. This involvement started with the control of weights and measures, extended into public health with the regulation of food and drugs sold to the public, and now has taken in such matters as the misdescription of goods and services, and the protection of purchasers against unsafe or inflammable articles or materials sold to them.

Under the Weights and Measures Act 1963, county councils and London borough councils are required to appoint qualified inspectors of weights and measures to enforce the law applicable to the supplying of short weights or measures of goods, and to provide the public with standards by testing and adjusting weights and measures in return for a charge according to a statutory scale of fees.

London boroughs and county councils have duties under the Food and Drugs Act 1955 which relate to the enforcement of standards applicable to the composition or ingredients, the labelling and description of foods and drugs which are offered for sale to the public. These food and drugs authorities, as they are called must appoint a qualified public analyst who tests that food and drugs are not injurious to health and are of the correct nature and quality required.

The above statute also gives the district councils various duties with regard to hygiene in dealing with food and the prevention of contamination of milk, ice cream, etc. Local authority officers may inspect premises where food is prepared or stored with a view to being sold to the public, and they may also take samples of the food, etc. for analysis. The districts, in effect, have a duty to round off the county services by making up any deficiency in coverage.

The enforcement of the Trade Descriptions Acts and various associated statutes is the responsibility of the counties and London boroughs which can provide information centres staffed by trained personnel whose duty it is to receive and investigate cases of grievance brought by the public in regard to goods and services alleged to be wrongly described.

The Consumer Protection Acts and the Consumer Safety Act 1978 also give duties to the same authorities to protect people from buying goods and materials which are harmful or dangerous in nature.

Education. The local authorities which are responsible for local educational matters are called local education authorities, and these are the I.L.E.A. and the London boroughs in London, and elsewhere, they are the non-metropolitan counties and the metropolitan boroughs. The Department of Education and Science has supervisory powers in England in respect of all facets of education, whilst the Welsh Office is responsible for Wales. The central departments can enforce the national policies by making regulations under the Education Acts and issuing directions on occasions when local education authorities fail to carry out their statutory duties.

The L.E.A.s are required to provide adequate primary, secondary and further education facilities, and to have regard to the need for nursery, special and boarding schools. To do this, they employ teaching and other staff, provide school and ancillary buildings and the necessary materials, equipment and furniture. They also supply a number of subsidiary services, such as clothing, meals and milk, facilities for recreation, social and physical training, transport to facilitate children attending schools, and, (where the L.E.A. operates it), the youth employment service. The L.E.A. makes bye-laws in connection with the employment of children and may be directed by the central department to provide teacher training facilities.

The local education authority must appoint an education committee and there is power to co-opt persons with experience in education or acquainted with local educational conditions on to it, but they must be in a minority. Whenever possible, all matters in connection with the authority's educational functions should be debated by this committee. A chief education officer must also be appointed.

Compulsory education operates for children between 5 and 16 years of age, and tuition, books, etc. are supplied free in the schools. Schools in the local education authorities' sector are county or voluntary. County schools are those provided by the L.E.A. from the rates, voluntary schools are those provided originally by religious bodies which are classified as aided, controlled or special agreement, according to the financial arrangements entered into between the L.E.A. and the religious denomination. There are also independent schools which are outside the state system but are subject to a measure of control of standards, etc.

Further education is provided mainly in colleges of further education, polytechnics and universities. The first two types of institution are in the local authority sector, whilst the last has its own direct arrangements for finance with the Department of Education and Science. Students are charged fees, and, in the case of many full-time courses, receive grants from the local education authority towards their living costs while studying.

Expenditure on a number of services of a relatively minor nature in the field of education which is incurred in the first instance by local education authorities is "pooled" because the activities involved are considered of benefit to the whole country and not merely to the authority spending the money. Such services include the training of teachers, the provision of advanced further education (mainly the cost of running the polytechnics), and the education of No-area children (i.e. those who do not belong to the area of any authority, for instance, when a child's parents are living abroad). The expenditure incurred by the individual authorities is repaid to them, and gathered together into national totals (i.e. pooled) by the central departments. These total amounts are then allocated among the authorities on the basis, mainly, of school population in each area, though rateable value plays a part. The idea behind pooling appears to be fair, but a disadvantage is that the individual education authority does not bear the burden of its decisions to spend as, ultimately, it only pays a part of what it has spent together with a proportion of the total sum incurred by all the other authorities. There is no direct benefit in being economical and, possibly, some gain (for instance, in the development of local amenities) in spending in excess of the average. This weakness has been long recognised and considered by the government, and, at present, the advanced further education pool is "capped". This means that the total sum available for reimbursement and allocation is limited as part of the drive to reduce public sector spending. As a matter of administrative convenience, all the sums reimbursed and allocated in respect of these pooled services are dealt with by augmenting or netting the payment of the Rate Support Grant.

The pooled services are grouped in the G.R.F. or County Fund revenue account as a separate section of the education committee's accounts. The expenditure items comprise the amounts charged to the authority from the pools. The credit entries represent the reimbursement of the expenditure of the authority, the amount of which has been obtained by analysing the various expenditure codes in teacher training, further education, etc.

Environmental Health Services

District and borough councils carry out most of the services which relate to the maintenance of adequate standards of public hygiene and sanitation so that the population may enjoy a healthy, disease-free environment and pollution-free, uncluttered living conditions.

These services cover a very wide range and include such duties as: −

The disinfestation of premises and articles

Refuse collection (English counties have the duty of refuse disposal)

The provision of mortuaries, public conveniences, baths, washhouses, parks, recreation grounds and bathing places

Street cleansing and the prevention of litter

The removal of abandoned vehicles from roads and open spaces

Airport and seaport health matters

The regulation of building and the control of insanitary, defective and dangerous buildings and of caravan sites

The removal of nuisances from smoke and the encouragement of clean air

The prevention of diseases of animals and damage by pests such as rats and mice

The abatement of noise

Health and safety at work, and home safety

The control of slaughterhouse and offensive trades.

Some environmental health matters are the province of other bodies. The regional water authorities are responsible for sewage disposal, pure water, etc. and the National Health Service operates preventive services (e.g. for the control of epidemics) which are for the good of the community rather than matters of personal health.

Fire Service

Under the Fire Services Acts, the county councils are responsible for the maintenance of fire brigades, though some areas are covered by schemes of amalgamation. The fire authority, as it is called, has to ensure that the fire fighting service is adequate for dealing with normal demands, that the personnel are properly trained, that water supplies are available for the fighting of fires, and that fire prevention methods are publicised and encouraged. Arrangements can be made for one fire authority to cover part of the area of another authority, or to reinforce another authority's appliances when required on the basis of a payment or mutual assistance.

The appointment of a chief fire officer is required by law, and the approval of the Home Secretary is necessary to the appointment. The fire brigade committee is no longer a statutory committee but is normally appointed.

The Home Office is responsible for the fire service nationally, and has power to make regulations to encourage the efficiency of the brigades in such matters as training requirements, equipment standards, discipline, etc. and to appoint inspectors to inspect and report on the condition of the brigades.

The services of a fire brigade are free for the fighting of fires and action taken in emergencies and life-saving, but charges may be made for other types of services, such as pumping out a flooded cellar.

Highways. Highways is a somewhat old-fashioned word which is used in local government to refer to all types of thoroughfares used by vehicular traffic. It includes roads, streets, avenues, groves, lanes, drives, closes, and, on occasion, even walks. There are also motorways and roads for specific types of vehicles. The counties are responsible as highways authorities for all the roads in their areas, except for trunk roads and motorways which are built and maintained out of central government funds. (Nevertheless, these are usually maintained by the counties as agents of the central government.) In addition, a district council can act as an agent of the county by agreement in maintaining any roads in the district's area, and, furthermore, may claim to maintain minor roads in its own area as of right. The county has to reimburse the district for the costs it has incurred on the maintenance of roads, both as agent or as claiming authority. The highways authority is also responsible for the lighting of roads and streets and this function also may be delegated by agreement.

The main legislation dealing with roads is the Highways Act 1959, which contains provisions for the creation of roads, their closure, the making up of private streets and their adoption for future upkeep by the highway authority, the making of deposits in respect of houses to be built on unmade roads to meet the cost when the road is made up, and the rights and duties of the public, owners of adjoining land, public utility undertakings and local authorities in respect to roads.

Traffic regulation matters such as the siting of pedestrian and school crossings, the restricting of speed and type of vehicles on specific roads, and road safety arrangements are functions of the county council. Parking places, both on-street and off-street, are also the responsibility of the county though a district council may provide them with the county's consent. Parish councils are also empowered to provide off-street car parks, if the county consents, and cycle and motor-cycle parks.

Housing

The Secretary of State for the Environment is responsible for the national policy in regard to housing and has duties of supervision over the programmes carried out by the local housing authorities.

The Greater London Council, the London boroughs, and, elsewhere in England and Wales, the districts or boroughs are designated as housing authorities under the Housing Acts. Although the G.L.C. is a housing authority, it is reducing its involvement in the provision and maintenance of accommodation and concentrating more on the overall aspects of London's housing problems such as overspill. The counties outside London are not housing authorities but if a district requests, or if it makes no request but is consulted by the Secretary of State, the county can provide housing in the place of the district.

A housing authority has a duty to review the housing needs and problems in its area and decide upon the action needed to either relieve or solve them. Such action is basically the supply of housing accommodation and the control of housing standards. The authority can provide rented accommodation by building new houses or acquiring, converting or improving older houses. It can only build on land which it owns, and, if the land is outside its area, the county must be notifed. It can help people to purchase and improve dwellings by making grants and loans to them. It can also make arrangements with local housing associations which ease the district's housing problems.

It has the power to require that privately-owned houses (either single or in areas or groups) which are considered to be unfit for human habitation, should be repaired, closed or demolished. It may also take over houses which are in multiple occupation, i.e. where several tenants live in one house, in order to bring the condition of repair and maintenance and sanitation up to standard.

Besides the operation of rent rebate schemes for its own tenants who have low income levels, it must also provide a rent allowance scheme for tenants of privately-owned residential accommodation.

During the post-war period, emphasis has been placed on slum clearance, and this has meant the wholesale demolition of unfit houses, singly, in groups, or in so-called "clearance areas", and often the acquiring by the housing authority of the sites after clearance in order to provide new accommodation or to develop the sites in some other way. A clearance area often includes properties which are not defective in themselves e.g. factories, shops, well-maintained houses, etc. but if these were left out, the area would not be in a suitable shape for proper overall planning. Compensation for an unfit house and its land is, fairly obviously, the value of the cleared site, and, in practice, the authority often pays for the demolition and levelling and the former owner merely gets a nominal sum for the site. In the case of industrial and commercial properties and well-maintained houses, the compensation is full market value, and in the case of churches and chapels, alternative reinstatement is required, the authority financing the building of a new premise elsewhere – this can be costly. Owner-occupiers, even when their houses are below standard, are treated favourably by being given extra allowances in the calculation.

The tide of slum clearance and the providing of new dwellings has now begun to ebb for several reasons. Most of the slums have been cleared, the high rise flats which replaced them have proved a disappointment in some areas, land is becoming scarce and expensive, the movement of population out of the towns has affected the distribution of the Rate Support Grant, and building costs have also inflated. Housing authorities are more disposed to encourage the existing owners of private dwellings to refurbish the existing stock, and this encouragement can take the form of loans and grants.

Grants payable by housing authorities to the owners of houses which are in need of renovation are of four main kinds. There are improvement grants which are given at the discretion of the authority for converting, improving, altering and enlarging houses so that older property is brought up to a high standard or additional accommodation results. A second category contains intermediate grants which are a matter of right and are designed to bring houses up to standard as regards basic amenities. There are special grants which are akin to improvement and intermediate grants but are applicable to houses which are in multiple occupation, and repair grants which are discretionary and intended to bring houses into a good state of repair. Repair grants are suitable for use in "General Improvement Areas" and "Housing Action Areas" where a neighbourhood is selected for treatment as a unit. General improvement areas are characterised by containing a close-knit permanent population who are living in houses which are basically in good condition, whilst the inhabitants of housing action areas suffer from poor housing conditions, environmental problems and social deprivation.

The Housing Act 1980 has introduced a new dimension to the making of improvement grants by extending the right to improve their homes to tenants of council and private residential property.

The authority can provide open spaces, shops, and other facilities and amenities for the residents of its estates and can sell furniture to them on hire-purchase terms. It has a general power to manage its property and to charge rents. Government subsidies are receivable in respect of the cost of providing the housing services.

There are a number of legal requirements affecting the way in which a housing authority treats the expenditure and income it incurs and receives on its various functions connected with housing.

The first of these is the duty to keep a Housing Revenue Account (which has its own Balance Sheet) which contains the items which arise from the carrying out of what are called "Part V" (i.e. five) duties. These are so called because that part of the Housing Act 1936 outlined them as the provision of accommodation in acquiring land to build on, the erection of houses to rent and the running of the housing estates including many of their amenities. The main items found in the Revenue Account are thus the repair and maintenance of council dwellings, supervision and management, debt charges on outstanding debt on land, houses, etc., and the income from rents, government subsidies and rate fund contributions in respect of rent rebates granted and any deficiency on the year's working. The level of rents charged must be reasonable and the Housing Revenue Account should not make a surplus, though a working balance of a not too excessive amount can be carried forward.

Other duties under the Housing Acts fall within the General Rate Fund for accountancy purposes. These include "Part III" functions and loans and grants made for the buying or improvement of houses under the Housing Act code. Again, Part III refers to the part of the Housing Act 1936 under which land occupied by substandard houses is cleared i.e. repair, closure and demolition orders, clearance areas, etc.

In addition to lending money under the Housing Acts, a local authority (i.e. a district or borough) may make loans under the Small Dwellings Acquisition Acts which require a separate set of accounts to be kept for the transactions involved. This code is more restrictive than that under the Housing Acts. The loans must be to persons wishing to buy houses in the local authority area for their own occupation. The loans are repayable over various periods with a maximum of thirty years, and interest is charged at ¼ per cent in excess of the rate of interest the authority pays to the Public Works Loan Board. In addition, the interest rate cannot be amended during the currency of the loan, and there is a limit to the annual loss which can be incurred on the whole scheme. These constraints have had the effect of making local authorities prefer to make loans under the Housing Acts for the buying of houses, particularly as the interest rate can be flexible.

Controversy has existed for a number of years over the question of the sale of council dwellings to their occupiers. On the one hand, it is argued that selling houses and flats to the tenants would relieve the authorities of the future maintenance costs which would increase as the properties grew older. On the other hand, the opponents of the sale of council dwellings consider that it would be a financial mistake, as the council would need to replace the properties sold by new ones built at inflated costs. In addition, people who needed accommodation but could not afford to buy, would suffer because of the reduction in housing stock, which, in any case, would become poorer in quality, as the better units would be bought. These points are countered, in their turn, by the claim that tenants who wish to buy their homes have usually resided there a number of years, and have no intention of moving. The housing stock is therefore already reduced for the foreseeable future, and the proceeds of sale are available to go at least some way towards financing any replacement considered necessary. Furthermore, every tenant should have the power to own his own home and this should apply to persons living in council property as well as to those in privately let accommodation. The attitude of the central Government, over the years, has reflected the views of the party in power at any one time, and has thus alternated between encouraging and restricting sales. The local authorities, exercising their independence from Government control to its greatest extent, have either sold dwellings or banned their sale from much the same motives.

The Housing Act 1980 now embodies the current legal position which is that the tenants of dwellings owned by local authorities, New Town Development Corporations and a number of non-charitable Housing Associations have the right to buy their homes if they wish, unless those dwellings were specially built or adapted for the purpose of accommodating elderly people. This proviso is intended to preserve the local authority housing stock for the aged, and, in addition, there is a restriction upon the resale of dwellings situated in National Parks to prevent profit being made from property speculations. Tenants electing to buy their homes are entitled to substantial discounts which begin at 33% after three years as a tenant and reach 50% after 20 years, and there is also a freeze on prices for two years from the passing of the Act. Tenants are also entitled to a guaranteed mortgage from the authority to finance the purchase.

Where an authority fails to carry out its duty properly, i.e. it refuses or blocks the tenants' applications to buy, the Secretary of State for the Environment has the power to take over the authority's functions under the Act, and to charge it with the expenses he incurs in doing this.

Libraries

The public library system is administered in London by the London boroughs, in the rest of England by the non-metropolitan counties and metropolitan boroughs, whilst in Wales, there is provision for either the county or the district to be the library authority in any one area.

The ruling statute is the Public Libraries and Museums Act 1964 under which a relationship was implied between libraries, art galleries and museums. The Local Government Act 1972, however, made a distinction between libraries and the other two services by making the provision and maintenance of art galleries and museums a concurrent power which both the county and the district can provide, whereas the library service is not. At present, the Chancellor of the Duchy of Lancaster and the Secretary of State for Wales are responsible for the overall supervision of the library authorities in England and Wales respectively. They are both assisted by Library Advisory Councils.

A library authority has the duty to provide (to the satisfaction of the central department) such buildings, equipment, staff, etc. as will supply a comprehensive, efficient and free lending and reference service in respect of books, journals, etc. for its inhabitants and for those people who are employed or receive full-time education in its area. Persons outside these categories can be charged a fee for the loan of books, but there are often mutual arrangements whereby library tickets of one authority can be used in the libraries of other authorities. Charges may also be made for any services which go beyond the lending of books. For instance, all users may be charged for the reservation and notification of books on their return from other borrowers, for delay in returning books, for the sale of printed material which becomes the purchaser's property, the loan of music cassettes, the hiring of rooms for private functions, etc.

Arrangements exist under the 1964 Act for joint action by library authorities in bodies such as regional councils for inter-library co-operation. In addition, one authority may make facilities available to another (for which it may charge), and any authority may make contributions to assist other persons or bodies (including another library authority) in providing public library services.

An important aspect of the library authority's work is to encourage all kinds of people, individuals or groups, to use the library's services and to see that co-operation exists within its area among all the bodies involved in library functions. To this end, a great deal of help is given to school libraries (which are the responsibility of the local education authority), and such events as story telling afternoons for children, book displays, local history exhibitions and lecture series are held.

Lotteries

The search for new sources of income for local authorities, either to replace the General Rate, or, at least, to augment it, has been singularly unfruitful, except, possibly, in the case of local government lotteries which, though moderate in the amounts they bring in, have raised some useful income for those authorities who have undertaken them. The central government hesitated for several years before allowing local authorities to follow the example of the Premium Bonds into the realm of gambling. The present legal position is set out in the Lotteries and Amusements Act 1976 and its supporting regulations. The local authorities which can run "local lotteries" under the Act are county councils, the G.L.C., London borough councils, district and borough councils, and parish (England) or community (Wales) councils. The lotteries may be for any purpose which the authority can do legally, including those on which it can spend the twopence rate under the Local Government Act 1972. The actual operation of the lotteries is subject to a complicated series of limitations, including the requirement that each lottery has to have its own lottery fund into which the net proceeds (i.e. proceeds less expenses and prizes) must be paid.

The local authority must register with the Gaming Board and must say to what purpose the net proceeds of the lottery are to be put. The maximum price per ticket is 25p, and tickets must be all the same price which must be printed on the ticket and the whole price must be paid for the ticket to be part of the draw, and no refunds are allowed. There must be at least seven days between each lottery being held and thus the annual maximum is 52. There are three categories of lottery — short-term, medium-term, and others — to which the following table applies: —

	Short-term	Medium-term	Other
Maximum Single Prizes	£1,000	£1,500	£2,000
Maximum Proceeds of Sales	£10,000	£20,000	£40,000
Period between Lotteries	less than one month	from one month to less than three months	at least three months

The value of the prizes in total must not be more than half the takings, and the expenses incurred in running the lottery are also subject to limits. Where the proceeds do not exceed £5,000, the maximum expenses must be one quarter (i.e. up to £1,250) and for lotteries with proceeds over £5,000, the maximum expenses are 15%, or such higher percentage up to 25% as the Board may decide. Thus at least one quarter of the money paid for the tickets is available for the purposes of the lottery.

There is also regulation of the circumstances under which the tickets are sold, who can sell them and to whom. For instance, tickets cannot be sold in an amusement arcade, by officials visiting persons at home, nor to children under 16 years of age.

At the time of writing, new regulations are being prepared to increase the financial limits applicable to lotteries.

Planning

The planning of the use and development of land in England is supervised by the Secretary of State for the Environment, and in Wales by the Secretary of State for Wales, but the local planning is the responsibility of the county or district. Local authority duties under the Town and Country Planning Acts are subject to a degree of overlap where the county and district have concurrent powers, but generally, the county as county planning authority is in charge of matters affecting the whole county or several districts (the structure plan), and the district as district planning authority is responsible for functions within its area (the local plan). The structure plan needs the approval of the central department which is not usually called for in respect of the local plan.

The local authorities' main duties thus comprise the preparation of the above two types of development plans, the control of new development so that it conforms with the plans and the law, the conservation of the environment in the same way, and the responsibility for paying compensation to persons who have a legitimate claim that they have suffered financial loss because of planning decisions affecting their land.

The Police Service

The police forces of this country are employed to protect members of the public and their property, and to preserve law and order. Their role includes the prevention of crime and disorder, the investigation of crime, and the delivery of accused persons to the courts for trial.

Under the Police Act 1964, the police forces are organised on a county basis except in those areas where amalgamation schemes cover more than one county. Each force is controlled by a police committee which is termed "the police authority" and consists of councillors and justices of the peace (i.e. magistrates) from the areas served by the force. One county councillor is nominated to act as official liaison officer between the police authority and his council, so that questions and answers are channeled through him. There is a separate fund for the police force's expenditure and income, and its needs are met by the county council, any disagreements being ruled upon by the Home Secretary. The police authority is responsible for the operational efficiency and adequacy of the force. It appoints the chief constable to control the force under its direction, lays down the strength of the various ranks, and provides the buildings and equipment up to the standard required.

The central authority for the operations of the police service is the Home Secretary who is responsible for the Metropolitan Police but has only a supervisory role in respect of the other police forces in England and Wales. The Home Office may make regulations regarding police matters such as appointment, promotion, resignation, retirement, conditions of service (pay, hours of duty, pension entitlement, etc.), equipment, and discipline generally. Inspectors of constabulary are appointed centrally to visit, review and report on the efficiency of the police forces. The Home Office also provides "common" services such as training centres, forensic science laboratories, radio stations and depots, and records offices. The Home Office also undertakes research into police methods and equipment.

Because of the national nature of the police service and the need to enforce adequate standards of service, the Home Office makes a grant of 50% of the net expenditure incurred on police duties. (Some duties such as poisons control, mortuary expenses and coroner's office costs are ineligible for police grant).

The Promotion of Industry and Commerce

Many government bodies, both central, regional and local, are involved in matters affecting the distribution of industry and commerce, and local authorities have their role to play in attracting employment to their areas. One may, of course, say that the level of amenities and the standard of services supplied by a local authority together with the rate in the £ levied is a factor here – the provision of houses, schools, parks, roads, bus services, etc. should without doubt affect a decision as to the siting of a projected factory. There are, however, a number of Acts which give local authorities specific powers to help industrialists.

The Town Development Act 1952 enables a district to arrange to receive people who are living in overcrowded conditions in another district by building houses, providing facilities for public worship, recreation and other amenities, and, furthermore, by providing accommodation for the carrying on of industrial and other activities.

Under the Local Authorities (Land) Act 1963 local authorities can erect buildings or carry out works on land for the benefit or improvement of their areas. They can lend money for the erection of buildings on land they have.

The Community Land Act 1975 empowered a local authority to acquire land for private development and to let it on a leasehold basis for industrial and commercial purposes. It could sell the freehold in the case of land for privately-built dwellings. (These powers were effectively repealed by the 1980 Act).

The Local Government Act 1972 permits a local authority to spend up to 2p in the £ of the rate proceeds for any purpose (not specifically illegal) which it thinks will benefit its area of inhabitants. This power may be used to relieve industry of part of their rate burden or to assist in other ways. Such ways may include the appointment of an industrial development officer and contributing to the costs of a local development group comprising councillors, estate developers, industrialists, etc.

Local authorities can use their powers for planning control and compulsory purchase of land under the Town and Country Planning Acts to promote development in their areas for industrial, commercial and central area improvement purposes. The redevelopment of a town centre with its shops, leisure complexes, multiple-storey and other types of car parks, integrated bus/railway station, etc. is an obvious addition to an area's infra-structure.

In recent years, there has been an increasing emphasis by the State upon the bringing back to life of the inner city areas in the major conurbations. Powers have been given to local authorities in those areas to carry out schemes for improving the environment, providing recreational facilities and encouraging industry and commerce. In several cities, "partnership" arrangements exist for carrying out schemes in which local and central authorities work together. There are also proposals to set up urban development corporations to revitalise areas such as Merseyside and the London dock areas, and to form a number of "enterprise zones" in industrial areas. These zones will be exempt from rates, subject to a relaxed planning code and the firms situated there will receive increased capital allowances for tax purposes.

Social Welfare

The personal social services are provided under the Local Authorities Social Services Act 1970 by the London boroughs, non-metropolitan counties and metropolitan boroughs. The authority must appoint a director of social services and a social services committee to administer the services dealing with the welfare of the elderly, physically and mentally handicapped, distressed families and children deprived of a normal home life.

The services to the elderly include residential accommodation in homes provided by the authority, and assistance where the senior citizen lives at home in the way of visits by social workers, meals on wheels, luncheon and other clubs, domestic help in household work, telephones, and in the case of blocks of council flats, the provision of warden services.

The authority has a duty to ascertain the number of physically handicapped or disabled people in its area and to make them and the public aware of the services available. They can receive similar services to those given to the aged, together with adaptations to their homes, and appliances to ease their disabilities, occupational workshops and holidays.

Mentally-handicapped persons when at home receive assistance from social workers, and after-care and preventative treatment by the provision of centres for care and training. Residential accommodation may also be provided.

The social workers assist families in need of assistance in respect of problems of incompatibility and inadequacy. The domestic helps can assist mothers, and children's officers ensure the welfare of children who are in need of care or ill-treated. Children may also be boarded out with foster parents or placed in community homes if home conditions are too adverse.

There is close co-operation between the social welfare departments of local authorities and the National Health Service via joint consultative committees and day-to-day collaboration by officers.

The Department of Health and Social Security is responsible for the supervision of the local authorities in carrying out the social welfare services. The Secretary of State is supported by a network of advisory bodies on various aspects of the services.

Sports and Recreation

Local authorities of all classes have powers to provide a great variety of community recreational services under a number of separate statutes. These services can take the form of public parks of several kinds, park games, recreation grounds or playing fields, pleasure walks, sports centres (indoor and outdoor), lidos and bathing places, camping facilities, public shows and entertainments, restaurants and refreshment facilities, and allotments.

The Public Health Acts give power to local authorities to provide, and to help to provide, parks, recreation grounds, etc. in which they can maintain amenities for sports and pastimes for which they can make charges (which are normally kept low to encourage the public to use the facilities). Refreshment facilities may be provided at these places and bye-laws may be made by the local authority to control the actions and behaviour of the users of the parks. The Countryside Act 1968 permits counties and districts to provide and manage country parks within easy reach of urban dwellers and to install facilities for countryside pastimes such as picnic areas, nature trails, fishing, etc.

Under the National Parks and Access to the Countryside Act 1949, the Countryside Act 1968 and the Local Government Act 1972, the county council is responsible for any National Park in its area. The county establishes a National Park Committee which appoints a National Park Officer. The county, via its committee and officer, makes the plans and carries them out. The amenities provided include accommodation, toilets, refreshment places, carparks, camping sites and a warden service, and similar facilities to those found in country parks.

The Local Government (Miscellaneous Provisions) Act 1976 gives very wide powers to local authorities to provide facilities within or outside their areas for land and water sports. Included in the powers, are the provision of premises, pleasure boats, instructors, parking amenities, and the supply of food, drink and tobacco, with or without charge. Local authorities can also operate restaurants under the Civic Restaurants Act 1947. Such restaurants can be licensed and whilst land can be bought compulsorily under this Act, an existing restaurant business can only be acquired by agreement. The number of authorities using their powers under the 1947 Act has decreased markedly in recent years because the powers are lost if a deficit is incurred for three consecutive years (separate accounts must be kept), and also wider powers exist under other Acts, some of which have already been mentioned.

The local education authority provides many kinds of amenities for physical education at its schools and other educational establishments which are for the benefit of pupils but may be rented to outside organisations and persons.

Where a district or parish council thinks that there is a need, it can provide small plots of land which local residents can spend their leisure time in cultivating and producing fruit and vegetables for the family table. Under the Allotments Acts, the local authority must fix reasonable rents and may be required to pay compensation to the tenant when the tenancy finishes.

Smallholders are a more commercial proposition than allotments as they are provided by both metropolitan and non-metropolitan counties under the Agriculture Act 1970 (and parts of the Smallholdings and Allotments Acts) for letting to persons who wish to be farmers. The local authorities have powers to manage smallholdings – agree tenancies, fix rents, assist the tenants in supply and marketing situations, make loans to them – and may be required to pay compensation to the tenant on the termination of the tenancy. The Ministry of Agriculture, Fisheries and Food has supervisory and default powers, and can make grants, mainly for improvements. The default powers mean that the Ministry can take over the functions if it is dissatisfied with the local authority's standard of service.

Finally, the Local Government Act 1972 empowers a local authority to provide entertainments which include dancing, theatre and concert facilities, the upkeep of a band or orchestra, developing arts and crafts, and the provision of refreshments on such occasions. This Act also gives a local authority power to spend up to a twopence rate on any matter which it considers is in the interest of its area or residents, but this expenditure must not be authorised by any other statute, nor be for an illegal purpose.

The Free Twopence

Local authorities in England and Wales are created by statute and thus can only spend money on doing those things which the law specifically authorises them to do. One small exception does, however, occur in S.137, Local Government Act 1972 which permits a local authority (i.e. a county, district or borough, or a parish or community council) to spend up to (at present) a twopence rate in any year upon lawful matters which it thinks are to the benefit of all or part of its area or inhabitants, provided that the authority has no authority to do these things under any other statute.

This relaxation also extends to the making of contributions to the expenditure of other local authorities under this section, and to contributing to charities, non-profit making bodies and certain public appeals.

A further condition is that the expenditure must be shown in a separate account, but the decision to operate under the section may be taken after the expenditure has been incurred.

It is a matter of interest that similar free funds can be found in the endowment funds of the National Health Service where they are used for the provision of comforts, assistance, etc, to patients and staff which are outside the ambit of exchequer funds, and in the "Common Good" funds of Scottish local authorities where they are used in the interests of the inhabitants of the area. In addition, prior to the 1972 Act, the municipal corporations (i.e. the boroughs) were not creatures of statute, and their legal position as regards the "ultra vires" rules was a matter of argument, and the central government was perhaps relieved of a problem when all the local authorities became completely subject to statute law.

Capital, Renewal and Repairs, and Insurance Funds

Before the Local Government (Miscellaneous Provisions) Act 1953 was passed, the position was that local authority funds which were formed to average out the amount levied in rates, one year with another, were, with few exceptions, held to be illegal following the decision given in Morgan v Cardiff Rating Authority in 1933. The exceptions were statutory funds such as the superannuation funds and those reserve funds for which the authority had Local Act power. Trading undertaking also were permitted reserve funds under the Acts which formed them.

The 1953 Act introduced legally-recognised Capital Funds and Renewal and Repairs Funds which could be used to meet future expenditure by accumulating current monies. These funds were subjected to restrictions, mainly because of their newness, as to maxima, the size of single transactions and other matters, which tended to reduce their usefulness and flexibility. This preliminary stage of central regulation has now passed, and the present position is now greatly relaxed and is contained in the Local Government Acts 1972 and 1976.

A local authority is now able to establish such funds as it considers necessary. There is no limit on a fund's size, nor on sums paid in, nor on payments out, though it must not be used for the purposes of a trading undertaking. Any money not in use should be invested in specified securities. The three main kinds of fund encountered under this arrangement are Capital, Renewal and Repairs, and Insurance Funds. Separate accounts have to be kept for the transactions of each fund.

A Capital Fund is used to finance capital expenditure which is not covered by a loan sanction, but it may also be employed in accelerating the repayment of debt. The payments out of the Capital Fund may be treated as advances to the service involved and repaid, with or without interest, over the life of the asset or assets acquired.

A Renewal and Repairs Fund is available to meet the cost of repair and maintenance and also the renewal or replacement of buildings, plant and equipment, vehicles and similar assets. Such a fund is usually managed in accordance with some long-term policy or it is used in addition to normal requirements (e.g. to take any extra burden off the revenue account). Here, also, repayments to the fund may be required, and, if so, these are based on the expected life of the asset or the work carried out.

An Insurance Fund gives a local authority the choice between insuring with an insurance company or within itself (i.e. self-insurance) in respect of the various risks which it runs. The fund may be opened with a contribution from the rates and then built up by payments from the services covered. The first contribution should be enough to cover any foreseeable losses in the early years, until the fund has grown. The surplus in hand should be invested until it is needed to pay any claims. Self-insurance appears to be advantageous in areas where premiums to insurance companies would be large whilst the risk would be relatively small. An example which comes to mind, is the insurance of council dwellings against damage by fire. In such a case, the premium, being based upon a large capital expenditure figure, would be equal to the cost of several houses being completely gutted – an unlikely event in any one year. However, where a local authority has high rise flats with lifts, the decision might well be to insure outside as damage could be much greater and there is an increased possibility of loss of life. Other risks can always be insured outside the fund, either directly by the departments involved or via the Insurance Fund acting as a centralised channel.

As a local authority is handling public money, it is prudent for it to insure against risks although normally there is no legal requirement for it to do so. For this reason, a local authority which insures for reasonable risks is unlikely to be accused of acting in an "ultra vires" manner. Two cases when insurance is compulsory are – the taking of security for officers handling money and fire cover on houses on which advances have been made under the Small Dwellings Acquisition Acts.

Insurance is an area where the assessment of the risks covered and the premiums charged by different companies, together with periodic reviews of policies, can result in great savings to a local authority. For this reason, authorities often employ qualified insurance officers.

The main classes of insurance risks which are met in local and public authorities include: –

Cash in Transit and in Safes – for the risk of loss and theft of cash.

Computer – for the risk of damage, cost of repair and of standby arrangements when needed.

Employers Liability – for the risk of injury, disease or death sustained by employees while working.

Engineering Inspection – for the risk of injury, loss or damage caused by breakdown, and also to fulfil legal requirements to inspect steam boilers, lifts, etc. Cover can also be given for the cost of repairs.

Fidelity Guarantee – for the risk of losses of cash, stock items, etc. from dishonesty by employees. The basis of the premium is an amount per head for "accounting officers" who handle money or stock, and a lower amount per head for other employees.

Fire – for the risk of fire damage to property.

Libel and Slander – for the risk of damages being awarded against councillors and chief officials for defamatory statements at meetings, in reports, etc.

Life and Personal Accident – for the risk of injury or death of councillors whilst carrying out or travelling on official duties.

Officials' Indemnity – for the risk of claims where members of the public have suffered loss because of negligence, error or failure to act on the part of officials.

Public Liability – for the risk of the authority (or its contractors) causing injury, death or sickness to members of the public or damage to their property accidentally in carrying out its functions.

Theft – for the risk of items of equipment, etc. being stolen, with damage to buildings and fittings.

Vehicle – for the risk of claims from other persons for injury, death and damage to vehicles or property, and for damage to the authority's own vehicles.

Superannuation

Local authorities are required by law to maintain schemes for providing retirement pensions and other benefits to various classes of their employees. The bulk of the whole-time officers and manual workers is included in the pension funds set up under the Local Government Superannuation Acts, and these are administered by the G.L.C., the London boroughs and the county councils. The county council schemes include the employees of the district councils in the county as well as the county's own personnel. The fund is a trust fund held by the administering authority on behalf of the present and future beneficiaries, and it has a separate Revenue Account and Balance Sheet.

The employees pay their contributions to the fund by a deduction being made from their pay – a basic 6% for officers and 5% for manual workers. The reason for the difference is that an officer receives increments per a salary scale and his benefits are related usually to his final salary, whereas a manual worker receives the rate of pay for the trade no matter how long he serves. The employing authority also contributes to the fund in the form of a percentage of staff pay. This percentage is declared as necessary by an actuary to keep the fund solvent in regard to future commitments. The actuary revises this figure every five years when a statutory valuation of the fund takes place.

Benefits are based on annual pay received towards the close of the employee's service and the length of time he has served in a pensionable position. They are usually an annual retirement pension and a lump sum which is payable on retirement. Arrangements exist for early retirement, transfers to and from funds, resignation and the freezing of rights, widow's and dependants' pensions etc. At the present, benefits are generally index-linked.

One major problem in the management of superannuation funds is the investment of surplus funds in an optimal manner which combines the need for income to accumulate as quickly as possible and the duty of the local authority to safeguard the fund's assets. The Trustee Investments Act 1961 allows investments to be divided between various classes of securities. At the present, a minimum of one-quarter of the investment must be in "narrower range" securities (which are not to any real degree speculative in nature) and a maximum of three-quarters in "wider range" (which are more speculative, but not excessively so). Superannuation money may be invested in the local authority, but the arrangement must be of a formal nature and the interest must be at a fair rate, and the money must be repayable if the pension fund needs it. The Act also regulates the position regarding the obtaining of proper professional advice about investment policy.

There are also local authority schemes for policemen and firemen. These are, however, "unfunded" as they are treated as part of the employing authority's main fund (i.e. backed by the county or district fund). Benefits are debited to the Revenue Account and the deductions from pay are credited, transfer values are both received and paid, but the balance either way is absorbed by the Revenue Accout. There is also a centralised scheme for teachers operated by the Department of Education and Science.

Questions
3.1 What is the doctrine of Ultra Vires?
3.2 Describe the nature and constitution of a local authority.
3.3 Who may vote in a local government election, and who may stand as a candidate?
3.4 Draw a diagram of the present system of multi-purpose local authorities in England and Wales.

3.5 What are the differences between the functions of metropolitan and non-metropolitan counties?

3.6 Which are the local authorities which are empowered to provide a library service and what are the statutory conditions ruling the service?

3.7 Give examples of the services which you would expect a parish council to carry out.

3.8 Outline the powers of local authorities to spend money in respect of disasters in their areas.

3.9 What are the duties of a fire services committee?

3.10 What are bye-laws and how do local authorities make them?

Chapter 4

Internal Structure and Organisation of Local Authorities

It is mainly a matter for a local authority itself to decide how it organises its internal arrangements to enable it to carry out the duties laid upon it by Parliament. It is true that there are a number of legal requirements, such as the need to form statutory committees to which certain duties must be given, the making of standing orders to regulate certain procedures, the observance of the rights of access to information by the public and press, but so long as it observes requirements of this nature, a local authority is free to choose its own form of organisation and mode of operation. The exercise of this discretion by local authorities means that each has its own unique internal arrangements which cloth the skeleton organisational requirements demanded by Parliament.

(a) *The Council*

The basic pattern of operation by local authorities is via the council, committees and departments. The councillors meet to decide policy matters with the help and advice of the staff, and the staff are responsible for carrying out what the members have decided should be done.

The council which is the authority's supreme decision-making body, is composed of all the councillors, and its meetings are presided over by the chairman or the mayor. Decisions on major policy formulation and changes are reserved to the full council, as it is called, together with the carrying out of statutory powers it is not allowed to delegate, such as the levying of a rate or the issuing of a precept, or the borrowing of a loan.

(b) *The Committees*

It is obvious that only a few matters can be considered and debated at the council meetings, and therefore, most council decisions are those taken in line with the recommendations made by the committees. The committees are meetings of relatively small numbers of councillors at which detailed discussion of the problems of a service (or of a number of related services) takes place. The committee system enables members to specialise in their areas of interest, to use that knowledge to better advantage, and to establish close working relationships with the officers who attend the meetings in order to advise the councillors and who eventually see to their decisions being carried out.

Where a problem requires special consideration, a committee may appoint a sub-committee from among its members to carry this out and to report back. The practice of co-option — the inviting of persons from outside the council to be members of committees by reason of their having valuable experience of a service or the area — assists in arriving at informed decisions. Variations occur in the statutes as to the maximum number of persons who may be co-opted to committees, the general limit being one-third of the total membership of a committee, but no co-option is permitted on the finance committee (or sub-committee) because of this committee's special responsibilities in the area of financial decision-taking.

A local authority may appoint such committees as it considers it needs to carry out its functions, but there is a requirement (where the authority is of the class charged with the service) to appoint an education, social service children's regional planning, and police committee (there are also a few minor ones), and to refer matters relating to the appropriate service to it, unless urgency prevents this. The council has the power to decide which councillors are to be members of its committees, and whilst it cannot force a councillor to attend a committee, it can remove him from a committee at any time.

In deciding what powers and duties the committees should have, the council can either refer or delegate specific decisions and matters to individual committees (always excluding rating, precepting and borrowing which cannot be delegated). When a matter is referred, then the committee resolution must be approved by the council before it can bind the local authority and be put into practice lawfully. This procedure is, of course, the normal way in which the authority goes about its business. Where the authority has the legal power to delegate, and does so, then it may arrange for the function to be carried out by a committee, which, if the council does not disagree, may pass the power to a sub-committee, which, if the council and committee do not disagree, may pass it once again to an officer. Delegation means that the decision can be carried out without going before the council for approval and that any action taken thus binds the authority in law.

Committees are sometimes classified in accordance with the nature of the task they are set. Standing committees run services which are of a continuing character, e.g. education, parks and amenities, etc. Education is, of course, statutory whilst parks and amenities is not. Special committees are appointed for specific tasks and then dis-banded on their completion, e.g. charter centenary celebrations. Joint committees may be formed to take decisions on matters of interest to several local authorities and are made up of councillors from each of the constituent bodies, e.g. National Park joint committee.

The committee structure of local authorities has been radically affected by the recommendations of the Bains Report "New Local Authorities: Management and Structure", 1972, which suggested the formation of a policy and resources committee with four sub-committees — land, personnel, finance and performance review. This committee's function would be to receive advice from its sub-committees and from officers' management teams (applying ideas of corporate management), control the spending committees (which supervise the running of the services), and thus co-ordinate all the authority's policies and finance decisions in an optimal manner.

Most local authorities have gone some way towards adopting the Bains Report recommendations but developments are still under way.

An example of a structure plan for committees is given below: –

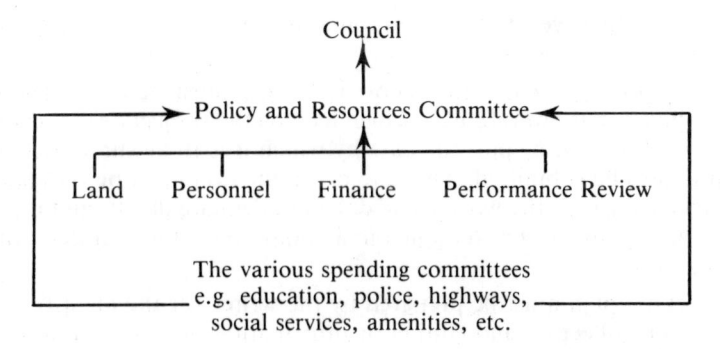

```
                            Council
                              ↑
          ┌─────────→ Policy and Resources Committee ←─────────┐
          │                   ↑                                │
          │         ┌─────────┼─────────┐                      │
          │    Land    Personnel    Finance    Performance Review
          │                                                    │
          │           The various spending committees          │
          └───────── e.g. education, police, highways, ────────┘
                      social services, amenities, etc.
```

The procedure for meetings, both committee and council, is fairly fixed in form. The minimum number of meetings of the council is laid down in the 1972 Act – usually four, including the annual meeting – but the council has a discretion as to how often each committee meets. It is normal practice to lay down a timetable of quarterly, bi-monthly, or monthly meetings, and the date of the next meeting is the last item on the agenda and in the minutes to provide an aide-memoire.

The agenda is issued a few days before the meetings and contains a list of items contributed by the various officers involved, together with supporting reports and the minutes of the previous meeting (which are to be approved as correct and any matters arising discussed). There may also be minutes from other committees to be considered and the final item, A.O.B. (i.e. any other business) is normally restricted by standing orders to unimportant matters in order to prevent its misuse.

The meeting starts at the prescribed time, date and place, and there must be enough members present to form a quorum according to standing orders. Each item on the agenda is discussed, usually in the order laid-down, though changes can be made. For instance, a chief officer may attend to report on two items which are not consecutive, and these may be brought together in order to save his time. Each decision is recorded by the administrative assistant and this record forms the basis of the minutes which the chairman ultimately signs as being correct at the next meeting. A manuscript minute book is often kept which contains items of confidential nature, such as the sums paid for property, and these are not included in the published version of the minutes.

Whilst reports are on occasion made in spoken form by officers to their seniors or to committee members, it is usual for written reports to be made on the more important matters, as a matter of record or to provide a basis for later discussion and decision-taking. Reports may arise in a number of ways. An officer may be required to report periodically by standing orders or he may himself decide that a report on a specific topic is timely. On the other hand, the report may be submitted in response to a request for information about a problem and its possible solution or solutions.

It is possible, however, to lay down some general advice for the preparation of most types of report: –

1. The purpose for which the report is needed must be clear. The writer must be given terms of reference which include the subject of the report, the use to which it is to be put, the date by which it is to be submitted, and to whom it is to be submitted. The date of submission must be far enough in the future to permit the work to be done in adequate detail, and it is usual for all these points to be contained in a committee minute or departmental memorandum.

2. A working plan must be prepared by the writer for the identification of sources, the collection and editing of information needed as a basis to the report. Forms may be prepared for extracting the data. Thought must be given to any factors which might be relevant to the issues involved in the topics under review, otherwise the report may prove to be incomplete because aspects have been missed or ignored.

Information may be forthcoming from previous reports on related subjects or on the same topic in past years. Other public authorities may be able to help where problems of a similar nature have been encountered already elsewhere – a questionnaire might be sent out to them on the matter.

3. The data must now be collected. Every attempt must be made to make them accurate, adequate and relevant (and this applies throughout the manipulations which they undergo until the report is finally drafted). The facts and figures should be arranged in the order called for by the report's objectives without any relaxation of standards of impartiality and clarity of presentation. Tables and graphs may be prepared to bring out the patterns in the collected data and be used later either in the body of the report or in appendices. All the implications in these edited figures should be absorbed by the writer.

4. The writer is now in the position to prepare the first draft of the report. A clear, easy style is recommended, with headings and numbered paragraphs which should lead on to one another and occasionally refer back to previous points made, so as to preserve interest and continuity.

The draft (and the finalised) report may be divided as follows: –

(a) The person or persons to whom it is addressed
(b) The date of preparation (of the final draft)
(c) The title of the report together with its purpose and terms of reference

(d) An introduction which summarises the way the terms of reference have been carried out, where and how the information has been obtained, any factors which have raised problems in preparing the report or limited the enquiries and might affect the results.

(e) The collected facts are now presented duly summarised in the body of the report. Their characteristics are analysed and used as a basis for the findings which spell out the essentials of the situation as revealed by the data.

(f) The writer now converts his findings into conclusions. He draws inferences from the data as to the causes of their characteristics. Whilst there may be room for statistical hypothesis testing of an unbiased nature, one cannot avoid being subjective in judging the situation indicated by the findings.

(g) The next step is for the writer to give his recommendations for future action (usually to improve the present situation revealed by his findings). Though these suggestions all call for actions which vary in effectiveness, cost and the use of resources generally, they must all stem from the same facts, findings and conclusions without distortions.

(h) Next come any appendices which are needed for data which is too bulky to be included in the findings in an unabridged form. Tables, charts, references and quotations may be found there.

(i) The final part of the report is often a summary which covers the essentials of the preceding sections. This is provided to inform the reader of the contents of the report, especially when he has not had the time to read it. (A necessary safeguard for a busy councillor, and it is hoped that he or she manages to read it during the discussion).

5. The second draft and later ones are now prepared until the final copy is reached and submitted to the persons for whom the report is intended.

Example of an abridged Report to a Committee.

To: Chairman and Members of the Cleansing Sub-committee
From: Director of Finance   14/7/ − 3
Subject: Sale of Salvaged Material from Refuse Collections.

1. Introduction: This report is submitted as required by Minute No. 123 of 4/6/ − 3 which required me to enquire into the current situation relating to the above-mentioned activity and to report upon future profitability.

2. Findings: The current position is that textiles, paper and metals are extracted from refuse and sold to scrap dealers for re-cycling. The current throughput, if continued, is estimated to show a net loss of £50,000 over the next four years. In the last few weeks, however, the economic situation in the re-cycling sector has suffered a fall in prices which may continue.

3. Conclusions: In view of the above-mentioned findings, there appears to be little prospect of this activity becoming profitable in the foreseeable future.

4. Recommendations: The activity should be suspended until the market situation improves. The staff should be moved to other work.

5. Appendices: Estimated running costs and sales for each commodity for the next four years, together with forecast Profit and Loss Accounts.
6. Summary: This report is into the profitability of the sale of salvaged materials from refuse and as no profit is foreseen for the next four years, it is recommended that the activity be suspended and the staff moved to other work.

(c) *Councillors*

As an individual, a councillor has little power, unless he is chairman of a major committee, but he is entitled to such information from the local authority as will enable him to carry out his committee duties adequately so far as participation in discussion and decisions is concerned. He has a statutory right to inspect and copy the accounts of the authority and its officers, and, if he is an elector for the area, he can inspect and copy the authority's minutes, orders for making payments and the abstract of accounts. Any other rights he has of access to documents arise from custom and implication under the common law. There have been a series of court decisions on the boundaries to the member's entitlement to information. Besides his duty to attend council and committee meetings (six months' unauthorised absence is grounds for disqualification from office), he also deals with complaints brought to him by the public and tries to prevent waste and to correct administrative errors committed by the local authority. He is required to disclose any interest of a financial nature he may have in any matter arising at meetings and should usually not take part in the discussion or any vote taken. Statements he makes at meetings have "qualified privilege" where he makes them as part of his duty and without malice. This means that he is normally protected against court action for libel or slander, but many local authorities, nevertheless, insure their members and chief officers against the possibility of such an action being brought.

Allowances are payable to councillors in respect of financial loss, travelling expenses and subsistence (i.e. meals and refreshments) which they have had to bear or pay for by reason of carrying out officially approved duties, such as attending council and committee meetings, local authority conferences, etc. Senior members can now be paid for special responsibility.

(d) *Staff*

A local authority has the power to appoint such staff as it considers necessary for the carrying out of its functions. There is thus great flexibility in the creation of staff posts and the allotting of duties and, indeed, titles, but, as in other areas of local government practice, there are statutory requirements to fulfil. Certain specified officers must be appointed by those authorities who are responsible for the relevant services. The chief education officer, chief constable, chief fire officer (and firemen), director of social services, and weights and measures inspectors are examples. There are also instances of central control as departmental approval is needed to the appointment of a chief constable, a chief fire officer, a director of education and a chief social services officer.

The personnel, as already mentioned, have the role of advising the councillors on policy matters at committee and council meetings, and of carrying out the policies once they have been decided by the members. The chief officers and senior staff of the departments attend the meetings and instruct the more junior grades of employees in the day-to-day running of the authority. To reduce the chance of confusion between the functions of members and officers the council usually draws up standing orders which lay down terms of reference indicating areas of responsibility and limits to the delegation of powers to officials, or, as it might be better put, those actions and decisions which are delegated as a matter of routine to the staff.

The Maud (1967) and the Bains (1972) Committee Reports have had an appreciable effect upon the staffing arrangements of local authorities. The former post of clerk to the council has been converted into that of chief executive, and its powers and duties radically changed and enhanced. Formerly, the holder of the office was usually a solicitor who was occupied with the legal and secretarial aspects of the council's work. Now he is, first and foremost, an administrator with the power to control the departmental chief officers' actions on questions of the efficient management of their departments and to regulate their collaboration with one another. The legal and secretarial work has now normally passed to a director of administration, thereby often relieving the chief executive of departmental work. The chief executive is also responsible for the successful operation of the corporate management teams of chief and other officers which help and advise the Policy and Resources Committee and its sub-committees in their decision-taking.

The removal by the Local Government Act, 1972, of the duty to appoint a treasurer was a traumatic event for the municipal accountancy profession. An authority need now only secure that one of its officers is responsible for the administration of its statutory financial code. The officer need not be a professionally qualified accountant, indeed, he could be the chief executive or any other officer. This financial officer, often called the finance director, is the council's financial adviser, accountant, collector and paymaster. His duties include running the finance division (the department dealing with financial matters) under the supervision of the finance sub-committee. Under the influence of the Maud and Bains Reports, he has become a member of a management team composed of chief officers, headed by the chief executive. Formerly, the treasurer was jealous of his independence of action, and though he still has duties which make him directly responsible to the citizens, he, as a member of a team, must compromise occasionally on matters of finance where the majority opinion differs from his. His role is now to ensure that the financial implications of any project under review are fully discussed and appreciated before a decision is reached on the advice to be given to the members.

The usual arrangement is for the management team to be composed of the chief executive, director of finance, chief planning officer (who is the officer in charge of area development), chief personnel officer (who is responsible for staffing), and other officers responsible for the departments involved in the items under discussion. In some local authorities, there is provision for teams of this advisory nature consisting of senior staff below chief officer grade, e.g. discussions on internal control or value for money to which the chief internal auditor is a party and from which reports are made to the performance review sub-committee.

The personnel employed in local government comprise administrative, professional and technical staff, teachers, policemen, firemen, and many classes of tradesmen and manual workers. Conditions of service, salary scales and wage rates are subject to national agreements.

Local authorities are required by law to maintain schemes to provide pensions and other retirement benefits to various classes of their employees. These schemes are all contributory, the employees paying a contribution based on a percentage of their salaries by deduction from their pay. The whole-time officers and most manual workers are included in funds operated under the Local Government Superannuation Acts 1937-72, whilst the police and firemen's schemes are financed out of the authority's main fund, and the teachers' scheme is run by the central government.

Benefits are normally based on the salary for the final year of service and the length of service. They take the form of an annual pension with the usual addition of a lump sum. Arrangements exist for early retirement on grounds of illness, for resignation and the freezing of rights, widow's and dependants' pensions, transfer of rights to other schemes on changing employment, etc.

Unlike the police and fire service schemes which are termed "unfunded" as their income and expenditure each year goes to the authority's revenue account, the local government schemes are "funded", which means that they are a form of trust fund with a separate existence from the other funds of the local authority. Superannuation was made a county function under the Local Government Act 1972 – the districts are thus employing authorities whilst the county is both an employing and an administering authority. In London, however, both the Greater London Council and the London boroughs operate superannuation funds.

(e) *Standing Orders and Regulations*

The council, committees and departments of a local authority require an atmosphere of order, routine and assurance in which to take decisions and to carry on the day-to-day work as efficiently as possible. For this reason, and because of the large scale of the operations of modern local government, a comprehensive code for the conduct of business is a necessity. In addition, this code has to take account of the public and political nature of local government, because public funds are used, and this gives rise to the duty to ensure that they are spent in proper ways, after sufficient open discussions have both taken place and been seen to take place.

A local authority's standing orders or instructions, as they are called, can be classified in three ways. Some are contained in the Acts of Parliament, especially the Local Government Act 1972, which gives detailed instructions regarding such activities as the holding of annual, extraordinary and other meetings, the quorum needed for business to be transacted at a meeting, the recording and signing of minutes and the election of a chairman. Some standing orders are required by law to deal with such matters as the making of proper arrangements for financial affairs and the ensuring of competition and the inviting of tenders regarding contracts, but their content is at the discretion of the local authority. The third type of standing orders are those made completely at the option of the authority to suit its own particular circumstances. A number of the instructions are often segregated under the title of financial regulations as they deal with receipts and payments, security of assets, etc. and are often more detailed in nature than other types of standing orders.

It is normal practice for a council to draw up its standing orders and financial regulations in the form of a booklet which incorporates any relevant extracts from the Acts of Parliament for easy reference by members and officials in cases of dispute or in the search for enlightenment. A brief list of the booklet's contents could be: —

The procedure for calling meetings and for conducting business at meetings; The constitution, powers and duties (or terms of reference) of the authority's committees;

The allocation of duties and functions to the chief officials and departments; The methods of inviting tenders, entering and executing contracts for the supply of goods or materials or for the execution of works;

The arrangements for accounting, budgetary control, incurring of liabilities, payments, receipt of income, safety of assets, internal audit, insurances, banking, borrowing, etc.

The appointment of employees and matters arising from their conditions of service.

It is usual for each councillor and senior officer to be given a copy of the standing orders on starting his duties, and this practice is to be recommended in an organisation which lives on whilst people come and go.

The External Relationships of a Local Authority

It is a self-evident that the world outside a local authority plays an important role in the way an authority shapes its structure, chooses its policies and makes its decisions. Parliament has created it, given it powers and, at any time, can take decisions which radically alter its form and purpose. It is one component in a two (and sometimes three) tier system of local government which interacts with an array of public corporations in providing services to the public. There are the public, press, political parties and pressure groups who make their points about the direction and quality of its services.

(a) *Other Local Authorities and Public Sector Organisations.*
It is suggested, with reason, that the freedom of action of a local authority is often restricted by decisions taken by other public bodies in the same or neighbouring areas. The provision of basic services (often called the infrastructure) – roads, housing, shopping precincts, crematoria, power and water supplies, etc. – by one body encroaches on the choices available to the others, both by reason of the overall limits to financial resources and the need to avoid over-providing services. The existence of such facilities, or the prospect of their being provided, can affect the manner and direction in which developments take place. Similar effects can be felt by differing levels of rates and industrial aid in neighbouring districts.

This is not intended to imply that public authorities are forever competing. There are many occasions where local authorities undertake joint action on matters of common interest. This can take the form of joint committees, joint boards (which are separate legal entities), arrangements to lend staff to one another, to supply one another with goods and services, and to act as agents in, say, highways maintenance. Co-operation is also necessary in such matters as planning – the district and county both prepare development plans which must be co-ordinated – and exercising concurrent powers. Local authorities, in addition, are members of various associations which represent them in discussions with the government.

(b) *The Central Government*
Central control of local authorities arises because the government considers it desirable and necessary to do so, in order to co-ordinate their activities, to share available resources according to national economic plans, to maintain minimum standards of service and public order, and, when persuasion fails, to enforce the carrying out of policies which are repugnant to individual authorities.

(i) *Control by Legislation*
Whenever local authorities are allotted duties by a statute, it is normal practice to include provisions which enable the Secretary of State of the department involved to enforce satisfactory compliance with the Act. He can often draw up regulations which lay down in detail how the duty is to be carried out, so that a local authority is in no doubt as to what it should do. So far as the authority is concerned these regulations are part of the Act, though, as they are delegated legislation, the law courts have the power to declate them unconstitutional – something that the courts cannot do to a statute. Courts can only interpret statutes i.e. apply them to particular circumstances.

The following methods which are available to the central departments, though based on express legal powers given by statute, are essentially administrative in nature.

1. Direction – the Minister may issue a direction to transfer a duty to himself or some other person or body, usually in cases of default by the authority (i.e. its failure to act as required by an Act).
2. Approval of schemes for providing services under the Act is needed before the authority can operate them. On a smaller scale, consent is necessary to certain individual decisions (e.g. expenditure incurred in relieving disasters). By-laws require confirming as valid before coming into operation. Of a similar nature, are the requirements that the appointment of certain chief officers be approved or conform with regulations (e.g. police, fire, etc.).
3. Inspections are carried by centrally appointed inspectors in the education, fire and police services, and local inquiries are used to hear objectors on matters such as compulsory purchase orders.
4. Under certain statutes, the Minister has the power to hear appeals from persons against decisions taken by local authorities, and to settle disputes between public bodies.

(ii) *Financial Control*

The income and expenditure of local authorities are components in the government's national economic plans, and, as the sums involved are quite large, the central departments have been equipped with powers intended to make local authorities conform with the desires of Whitehall. To this end, the government operates three main controls – the grant system, control over capital expenditure and external audit.

1. *The Grant System*

This is designed to enable the central departments to change the rate or direction of the local government services – to accelerate, retard or stop developments, or to change emphasis from one aspect of a service to another – as required by economic or political motives. It can be used to encourage the undertaking of new services, to enforce a national minimum standard of service, to retain some measure of control over services of national importance, such as the police and civil defence, and to share the grant monies among the authorities in accordance with the government's assessment of the relative needs.

Grants may be paid to local authorities in respect of individual services, when they are called specific grants, or they may be made in respect of all services, when they are called general grants. They may be further classified according to the basis of calculation – a percentage of net expenditure, a sum per unit of service provided, a block amount decided by the government. There are also assignable revenues which meant that the government allots the proceeds from a tax to the local authorities. These are now quite insignificant and have become few in number, as their yield almost always fell behind the services costs they were supposed to meet.

2. Control over Capital Expenditure

Local authorities usually need to borrow money to pay for schemes which involve expenditure on a large-scale resulting in the creation of assets which are expected to have a long life. If this were not done, the income received each year from the rates would not be enought to meet the capital costs incurred in the same year unless the rate in the £ became astronomically high. It is now sometimes argued that, if "Pay-as-you-Go" (i.e. paying for schemes out of revenue) had been introduced from the beginning, the present portion of the rate income which is used to repay debt is equivalent to a year's capital expenditure, and thus "Pay-as-you-Go" would have been a more foresighted policy. This argument overlooks the fact that, by borrowing, the local authority has provided amenities years earlier than would be the case if they were provided out of revenue. The bringing forward of schemes must have been of immeasurable benefit to the people of the time, and whilst their costs are a burden on future ratepayers, the assets will still be there for future generations to enjoy and should therefore be partly borne by them.

In view of the magnitude of the sums involved in the capital projects of the local authorities of the country, the Government is required to operate measures of control in order to keep them in line with national economic plans. It must be remembered that, up to the present, local authorities have always been free to rate for deficits, and any excess of the cost of schemes above the money borrowed can be met out of revenue, capital funds and capital receipts (e.g. the proceeds of selling longlife assets). "Pay-as-you-Go" is thus always open to the authority to adopt when desired, bearing in mind the effect it would make on the rate in the £.

Before the Local Government, Planning and Land Act 1980 was passed, the Government adopted the policy of controlling the amounts of money which the local authorities borrowed to finance their capital schemes, rather than the actual expenditure incurred on those schemes. This meant that authorities could pay for capital items out of revenue and thus escape the controls to that extent. The 1980 Act has now transferred Government control from borrowings to the capital expenditure itself, so that the way in which it is financed (i.e. from loans or revenue) is for the most part irrelevant. (As a matter of interest, the old system of the control of borrowings is summarised at the end of the chapter).

The current arrangements apply to the capital expenditure on most of the locally-provided services, but the police service, probation of offenders and magistrates' courts are outside their scope, apparently because they already have their own system of controls and are regarded by the Government as needing special treatment in the current climate of encouraging the maintenance of law and order.

Each local authority is given an annual allocation in respect of all its capital expenditure on services, given the exceptions already mentioned. This allocation is divided into five blocks, covering education, housing, personal social services, transport, and "other services" for the residue. The division into blocks is based on plans submitted by the authority for the schemes it envisages carrying out over a number of years. The authority has complete discretion, however, as to how it makes virements between the blocks, so long as they are within its total allocation as prescribed, although there is flexibility as a maximum of 10% of this total annual sum can be transferred between years, so long as the authority balances these out over the years. A local authority's entitlement may also be augmented by some part of the capital receipts it receives from the sale of land and other assets being designated by the Secretary of State as being available to meet capital expenditure. Finally, authorities may assist one another by transferring part of their allocation from one to the other.

Local authorities are thus free to exercise their discretion in deciding on how and with what order of priorities they lay out their money on the various schemes which they have chosen to include in their capital programmes, except for some powers exercised by the central Departments to review or investigate particular schemes or to give local authorities directions of a general nature. In particular, the Department of the Environment has the power to monitor the capital expenditure of each local authority and to give orders to it when it overspends its allocation or is in danger of so doing. The Department also has the duty to prevent the pattern of expenditure which the Government has envisaged in its economic plans being disrupted by the local authorities in using their legitimate right to make transfers between services within their approved global allocations. Where a local authority takes no notice of a direction from the Government and proceeds to overspend, the amount overspent is declared to be ultra vires by the Act. Thus, whilst the nature and purpose of the excess payment is as legal as the rest of the sum spent, the excess is held to be illegal because it breaches the law as regards its size. This calls to mind the Poplar case of 1925 (i.e. Roberts v Hopwood) where the amount paid in wages above the agreed national scale was held to be ultra vires and an unreasonable use of discretion on the part of the local authority, and a matter for disallowance and surcharge by the district auditor under the law as it stood at the time.

In changing from controlling borrowings to controlling capital expenditure, the Government has had to define what it means by capital expenditure, and while there is general agreement as to the meaning of the term, the definition also includes the acquisition of interests in property or a right to the future use of property. Assets obtained by leasing are held to be included where their ownership is transferred to the local authority under the agreement, whilst examples of transactions excluded from the controls are items of equipment costing less than £5,000, payments made out of capital funds built up for specific schemes, and expenditure of a capital nature by parish councils.

3. *External Audit*
Each local authority has to submit its accounts to a district or approved auditor under the Local Government Act, 1972. There is a set procedure for the audit and the auditor has certain duties allotted to him by statute, regulations and an audit code. He must be satisfied that the accounts are properly prepared and conform with the law. He has to act as prescribed in cases of unlawful expenditure or losses, and have concern for the cases of waste arising from a wide variety of causes. So far as the central departments are concerned, one might also say that the external audit acts as a check upon the use to which a local authority has put the grant money it has received, as the district auditor signs certain grant claims whichever the type of audit.

4. *Returns and Reports*
The central departments are empowered to demand various returns on services and financial matters which given an insight into the affairs of individual local authorities. Examples of these are returns of capital and revenue outturn (i.e. expenditure and income), the preparation and publication of an abstract of accounts (i.e. a summary of the financial accounts), besides claim forms for grants. The Local Government, Planning and Land Act 1980, in particular gives the central departments the power to order each local authority to provide information in an annual report on the costs of its main services. These statistics are in a form which makes it easy for ratepayers, councillors, officers and others to compare the cost of providing services by one authority with that of other authorities with similar characteristics. Figures required include the cost per thousand of population for services such as fire, roads, libraries and refuse collection, education costs, such as cost per pupil, pupil/teacher ratios, social welfare costs such as the cost of children and old people in care and their numbers, and information on rent levels and rent arrears in respect of council dwellings.

(c) *The Law Courts*
Local authorities are subject to the control of the ordinary courts of law in respect of their actions, rights and liabilities, in much the same way as any citizen. They can be involved in cases dealing with acts of tort (these are wrongs for which the remedy is compensation or the payment of damages), infringement of rights, actions which are ultra vires, failure to carry out statutory duties, breach of contract, etc. Where an Act lays down a fine for a contravention of its provisions, this introduces the criminal law, and an authority may be fined because its members or officers have committed the offence on its behalf. As a local authority is only a legal person, not a real one, certain laws do not apply to it, such as matrimonial, homicide, etc. A local authority cannot commit bigamy, murder or treason.

It is normal for Acts of Parliament dealing with the control of the activities of public bodies to include specific remedies which the courts can apply in cases brought before them by aggrieved citizens. There are, however, occasions where the remedy given in an Act is inappropriate or the provisions of the Act may even be defective, and thus the courts have a duty to provide their own remedies. This they do by issuing orders of various types which a local authority should only ignore at its peril.

1. Mandamus (which is Latin for "we command") is an order issued by the High Court telling a local authority to carry out a public duty. There is usually no other way of making the authority carry out the duty and no other remedy open to the person who has complained. In addition, the person bringing the case must suffer personally in some way if the authority fails to act. Mandamus obviously applies to mandatory functions – i.e. those which the law says shall be done. Where a local authority has a discretion as to whether it will provide a service, the court can only make the authority formally consider the matter and if the council decides not to implement the service, that is the end of the matter.
2. Prohibition stops a lower court (or, in this case, a local authority which is acting in a judicial capacity in, say, a planning matter) from proceeding with a case. The usual reason is that the case is outside the authority of the lower court.
3. Certiorari (which is Latin for "to become more informed") is an order which makes a lower court hear a case once again or transfers it to a higher court. It occurs where a person complains with justification that he has not had a fair hearing. Again, a local authority acting as a court would be affected.
4. Declaration and Injunction are usually used together. The court may issue a declaration in which it sets out its view of the legal aspects of an application brought before it and states the rights of the persons involved. If this is not enough to stop the person or body complained against, the court will go further and issue an injunction ordering the person or body to remove the cause of complaint.

(d) *The Public, the Ombudsman and the Press*

Local authorities are in contact with the public via their members and officers, and their reactions to the indications they receive are a measure of their flexibility in policy-making. It is the councillors who are most affected by the comments, desires and demands of their electors, either as individuals or in groups such as residents' and ratepayers' associations, chambers of trade or commerce, trade councils, and, of course, political parties. This often means that local authority members become involved in relatively minor matters instead of applying themselves to the consideration of major policy. Ratepayers visit the town hall and are attended to by officers, and as the rate is a compulsory levy and thus somewhat resented, they look for evidence there and in the streets, that their burden is no heavier than necessary.

Public participation in local government and the publicising of their own actions by local authorities have received increasing emphasis in recent years. The public must be involved in the preparation of structure plans for their area. The idea of neighbourhood councils has been tested in a few urban areas. There is the right of inspection of accounts at all audits. The Public Bodies (Admission to Meetings) Act 1960 gives the public and press the right of access to local authority council and committee meetings, subject to their being excluded by a resolution of the meeting in respect of matters where publicity would prejudice the public interest or for some special reason such as discussing the pay of individual officers and receiving reports from officers.

For many years, the Scandinavian countries have appointed officials whom they call "Ombudsmen" to investigate complaints by members of the public about actions taken by administrative bodies. This idea has been adopted for local government in this country under the Local Goverment Act 1974. A system of local commissioners (each responsible for a region of the country) was established and these officials were given the duty of investigating complaints of alleged maladministration by local authorities. (The system of commissioners applies to other areas of government besides local authorities – there are the Parliamentary Commissioner, and the Health Service Commissioner (who is at present the Parliamentary Commissioner) – and the local commissioners deal with police and water authorities also but, strangely enough, parish councils are outside their ambit).

A citizen wishing to complain must first write to a councillor of the particular authority. If this councillor cannot remedy the matter, he can be asked to pass it to the local commissioner. If he fails to do this, the citizen can approach the commissioner direct. Certain matters are outside the scope of the commissioner's duties. He cannot investigate matters affecting all or most of the inhabitants of a local authority's area, nor matters affecting staff terms of employment, commercial and contractual arrangements. He should not act in cases where alternative means of satisfaction are available. In the absence of maladministration, he must not criticize a decision which has been properly taken.

The commissioners' role is intended to remove causes of grievance and bring local authorities and private individuals nearer together by improving the quality of administration. As yet, the commissioner has no legal power to make the authority accept responsibility for injustice arising from what he considers to be maladministration, though the council may make a payment or give benefits in such a case. However, if the authority fails to remedy the situation, the publicity given by the press, especially the local newspapers to the commissioner's report can be a potent weapon.

This leads on to the local authorities' relationship with the press. Some councils have appointed public relations and press officers whose duty it is to publicise the items which the authority wishes the public to be aware of.

These officers are often responsible for newspapers financed by the authority which contain local news and are delivered free to all the addresses in the area covered. In addition, the professional touch must often tone down unguarded and ill-expressed statements made by members and officers. Nevertheless, the press often print stories which do not reflect credit upon the authority involved, and this can lead to second thoughts on intended actions and improvements in administrative procedures.

As has been mentioned already, the press has the right of access to local authority council and committee meetings, unless the public is expressly excluded by resolution. Any newspaper may, on paying the postage, demand committee agenda papers concerning public items and any other information which will enable it to decide the nature of those items. Where such a demand is made, and the papers contain a libel which is subsequently published without malice, the local authority and the newspaper have a measure of protection against being sued. Reports of statements made at meetings are similarly protected. The authority is also required to provide reasonable facilities to newspapermen (and women) for taking down reports of proceedings and for making telephone calls (for which they pay).

Supplement

Summary of the arrangements for the control of local authorities' borrowing previous to the operation of the Local Government, Planning and Land Act 1980: –

Local authorities were given the power under national and local laws to spend money upon providing their services. Such expenditure is capital or revenue in nature and, in both cases, the authority had the right to finance it from revenue income, i.e. the rates or other current receipts. Where a scheme was on too large a scale to permit it to be met from revenue, or capital monies, such as sales of assets, the authority was forced to borrow to finance it, and, it was at this point that the Government applied its main control measures.

Capital schemes were divided into three main sectors, the Key Sector, the Subsidiary Sector and the Locally Determined Sector.

The Key Sector services included education (schools, etc.), principal roads, social services, police, etc. and these schemes needed specific approval (sometimes called a "loan sanction") from the appropriate central Department.

The Subsidiary Sector services contained the acquisition of land for education, social services, etc. and the purchase of buses. These had general automatic approval, as they mainly linked up with the Key Sector schemes.

The Locally Determined Sector services included all those schemes not included int he first two sectors – fire service, libraries, central area development, amenities and recreation, etc. – and were covered by a block borrowing allocation which was notified to the local authority annually. As the title indicates, the local authority had the power to use this block allocation as it wished for schemes which were optimal for the development of its services and the benefit of the people in its area. Each project in the L.D.S. was assessed according to an official scale as to the estimated length of life of the asset created or the works carried out. The repayment period of the borrowing related to the project was then based upon this estimated life, e.g. a vehicle would be paid for over 10 years, a purchase of land over 60 years, and so on.

Housing had been part of the Key Sector but had later been separated in the form of Housing Investment Programmes which were already based on capital payments, instead of borrowings, as the controlling factor.

There was also a general consent for Key Sector schemes to be borrowed for without sanction being needed up to a ceiling of a penny rate, with a limit of £5,000 for any one transaction.

Questions
4.1 Describe the various categories of committee encountered in a local authority.
4.2 What are the advantages and disadvantages of co-option of persons other than councillors on to committees?
4.3 Discuss the dividing of duties between members and officers in the administering of a local authority's affairs.
4.4 How far does central control remove the local authorities' powers to make important decisions?
4.5 How may a law court influence the actions of local authorities?
4.6 What rights are given by law to the press in respect of attendance at meetings of local authorities and their committees?
4.7 In what way can the Local Ombudsman assist the public?
4.8 Make a brief list of the matters which one would expect to see dealt with in the Standing Orders of a local authority.
4.9 What advantages are expected to accrue from adopting various recommendations of the Bains Report?
4.10 Prepare an example of a committee agenda of a local authority.

Chapter 5

Sources of Income of Local Authorities

It is a common practice to present a simplified picture of the difference between private business and local authority finance in the following manner. Commerical firms first of all consider the size of the market which can be expected and estimate the sales in the coming period of their goods and services. Thereafter, they proceed to plan how much they need to spend to produce enough goods or a sufficient level of service to meet the expected demand. Local authorities, however, are regarded as approaching the problem from the opposite direction. They start by estimating how much they will spend on their services, and then calculate the charges, the government grants, and, finally, the rates needed to meet the proposed expenditure. To be sure there are some minor exceptions to this procedure in the shape of trading undertakings and central servicing and works departments where the commercial approach is encountered, but for the non-trading services which are predominant in local government, the rate levy is tailored to their needs. In actual practice, there is usually a system of giving prior warnings to spending committees as to the total expenditure available to them for the coming year, but, before the Finance Sub-committee recommends a rate in the £ to the council, there have been reductions, deletions and re-calculation of many of the items as a result of many hours of discussion and bargaining. An authority's revenue expenditure is thus met out of income from charges for goods and services, government grants and subsidies received to support the running of the services, and the rate money from the ratepayers.

A somewhat similar situation is found in respect of the acquisition and creation of capital assets. Capital schemes are brought together in a capital programme, covering a number of years into the future, and their costs are calculated and arrangements made to meet them, firstly, out of borrowed money, and then by providing in the annual rate estimates for the repayment of those loans over the expected lives of the various schemes. The bulk of the capital payments is thus met out of some sort of borrowing, though the authority can pay for capital items out of current income if it so wishes and the rate levy is adequate. The spending committees and the Finance Sub-committee are thus concerned with two aspects. The first is the amount which can be spent on capital schemes, and the second is the effect of this plus the running costs of the schemes when operational upon the amount of the rate which the authority can impose upon its ratepayers.

The next pages therefore deal with the sources of income available to local authorities in the following order: — rates, grants, miscellaneous charges, and borrowings.

(For the sake of completeness, a mention should be made of revenue and capital funds which can be built up and then used to meet expenditure. However, considering how large a local authority's scale of operations is, the transactions financed in this way are relatively minor in nature).

The General Rate

The rates, as they are called, are a form of local taxation levied by a rating authority upon the occupiers (and sometimes the owners) of land and buildings in its area. The rating authority is the district or borough council and the proceeds of the rates go to meet the costs of its own services as well as those of the other local authorities who operate in the area. These other authorities include the county council, any joint boards, parish councils, etc. and are called precepting authorities because they precept (i.e. demand that a rate be levied) upon the district for their requirements. There are arrangements whereby expenses (including precepts) chargeable on part only of the district form additional items to the general rate levied in that part.

The amount of rates which a ratepayer is required to pay is a number of pence in the £ of the rateable value of the property he occupies. The number of pence in the £ (or the rate poundage) is obtained by dividing the total amount needed by the estimate of what a penny rate would bring in. The penny rate product, as it is called, is one hundredth of the district's total rateable value after deductions for losses and some minor costs of collection. The rateable values of all properties are fixed by valuation officers of the Department of Inland Revenue and included in valuation lists which the rating authorities use as the basis for collecting the rates.

As a simple illustration of the system, let us assume that a district has a total rateable value of £22,000,000, and that losses on collection (e.g. empty properties, demolitions, etc.) amount to the equivalent of £2,000,000 of rateable value. The penny rate product is thus £200,000, i.e. £20,000,000 divided by 100. If the total needs of the rating and precepting authorities for next year amount to £16,000,000, then the rate in the £ is 80p i.e. £16,000,000 divided by £200,000. The occupier of a property with a rateable value of £150 would be required to pay £120, i.e. £150 @ 80p per £.

An occupier is only responsible for the rates for the period during which he actually occupies the property, and, formerly, an empty property always escaped the rates. Rating authorities now have the power to levy rates on the owners of unoccupied properties, if they so decide. They have a wide discretion as to the proportion of the rate to charge, the classes of property to designate, and reductions to make in case of hardship being caused. For unused commercial properties, there is a duty to impose a surcharge on the owner where he has not tried his best to let the property. This surcharge is additional to any empty property rate charge and is 100% of the normal rates for the first year, and rises by a further 100% for each following year until the place is let. The measure is obviously intended to reduce superfluous office accommodation (which was a problem at the time) but the rating authority can also in this case give relief where hardship or genuinely unsuccessful attempts to let the building are proved. (These requirements have been so easy to meet that the Government has dispensed with the compulsory surcharge as uneconomic, and also set a maximum of 50% to the empty non-domestic property rate).

As indicated previously, the owner of a property can sometimes be rated instead of the occupier. The rating authority can do this compulsorily in the case of small properties, and by agreement for any properties where the rent is paid oftener than quarterly. The owner receives a compounding allowance in either case. If the owner fails to pay, the occupier can be approached, and if he does not pay, there is provision to demand the rate from lodgers.

There are some properties which are completely or partly exempt from rating. Farm land and buildings (barns, etc.) do not even appear on the valuation lists — one of the arguments against rating them is the tremendous task of valuation it would entail. Crown properties are exempt because the Crown is above the law, but though no rates are paid, the Treasury pays contributions of equivalent amount in lieu of rates. This applies to premises occupied by central departments, the more local type of property such as police stations and law courts have rateable values and rates are paid in respect of them. The operational installations of the railways and canals are also paid for by contributions in lieu. Places of public worship — churches, chapels, etc. — are exempt. Charities are entitled to 50% reduction and may be relieved from the rest. Non-profit making societies for religious, cultural and recreational purposes can be wholly exempted.

Other cases of exemption are public parks, public highways and bridges, lighthouses in operation, sewers and drainage works, residences of foreign ambassadors and their diplomatic staff, and rebates exist for premises adapted to meet the needs of disabled residents and premises occupied by organisations for welfare purposes.

The government has made modifications in the rating system, especially in recent years, to make the payment of the rates less of a burden to the occupier of a dwellinghouse (i.e. the so-called domestic or residential occupier) whose income often bears little relationship to the size of his rate bill. Firstly, there is a charging of a lower rate in the £ on dwellings than on other classes of property. The government recompenses the rating authority for the loss of income via the domestic element of the Rate Support Grant. Secondly, there is the rate rebate system which is designed to help domestic ratepayers with low incomes. The amount of the rebate depends on a national scale of income level, family circumstances and rates payable and there is a 90% grant towards it. Thirdly, for those who pay their rates direct to the rating authority, domestic (and some non-domestic) ratepayers have the right to pay their rates in a minimum of ten monthly instalments —

April to February. Failure to pay any due instalment means that the rating authority can demand the whole amount outstanding. Fourthly, although the rating authority has been empowered for many years to give a discount for prompt payment to all ratepayers, now it may limit it to domestic ratepayers only. It is arguable whether this step assists the poorer ratepayer, but the earlier receipt of rate monies would bring down costs of operation of services which would reduce the future rate poundage.

The Making and Collection of the Rates

A rating authority (i.e. a district or borough council) has a duty to levy a rate to meet its own needs as well as the precepts it receives from the county, parishes and any other bodies operating in its area. There is no legal requirement to prepare detailed estimates but there is a legal duty to arrange for its financial affairs to be properly carried on. From this, it might be suggested that without a system of detailed budgets, (of which the rate estimates is one), there is no proper measure of control.

Rates are usually levied for a year at a time, i.e. from the 1st April to the 31st March, although they can be for any period of time, and each new rate period is regarded as starting immediately the previous rate period ends, so that a delay in making the rate has no effect.

The estimates of the expenditure and income of the council's departments are the basis of the rate levy calculations, and are prepared jointly by the chief officer of each department and the finance director. A timetable is laid down for their preparation, and while starting times vary, the procedure must be well on the way by the January committee meetings.

Columnar schedules are drawn up for all the departments in the following form: –

(1)	(2)	(3)	(4)	(5)	(6)	(7)	(8)
Budget Code	Particulars	Actual 19-1	Estimate 19-2		Revised 19-2		Estimate 19-3
				To Date	Balance	Total	

The finance division completes the first five columns to show, analysed over the budget codes, the actual expenditure and income for the financial year just ended, the estimate for the current year, and the expenditure and income to date for the current year as given by the accounting records. The sixth, seventh and eighth columns are also completed by the finance staff in respect of such items as central administration charges, debt charges, certain superannuation charges, etc. The provision for debt charges includes both existing schemes and those intended to commence soon enough to affect the estimates of the loans fund for the coming year. Details of these projected schemes are obtained from the capital budget.

Expenditure is usually assumed at the level of prices applicable to November (in the revised year), and a contingency provision is brought into the summary in the later stages with the aim that it will prove sufficient to meet the increases in price levels from inflation in the coming year.

The schedules are passed to the appropriate department where the vacant spaces are filled in after due consultation. The departmental estimates are now drawn up from the balanced, totalled schedules (columns 5 and 6 disappear in the final form) and then considered and finally approved by the relevant executive committee which is advised by the officers' management team. The estimates for all the departments are now brought together and submitted to the finance sub-committee which considers them in conjunction with a report from the officers' team containing recommendations on the total estimates, the rate level and other financing matters. The finance sub-committee ultimately recommends a rate in the £ based on the approved estimates (which now include amounts for contingencies and working balance) to the policy and resources committee. This committee usually accepts the recommendation and passes it to the council where it is turned into a resolution making the rate as required by the law (the power to levy a rate cannot be delegated).

To turn for a moment from the rate making procedure, the estimates are now used as a standard against which expenditure and income for the rest of the current year and the whole of the coming year are measured and controlled and, where necessary, adjusted by supplementary estimates and virements.

After the resolution making the rate has been passed, there is a period of twenty-one days in which the date must be published, usually in the local press. The next step is to demand the rate by sending the rate notice to the ratepayer. This is necessary because the authority cannot start the recovery proceedings until seven days after the rate has been demanded.

The basic particulars to be given on the rate demand notice sent to a ratepayer used to be laid down by law but this has now been replaced by a predominantly voluntary code which the local authorities can interpret with some discretion to meet their particular circumstances. In the first place, the notice should include (or be accompanied by) such details as the address of the property, the rateable value, the poundages levied, the rate period covered, amount due, the times, methods and places available for payment, and reliefs and rebates available to individual ratepayers in respect of their personal circumstances. Information should also be given in regard to such matters as the factors which have affected decisions on the level of the rate, the costs and income of the main services, the burdens falling on the various categories of ratepayer, and the details and use of manpower. The code is open-ended, as the authority can add such information to that suggested as it desires.

The ratepayer may arrange to pay the rates by instalments as of right under the General Rate Act 1967 (ten monthly payments ending in February) or in some manner expressly or implicitly agreeable to the rating authority. After a certain delay in paying or default in paying instalments, the authority finds it necessary to start the procedure to enforce payment of the amount still due. Notices are sent culminating in a final demand. The rating authority has the power to excuse payment of all or a part of the rate on the grounds of the poverty of the ratepayer. Some ratepayers who are known to be permanently poverty-stricken are excused each year, but in other cases, excusal is left until the result of the hearing of the warrant of commitment is known (see later). Assistance given under social welfare legislation has reduced the need to write-off sums because of poverty.

The next step is a complaint to a justice of the peace by the rating authority that the amount is due and an application for him to authorise the issue of a summons requiring the ratepayer to attend before the magistrates' court to explain why he has failed to pay. If he pays the sum due and the costs of the summons, the matters ends. If he still does not pay, then there is a hearing in the court before two justices. If the ratepayer appears and offers a good defence, no further proceedings take place. Valid defences include — the rate is already paid, he is not the occupier, the rate is already excused on account of poverty, there is a defect in the publishing of the rate or it has been illegally altered. If there is no valid defence or the ratepayer does not attend the hearing, the justices are required to issue a distress warrant for the amount and costs. The distress warrant authorises the taking of the ratepayer's goods and possessions up to the value of the amount due, holding them for five days, and if the money is still not paid, selling them at public auction. If there is a net surplus on the sale, it must be paid to the ratepayer.

If the amount raised is not enough to pay the debt and costs, the warrant is returned marked "no goods or effects" or "goods insufficient", the rating authority may now report this to the court and ask for a warrant to commit the ratepayer to prison. Before the justices can issue a warrant of commitment, as it is called, they must enquire into the ratepayer's circumstances in his presence (having him brought to court, if necessary), and if they decide his non-payment did not arise from his wilful refusal or culpable neglect, they may refuse to issue the warrant. In other words, the court will not imprison a person who cannot pay the rates due because of lack of means, and if the rating authority itself does not now resolve to excuse payment on the grounds of poverty, the court can relieve the ratepayer of all or part of his liability. Where the justices refuse to issue the warrant but do not excuse him the debt completely, the rating authority can re-apply to the court if the ratepayer's financial condition improves afterwards.

The justices can order the imprisonment of a defaulting ratepayer for a maximum period of three months. However, whatever sentence they do give can be reduced (a) by payments made during the committal procedure, when the court can delay the issue of the warrant for this purpose, or (b) by payments made after committal (which is immediate, once the warrant is issued) which reduce the sentence pro rata to the total period. After the prison term is served, legal opinion is that the ratepayer who was proceeded against no longer owes the rates involved, even if it is found he had hidden money, because the rating authority has completed the procedure for recovery laid down for rates.

Valuation for Rating

The Inland Revenue employs valuers who value properties for rating purposes, and prepare and amend valuation lists which are the official record from which the rating authority derives its right to levy the rate in the £. The function of valuation was transferred in 1948 from the local authorities with the intention that centralisation should bring nationally uniform standards. The rating authorities have the right to be informed of all alterations to the list, can propose amendments and object to proposed amendments, and have a duty to give the valuation officer any information they receive which might require the list to be altered.

Over the centuries, during which the basis of valuing land and buildings changed and developed, even at one point apparently becoming a kind of wealth tax (the rateable value being calculated on the land, buildings and contents), the practice grew to value property at its rent for a year or, if no rent were paid, at the rent that would be paid for it, if the occupier maintained it and had the prospect of staying in occupation for the foreseeable future. This value is called the net annual value and, at the present, is the same as the rateable value for most properties. It can be arrived at direct for premises where the tenant repairs the property, such as a factory, but in most cases, the landlord repairs the property and recoups himself out of the rent he receives. The rent paid in such circumstances is called the gross value and instead of the actual costs of maintenance being deducted, a scale figure is taken off (this is called a statutory deduction or "statutable") to arrive at the net annual value. An example where the net annual value and the rateable value differed was an empty office block which was subject to the penal surcharge.

Various methods of valuation are used, each having advantages for different situations and types of property. Many unexpected forms of property are rateable, e.g. shooting rights, moorings, and in the case of machinery, that for manufacturing is usually exempt unless it is self-standing i.e. it is itself a type of building.

Some of the main methods are as follows: –
1. The rental method whereby the actual rent paid is suitably adjusted to give a gross or net annual value according to the nature of the property, is the most frequently used. The rise in numbers of owner-occupiers of dwellinghouses has meant a loss of data about rents which would be of use in making comparisons and difficulties can arise where the actual rent is affected by services given in lieu of rent, increasing rent is paid for succeeding years of a lease, relationships which mean the transactions are not at arms-length, etc.

2. The method of zoning is a variation on the rentals method whereby the floor area is divided into zones and each zone is given a unit value according to its position and attractiveness to a possible occupier. It is found in use for valuing large shops, etc. The unit charges are based on evidence of local rent levels.
3. Two similar methods are based on the units of accommodation provided (e.g. a sum per bed in a hospital, per seat in a cinema, per desk in a school — using area average rents, etc.) or the units of output for the year (e.g. a sum per ton of ore from a mine extracted in the future — using rents, royalties payable, etc.).
4. The accounts (or profits) method is used where there is a measure of monopoly and rental evidence is either lacking or deceptive. The rent (on which the rateable value is based) is considered as being decided by the profit (suitably adjusted) as shown by the accounts.
5. The contractor's test which is also called the value on cost method is used when none of the previous approaches seems applicable. It assumes that a builder would only incur the capital cost of a property if he is sure of a return on his expenditure at least equal to what he would get from an investment of the same amount.
6. What are called formula assessments are applied by the government under rules laid down by statute to a variety of public sector bodies which operate nationally or over several rating areas, e.g. gas, electricity, railways, coal, water, etc. The total rateable value of the operational land, assets, etc. is agreed and adjusted in accordance with levels of output, services, etc. and then divided over the rating areas in the area of operation. Ordinary properties — houses, hotels, shops, showrooms — are valued and rated in the normal manner.

A proposal written in a prescribed form may be given at any time to the valuation officer by the owner or occupier of a property, the rating authority or any other aggrieved person to amend that property's value in the list. The valuation officer must notify all persons whose interests are affected by the proposal, and they may object to it. If the proposal is agreed by all those involved, the valuation list is altered by a direction from the valuation officer. If there is disagreement, then the proposal goes to the local valuation court which directs what should be done. There is a right of appeal to the Lands Tribunal, and, with permission, further to the Court of Appeal and the House of Lords. An alternative procedure can be followed of agreeing to arbitration instead of going to the local valuation court.

Future Developments in Rating

The General Rate has been criticised for many years as being regressive in nature because it is not related to income and is a greater burden upon the poor than the rich. Despite the introduction of rate rebates and the right to pay by instalments, together with the domestic relief, the complaints have continued. It is argued that it is unfair to charge people for the cost of services which they do not use, such as education and childless couples. Against these arguments, the points are made that the rate is only one tax among many, and any inequity in it may be balanced elsewhere in the whole system, and it is essentially a tax and not a charge for services. As a tax, the rate has several advantages. It is economical to collect, as the costs incurred are a small fraction of the total sum collected. The ratepayer is certain as to his liability – how it is arrived at, and when, in what way, how much and to whom he should pay (although he may not understand what a rateable value is and fail to claim his rightful rebates). It is flexible, as the amount in the £ can be altered by the rating authority as needed, though it is not buoyant like income tax and VAT, as it does not increase automatically with inflation, except when rateable values rise in the new lists on re-valuation. Other criticisms are that its payment is not convenient to the payer as it involves distinct payments unless an inclusive rent is paid, and that differences in rate levels between localities can attract or repel industry and commerce which are subject to the full poundage, unlike residential property.

The government has given consideration at various times to reforms (some of which have been carried out) and even the abolition and replacement of the rating system. Suggestions for reform at present take two forms. The first is to strengthen what is after all local government's main independent source of income by re-rating agricultural land, more frequent re-valuation of property, adopting capital or site value of land instead of rent, etc. and further, to give additional sources of income – local sales tax, entertainment tax, bicycle tax, dog licences, etc. – which have all been rejected as inappropriate. The second is to provide an alternative to the present system – local income tax (favoured by the Layfield Committee), a poll tax of an amount per head for residents, diversion of some national insurance contributions from central government funds, etc. – which have all been unacceptable. The present position appears to be that, whilst it is the intention to replace the rates by another system, no action is likely in the near future. It must be remembered that the total sum produced by the rates over the country is very large and any new tax created to replace it must have a large impact upon the public.

Government Grants

The present system of grants paid by the central Government to local authorities consists of a large block grant and a number of much smaller specific grants. The block grant is intended to benefit the whole of an authority's services and to be used as an item of general income towards meeting total costs. Specific grants, on the other hand, assist individual services, and are treated as items of income to those services. The statement is sometimes made that somewhat more than 60 per cent of local authority expenditure is financed from Government grants and subsidies, and that the balance, roughly 40 per cent is met by the proceeds of the General Rate. This statement is debatable, because it omits to mention the existence of charges for services and miscellaneous income receivable by a local authority in respect of its various services. The expenditure taken for grant purposes is net, i.e. these income items have already been deducted, and the proportions might be better expressed as nearer to 30 per cent charges and other income, 30 per cent rates, and 40 per cent Government grants, though the figures will vary for individual local authorities.

So far as the history of grants is concerned, the first were specific in nature and stemmed from the mid 1800s. Examples included the grants towards the costs of borough police forces and sums given to help agriculturists when they lost income upon the repeal of the Corn Laws and were unable to pay their rates. These were mostly percentages of net expenditure, but about 1888 a system of "Assigned Revenues" was introduced to meet (inter alia) technical education costs. In essence, the proceeds of those taxes which were assigned to local authorites, arose from the sale of liquor. Thus it is said that higher education in this country owes its origin to a "whisky tax". Of course, in the usual nature of assigned revenues, the costs of the service soon outstripped the grant income. The first block grant was introduced in 1929 to replace the loss of rate income to local authorities because agricultural and industrial properties were relieved of rates either wholly or partly.

Parliament votes money each year to be paid in the form of grants and subsidies to local authorities during the following financial year. Account is taken of the trends occurring in expenditure, prices and pay levels, changes in the level of demand for the various services, and other relevant matters, such as the economic state of the nation. A global sum is decided and approved by the Government, and, out of this sum, amounts are taken for grants for specific services, and the remainder is allocated to the block grant.

One of the main purposes of the Local Government, Planning and Land Act 1980 was to change the pattern of grant payments made by the central Government to local authorities in a fundamental manner. It introduced a new form of block grant which took the place of the resources and needs elements of the pre-1980 Act Rate Support Grant but the domestic element in that grant continued. (The summary at the end of this chapter contains the main characteristics of the former arrangements).

The idea for a new block grant, at that time referred to as "unitary", was considered in the Layfield Report which was published in 1976, but the Committee made no proposal for its adoption, mainly because the members had reservations as to its possible effects upon relations between the central Government and the local authorites. This new block grant is intended to enable each local authority to provide services up to a national standard while levying a rate in the £ laid down as the norm for the authority's class, i.e. the norm varies according to whether it is a county or district, in London or a metropolitan or non-metropolitan area.

The calculation of the grant can be envisaged as being composed of three steps. First, the central departments assess the coming year's expenditure requirements for each local authority. Several major Ministries are involved in this – Environment, Education and Science, Health and Social Security, Transport and the Home Office – as well as a number of minor ones. Their staffs are occupied in ascertaining the costs of the various services and in finding ways of defining and then measuring the particular characteristics of population, etc. which influence local government expenditure patterns. Examples of such factors are the occurrence of above average numbers of old people, schoolchildren or one parent families in an area. In carrying out these grant related expenditure assessments, various bases have been tried, including population, past expenditure and the unit cost of so-called "client groups", according to the nature of the services. Overall, the spending needs of local government are related to the level of services envisaged in the PESC (the national economic plans) for the next financial year with an inbuilt cash limit to cover inflation.

Having decided the global sum available for the block grant, the Government proceeds to its distribution. To do this, it sets a standard rate in the £ for each class of local authority (i.e. county or district, metropolitan, non-metropolitan or in London), and this, multiplied by the rateable value of the authority's area, gives the rate product for the authority. The final step is the deduction of this calculated rate product from the authority's expenditure assessment which gives the provisional block grant payable to the authority.

The authority's grant entitlement is, however, affected by deviations from the estimated expenditure as assessed by the Government. If spending goes above a given threshold, the block grant entitlement starts to taper off (by altering the above-mentioned multiplier) as the overspending grows, and the resultant deficiency has to be met by the ratepayers.

The new system provides for revisions of calculations in respect of the global entitlement where, for instance, inflation varies significantly from the expected rate, and in respect of individual authorities where actual expenditure when known varies from the budget figures originally submitted. There is also provision for limiting variations in the amount of block grant from one year to another so far as each local authority is concerned.

The advantages claimed for the new system are claimed to be simplicity, (i.e. avoiding the mathematical complexities of the old Rate Support Grant), the removal of the tendency under the old system to encourage the overspending authority by paying more grant as expenditure rose, and the control which now exists on the extravagance of a small number of authorities who refuse to economise.

Opponents of the new grant argue that the complexities are still there but have been moved into the central departments which have to calculate spending needs and standard rates in the £ for all the local authorities in the country. In addition, the situation involves several departments which may tend to promote the interests of the services that each is responsible for in competition with the others. Furthermore, local authorities may be forced into a pattern of average spending on individual services owing to the conflicting influences of the departments, and thus progress in the development of new ideas in local government may be stifled. The point is also made that the central-local relationship is still unsatisfactory, as local authorities can blame the Government for cuts in the services caused by the cash limits, while the Government can hold the local authorities as responsible for high levels of rate levy.

It is finally argued that the replacing of local responsibility by decisions made at the centre in respect of rate and service levels may result in the demise of democratic local government and the birth of a centralised State. The Government refutes such criticisms and argues that local government should be strengthened by operating its finances in a responsible manner at a time when reductions in public sector expenditure are vital to the economic well-being of the country.

Grants by the Government towards the costs of individual services (i.e. specific grants as they are called) are now a very small part of the total state subsidies to local authorities.

The following table gives a brief description of the more important of these grants: —

Housing Subsidies	— a revised system of grants in support of the Housing Revenue Account has been introduced by the Housing Act 1980. The intention is for the Government to meet any deficit arising between recognised costs of providing accommodation and the income from housing and local authority sources (e.g. rate contributions).
	— rent rebates — 75% of the standard laid down nationally for rebates.
	— rent allowances — 100% re-imbursement.
	— housing improvement and renovation (i.e. intermediate, repairs and special) grants — 75% of the notional loan charges (90% is paid in Housing Action and General Improvements Areas).
	— slum clearance — 75% of the loan charges on the net annual loss incurred on schemes.
Police	— contribution to service costs — 50% of net expenditure.
Magistrates' Courts	— contribution to costs — 80% of net expenditure.
Education	— mandatory awards to students — 90% of expenditure.
Probation and After-care	— reimbursement of costs — 100% of expenditure.
Various	— urban programme — 75% of approved expenditure.
Rating	— rate rebates — 90% of total allowed.
Commonwealth Immigrants	— contribution to costs — 75% of expenditure.
Environmental Health	— clean air — 40% of approved costs.
Transport	— transport supplementary grant — per formula.

Charges and Miscellaneous Income

Local authorities receive current income from many sources besides rates and government grants. It is estimated that about one-third of the total expenditure on revenue account made by local authorities is met out of this class of income, which may be divided into charges for work done or services provided for socially desirable purposes, and contributions from services which are run for profit on broadly commercial lines.

The first category of charges includes, as its largest component where the authority provides housing, the rent income from council houses and flats, and other examples are accommodation charges in old persons' homes, library charges, fees for games in parks, charges for unblocking drains, etc.

The second category contains charges for cemetery and crematorium facilities, transport, caravan sites, car parks, airports, race courses, trading estates, licensed and unlicensed restaurants, the leasing of development land, proceeds from lotteries, lido's, etc.

Even within the services which are provided because they are regarded as socially desirable, there is a medley of bases upon which charges are levied. Some are purely nominal, e.g. fees for library books retained beyond the due date for return, especially when pensioners are usually exempted from such fines, anyway. Other charges are related to the means of the person paying, e.g. council house rents which are subject to rebates based on the tenants' circumstances, parental contributions to children in care, and accommodation charges to residents of hostels and homes. There are also fees and charges which are laid down by law, e.g. licence duties, and, in the trading sector, there are maxima laid down, e.g. bus fares.

Most local authorities have been reluctant to increase charges in line with rising costs because of the social nature of their work and the fear that the people who need the services most might not use them because of the increased cost.

There is also the desire on the part of elected members not to lose the votes of possibly an appreciable proportion of their electors by raising rents, evening school fees, bus fares, etc. The result of this reluctance to increase charges has led over the last few years to a fall in the relative proportion of these other income sources as a proportion of the total current income of local authorities. Whether this tendency will be stopped or reversed in the future is a matter or conjecture.

The procedure for the amendment of charges for services or facilities is usually laid down in the authority's financial regulations. These require a periodic review of charges by the committee which supervises the running of the service and the head of the department involved may also report to the committee whenever he considers it necessary on the question of scales of charges. All amendments to charges are normally prepared in consultation with the director of finance, and the proposal must go to the finance sub-committee for consideration before going before the council. Certain types of charges are subject to measures of central control, though this has tended to slacken in recent years, and any such alterations require the necessary approval from outside bodies, e.g. bus fares require the approval of the Traffic Commissioners who must ensure that they are reasonable.

Loans

Different forms of borrowing are used to meet the bulk of a local authority's capital expenditure, and, unlike the capital which a company raises to finance its purchase of fixed assets, every loan borrowed must be repaid during a period related to the estimated life of the assets acquired, e.g. 12 years for vehicles. Thus, by way of the charging of annual debt charges to the revenue account (and specifically the "repayment of principal" or "sinking fund provision"), the capital expenditure is eventually paid for out of revenue.

Local authorities' powers to borrow are contained in the Local Government Act 1972 (as a general power) and in a number of other Acts relating to borrowing for specific services (education, police, fire, etc.). A temporary loan or overdraft can be incurred without the need for government approval if it is to meet expenses pending income (e.g. rates) coming in, or whilst a long-term loan is being raised. In practically all other cases, approval is needed to the borrowing, and the method used must conform with the 1972 Act or be otherwise approved by the Treasury. The 1972 Act also empowers local authorities to borrow from abroad or in foreign currency but Treasury consent is needed.

The forms of borrowing available to local authorities include the following: –

(a) *Mortgages*. These are in the form of a deed in a prescribed form, duly sealed, etc. There are two sources – local investors who invest small sums for a period of years, and large institutions which lend much larger amounts for, on occasion, longer periods. There are many variations in the ways interest is calculated and repayment made. The loan may be an escalator or liquidity mortgage where the interest rate rises as the loan's term lengthens. It may include break or stress clauses which allow the terms to be re-negotiated at specific dates or allow the investor to ask for the loan to be repaid in a time of financial stress. Repayment may be at the end of the term of the loan (i.e. maturity), by instalments (yearly and half-yearly) which repay the loan in equal amounts over its life, or by the annuity method under which the borrower pays a constant amount made up of principal and interest.

(b) *P.W.L.B. Mortgages*. The Public Works Loans Board which is now part of the National Loans and Investment Office, was originally formed to lend to smaller local authorities who were required to pay higher interest rates than were demanded from larger, more secure, authorities. The re-organisation of local government have brought about the disappearance of small authorities and changed the role of the P.W.L.B.. It now lends to any local authority up to a quota (i.e. a proportion of the authority's borrowing needs) at interest rates fixed by the government. The Board can also lend outside the quota, when the interest rates are based on market rates (higher than for "quota" loans) – this is known as acting as the "lender of last resort". Loans can be for new capital schemes or to replace other loans falling due for repayment and their terms usually run from 10 years up to 40 years for loans which will be repaid at maturity and 80 years for loans repaid by instalments or annuity payments. Loans (especially maturity) may be advanced for less than 10 years for good reasons, e.g. the loan sanction is for less than that period, but there is no requirement to link the amounts borrowed with particular loan sanctions or allocations and they are taken into the loans pool. The local authority has a choice as to how it will repay the loan – maturity (i.e. the full sum is owed throughout the loan period and then repaid at the end, although interest is paid half-yearly and charged to revenue, accompanied by an annual provision for the ultimate repayment of the principal which is actually based on the loan fund advance and the period of the sanction), instalment (i.e. an equal instalment of the loan is repaid half-yearly with interest on the reducing balance), and annuity (i.e. an equal sum paid each half year in respect of interest and principal, annuity table being normally required for the ascertainment of this sum). It is pointed out that payments to the P.W.L.B. are, as you may have noted, half-yearly though this was not always the case, and that to repay loans by the annuity and instalment methods means that the sums paid have to be replaced by other borrowing or some other way.

(c) *Stock*. Local authorities which are faced with large capital programmes to finance can use stock issues to obtain substantial amounts of money over long periods. Stock can also be used to "fund" debt by replacing a number of fairly short-term mortgages, bonds, temporary loans, etc. by one long-term issue. An element of stability is thus introduced into the interest rate payable on that part of the total debt for a number of years and the local authority is to that extent less at the mercy of market conditions, even though the rate payable may prove somewhat high if interest rates ease later. The preliminary expenses incurred in issuing the stock and in its annual management can be high and there is a minimum amount of £3,000,000 for any issue at the present. Holdings of stock can be bought and sold on the stock exchange, and terms of issue can be finely adjusted to meet market conditions at the time of offer. For instance, there can be a premium on the issue – the investor paying, say, £98 for a £100 holding. A stock has two dates in its title, the first being the optional repayment date, the second the compulsory repayment date (which must give at most a life of 60 years to the stock). The authority therefore has a period of years in which to choose the best time for it to repay and replace the particular issue. The Bank of England and the Treasury control the timing and terms of stock issues, and regulations prescribe most of the aspects of stock management and accounting methods.

(d) *Local Authority Bonds*. This form of borrowing was introduced under the Local Government (Financial Provisions) Act 1963 with the intention of opening up a new source of loans for local authorities which, at that time, were restricted in their access to the P.W.L.B.. This new method has proved a success, and the bonds have acquired various designations, such as general bonds, local bonds, yearling bonds, negotiable bonds, etc. dependent upon how and where they are issued. They can be sold "over the counter" in quite small sums to local people who wish to invest in their town or others who are attracted by the terms offered (when they are called local bonds), or they can be issued in much larger amounts via the money market, that is through discount houses and the Stock Exchange (when they are called negotiable bonds and are subject to a maximum quota for each authority). In the first case, the local authority offers a rate of interest over a period. In the second, the Bank of England and the Treasury decide the date of issue and the terms, though, (as with stock), the authority may refuse to proceed with the issue if the terms are not to its liking. The term must be at least one year but terms can be agreed for renewal at the end of the original period. The bond is in multiples of £5 and is represented by a certificate. It is much more flexible and easy to administer than a mortgage and because of this many authorities have opted to use bonds instead of mortgages, especially for small investors.

(e) *Foreign Loans*. These can, of course, be in various forms but it is of interest to consider the need for expert advice on international aspects of finance and the existence of a gamble on the value of the £ at the advancing and repayment dates. As mentioned above, this type of borrowing is closely controlled by the central departments involved.

(f) *Temporary Loans*. These are obviously for short terms, another name being short-term loans, and can be merely overnight from one day to the next, or up to 364 days (365 in a leap year). They may be for a fixed period only, such as three months. They may be on notice only, such as 7 days' notice, or they may be for a fixed period and then on notice, such as three months certain and thereafter at 7 days' notice. Notice refers, of course, to the warning given of the desire for repayment given by either the lender or the borrower. These loans are evidenced in the form of a simple receipt (called a deposit receipt − another term used for these loans), even for quite large amounts but they are supported by the evidence of correspondence with brokers, etc. If the loan is to meet expenses pending the receipt of income (either capital or revenue), no consent is needed from the central department. The total amount of temporary borrowing is subject to a control, however, as to its proportion of the local authority's whole debt. Thus, as regards the whole debt, at most 20% must be for less than one year, and at most 15% must be for three months or less. Temporary loans are usually obtained via brokers or loans bureaux, and interest is usually paid half-yearly, and on repayment. They have the advantage of low interest rates but their handicap of short notice generates much administrative work. At certain times of the year, i.e. the customary financial year-ends, − 31 March, 30 June, 30 September and 31 December − window dressing can cause the funds to dry up, forcing authorities into bank overdraft for a few days.

(g) *Internal Funds.* A local authority can utilise its internal fund balances to finance capital schemes instead of borrowing from outside. Such funds include superannuation, insurance, capital, repair and renewal, reserve and funds for the repayment of debt. Such sums borrowed must be repaid if the internal fund needs them for its own purposes, and an adequate rate of interest must be paid. Balances on revenue funds may also be lent temporarily to the loans pool but in practice this is often done on a notional basis, the capital schemes being charged with an interest calculation on an annual basis in respect of their individual underfinancing.

(h) *Bank Overdraft.* This is mainly a matter of negotiation between the local authority and its bank, though the Treasury can lay down limits to its amount. The rate of interest which is generally related to the base rate, and the period are also agreed. The bank is often the lender of last resort in times of shortage of funds and the local authority may occasionally be forced into overdraft without being able to give the bank manager what he considers is fair warning.

(i) *Money Bills.* The power to issue bills (which are similar to bills of exchange or Treasury Bills) was originally given to local authorities only under Local Acts. The Local Government Act 1972 has extended this power to larger authorities (who rate-derived income exceeds £3,000,000) to issue bills for revenue and capital purposes for periods up to 12 months. The maximum amount of bills issued must not exceed one-fifth of the local authority's income from the rates. At present, these powers are restricted – maximum period of issue is six months and the bills must be for revenue purposes only. The method of borrowing has a relatively low cost of issue and management and because of the authorities being large in size and resources, interest rates are lower than for other types of loans. If certain conditions are fulfilled, the bills can be discounted at the banks. (Discounting a bill means that the original lender or someone to whom he has passed it, sells it before it is due for repayment to a bank at a value which is discounted, i.e. at a value at which the bank is given its due profit when the bill is finally paid).

The Principles of Loans Fund Operation

Under the provisions of the Local Government Act 1972, a local authority has power to borrow money to enable it to carry out its functions, and can establish a loans fund (to which the borrowings are taken) to finance its capital expenditure and to repay loans when they fall due. All money borrowed is charged indifferently on all the authority's revenues and all loans rank equally, i.e. no loan has any priority over others.

A loans fund is a device which divorces the raising and repayment of loans (between the authority and the outside world) from the internal transactions (between the loans fund and the services or departments needing advances to finance their capital schemes). It introduces simplicity and a measure of fairness by gathering all costs together and charging them out to the departments at average (or "pool") rates for interest and administration expenses.

The main features of a loans fund scheme are as follows: −

1. All sums borrowed (by mortgages, etc.) go straight into the loans fund which pays the interest due on them and incurs the costs of managing the fund (salaries, office supplies, brokers' commission, etc.).
2. The loans fund makes advances to the departments (which are called "borrowing accounts") to meet the needs of the capital schemes which are approved for financing from loans. Advances can be made monthly, quarterly, half-yearly or annually, in such amounts as the schemes need.
3. The loans fund allocates the interest and its management expenses at pool (average) rates over the outstanding advances held by the departments. The fund's revenue account is thus balanced − expenditure equals income and recharges.
4. The borrowing accounts repay proportions of the advances to the loans fund in order to conform with the legal requirement that a local authority must make annual charges in its accounts sufficient to repay the principal of each loan by the end of the loan sanction period. These repayments may be calculated either on a straight-line or on an accumulating basis. Straight-line (or "equal annual instalments") means that each year bears an equal charge − the total advance is divided by the number of years of the sanction period. Thus an advance of £100,000 with a sanction for 5 years creates a charge of £20,000 in each of those years. The accumulating basis assumes that the annual repayments earn a prescribed rate of interest. Tables are needed to obtain the figures, but a similar advance as that above would create charges of £18,097, £19,002, £19,952, £20,950 and £21,999 in the five years, taking the present maximum prescribed rate of 5%. These repayments by the departments to the loans fund can be used to make new advances to them.

The loans fund repays outside loans when they fall due, possibly, out of new borrowings. Loans can be instalment, annuity or maturity in nature. Instalment loans are repaid in equal annual instalments of principal, annuity in equal annual payments of principal and interest combined, whilst maturity loans are repaid in full at the end of their terms. Annuity loans can be repaid at half-yearly or quarterly intervals as well as annual.

The modern form of loans fund is entitled "Consolidated Loans Fund" and in these days of large-scale local authorities it is now almost certainly universal.

The continuing high rates of interest on borrowings has over the past few years caused the average period of loans to local authorities to shorten dramatically, as the treasurers adopt the dictum "interest high, borrow short". The Government became uneasy at this occurrence as it meant that local government was subject to instability from erratic interest rates on the short-term loans. To avoid the threat of central governmental regulation, the local authority finance officers drew up a voluntary code under which they would progressively lengthen the average life of their authorities' debts over a period of years. The final stage in the code is to maintain the average term of a local authority's debt at seven years or more.

The Nature of Local Authority Expenditure and Methods of Financing it

Local authorities are a creation of Parliament which has allotted various duties to them in relation to the provision of services and amenities. Some duties are mandatory upon the local authorities — they "shall" do them — whilst others are discretionary — they "may" do them, but, in all cases, the payments made by the authorities must be "intra vires" i.e. within their legal powers. The payments made by the councils upon the services they provide are divided into two categories according to how quickly the benefit arising from a particular payment is exhausted.

The first kind is called revenue expenditure (bearing in mind that payments adjusted for accrued items equal expenditure) and the return on it is experienced and exhausted immediately or within a fairly short period, i.e. before the end of the financial year in which it is incurred. The second class is termed capital expenditure and the return on this is of longer duration. Its benefit is felt for, possibly, many future financial years.

The theoretical position, however, is subject to some practical difficulties of interpretation: —

1. Payments of the same subjective nature may be of either category, according to the purpose for which they are made. Wages paid to a tradesman who carries out repairs are revenue expenditure, whereas wages paid to the same tradesman employed on building a new council dwelling are capital expenditure. Thus a telephone call by a surveyor or the purchase of the first tablets of toilet soap in a community home can be regarded as capital in nature.

2. Capital expenditure is generally regarded as being incurred on the creation of some revenue-earning, benefit-giving, permanent asset which will give service throughout its life. Borrowing powers are normally only granted by the central departments in respect of financing capital expenditure, but these can include items such as compensation, costs of obtaining Local Act powers, etc. which do not apparently bring future tangible benefits. It can be argued that their cost should be spread over several years because to charge one year is even more unfair to the current ratepayers.

3. Capital expenditure is charged to capital accounts and revenue expenditure to revenue accounts, as a general rule. Assets of relatively small value are sometimes charged to the revenue account, and no record appears of their acquisition in the capital account, though the omission is covered by requiring inventories to be kept of such items which are checked

periodically. Typewriters, tape recorders and calculators are examples of this type of item.

It must be remembered that, up to the present, a local authority has the power to charge any intra-vires expenditure to revenue without regard to whether it is revenue or capital in nature. It just means that the ratepayers' burden is increased in the particular year. The opposite does not apply — revenue expenditure cannot be charged to capital except in one rare instance where a local authority can borrow to meet interest on the debt incurred on a new revenue-producing undertaking for a limited period — i.e. until it starts giving returns.

Revenue expenditure may thus be financed out of the general rate, government grants and other local authority sources such as rents, fees and miscellaneous charges.

Capital schemes may be financed in various ways besides the principal source supplied by borrowings. The sources include the following: —

(a) Revenue contributions to capital outlay can be made as a matter of policy. A rate in the £ can be earmarked for capital schemes either within committee estimates or as a global sum, schemes costing below a given figure can be charged automatically to revenue, or individual items can be charged as they occur. This method is sometimes called "Pay-as-you-Go" and whilst it saves interest charges and administrative costs, it may cause waste as no central control operates with regard to the financial aspects of the schemes.

(b) Advances from capital and other reserve funds may be used to meet capital expenditure. Such funds are built up by earmarking rate monies, paying in the proceeds of the sale of assets, etc.. These funds are intended to reduce the need to borrow, so their advantages and disadvantages are similar to those of charging revenue direct, except that a fund can be built up over several years to avoid fluctuations in the rate level. Inflation is a factor to be considered, as its effect is to reduce the burden of future debt and thus immediate payment may prove the more costly.

(c) Capital receipts from the sale of assets which were originally acquired out of loan can be used to meet capital expenditure, either directly by application to the scheme, or indirectly, by being paid into some capital fund. The consent of the Department of the Environment is needed to the use of large sums realised from sales for purposes unconnected with new and existing capital expenditure. It is unusual for any substantial capital receipts to be permitted to be credited to the revenue account.

(d) Capital grants from government departments are given in respect of projects of national importance, either to encourage local authority action or because the cost is too heavy for the authority without assistance. At present, this class of grant is insignificant in amount.

(e) Company Formation and Partnership Schemes may be used to redevelop areas. A company may be formed in which the local authority is the majority shareholder. In the case of a partnership, the authority and a private developer may provide the land and the finance respectively, and after the agreed period has run, the assets revert to the authority. Many variations are possible.

(f) Leasing is employed to avoid the need to incur heavy capital expenditure on equipment (buildings have always been the subject of leasing, this is just an extension of the practice). The payment is revenue in nature, as the firm supplying the equipment, machinery, vehicles, etc. bears the cost of purchase and maintenance. It might be argued that this method is dearer than if the authority financed direct but there is the point that such an arrangement was outside the control of borrowing limits, though it can be expected to fall within the definition of capital expenditure under current legislation.

Supplement

Summary of the Rate Support Grant system previous to the Local Government, Planning and Land Act 1980: –

After the amounts for specific grants were taken out of the global sum approved by Parliament, the balance was allocated to the three elements of the Rate Support Grant. It was first allotted to the domestic element, then to the resources element, and the residue went to the needs element. The domestic element was the smallest and the needs element the largest in terms of money.

The domestic element was intended to reimburse fully the loss in rate income arising from the reduction in rate poundage levied on domestic ratepayers compared with other classes of ratepayers. This grant element was paid to rating authorities, i.e. district or borough councils, and was credited to the rate income and appropriation account.

The resources element was a form of notional rate payment by the government to meet the deficiency in rate income suffered by a rating authority because its rateable value per head fell short of a national standard. The calculations were somewhat involved and the following illustration is given: –

Population of the rating authority = 500,000

Total net expenditure (including precepts) for the next year – £80,000,000

Actual local rateable value = £95,000,000

National standard rateable value per head = £200 (prescribed for the next year)

National standard rateable value for the area = £200 × 500,000
= £100,000,000

Shortfall in rateable value for the area = standard – actual = £5,000,000

The government pays $\frac{£80,000,000}{£100,000,000}$ i.e. 80p in the £ on £5,000,000 = £4,000,000 as the resources element.

As implied above, this element was paid to rating authorities and was credited to the rate income and appropriation account.

The needs element was made up of a number of payments based on factors which were considered as representing various conditions affecting local authorities which called for a higher level of expenditure on services. The overall aim of this element was to enable all local authorities to supply a standard level of service at an equal cost per head of their population. The factors upon which the payments were made could be varied year by year as experience was gained on the working of the various formulae used. Most of the factors were fairly complicated and related the grant payment to an excess of specific characteristics possessed by an area or its population over nationally-chosen norms. Attributes taken into the reckoning included the number of inhabitants, the degree of sparsity of the population over its area, any decline in population in recent years, the number of old people who lived alone, the number of persons living in densely-inhabited areas or without basic amenities, the number of one-parent families, the number of pupils at school and other educational establishments, etc.

The needs element was originally paid to non-metropolitan counties, metropolitan and London boroughs, but in recent years, the non-metropolitan districts had begun to receive part of the county's quota direct. This apportionment was based on the district's share of the combined expenditure of both county and its districts. Where the factors and formulae gave what were considered unfair results if rigidly applied, there was provision to use damping factors called "safety nets" (where there would be an excessive fall from one year to the next) and "claw-back" (where the rise between two years would be too sharp) so that variations in distribution from year to year were reduced.

An advisory body composed of representatives of central and local government entitled the Consultative Council on Local Government Finance has played a role for a number of years in advising the Government in respect of the method of allocation of the Rate Support Grant among the local authorities. The Government would inform the Council of the global sum available for the year's R.S.G. and the Council would offer suggestions as to its distribution. It was supported in its deliberations by a number of sub groups dealing with particular aspects of the problem, the main sub group being the Grants Working Group. The introduction of the new block grant system has still involved the Council via its sub groups but its role in the future appears likely to be more restricted than under the former grant arrangements as the allocation of the block grant to individual local authorities is now a centralised matter. Nevertheless, the Government has said that, in its opinion, the Council still has a useful part to play as a forum for the discussion of matters involving the joint interests of local and central authorities and the need for co-operation between them.

Questions

5.1 What are the main forms of income receivable by a local authority?

5.2 Indicate the various types of grant payable to local authorities by the central government.

5.3 Describe briefly how the product of a penny rate is calculated.

5.4 Outline the main methods of valuing properties for rating purposes.

5.5 Outline the procedure for levying and collecting the General Rate.

5.6 What considerations may affect the level of charge for a service supplied by a local authority?

5.7 In what ways may a local authority borrow money to finance capital expenditure?

5.8 Besides the use of borrowed money, in what other ways may capital expenditure be financed by a local authority?

5.9 What are the main ways in which loans may be repaid to investors by a local authority?

5.10 Explain briefly how a loans fund works.

Chapter 6

Financial Control of Local Authorities

We live in a universe of infinite variation, in which no two articles are actually identical, although, at first sight, there appears to be no differences between them. This fact is brought home to all students of statistics and quality control inspectors. In the same way, each local authority possesses its own individual pattern of organisation, functions, committees and officers. Many factors have combined to make every local authority unique. An authority may be a county, district, parish, community or ad hoc. It may be in a metropolitan or non-metropolitan area, or in Greater London, Wales or elsewhere. All this affects the span of duties which Parliament allots to it. There are also differences in geography, and in the age pattern and distribution of population − whether a locality is urban or rural, compact or dispersed, has a relatively young or old population − and these factors influence the way in which an authority deploys its staff and money on services, and how it organises itself to do the best it can. In addition, a whole host of variations grow out of the history of an area and the way local government has developed there, especially when this is allied with the central government's policy of allowing local authorities a measure of discretion in arranging their internal affairs.

Any attempt to give an outline of a financial control system applicable to local authorities of such differing natures must therefore only be of a general nature, and in some respects, such as the titles and roles given to committees, differences in the use and meaning of terms must arise between the text and actual examples which the reader may know from personal experience.

The component parts of the control system for the financial work of a local authority may first be divided into internal and external controls. These may be further subdivided for ease of treatment, as shown in the following listings.

Internal
1. The Finance Sub-committee
2. The Director of Finance
3. The Finance Division
4. The Departmental Finance Officers
5. Standing Orders and Financial Regulations
6. Budgetary Control Systems
7. Accounting Procedures
8. Costing Methods
9. Management Services
10. Evaluation of Capital Projects
11. The Internal Audit

External
12. The External Audit
13. Central Government Controls
14. Public Opinion
15. The Commissioner for Local Administration

This section of the book deals with the first ten elements of internal control given in the above tabulation. The internal audit function and the external elements of financial control are treated in their respective parts of the book to avoid repetition.

1. *The Finance Sub-committee*

Although the council of a local authority is its ultimate decision-making body, for the majority of the time it follows the recommendations made by the policy and resources committee with only a small amount of debate in council because of lack of time and pressure of business. The policy and resources committee, in its turn, normally refers the bulk of the discussion and detailed consideration of financial matters to its finance sub-committee.

The functions of the finance sub-committee include such matters as: –

(a) the supervision of the operation of the local authority's financial control system, such as receiving the reports of the director of finance and overseeing the finance division, reviewing, considering and advising on revisions in financial regulations, regulating scales of charges, supervising borrowing, banking, fund investment and insurance arrangements, receiving reports from the authority's external auditor and giving them due consideration, dealing with questions of interdepartmental disputes and major irregularities of a financial nature.

(b) the allocation of the local authority's resources over its various services in line with a pre-determined policy designed to make the best use of those resources and to review the adequacy of such resources for the requirements of the programmes. This comprises such matters as considering the annual estimates of expenditure and income on revenue and capital account, recommending the rate levy or precept, and deciding whether to approve or refuse proposals for new projects, supplementary estimates, and virements.

(c) the consideration of the effects which new legislation might have upon the finances of the local authority.

2. *The Director of Finance*

This officer has a number of titles – treasurer, chief financial officer, comptroller, chamberlain (in Scotland) – besides the current favourite of director of finance. He is the council's accountant, receiver of monies, paymaster and financial adviser. His duties are to control the day-to-day operations of the finance division, and to report to and take instructions from the finance sub-committee on all matters within its terms of reference. It is normal procedure for certain matters to be within the power of the director under financial regulations, e.g. minor supplementary estimates and transfers between votes (i.e. virements), administration of the loans fund, payment of all accounts properly certified, institution of recovery proceedings for all debts, writing off minor bad debts, controlling the use of the computer installation, implementing national pay awards and keeping insurance matters up to date.

A local authority is charged under the Local Government Act, 1972, with the duty to make arrangements for the proper administration of its financial affairs and to secure that one of its officers is responsible for administering those arrangements. No title is given in the Act, though the Accounts and Audit Regulations, 1974, refer to this officer as the "financial officer" and allot him the duty of maintaining an internal audit of the council's operations. It is nowhere required that he be a professionally qualified accountant, though as far as is known, no gifted amateur has been appointed to date.

The Bains report recommended the formation of management teams of chief officers (and, incidentally, of other officers also) as a part of a corporate management structure for local authorities. The chief officers' team is intended to carry out the following functions — consideration of the actions needed to meet future changes in circumstances and their resultant problems, and advising the council accordingly, and speeding up the running of the local authority by joint effort at the top level. Most councils have adopted in one form or another, the suggestions of Bains that the director of finance acts as a member of a team, instead of, as under the earlier arrangements, regarding it as a duty to argue the case for efficiency and probity in finance independently, in view of his direct legal responsibility to the ratepayers. It is now his role to ensure that the financial aspects of matters are fully explained to, and explored by the team but to acquiesce in majority decisions. The problem of his relationship with the citizens whereby he is directly answerable to them for the results of any unlawful act he may commit, is still present, according to expressed legal opinions. In the main, however, the success or failure of the new arrangements may rest on the ability to avoid clashes of temperament whilst promoting collaboration.

3. *The Finance Division*

The detailed financial work of the local authority is centred in this department which is headed by the director of finance. Traditionally, the division has been split into sections which each carry out stages or aspects of the operations of all services, especially with regard to those operations creating or affecting cash flows. The titles of these sections indicate their functions — cashiers and collection, credit income records, payments and expenditure certification, salaries, wages and personnel records, internal audit, loans and investments, management and financial accountancy, management services, computer, etc. The emphasis on the optimal use of resources and value for money in recent years has caused a move to divide the accountancy function into (a) budgetary control — the day-by-day recording of transactions, and (b) financial planning — the forecasting of future needs and the evaluation of projects. Internal audit also has been affected by this new emphasis.

The finance division's involvement with all departments make it essential that there are recognised procedures for inter-departmental co-operation and the apportioning of responsibility for ensuring they are complied with. Normally, a transaction is originated in a service department and its financial aspects passed over to the finance division to deal with, e.g. payment or collection of the sum involved. The personnel of each department should be certain as to where their responsibilities begin and end for the various tasks in the particular procedure, otherwise omission or overlapping of duties may occur.

4. *Departmental Finance Officers*

The scale of operations in most local authorities is now so large that the need has arisen for a measure of decentralisation of financial duties by integrating some procedures which normally fall within the province of the finance division into the larger executive departments.

Departmental finance officers are appointed who carry out detailed work on salaries, costings, etc. and forward listings and summaries to the finance division. One advantage is that errors are reduced as these officers have specialist knowledge of a departmental nature but the arrangement is criticised on the grounds that officers may fail to be completely objective in carrying out their duties because of a feeling of loyalty to their department, e.g. introduction of bias into progress reports on projects.

It must be remembered, in this connection, that every member of staff has a duty to conform and require conformance with standing orders, including those applicable to financial control, so far as they affect him, even when he is not, in effect, carrying out financial work. An employee in control of stores which he must protect in accordance with laid-down instructions, is not a finance officer (though perhaps an accounting officer) but his work has financial undertones.

Indeed, one might say that there is a no more certain way of making sure that a new financial code, accountancy system, costing procedure, or computer installation will fail than to either antagonise, ignore or frighten those who will have the duty to supply data to the system, operate it or use the output. Lack of consultation may be the root of an array of reactions by the staff including the fear of redundancy, failure to discern any benefits or injured pride reflected in working to rule. An example of this occurred, it seems, in English local government in a large northern town during the 1930s. A new mechanised rating system was introduced (this was in pre-electronic computer days) and possibly because of failure to educate the staff, within eighteen months the system was in complete disarray and nobody knew who owed what. It is said that this event held up the development of mechanised methods in local authority finance for several years, in fact, until the 1939-45 war forced the adoption of machinery, as staff became depleted by the call-up.

Suggested Organisation Chart for the Finance Division of a Local Authority

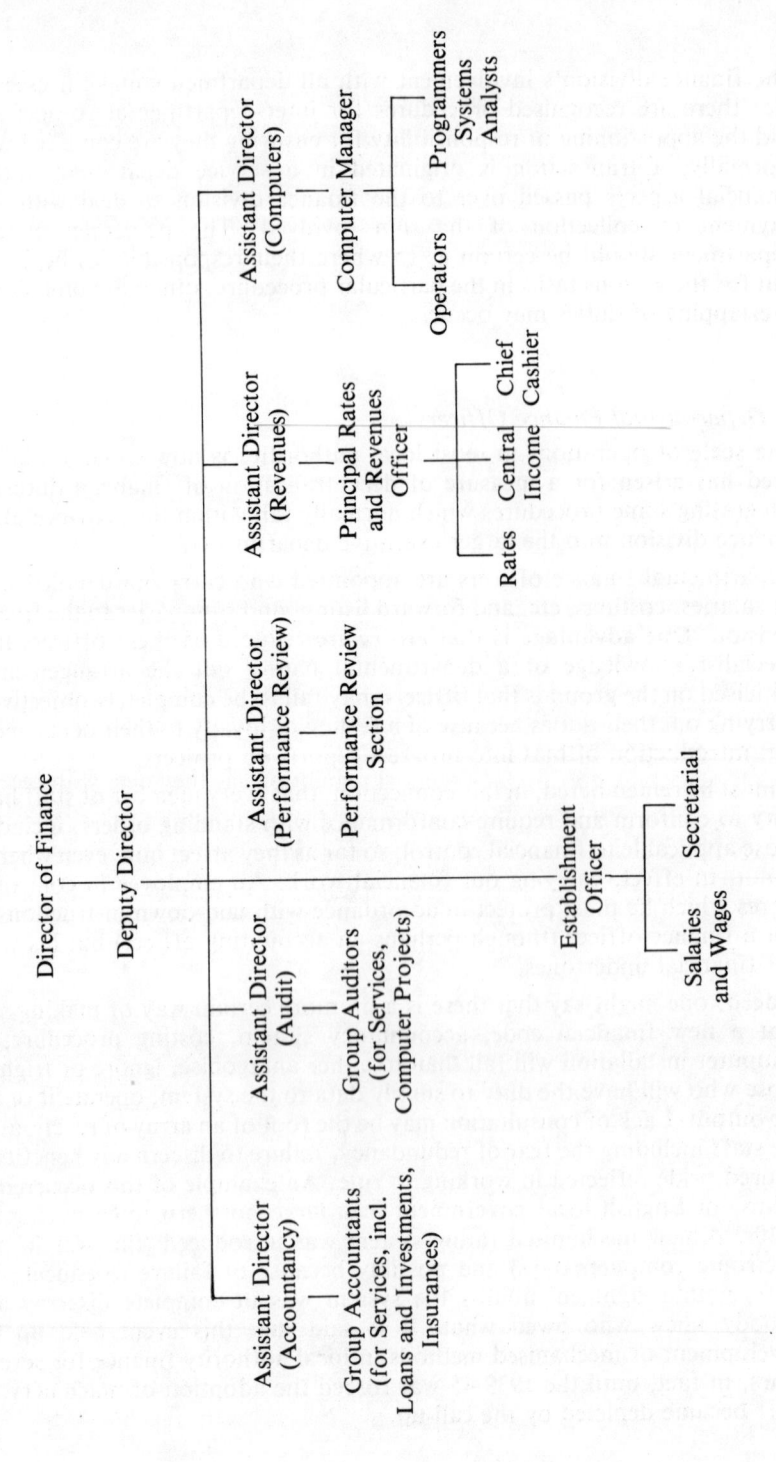

```
                              Director of Finance
                                     |
                              Deputy Director
                                     |
    ┌────────────┬──────────────┬────────────┬──────────────┬──────────────┐
Assistant    Assistant     Assistant    Assistant     Assistant     Establishment
Director      Director      Director     Director      Director       Officer
(Accountancy) (Audit)   (Performance  (Revenues)    (Computers)
                           Review)
    │            │            │             │             │           ┌────┴────┐
Group        Group       Performance   Principal    Computer     Salaries  Secretarial
Accountants  Auditors    Review        Rates and    Manager      and Wages
(for Services, (for Services, Section  Revenues         │
incl. Loans   Computer                 Officer      ┌───┴───┐
and Investments, Projects)                │         │       │
Insurances)                          ┌────┼────┐  Programmers Operators
                                   Rates Central Chief  Systems
                                         Income Cashier Analysts
```

5. Standing Orders and Financial Regulations

The council, committees and departments of a local authority require an atmosphere of order, routine and assurance in which to take decisions and to carry on the day-to-day work as efficiently as possible. For this reason, and because of the large scale of the operations of modern local government, a comprehensive code for the conduct of business is a necessity. In addition, this code has to take account of the public and political nature of local government, because public funds are used, and this gives rise to the duty to ensure that they are spent in proper ways, after sufficient open discussions have both taken place and been seen to take place.

A local authority's standing orders or instructions, as they are called, can be classified in three ways. Some are contained in the Acts of Parliament, especially the Local Government Act 1972, which gives detailed instructions regarding such activities as the holding of annual, extraordinary and other meetings, the quorum needed for business to be transacted at a meeting, the recording and signing of minutes and the election of a chairman. Some standing orders are required by law to deal with such matters as the making of proper arrangements for financial affairs and the ensuring of competition and the inviting of tenders regarding contracts, but their content is at the discretion of the local authority. The third type of standing orders are those made completely at the option of the authority to suit its own particular circumstances. A number of the instructions are often segregated under the title of financial regulations as they deal with receipts and payments, security of assets, etc. and are often more detailed in nature than other types of standing orders.

6. Budgetary Control Systems

Local authorities prepare various forms of budget, each designed for a different purpose but united in embodying the implementation of the council's policies. The main types of budget prepared are (a) the revenue budget, (b) the capital budget, (c) the manpower budget, and (d) the cash flow or financing budget.

There is also budgeting called P.P.B.S. − planning, programming, budgeting systems − where objectives are set out, alternative methods of attaining them are evaluated, capital and revenue aspects of cost and financing are combined, and departmental boundaries are ignored. Thus a project might have as objective the provision of 500 car parking spaces. This could involve on-street parking, appropriation of vacant land owned by any committee of the council, purchase of land by agreement or compulsorily, encouragement to private land owners to provide space for parking and to charge, multi-storey car parking either by the council or privately, etc.. All these alternatives need evaluation as to relative costs − capital and revenue − and several committees could be involved.

The Revenue Budget. This is a series of financial statements which contains the detailed estimates of current expenditure and income on the services operated by the local authority for the coming year. It represents in terms of money the local authority's policy as to the allocation of its resources. Besides showing how the money is to be spent, it is used to fix the rate or precept – the law requires the authority to levy a rate or precept sufficient to meet its net expenditure, plus any deficiency for last year, and to include a working balance.

A local authority can authorise supplementary estimates during the year for items which are, or are going to be, overspent, and virements where a transfer may be made from an underspent vote to one where the money is needed.

The Capital Budget. This is the approved co-ordinated programme of the local authority's future expenditure on long-term assets, buildings, works, etc.. By giving an overall view of total requirements, it facilitates variations in the pace of developments, decisions on priorities and the effect upon the rate levy. It gives details of the projected schemes over the next few years (usually five), and enables the revenue cost to be estimated in respect of debt charges and running costs on completion for each scheme. It also permits consideration of methods of financing and the provision of staffing and supplies. Local authority capital budgets are usually of a "rolling" type – a year is added annually to the far end of the budget period while a year is dropped from the beginning. It must be remembered that the inclusion of a scheme in the capital programme is not the final word on approval – finance sub-committee recommendation and council approval is still needed when the time comes. One difficulty of the rolling type of programme is that delays in present ongoing scheme developments and uncertainty about the not-too-near future can cause congestion in the early years and sparsity in the later.

The preparation of the Structure Plans which is a requirement of the Town and Country Planning Acts appears to some extent to be capable of being combined with the work on the capital budget. These plans are blueprints for the development of the local authority's area for the coming decade or two. They deal with land use, transport facilities, housing, shopping facilities, industrial development, and amenities generally, incorporating financial estimates of costs which, however, include investment from the private sector besides that of public monies.

Manpower Budget. This is intended to enable the local authority to control the numbers of staff it employs, by relating the departmental provisions in the budget for salaries and wages to the authorised establishments which are the basis of the estimates. Thus, as only authorised increases in staff are allowed to be added to the previous official total of employees, any discrepancies are revealed.

There may have to be measures of relaxation in respect of departments employing large numbers of manual workers or casual or part-time staff, mainly because of the difficulties of maintaining levels of employment where there is competition elsewhere for labour, and work is subject to variation in availability. Examples of such departments are direct works, highways and parks. Lump sum provisions are made which are based on an estimated number of employees considered sufficient to do the projected workload, and the departmental head has power to take on labour within those limits.

Cash Flow or Financing Budget. The high level of interest rates forces a local authority to manage its cash flows efficiently. This is achieved in two ways. Firstly, the loans fund estimates which are drawn up in advance of those for departments, provide for loans falling due for repayment, and new loans to meet the projected capital scheme payments, including temporary borrowings and the use of surplus internal funds. Secondly, throughout the year, a daily or weekly record is kept which forecasts receipts and payments for the coming few weeks and the movement in the bank balance, so that borrowings can be planned if in deficit, or money lent out if in surplus. The record is constantly updated.

7. *Accounting Procedures.* The operation of budgetary control requires means of measuring how far the objectives envisaged in the plan have been attained. The accounting system provides these means – reliable and accurate records of income and expenditure on revenue and capital account, equitable allocations of costs, commitments undertaken (e.g. orders issued and contracts signed), etc.. These records are checked against budget votes to signal any unexpected variations in pattern which might call for corrective action, such as obtaining authority for a supplementary estimate or a virement. It must not be imagined that the budgets are cast iron in nature, but they are in fact subject to continual amendments, and the accounts supply the basis for correct decision-taking in respect of both current events and future plans.

Although a local authority is one legal entity – a public or statutory corporation – it is required by a number of statutes to keep separate accounts in respect of certain services, funds, activities, etc.. This introduces an appreciable degree of complication into the accounting arrangements which is administratively inconvenient, confusing to the layman but legally unavoidable. Examples of the services and funds which require separate accounts are: – the Housing Revenue Account, the loans fund, the superannuation fund, the local lotteries, the Capital Fund, the Renewal and Repairs Fund, the Insurance Fund, house purchase (the Small Dwellings Acquisition Acts code), allotments, the free 2p. rate allowed under the Local Government Act 1972, and direct labour projects of major size (carried out by what the government now calls Direct Labour Organisations or D.L.O.s).

The main fund of a county council is called the county fund, that of a district or borough is called the general rate fund, whilst a parish has a general fund.

Notes on the Accounting Methods in a Local Authority

(a) *The Cash Account*

The cash accounts operated by local authorities are essentially the same as those kept in commercial accounts. It should be realised that all the receipts and payments are bank figures, so the cash account is, in effect, the bank columns of a cash and bank account as taught in commercial bookkeeping. Owing to the need to keep separate accounts for certain funds, the account is columnar in form, having a Dr. and Cr. column for each fund. It is customary for a local authority to keep one bank account and the entries on the pass sheets relating to it are reconciled with the total of the Dr. and Cr. columns in the cash account. The Dr. and Cr. entries for each fund are balanced and the fund cash balance brought forward monthly.

Some authorities keep a group of bank accounts and each is reconciled with its cash account. This system can be complicated in actual operation and a bank transfer journal is essential for transfers and correction of errors in bankings or withdrawals.

Subsidiary bank accounts may be sometimes be kept which are on an imprest basis or for the purposes of suspense of items. For instance, when the half-yearly loan interest cheques are despatched, their total cash value is transferred to an imprest account at the bank. The interest cheques (which are in their own special form and sequence of numbers) are presented against the imprest, and the imprest balance at any time equals the unpresented cheques. In the case of a suspense, the daily bankings of receipts might be credited to a special account at the bank, and at month end, the total monthly receipts are analysed and transferred to the main bank account or, if a group is operated, to the respective individual fund bank accounts.

The cash account may take the following form: –

Dr. Cr.

Date	Details	Fo	G.R.F.	Rates	Loans	Total	Date	Details	Fo	G.R.F.	Rates	Loans	Total

Only three analysis columns are given here because of lack of space, but in practice there will be as many as necessary to meet legal requirements for the separation of funds. This example is for a district, a county would have County instead of G.R.F. (General rate fund) and have no rating columns.

Balances Brought Forward

These are the opening entries in the cash account for any period though balances are usually brought forward each month. Each fund balance is entered in its appropriate column, usually the debit side as an amount in hand, but credit entries do occur when amounts overdrawn are brought forward. The fund balances add across to agree with the total column of the cash account.

Cash Received

Receipts are entered on the debit side of the cash account in total each day for each fund. These totals are obtained from the records of the payments into bank which are duly summarised and supported by analyses into budget codes so that the corresponding credit entries to complete the double entry can be made (usually in total at the month end) to income (i.e. nominal) accounts, sundry debtors, contra-expenditure, etc..

Payments Made

The credit entries made to the cash account are the totals of the schedules of invoices for payment approved by the committees. These schedules contain creditors' accounts for supplies and work done, for which cheques are drawn, salaries and wages, which are paid in cash or by bank credit, and petty cash reimbursements and emergency payments, which are both paid by cheque. As with the receipts, the schedules are analysed over the funds per the columns in the cash account. They are also analysed to budget codes so that the corresponding debit entries to complete the double entry can be made monthly, firstly, in total to the sundry creditors' accounts of the various funds, and then the record is completed by debiting all the expenditure accounts (revenue, capital, contra-income, etc.) per budget vote in detail, and crediting the sundry creditors' accounts of the funds. The sundry creditors' account of each fund is thus a control and total account which facilities the ledger being sectionalised, especially for trial balance purposes.

In the case of the schedules of invoices for payment approved by the committees in the months just following the financial year end, e.g. April and May, the entries in the cash account are made in total in the new year's account − Dr. sundy creditors' account, Cr. cash account. The schedules, however, contain invoices for liabilities incurred before the old year ended, and thus the total value of those items relating to the previous year is extracted, and the same is done with those accounts chargeable to the now current year. Each of these two totals is credited to the sundry creditors' account in its particular year, and the corresponding debits go to the nominal accounts in detail in the same year. An adjustment has to be made in the cash account for those items on the April schedule (salaries, wages, emergency payments, etc.) which were actually paid before the 31st March. These are debited in total to the sundry creditors' account and credited in total to the cash account, both entries being in the old year. This nets down the sundry creditors on the April schedule to those which had not been paid by the year end, but leaves the amount charged to the old year's revenue (and capital) account and the cash balance correct.

Finally, a provision is made for liabilities which are still outstanding after the May schedule. A list is drawn up for each fund and totalled. This is debited to expenditure per budget code and credited in total to the sundry creditors' account. (Some authorities may credit a provision for outstanding liabilities, but this is unusual). The provisions are used up as the liabilities are eventually paid, small adjustments are often needed where estimates differ from the actual amounts. Of course, where no provision is made for a previous year's liability, it is a charge on the new year's accounts when it is paid.

As will be apparent from the preceding sentences, the payments made are analysed to either revenue or capital expenditure codes. What are called contra-income items also occur, such as the refund of charges for services, and in the preparation of the final accounts, these are netted from the appropriate income headings.

The treatment of the petty cash imprests is also worthy of explanation. Petty cash accounts are used to meet small items of expense normally paid in cash and the term imprest means that the amount held by the holder of the account (or, as he or she is sometimes referred to, the petty cashier) is limited to a fixed sum. Thus, at any time, the cash in hand plus the vouchers paid should add up to the value of the imprest. The imprest is recorded as a type of debtor when it is first advanced, usually in the form of a cheque payable to the imprestholder via the committee schedule of invoices for payment. The entries are the same as for other such invoices, i.e. Dr. petty cash imprestholders' account, Cr. sundry creditors' account, and Dr. sundry creditors' account, Cr. Cash. This is thus an example of a personal account occurring in the expenditure analysis, and, unless it is repaid at the end of the year, will appear as a debtor or asset (as part of the item "cash in the hands of officers") on the Balance Sheet. When the imprestholder applies for reimbursement of the money spent out of the imprest, the petty cash vouchers are collated, coded and totalled, and their total sum is paid to the holder by cheque. The vouchers are included in the next payments schedule in the same way as other invoices from creditors. The book entries are thus within the schedule total, i.e. Dr. expenditure per budget code, Cr. sundry creditors' account, and Dr. sundry creditors' account, Cr. Cash. The original imprestholders' accounts thus remain unaffected and untouched by the entries involved in their reimbursement, i.e. they are always at their maximum value until they are finally repaid by the holder to the authority.

Balances Carried Forward

These are the differences between the debit and credit entries in the cash account at the end of the period, in respect of all the funds for which separate columns appear in that account. They are carried forward to the new period, usually the next month. The balances carried forward are reconciled with the bank balance in total, the main difference being the cheques issued but not yet presented to the bank by the payees. The local authority's financial procedures require the frequent updating of the bank reconciliation statement to prevent or minimise error or fraud, and to show the true amount of money at the disposal of the authority.

Examples of the Cash Account

To assist the reader to understand this somewhat lengthy and involved explanation, and at the same time to give some indication of the general form of cash account encountered, two examples are given, the first dealing with the entries generally, whilst the second concentrates on the year end adjustments. The reader is recommended to trace all the entries and to give the examples his or her full attention.

Examples of the Posting of Cash Book Entries

			£
Balances in hand brought forward 1 July 19-3			
General Rate fund			490,000
Rating			105,000
Loans fund			1,800,000
Housing Revenue account			115,000
Receipts, 1 to 31 July 19-3 (Cash Analysis)			
General Rate fund	Sundry debtors	40,000	
	Cash income	35,000	75,000
Rating	Ratepayers		851,000
Loans fund	Borrowings	2,473,000	
	Fees	1,000	2,474,000
Housing Revenue account	Rents		90,000
Payments (committee schedule totals)			
General Rate fund	Sundry creditors –		
	Revenue expenditure	242,000	
	Capital expenditure	101,000	
	Contra Income	2,000	345,000
Rating	Revenue expenditure	40,000	
	Refunds	3,000	43,000
Loans fund	Revenue expenditure	6,000	
	Loans repaid	900,000	906,000
Housing Revenue account	Revenue expenditure	20,000	
	Capital expenditure	123,000	143,000

Dr.   Cash Account – Debit Side

Date	Particulars	Folio No.	General Rate Fund £	Rating £	Loans £	Housing Revenue £	Total £
19-3							
Jul 1	Balances	b/f	490,000	105,000	1,800,000	115,000	2,510,000
Jul 1 to Jul 31	Cash Analysis	CA1	75,000	851,000	2,474,000	90,000	3,490,000
			565,000	956,000	4,274,000	205,000	6,000,000
19-3							
Aug 1	Balances	b/f	220,000	913,000	3,368,000	62,000	4,563,000

101

Cash Account – Credit Side

Date	Particulars	Folio No.	General Rate Fund £	Rating £	Loans £	Housing Revenue £	Total £
19-3 Jul 1 to Jul 31	Sundry Creditors	SC1	345,000	43,000	906,000	143,000	1,437,000
Jul 31	Balances	c/f	220,000	913,000	3,368,000	62,000	4,563,000
			565,000	956,000	4,274,000	205,000	6,000,000

General Rate Fund Ledger

Dr.   *Sundry Debtors*   **Cr.**

19-3
July   Cash Analysis   CA1   40,000

Income per Budget Codes (Revenue or Capital)

19-3
July   Cash   CB1   35,000

Sundry Creditors

| 19-3 July | Cash | CB1 | 345,000 | 19-3 July | Expenditure per budget codes | E1 | 345,000 |

Expenditure per Budget Codes

19-3
Jul   Sundry Creditors SC1
       Revenue   242,000
       Capital   101,000
       Contra income   2,000
(all in greater detail)

Rating Ledger

Dr.   *Total Ratepayers' Account*   **Cr.**

19-3
July   Cash Analysis   CA1   851,000

Sundry Creditors

| 19-3 July | Cash | CB1 | 43,000 | 19-3 July | Expenditure per budget codes | E1 | 43,000 |

Expenditure per Budget Codes

19-3
July   Sundry Creditors SC1
       Revenue   40,000
       Contra income   3,000
(all in greater detail)

Loans Fund Ledger

Dr.   *Lenders' Account*   **Cr.**

19-3				19-3			
July	Transfer from Expenditure per budget codes	E1	900,000	July	Cash Analysis	CA1	2,473,000

Income per Budget Codes

				19-3			
				July	Cash Analysis	CA1	1,000

Sundry Creditors

19-3				19-3			
July	Cash	CB1	906,000	July	Expenditure per budget codes	E1	906,000

Expenditure per Budget Codes

19-3				19-3			
July	Sundry Creditors SC1 Revenue Capital		6,000 900,000	July	Transfer to Lenders' Account	L1	900,000

Housing Ledger

Dr.   *Income per Budget Codes (Rent)*   **Cr.**

				19-3			
				July	Cash Analysis	CA1	90,000

Sundry Creditors

19-3				19-3			
July	Cash	CB1	143,000	July	Expenditure per budget codes	E1	143,000

Expenditure per Budget Codes

19-3			
	Sundry Creditors SC1 Revenue Capital (all in greater detail)		20,000 123,000

Example of the Year-end Entries dealing with Liabilities

		£
April 19-2 to March 19-3	Total of schedules of payment (including £43,000 applicable to 19-1/2)	793,000
April 19-3	Schedule of payments (including liabilities for 19-2/3 of £31,000 of which £6,000 had been paid before 31st March 19-3)	60,000
May 19-3	Schedule of payments (including liabilities for 19-2/3 of £5,000)	45,000
May 19-3	Estimate of total liabilities still outstanding for 19-2/3	14,000

Dr.   *Cash Account*   Cr.

		April 19-2 to March 19-3	Sundry creditors	750,000
		March 19-3	Sundry creditors	6,000
		April 19-3	Sundry creditors	54,000
		May 19-3	Sundry creditors	45,000

Sundry Creditors' Account

April 19-2 to March 19-3	Cash	750,000	April 19-2 to March 19-3	Expenditure per budget codes	750,000
March 19-3	Cash	6,000	April 19-3	Expenditure per budget codes	31,000
			May 19-3	Expenditure per budget codes	5,000
31 March 19-3	Balance c/f	44,000	May 19-3	Expenditure per budget codes	14,000
		800,000			800,000
April 19-3	Cash	54,000	1 April 19-3	Balance b/f	44,000
May 19-3	Cash	45,000	April 19-3	Expenditure per budget codes	29,000
			May 19-3	Expenditure per budget codes	40,000

Expenditure per Budget Codes (Revenue and Capital)

April 19-2 to March 19-3	Sundry creditors	750,000
April 19-3	Sundry creditors	31,000
May 19-3	Sundry creditors	5,000
May 19-3	Sundry creditors	14,000
		800,000
April 19-3	Sundry creditors	29,000
May 19-3	Sundry creditors	40,000

Arrangements with Banks

The services provided by the commercial banks which are used by public authorities include: –

Current account facilities – the payment of cheques, salaries and superannuation allowances, and the collection of cheques due to the authority; the receipt of cash deposited by cashiers and collectors; the payment of standing orders; the management of credit transfers by bank giro; the receipt of grants from the Government via the Bank of England; the making of overdrafts and bridging loans; the provision of cash for wages.

Deposit account facilities – interest paid on surplus cash at bank.

Night safe facilities — the after-hours banking of cash income by cashiers and collectors at branches near their offices.

The printing of cheques and other documents, such as paying in books for the authorities' use.

The arrangements for settling temporary loans to and from authorities; the purchase and sale of investments via the Stock Exchange (i.e. acting as a stockbroker); arranging stock issues and acting as a registrar of stock on behalf of authorities.

The provision of bankers' references in respect of financial enquiries into the standing of firms with which authorities have dealings, e.g. tenderers for contracts.

Foreign currency transactions which include the advancing and repayment of loans from abroad, the purchase of foreign made products or foreign literature, and members' expenses for overseas conferences and official visits.

So far as bank charges are concerned, there appears to be a considerable amount of variation, especially in the bases available. These may include combinations of various elements, such as lump sum charges for services over a period; charges based on numbers of cheques paid, deposits received; an agreed minimum balance in hand which cancels the charges (i.e. it earns enough interest to equal the charges); and charges based on the sums paid in and withdrawn.

Besides the traditional joint-stock banks (also called clearing or deposit banks), there is the National Girobank which was formed in 1968. Despite a somewhat slow start (possibly because of a crop of frauds early in its history and a reluctance to have a governmental body handle one's money), the bank has increased its number of accounts with persons and organisations together with a growth in the range of the services offered. Authorities are mainly interested in the Girobank's facilities for rent, rates, water, gas, electricity and other charges being collected and transferred to the authorities involved, and for the payment of salaries, wages and various benefits.

(b) *Expenditure Accounts*

The payments made by a local authority are in respect of goods and services invoiced by suppliers, salaries and wages paid to employees, and petty cash vouchers reimbursing imprests. These are all checked for accuracy, certified as authentic, analysed to budget codes, scheduled, totalled and approved for payment at the usual interval of one month.

The entries in the books are as follows: —

Sundry Revenue and Capital Expenditure (and Contra Income)
    Accounts   Dr.
        To Sundry Creditors   Cr.
(The recording of the liabilities — a total expenditure account may be used as an intermediate step)

Sundry Creditors Dr.
    To Cash Cr.
(The payment of the liabilities)
Each of the four entries balances with the total of the schedule.

It is the practice to omit any record of cash discounts deducted from the amounts of invoices when entering up the financial accounts. For instance, a bill for £100 with a 5% cash discount is recorded merely as a payment of £95. There is no column for recording cash discounts as part of the double entry as is encountered in cash accounts in commercial book-keeping text books. The only occasion attention is directed to cash discounts is in the cost accounts dealing with rechargeable work, and in exercises to review the efficiency and logic of an authority's policy in respect of early payment in return for cash discount. Some local authorities automatically deduct 2½% from any supplier's invoice, unless it is marked "strictly nett" or has discount terms stated on it. Suppliers who disagree with the deduction may claim it later, of course.

(c) *Income Accounts*

The various kinds of income received by a local authority can be classified into two main types for book-keeping purposes.

Firstly, there are those sources of income which are received in cash immediately the service is rendered or the goods handed over. They are often called "cash receipts" and because of the fleeting nature of the debt and the impossibility of the debt proving bad and having to be written off, no personal aspect of the transaction is recorded in the accounts. The entries are thus: –

Cash Dr.
    To Income (analysed to budget codes) Cr.
(The recording of the receipt of the cash)

Secondly, there is the class of income which requires the submission of an invoice because payment is not made immediately the service is rendered or the goods provided. There must be a record of the person owing the sum due together with details of the nature of the debt and its value. This personal aspect of the transaction is recorded on a multi-copy invoice – top copy to the debtor, second to the finance division for collection and recording, and the third held on file by the service department. The file of copy invoices kept by the finance division is the equivalent of the "sales book" used in commerce. The invoices are usually listed, totalled and analysed per budget code every month, and it is these totals which are recorded in the accounts. For ease of explanation, the following book entries relate to the recording of one invoice, its payment or allowance, and the issue of one credit note. In practice, such entries would relate to the figures for a whole month's transactions. The entries are thus: —

Sundry Debtors   Dr.
    To Income (analysed to budget codes)   Cr.

(The recording of the creation of the debt which is due to the authority) and if, and when, the debtor pays,

Cash   Dr.
    To Sundry Debtors   Cr.

The recording of the receipt of cash)

If the sum paid settles the account in full, then the copy invoice is marked "paid" and usually transferred to a "paid invoice" file. Where no payment or only part payment is received, and despite attempts to collect it the amount proves irrecoverable, then the entries needed to record the "write-off" or allowance — which normally requires committee approval — are as follows: —

Income   Dr.
    To Sundry Debtors   Cr.

(The recording of the amount allowed)
and the copy invoice is so marked and moved to the "paid invoice" file. Occasionally, errors are made, or goods returned, and credit notes have to be issued to correct the amount of the original invoice. The entries are identical to those for allowances and the copy invoice is marked and transferred in the same way: —

Income   Dr.
    To Sundry Debtors   Cr.

(The recording of the credit note issued)

Reference back to the example of the cash account will show the difference in treatment between cash receipts and credit income in the accounts. From a control point of view the rendering of an invoice is obviously preferable to treating the item as cash i.e. the first recording being the cash coming in, but in some cases, for instance, parental contributions for children in care, the non-payment rate can be so high as to make the preparation of invoices ludicrous. Thus details of the amounts due would be kept in memorandum form and the money the parents pay treated as cash receipts.

(d) *Personal Accounts*

Local authorities have lasting commercial or financial relations with persons, firms, other public authorities, central government departments, etc. and this requires the opening of individual personal accounts outside the system of total debtors' and creditors' accounts, as it is necessary to keep a separate record of the dealings with the person, firm, etc. Examples are accounts for government departments in respect of grants payable to the authority, or joint operations with other authorities in, say, running a community home for children and dividing the costs on some agreed basis. Such an account would appear as follows: —

Extract from the accounts of a local authority running a community home.

Dr.   Cr.

X District Council (Share of the Costs of Community Home) Account

19-3		£	19-3		£
April 1	Balance b/f	940	September	Cash	37,400
19-4					
March 31	General Rate Fund – Social Services – Community Home – Costs Recharged	40,210	19-4 March 31	Balance c/f	3,750
		41,150			41,150
19-4					
April 1	Balance b/f	3,750			

General Rate Fund – Social Services – Community Home – Revenue Account

19-4
March 31 X District Council
Share of Costs   40,210

The X District Council had underpaid its share of the costs of the community home for 19-2/3 by £940. In September 19-3, it paid £37,400 as the balance due from the previous year plus the estimate of its share for the current year. At the year end, the costs of the home were ascertained and the share of costs chargeable to X District were £40,210. The amount of £3,750 is thus still due and is included on the balance sheet as at 31 March 19-4 as a debtor.

Although it is possible to render an invoice via the sundry debtors' system, the amount is usually demanded by letter accompanied by a proforma invoice. The book entries are made by journal: –

	Dr. £	Cr. £
X District Council (Share of Costs of Community Home) Dr.	40,210	
To Social Services – Community Home Cr.		40,210
(Recording of costs of community home due from X District Council for 19-3/4)		

As has been mentioned, ordinary debtors are consolidated into a total account, entitled "sundry debtors" which contains entries comprising monthly totals only. Thus to find out the position relating to an individual debtor, one must turn to the invoice file. The invoices are usually filed in departmental sections in number order, and debts due from the same person are not brought together as part of the system, though if they are observed, joint notices, etc. may be sent.

The sundry debtors' account takes the following form: —

Dr.	Cr.
Balance brought forward (total debtors, 1st April) Income account — total of invoices issued for each of the twelve months — (April to March)	Cash — total receipts for each of the twelve months — (April to March) Allowances — total receipts for each of the twelve months — (April to March) Balance carried forward (total debtors, 31st March)

Balance brought forward (1st April)

(e) *Suspense or Holding Accounts*

Local authority accounting makes great use of suspense or holding accounts by means of which large amounts of expenditure by one department or service are accumulated and then allocated over all or various services on some equitable basis. Income can be similarly treated but less often. There is some similarity between these accounts and the total accounts previously mentioned, as their use assists sectional balancing. In effect, trial balances are extracted progressively, before the allocations are made, and afterwards.

Examples of holding accounts are those containing "pooled expenditure" of administrative departments which is allocated as central establishment charges to the various local authority departments and services. Thus the costs of the chief executive's department, the finance division, the architect and engineer's department and the town hall and offices are recovered from the executive departments pro rata to the value of the services they render.

The bases of allocation of costs vary with the nature of those costs. For instance, taking the Finance Division, the following bases could be used: —

Section	Basis of the Recharge to User Departments
Accountancy	on the basis of staff time
Audit	on expenditure (excluding loan charges) and income (excluding grants)
Wages and Personnel	on staff numbers
Computer	on the basis of computer time

The services of the Division of Administration could be recharged to departments on staff time and numbers of resolutions passed by committees. The administrative offices could be charged for on the basis of floor area, suitably weighted for the purposes for which the area is used, i.e. office work, storage, etc. The technical staff — architects, engineers, etc. may be charged for on a time basis to capital schemes and revenue work.

(f) *Revenue Accounts*

Comments have already been made about the keeping of expenditure and income accounts which are, in effect, the basic elements in the revenue (and also capital) account.

The running costs and the ordinary income of a service or department are required to be included in a revenue account which is intended to show the financial result of the operations for the period covered by the account as a surplus or a deficit. The revenue account is thus the non-trading alternative to the profit and loss account (including the manufacturing, trading, and appropriation accounts where applicable), and the surplus/deficit replaces the profit/loss of commerce.

The items debited to the revenue account are usually "subjective" in nature – salaries and wages, repairs and maintenance, rent, postages and telephone, interest and debt repayment, etc. Sometimes, the expenditure is analysed "objectively" e.g. the costs of a civic concert, and there are also objective headings, such as "Acme Park", under which its subjectively analysed expenditure – salaries and wages, trees and shrubs, etc. – is itemised.

The items credited to the revenue account depend for their nature upon the type of service involved, but examples of typical entries are: – government grants, sales of materials, fees and charges, etc.

Separate revenue accounts are kept for individual services because (a) the law requires a fund to keep separate accounts, or (b) it is convenient for detailed control – the general rate fund revenue account may be divided into sections e.g. education, environmental health, etc. and total expenditure and income figures are transferred into a final summary which shows the balance carried forward.

(g) *Capital Accounts*

As is the case with the revenue accounts, the capital accounts are derived from the analysed expenditure and income headings, but in this instance, it is the items of a capital nature which are segregated.

The capital accounts thus include those transactions which arise in relation to the creation and acquisition of assets which will be useful or otherwise of benefit to the local authority and its inhabitants for an appreciable number of years. They also include income (i.e. capital receipts) arising from the disposal of such assets, loans advances, etc.

There is a parallel with the practice in commerce of operating accounts for fixed assets (which are defined as those assets used in running the business). The differences between local authority and commercial procedures mainly arise, however, in the way the payments are financed.

The capital accounts thus contain such items as land and buildings (schools), machinery (refuse incineration plant), vehicles (fire engines), roads and streets, the landscaping of parks, etc. Assets which have a saleable value are called "capital outlay", whereas those which are unsuitable for sale or which nobody would seriously consider buying, are called "other long-term outlay". (There is also a third class of capital expenditure known as "deferred charges" which might be described as money paid for future benefit without creating any actual asset or as a device for making the balance sheet balance by creating a debit item equal to an outstanding loan where no corresponding asset exists).

Where a local authority has spent £500,000 on a new central garage, and £64,000 on roads, the entries are as follows: –

General Rate Fund Ledger

Cash Account

		£
	Sundry creditors	564,000

Sundry Creditors' Account

	£		
Cash	564,000	Expenditure per budget vote –	
		Capital outlay	500,000
		Other long-term outlay	64,000

Capital Outlay Account

	£
Sundry creditors	500,000

Other Long-term Outlay Account (Highways)

	£
Sundry creditors	64,000

Turning to the question of financing this expenditure, or, as it is sometimes called, discharging it, there are several alternative methods available.

(i) Items of relatively small value (e.g. typewriters) may be paid for out of revenue, and thus treated as though they are running expenses. They are debited to the revenue account for the year in which they are bought and there is no record in the capital accounts. An attempt is made to safeguard such items by placing them in an inventory register which is checked periodically.

(ii) Larger schemes also can be financed from revenue according to the resources of the authority. The expenditure is debited to the capital account of the fund involved, and a "revenue contribution to capital outlay" is debited to the fund's revenue account and credited to a revenue contributions to capital outlay account. In the case of a capital scheme which costs £4,650 and is met out of revenue, the entries are as follows: –

Capital Outlay Account

	£
Sundry creditors	4,650

Cash Account

		£
	Sundry creditors	4,650

Sundry Creditors' Account

Cash	4,650	Expenditure per budget code – Capital outlay	4,650

Revenue Account

Revenue contribution to capital outlay	4,650		

Revenue Contributions to Capital Outlay Account

		Revenue	4,650

The journal entry format applicable is as follows: –

		Dr. £	Cr. £
Revenue Account	Dr.	4,650	
To Revenue Contributions to Capital Outlay	Cr.		4,650

(The recording of the financing of the scheme from revenue)

(iii) The main way of financing capital expenditure on local government services is by loans which the authority must have power to borrow. It is the practice for borrowed monies to be paid firstly into a loans fund and then advanced out of the loans fund to the services. These advances to the services must be repaid to the loans fund over a period loosely related to the life of the asset involved. The repayments are made annually, with interest on the balance of the advances, and these debt or loan charges plus loans fund expenses allocated are debited to the service revenue accounts.

Taking the example of a school costing £300,000 to build, for which a loan sanction is available for the full cost and the repayment period is fixed at 40 years, the entries may be as follows: –

The Year of the Completion of the School (19-2/3)
Ledger Entries (General Rate Fund)

Dr.	Cash Account £		Cr. £
Loans Fund	300,000	Sundry Creditors	300,000

Sundry Creditors' Account

	£		£
Cash	300,000	Capital Outlay	300,000

Capital Outlay Account

	£		
Sundry Creditors	300,000		

Loans Fund Account

			£
		Cash	300,000

Items appearing in the General Rate Fund Balance Sheet as at 31st March 19-3

	£
Capital Outlay – Education	300,000
less Loans Fund Advances	300,000

The Following Year (19-3/4)

		Dr. £	Cr. £
Journal Entries (General Rate Fund)			
Revenue Account – Repayment	Dr.	7,500	
– Interest	Dr.	30,000	
– Loans Fund Expenses	Dr.	300	
To Sundry Creditors			37,800

(the recording of the repayment due – 1/40th of £300,000, interest @ 10% p.a., expenses @ 0.1% p.a.)

Sundry Creditors	Dr.	37,800	
To Cash			37,800

(the cash transfer to the Loans Fund)

Loans Fund	Dr.	7,500	
To Loans Repaid			7,500

(the recording of the change in the capital provisions)

Ledger Accounts. (General Rate Fund)

Dr.   *Loans Fund Account*

		£			£
Loans Repaid		7,500	Balance	b/f	300,000
Balance	c/f	292,500			
		300,000			300,000
			Balance	b/f	292,500

Loans Repaid Account

Loans Fund	7,500

(Cash is £37,800 less, and the revenue account has a debit of £37,800).

Items appearing in the General Rate Fund Balance Sheet as at 31st March 19-4

	£	£
Capital Outlay – Education		300,000
less Loans Fund Advances	292,500	
Loans Repaid	7,500	300,000

(iv) Other methods of financing capital expenditure include the use (or, as it is called, the application) of reserve fund or capital fund monies, government grants, gifts from individuals, and capital receipts (i.e. money received from the sale of fixed assets). The entries in the accounts are essentially the same for all these sources. The fund, grant, capital receipt account is debited with the amount involved, and the credit entry goes to a fund, grant, capital receipt applied account. Taking the example of a number of vehicles costing £45,000 which are to be financed out of reserve fund to the amount of £27,000, and out of a capital receipt for the rest, the entries may be as follows: –

Journal Entries

		Dr. £	Cr. £
Capital Outlay – Vehicles	Dr.	45,000	
To Sundry Creditors	Cr.		45,000
Sundry Creditors	Dr.	45,000	
To Cash	Cr.		45,000

(the recording of the incurring of the liability and paying for it)

Reserve Fund	Dr.	27,000	
To Reserve Fund Applied	Cr.		27,000
Capital Receipt	Dr.	18,000	
To Capital Receipt Applied	Cr.		18,000

(the recording of the contributions to the financing of the vehicles)

Items appearing in the Balance Sheet

	£	£
Capital Outlay – Vehicles		45,000
less Reserve Fund Applied	27,000	
Capital Receipt Applied	18,000	45,000

Local authorities do not normally depreciate their fixed assets – they are kept at their original (i.e. historical) cost and the accumulated repayments of loans fund advances which are based on the estimated life of the assets, are regarded as the equivalent of depreciation. As regards the replacement of assets, a local authority can build up its capital and renewal and repairs funds and, of course, borrow anew to meet inflated costs. There is, however, a class of fixed assets, known as "deferred charges" which have already been mentioned. These are written down in value each year by the repayment of the loan advances covering them, until they disappear from the balance sheet. Such assets include stock issue expenses, Local Act promotion expenses, and "continuing liabilities" i.e. the outstanding debt on assets which have been transferred by law to another public or local authority must be balanced in the accounts by an, in effect, fictitious asset, or, perhaps, a debt due from the transferee authority.

Taking as an example that the promotion expenses of a Local Act amount to £20,000, and that there is a loan of £20,000 sanctioned for a period of 10 years to meet them, the book entries may be as follows: –

Journal Entries

		Dr. £	Cr. £
Deferred Charge – Local Act Promotion Expenses	Dr.	20,000	
To Sundry Creditors	Cr.		20,000
Sundry Creditors	Dr.	20,000	
To Cash	Cr.		20,000

(the recording of the incurring of the liability)

Cash	Dr.	20,000	
To Loans Fund	Cr.		20,000

(the making of the advance from the Loans Fund)

Items appearing in the Balance Sheet.

	£
Deferred Charge	20,000
less Loans Fund Advances	20,000

The Following Year
Journal Entries

Revenue Account – Repayment	Dr.	1,000	
– Interest	Dr.	2,000	
– Loans Fund Expenses	Dr.	20	
To Sundry Creditors			3,020

(the recording of the repayment due – 1/20th of £20,000, interest @ 10%, expenses @ 0.1% p.a.)

Sundry Creditors	Dr.	3,020	
To Cash			3,020

(the cash transfer to the Loans Fund)

Loans Fund	Dr.	1,000	
To Deferred Charge	Cr.		1,000

(the recording of the writing down of the deferred charge and the advance)

Items appearing in the Balance Sheet

	£
Deferred Charge	19,000
less Loans Fund Advances	19,000

The deferred charge will be progressively written down until it completely vanishes from the balance sheet in nineteen years' time.

Another important use of deferred charges is on those occasions when an asset is sold before the outstanding debt on it has been paid off, and the amount received from the sale is less than the debt still due. To keep the books in balance, a non-existent asset has to be debited in order to offset the loan advance outstanding on the balance sheet.

For example, a plot of land which cost £5,000 to acquire and which was financed by a loan of £5,000, of which £3,000 is still outstanding, is sold for £2,500. The book entries may be as follows: –

Journal Entries

		£	£
Debtors	Dr.	2,500	
To Capital Receipt	Cr.		2,500
Cash	Dr.	2,500	
To Debtor	Cr.		2,500

(the recording of the sale and the receipt of the cash)

		£	£
Loans Repaid	Dr.	2,000	
Capital Receipt	Dr.	2,500	
Deferred Charge	Dr.	500	
To Capital Outlay			5,000

(the writing out of the books of the land sold, the debt repaid and the capital receipt, and the creation of a deferred charge in respect of the £500 loan still outstanding)

		£	£
Loans Fund	Dr.	2,500	
To Sundry Creditors	Cr.		2,500
Sundry Creditors	Dr.	2,500	
To Cash	Cr.		2,500

(the payment of the capital receipt monies over to the Loans Fund to repay £2,500 of debt)

The Form of the Published Accounts

Whereas the form of the accounts of some of the public authorities are prescribed in detail by statute or regulations, those of local authorities are in a form left to the discretion of the council subject to the observance of general requirements and the inclusion of specific items. Within a local authority's own circumstances, there is a measure of standardisation of format and phraseology based on recommendations made by the Chartered Institute of Public Finance and Accountancy.

The Account and Audit Regulations 1974 require a local authority to prepare an abstract of accounts as soon as possible after the accounts have been audited. The accounts contained in the abstract are affected by the statutory duties allotted to the class of the authority, and also vary according to the discretionary functions that it resolves to carry out. The opening item is a report in which the accounts are commented upon and accounting policies are stated. Then comes the auditor's report on the accounts followed by the revenue account, balance sheet and capital statements for the General Rate Fund (or County Fund); Rating (if a district or borough); Housing Revenue Account (if a district or borough); Loans Fund; trading undertakings (e.g. markets, crematoria, etc.); Capital, Renewal and Repairs, and Insurance Funds; trust funds (including Superannuation, if a county); and, finally, a consolidated balance sheet. Corresponding amounts for the previous financial year are a legal requirement.

The General Rate Fund or County Fund is operated by districts or counties, respectively, under the Local Government Act 1972 which requires them to pay all receipts into it and to make all payments out of it, except where specific activities require a separate fund under this Act or another. This fund therefore includes the expenditure and income arising from the operations of the majority of the council's committees and departments in its revenue account, whilst the assets and liabilities involved appear in the balance sheet. It is customary for the expenditure and income of each committee to be detailed separately and totalled, and for these totals to be carried to a summary revenue account which also includes items of a general nature, such as the Rate Support Grant ("block" element), the income from the General Rate, and contributions to capital funds, before arriving at the surplus or deficiency for the year. This is carried to an appropriattion account (called a surplus or deficiency account), the balance of which appears on the balance sheet. The items on the balance sheet include fixed and current assets, deferred charges, and other debit balances, such as debtors and cash, on the right hand side, whilst, on the left hand side, they are financed by long-term loans, loans repaid, creditors, the revenue account cumulative surplus and other credit balances.

The Rating Accounts consist of the rate income account, the rate income appropriation account and the balance sheet. The rate income account is charged with some minor items of expenditure on the collection of the rate. It is credited with the gross amount of money which is due from the ratepayers (called the gross rate income) from which are deducted various items which include allowances to owners, allowances for empty (void) properties, relief to charities, reductions on appeal, and irrecoverable items. Other credits are the domestic element of the Rate Support Grant and contributions in lieu of rates from Crown properties. The balance on this account (called the net rate income) is transferred to the appropriation account where it is divided between the general rate fund and the precepting authorities in accordance with their respective rate poundages. The appropriation account is usually cleared, i.e. no balance is carried forward. The balance sheet is fairly simple, as it contains as assets, sundry debtors (usually the arrears of rate), and cash, whilst the liabilities side contains sundry creditors (such as rates received in advance and outstanding expenses).

The Housing Revenue Account consists of the supervision and management account which bears the costs of administration of the housing properties and of the common services supplied to their occupiers, such as staircase lighting and the maintenance of grass verges (the first class of costs is called general expenses, whilst the second is termed special − though the division is somewhat arbitrary), and the revenue account proper which is debited with the repair and maintenance of dwellings, etc., debt charges on their capital financing, the balance from the supervision and management account, and establishment expenses, and credited with any surplus brought forward from the previous year plus rents, government subsidies, and rate fund contributions. The balance carried forward on the revenue account (if any, in which case it must be a credit sum of reasonable size) appears on the balance sheet. The assets on the Housing Revenue Balance Sheet include the costs of building houses and flats, sundry debtors (for rent due), cash at the bank and in hand, and these are balanced by outstanding loans, sundry creditors for goods and services supplied, the revenue account balance and capital provisions, such as repaid debt.

The Loans Fund accounts consist of the revenue transactions account, the capital transactions account, the balance sheet and supporting statements. The revenue transactions account is charged with the interest paid on loans and the management expenses incurred in dealing with the authority's borrowing needs, and the account is cleared by being charged to the departments. The capital transactions account shows the details of the external loans raised and repaid, and the advances made to and the repayments made by the departments. It is balanced by adjusting the cash figure (which is usually an overdraft). The balance sheet shows the assets as the advances owed by the departments, debtors (for interest due on surplus funds lent out, if any), and the liabilities as the borrowings from outside (e.g. from the P.W.L.B. and bondholders), creditors (for items such as interest and services supplied) and, usually, cash overdrawn. Statements may be included giving details of external loans – their type, interest rates, amounts and repayment dates – and of the total outstanding advances – amounts advanced, amounts repaid and periods of repayment.

The accounts of trading undertakings vary in layout according to the nature of the service provided and the existence of any legal requirements applicable to the service and its published accounts. There is usually a revenue account, a balance sheet, and, if authorised, a reserve fund account. A net revenue or appropriation account may sometimes be included. The revenue account bears the operating costs and financing charge re loan debt, and is credited with the trading income. The balance on this account may be taken to the appropriation account from which contributions may be taken to the undertaking's reserve fund or to the general rate or county fund. The reserve fund is built up by contributions, as stated, and, possibly, investment income, and it is debited with such charges as major improvements or purchases of fixed assets. The balance sheet contains fixed assets such as buildings, equipment, vehicles and other operating plant, and current assets such as buildings, equipment, vehicles and other operating plant, and current assets such as stock in hand, investments, debtors, and cash. The liabilities on the balance sheet would include outstanding loans, loans repaid, creditors and amounts received in advance, and the reserve fund balance. The accounts may be traditional in form i.e. double columnar, or narrative, i.e. the liabilities deducted from the assets to show the total finance needed and its sources.

The published accounts of Capital, Renewal and Repairs, and Insurance Funds are similar to one another. There is a fund account which is credited with the balance brought forward from the previous year, general rate fund contributions, and other income (for the first two funds − repayments of advances, for the third type of fund − premiums paid by departments). The debit entries are expenditure on the fund purposes (Capital Fund − advances for buying new capital assets or to expedite debt repayment, Renewal and Repairs Fund − advances for the purposes stated, and Insurance Fund − meeting claims for losses arising from risks insured with the fund). Income from investment of surplus funds may arise in each case. The funds appear on the General Rate Fund balance sheet, the fund balance in each case appearing among the reserves, and the assets − cash and investments − are indicated on the other side.

The accounts of Trust Funds, of which the Superannuation Fund is the most important example, each possess a revenue account and a balance sheet. This segregation is usually required by the terms of the deed or legacy creating the fund or by Act of Parliament. The revenue account is debited with the expenditure upon the purposes of the particular fund, and the income is often investment income, though in the case of superannuation, there are contributions from employers and employees, and transfer values. The balance sheet contains the assets of the fund − property, investments, debtors, cash, etc. − and these are balanced by the creditors and the fund balance carried forward.

The local authority is required to prepare a consolidated balance sheet which the treasurer must sign and submit to the auditor together with the accounts it relates to. The consolidated balance sheet contains all the assets, liabilities and reserves of the individual fund balance sheets, with the exclusion of internal liabilities i.e. the sums which one fund owes to another − debtors, creditors, loans fund advances, etc.. The superannuation fund and other trust funds are also excluded as these monies are held on trust by the local authority. The intention in preparing such a balance sheet is to show the financial state of the authority as a whole.

Costing Methods

The aim of a costing system is to charge as accurately as possible to each chosen unit, the costs incurred in producing it. This calls for a decision as to a suitable unit of cost and for a system of cost accounts designed to give more detailed information than that found in the financial accounts, so that the expenditure on any particular unit of service or output can be easily identified. For the purpose of analysis and allocation, costs are classified as follows: −

(a) Direct costs
   (i) Direct wages are identifiable with a specific unit of cost, usually being paid to the employee who actually makes the product or renders the service, e.g. the tradesman's wages.
   (ii) Direct materials are either used up in the product or on the service in such a way as to be related with each unit, e.g. the glass used to repair a window, the rat poison used at one premise by a rodent control officer.

(iii) Direct expenses are similarly spent on a particular unit of cost, e.g. the hire of special machinery for a specific contract, annual road tax licence on a vehicle.

The total direct costs are called the prime cost.

(b) Indirect costs (also called "overheads")

These comprise wages, salaries, materials costs and expenses which cannot be allocated to an identifiable unit of cost. They are usually collected under the following headings.

(i) Production, factory or works costs, e.g. foreman's wages, lubricating oil for machinery, cost of lighting shopfloor.

(ii) Administrative costs, e.g. salaries of office staff, stationery and office materials, external audit fees.

(iii) Selling and distribution costs, e.g. salaries and commission of salesmen, packing materials, charges for press advertising.

The prime cost plus the works overheads is called the works cost. The works cost plus the administrative overheads is called the cost of production. The cost of production plus the selling and distributive overheads is called the total cost.

Occasional variations from the above classifications are found in practice. It may be more convenient to treat an item of small value, e.g. a washer, which is theoretically a direct cost in a manufactured article, as an element of indirect cost and include it in production overheads.

The charging of the direct costs to output presents little difficulty but, in the case of indirect costs, there is a variety of approaches available. These overheads are usually allocated to the products, jobs, etc. as a percentage of wages, materials, prime cost or cost of production (as appropriate) or on a time basis, e.g. an amount per hour of labour or machine usage. These percentages and time rates are called oncosts. Their calculation is carried out in advance of the production (by using a budget) and if costs and production levels differ from those expected, then there is a variation between the costs incurred and those charged to the output. The reason for this is that costs are broadly divisible into fixed and variable. Fixed costs are incurred whether anything is produced or not. Variable costs are related to the level of output, the relationship usually being assumed to be in direct proportion. Direct costs, by their very nature, are mostly variable, though examples of a fixed nature may be found, e.g. the fee charged by a consultant in preparing plans for a construction scheme – which is payable even if the scheme is not carried out. Indirect costs contain many examples of both types, fixed – rent of the factory, variable – electrical power for the machinery, and even some of mixed nature – telephone charges where the rental is fixed and the cost of calls is variable. Thus while the variable costs should be automatically recovered by a suitable oncost (given that there have been no unexpected increases in the level of costs), the calculation of the oncost for the fixed expenses depends on the estimated volume of output and if the actual volume varies from this, wide discrepancies can arise in the period. In other words, the fixed costs could be significantly under- or over-recovered and the management must decide whether to raise or lower the oncost rates in the following period or debit or credit the discrepancy to the profit and loss account for that period.

Much of what is said above refers mainly to commercial-type undertakings, such as gas and electricity supply, as there are many public sector organisations which do not incur sales costs, and indeed, their costing systems are based chiefly on a detailed analysis of the figures which appear in the financial accounts.

The main costing methods used in the public sector may be classified as follows: –

1. Job costing is operated when an item is manufactured, or a specific piece of work is done, and the cost of the item or work, i.e. the job is calculated separately. An example would be the carrying out of repairs to a domestic water supply, the cost of which is charged on the owner or occupier.
2. Batch costing is a form of job costing where a number of identical items or jobs are costed together and the total charge is averaged among them. An example would be the making of pavement-crossings for cars at a number of houses on a street in one operation.
3. Contract costing is a larger version of job costing where the cost of a scheme is segregated. Such a scheme would require a fairly long period for completion and its costs usually would usually be in five or more figures. The erection of a town hall by a direct works department (or D.L.O.) is an example.
4. Output costing is similar to batch costing but is applicable where one standard product is made. The total costs of the whole undertaking are divided by the units produced, giving an average cost per unit for a period. Produce from a hospital or sewage works farm might be dealt with in this way, or it could apply to refuse collection or disposal (the cost per ton of refuse).
5. Operation or operating costing is applicable when a single type of service is supplied, and, as with output costing, the total cost for the period is divided by a suitable unit of service. Examples are passenger transport (cost per passenger-mile) and street cleansing (cost per mile of road).
6. Process costing is a form of output costing where the production involves a series of processes and the output of one process is the input of the next. An example is the treatment of sewage where charges are made for treating industrial effluent.

Methods 4 and 5 are sometimes called unit costing, and use is also made in public authorites of marginal and standard costing techniques.

Marginal costing (also called direct costing) is used to avoid the problem of allocating fixed overhead expenses, i.e. those costs which are incurred whether there is any production or not, by leaving them outside the costs charged against the output. Thus, any surplus of income over the costs charged is regarded as firstly as a contribution to fixed expenses, and any remainder is profit. Taking the case of a civic restaurant undertaking which operates several cafes from a central office, the costs of the central office would not be allocated over the cafes (one basis could be according to turnover), but charged against the whole enterprise. In this way, the problem of an equitable allocation of the central office costs is avoided, and the degree of profitability of each cafe is indicated by the amount of its contribution.

Period 1	Cafe A £	Cafe B £	Cafe C £	Total £
Sales	10,000	15,000	12,000	37,000
Costs (wages, provisions, etc).	8,000	11,500	9,500	29,000
Surplus	2,000	3,500	2,500	8,000
Costs of the central office				7,500
Profit for the period				500

Standard costing means that detailed estimates are prepared of the costs which would be incurred in giving a normal level of output or service in an efficient manner. The actual costs and performance figures are compared with the standards, and enquiries made into the possible causes of any differences. Corrective action or improvements in operation may then be possible.

Standard costing thus aims at providing the means of comparing pre-determined or budgeted costs for specific tasks or units of output with the costs which have actually been incurred. The differences (known as "variances") revealed by the comparison can thus be identified, quantified and investigated. In addition, under the budgetary system which provides the basis for the standard costs, responsibility for unfavourable variances can be fixed upon the officers accountable whilst, at the same time, credit for favourable variations can be given.

This type of costing can best be used where the output of the service or process can be measured in an objective manner. Public authorities may thus apply it to such matters as the erection of buildings, the laying of underground services, and the construction of roads. There are difficulties in using it for costing services of a personal nature, such as home visiting, education, and residential accommodation, where subjective thinking comes into the assessment of results, particularly quality of service.

Standard costing as used by local authorities does not possess the highly developed form which one meets in manufacturing companies in the private sector where standards are often set at an ideal level of complete efficiency. The standards set in local government applications are usually capable of being realised with reasonable diligence because the budgets underlying them are attempts to forecast the actual outturn for the period involved and the officers and foremen supervising the system are helped psychologically by the knowledge that the targets can be reached and, perhaps, surpassed. In addition, standards are normally restricted to direct costs — direct wages, materials and expenses — while overhead expenses are dealt with by more traditional costing methods.

Worked examples of the main types of costing encountered in local government and its allied sectors are given in Appendix II to which the reader is referred.

9. *Management Services*

These are a range of functions carried out by a section of the staff who have the responsibility of making management more effective. They apply such techniques as organisation and methods, work study, operational research, network analysis, etc. The chief management services officer may be of chief officer status or he may report to the chief executive or the finance director. There are resemblances between the work of the management services section and the internal audit staff. For this reason, the suggestion has been made for their amalgamation, but management services is involved in planning non-financial procedures which may fall outside the ambit of the internal audit, are advisory only in status, and do not carry out the continuous check on procedures they have recommended, which is expected from internal audit in regard to financial matters. There is, nevertheless, ample scope for co-operation between the two sections, and any criticism of systems by the internal audit might be discussed with the management service personnel involved before a report is made.

10. *Evaluation of Capital Projects*

The optimum use of resources is a major problem of public organisations and one particular aspect of this is the need to evaluate projects in accordance with a common standard of financial return or benefit. Proposed schemes may be compared with one another (especially when they are alternative approaches to the same problem) and measured against an acceptable minimum return on capital — perhaps the ruling cost of borrowing or the internal rate of return appropriate to the activities of the organisation or ruling in the particular industry.

The actual process of evaluation may be undertaken in several ways, such as: —

1. The pay-back period,
2. The return on investment,
3. The net present value,
4. The discounted cash flow.

(Methods 1 and 2 may be designated "non-discounting" techniques, as they ignore the proposition that present cash is worth more than future cash. Methods 3 and 4, on the other hand, are discounting techniques).

These procedures may be used in isolation, collectively, or in conjunction with other evaluation methods not listed here. In addition, variations exist in the manner in which the techniques may be applied, but the essential point is that, where comparisons are made, a technique must be used consistently on all the projects being considered.

The Pay-back Period

This is the period of time needed to recoup the original investment. The expenditure is divided by the average annual net receipts or earnings, or the receipts are progressively deducted from the outlay until it becomes zero.

Example

A machine is bought for £10,000 and its life is estimated to be 4 years. It is also calculated that it will earn: −

	£
In the first year	4,000
In the second year	5,000
In the third year	4,000
In the fourth year	3,000

(a) Dividing the expenditure by the average annual earnings: −

$$£10,000 \div \frac{£(4,000 + 5,000 + 4,000 + 3,000)}{4} = \frac{£10,000}{£4,000}$$
$$= 2½ \text{ years.}$$

(b) The expenditure less accumulated earnings: −

£10,000 − (first year) £4,000 = £6,000
£ 6,000 − (second year) £5,000 = £1,000
£ 1,000 − (third year) £1,000* = 0   i.e. 2¼ years.

*Earnings are assumed to accrue at a constant rate during the year, i.e. ¼ of £4,000 earned in the first quarter of the third year.

The Return on Investment

This can be calculated as the percentage which the average annual earnings or incomings bear to the original investment, but variations occur in the non-averaging of earnings, weighting of income, differing definitions of investment and expenditure, etc. The return on average investment is also encountered − the average being the mean of the unrecouped investment balances at each year end, though this is not always certain to be the case.

It must be repeated that constancy of method is vital if comparisons are to be to any degree valid.

Example

£1,000 is invested for three years and earns £300 in the first year, £200 in the second year and £100 in the third.

Thus annual average earnings as a percentage of investment is: —

$\dfrac{£300 + 200 + 100}{3}$ as a % of £1,000

$= \dfrac{£200}{£1,000} \times 100\% = 20\%.$

As the Accounting Rate of Return occurs in non-discount and discounting mode, it is given at the end of the chapter in both forms.

The Net Present Value

This method uses a selected rate of interest (the chosen minimum return, for instance) to discount the scheme's cash flow items (receipts and payments) into their respective present values. The net sum of these present values is compared with the original outlay and the excess or deficit arrived at.

The formula for discounting is: —

$$PV = A \times \left[\dfrac{100\%}{(100+r)\%} \right]^n$$

PV = the present value.
A = the amount of the receipt (+) or payment (−).
r = the selected rate of interest as a %.
n = the number of years in the future.

Example

A van is purchased by local authority for £8,000. Payment is to be £5,000 immediately and £3,000 in one year's time. Net earnings are expected to be £2,000 per annum for 4 years, at which time it is intended to sell the van for £2,000. For simplification purposes, the earnings are assumed to accrue at the year end. The discount rate is 10%.

	Payments £	Receipts £	Net Amount £	Discounting Factor		Present Value £
Date of Purchase	5,000		−5,000	1.000		−5,000
End of Year 1	3,000	2,000	−1,000	$\left[\dfrac{100}{110}\right]$	.909	−909
End of Year 2		2,000	+2,000	$\left[\dfrac{100}{110}\right]^2$	.826	+1,652
End of Year 3		2,000	+2,000	$\left[\dfrac{100}{110}\right]^3$	.751	+1,502
End of Year 4		4,000*	+4,000	$\left[\dfrac{100}{110}\right]^4$	.683	+2,732
(*£2,000 earnings, £2,000 sale proceeds).				Deficit		− 23

On the basis of these figures, the projected investment appears to break more or less even. It cannot be said to be attractive, but comparison with other methods of purchase, estimation of life, etc. should be made. In addition, evaluation of alternative uses of the capital may be needed.

The Discounted Cash Flow

This technique (also called the yield method) is intended to arrive at the rate of return at which a project's discounted incomings and outgoings will balance. The procedure is by trial and error – various levels of interest are tried and interpolation can be carried out between the appropriate results flanking the optimum balancing position, although it is normal practice just to state the result approximately.

Example

It is suggested that a short-term tipping site cost £50,000 be acquired. It is estimated that, over the next three years, it will bring in a net cash income of £30,000 in the first year, £25,000 in the second and £20,000 in the third when the site will be fully tipped. The suggestion is accepted on condition that the rate of return on the scheme is at least 22½%.

	Payment £	Additional Cash Income £	Discounted at 20% £	25% £	30% £
Acquisition of Site	−50,000		−50,000	−50,000	−50,000
End of Year 1		+30,000	+25,000	+24,000	+23,070
End of Year 2		+25,000	+17,350	+16,000	+14,800
End of Year 3		+20,000	+11,580	+10,240	+9,100
			+3,930	+240	−3,030

(The position has been simplified by making the total payment at the start and accruing the cash income at the year ends).

The rate of return in just over 25% and the condition is thus fulfilled.

The Accounting Rate of Return

The simplest form of this method uses the non-discounted yield figures. This is $\frac{\text{Average Yield} - \text{Depreciation}}{\text{Investment}}$; Depreciation is $\frac{\text{Investment}}{\text{Life of Asset}}$

The formula can be symbolised in various forms.

Example

£1,000 is invested in a revenue-earning asset which has a five year life and no scrap value at the end. The earnings average £400 a year.

$$\text{Accounting Rate of Return} = \frac{£400 - (£1,000 \div 5)}{£1,000} = 20\%$$

A more sophisticated form uses the average discounted net yield. Thus: —

Example

£3,000 expended on an advertising campaign for a crematorium service is estimated to bring in £2,000 p.a. during the following three years. The incoming cash is assumed to be received at the year-end. The discounting rate is taken as 5%.

	Payments £	Receipts £	Net Cash Flow £	Discounting Factor £	Net Present Value £
Start of Year 1	3,000		−3,000	1.000	−3,000
End of Year 1		2,000	+2,000	.952	+1,904
End of Year 2		2,000	+2,000	.907	+1,814
End of Year 3		2,000	+2,000	.864	+1,728
					+£2,446

Note that the depreciation is already recouped in the calculations made above.

$$\text{Discounted Accounting Rate of Return} = \frac{\text{Discounted Net Yield}}{\text{Investment} \times \text{Life of Asset}}$$

$$= \frac{£2,446}{£3,000 \times 3}$$

$$= 27.2\%$$

$$\left(\text{The formula can, of course, be given as } \frac{\text{Average Discounted Net Yield}}{\text{Investment}}\right)$$

Summary of Present Values at Various Discount Rates.

Year	5%	10%	20%	25%	30%
1	.952	.909	.833	.800	.769
2	.907	.826	.694	.640	.592
3	.864	.751	.579	.512	.455
4	.823	.683	.482	.410	.350
5	.784	.621	.402	.328	.269

Questions
6.1 Outline the matters which are normally referred to the Finance Committee of a local authority.
6.2 What are the duties usually allocated to the Director of Finance?
6.3 Why does a local authority prepare a revenue budget?
6.4 What are the main classes of items dealt with in Financial Regulations?
6.5 Describe briefly the main methods of costing encountered in local government.
6.6 Outline the various types of ledger accounts used in the accounting systems of public authorities.

6.7 Draw up a system of control for the safekeeping of the valuables and other personal property of residents in a home for the elderly.

6.8 Give a brief description of the way in which the revenue budget of a local authority is prepared each year.

6.9 Discuss the benefits and drawbacks to a local authority of setting up a central purchasing department.

6.10 Discuss the use of inventories in a large public or local authority.

6.11 Record the following transactions in the form of journal entries: –
   (a) Library books are delivered to a public library, the invoice for them amounting to £1,200 is received and paid,
   (b) The cost of running the central greenhouse complex in a Parks Department amounts to £43,000 and this sum is rechargeable as follows: –

Queen's Park	40%
Prince's Park	60%

6.12 The following transactions occurred in connection with the operation of a transport undertaking. You are required to show each in the form of a journal entry.

   Obsolete buses were originally bought for £250,000 and financed out of loan advances which have all been repaid. The sale of these buses realised £10,000 and the proceeds were credited to the Reserve Fund. New buses were then purchased for £400,000 and were financed out of the Reserve Fund.

6.13 Record the following transactions arising in a market undertaking and show the ledger entries in the form of journal entries and post them to the appropriate ledger accounts: –

   Capital outlay on market stall fittings which originally amounted to £7,500 were scrapped. They were bought from revenue and were of no value when they were disposed of.

   A sum of £1,400 owing in respect of stallholders' rent was written off as irrecoverable.

   Rates amounting to £2,600 due on the market hall had not been paid and had not been provided for in the accounts.

6.14 Draw up the following data in the form of a marginal cost statement.

Direct Charges –		£
Wages,	Activity A	4,600
	Activity B	2,100
	Activity C	3,400
Materials,	Activity A	3,000
	Activity B	4,000
	Activity C	3,500
Expenses,	Activity A	1,400
	Activity B	900
	Activity C	1,100
Sales,	Activity A	12,500
	Activity B	10,000
	Activity C	11,500

Variable expenses – 20% of Direct Cost.
Fixed expenses for the period   4,000

6.15 The following figures refer to a contract which was started by a Direct Labour Organisation on the 1st October 19-3 and completed on the 31st March 19-4 on behalf of the Recreation and Amenities Committee of a District Council: –

	£
Material supplied to contract	100,000
Materials in hand, 31st March 19-4	4,000
Direct Labour	70,000
Direct Expenses	20,000

Prepare the contract account recharging the full cost of the contract to the committee, given that plant valued at £300,000 was used and was chargeable at a rate of 10% per annum of its value, and that central administrative charges of £11,000 were allocated to the contract.

6.16 A reprographic machine is operated in a College of Further Education. The following data is available regarding its operation: –

	£
Operator's Wages, National Insurance, Superannuation, etc.	2.50 per hour
Running Costs: –	
Paper and other Variable Costs	4.00 per 1,000 sheets
Fixed Costs	21.00 per week

The charge for the service is 2p per sheet of paper supplied. You are required to calculate the output at which costs and income break even.

6.17 Draw up an operating cost sheet for a local authority swimming pool showing the total and unit costs for each head of expenditure and income for the year ended 31st March 19-3: –

	£
Wages, etc.	53,000
Administration	3,000
Water, etc.	10,000
Electricity	8,000
Rates	5,000
Maintenance and Repairs of Buildings	15,000
Loan Charges – Interest	6,000
Repayment of Principal	11,000
Maintenance and Repairs of Plant	7,000
Charges for Admission	125,000

The number of admissions in the year was 250,000.

6.18 The management of a public authority are faced with two possible lines of action.
(a) The purchase of machine A for £5,000. This has a life of five years and should earn £2,000 p.a. and sell for £500 at the end of its life.
(b) The purchase of machine B for £2,000. This has a life of three years and should earn £1,000 p.a. and sell for £200 at the end of its life.
There is no difference in the quality of output.
Assuming the cost of capital to be 10%, and that the earnings accrue at the year ends, calculate the net present value and the accounting rate of return (both methods) and comment on the results in respect of both machines.

6.19 Kiadpenz Inc. Public Utilities Ltd decide to invest in a project costing £100,000 which will bring in the following cash sums at each year end, thus: —

	£
End of Year 1	30,000
End of Year 2	40,000
End of Year 3	50,000
End of Year 4	60,000

What is the rate of return on the project as calculated by the discounted cash flow method?

6.20 An internal telephone system is being offered to Felhiv B.C. on any one of three bases: —
   (a) Outright purchase for £3,500 paid immediately,
   (b) Hire for 5 years at £1,000 per annum payable in advance,
   (c) Purchase by paying £1,000 immediately, £1,000 after one year, and £3,000 after two years.

Assuming a discount rate of 20%, calculate which alternative would be cheapest and comment on what other information you consider you need for proper consideration of the problem.

6.21 The Brokenspring highways authority is under a duty under the Highways Act, 1959 (as amended by the Local Government Act, 1966), to resurface a length of roadway which is in a state of disrepair. The engineer places three choices before the members, viz: —
   (a) Annual repairs, renovation, patchings, etc. of parts of the road for the next five years at £2,000 per annum incurred at the end of each year.
   (b) Total resurfacing immediately at a cost of £8,000.
   (c) Resurfacing in two convenient sections — £4,000 immediately, and £5,000 in two years' time.

As treasurer and accountant, you are required to report on these alternatives, using the knowledge that the authority is paying 10% on monies borrowed and no alteration in this rate is envisaged over the relevant period.

6.22 A local authority borrow money on the understanding that they will repay the sum less a premature repayment fee if the investor dies. This premature repayment fee is based on the difference between the present values of the interest which would have been paid on the loan and the interest which becomes payable on its replacement by a loan at higher interest rate. — for the balance of the period.

Mr. Heredonto inherits a £1,000 bond under his uncle's will and applies for repayment. The bond has 3 years to run. Interest is payable at each year end at 5% per annum. The current borrowing rate for 3 year money is 10%.

Calculate the premature repayment fee.

Chapter 7

The External Audit of Local Authorities in England and Wales

The arrangements for the external audit of local authorities in England and Wales are embodied in the Local Government Act 1972 which is supported by the Accounts and Audit Regulations 1974 and an audit code of practice issued by the Department of the Environment. The Act lays down the general framework of the audit procedures whilst the regulations and the code go into greater detail as to the legal requirements and the auditor's responsibilities. The audit under the 1972 Act applies to the accounts of counties, districts or boroughs, parish or community councils or meetings, their committees, joint committees and officers. (Other Acts also apply this type of audit to regional water authorities and passenger transport executives).

A local authority is free to choose between district audit or approved audit for its accounts, and it may do this by arranging for one of them to apply to part of its accounts whilst the other covers the remainder. It can alter its arrangements whenever it wishes, subject to the rights of the auditor (or auditors) being respected and the consent of the Secretary of State of the Environment being given.

The Secretary of State appoints the district audit staff who are therefore civil servants and thus responsible to him for their diligence in carrying out their allotted tasks, but, nevertheless, they possess a fair measure of independence from the department in respect of the way in which they interpret their duties and the actions and decisions they take in following their employment.

The district audit originated under the Poor Law Amendment Act 1834. A central body (the Poor Law Commissioners) were given the power to make regulations and give orders regarding the administration of the Poor Law at that time, including the way in which the accounts were to be kept by the local guardians, and how the account books and forms were to be audited. The commissioners could make the guardians appoint auditors and pay them, and the persons appointed had to be satisfactorily qualified in accountancy and auditing. Furthermore, the auditors' conditions of service and their range of duties were also laid down centrally. To provide support for the auditors (who began to be referred to as "district auditors"), the justices of the peace were ordered to enforce the provisions of the Act against the guardians and their subordinates by disallowing any payments made by them which did not conform with the regulations. As a disallowance arising from the misuse of funds has by tradition meant that the person responsible has to make up the missing sum, this has developed into the practice of "surcharge". In earlier times, it was usually quite clear as to which person was responsible for wrongful payments, nowadays the courts have to consider more complicated situations in allotting responsibility. For a period, the power of disallowance and surcharge was passed to the district auditor, but the Local Government Act 1972 has returned it to the courts.

The district audit service is at present operated by the Audit Inspectorate which is headed by the Chief Inspector of Audit who co-ordinates the work of a number of District Auditors who are each in charge of an audit area in England and Wales. The senior staff in each area — deputies, assistants, audit examiners, etc. — are (like their chiefs) trained in the law, finance, accountancy and auditing applicable to their duties and usually become professionally qualified accountants by examination. The standards of the service are maintained by reviews carried out under the instructions of the Chief Inspector of Audit, which provide for Audit Inspectorate staff making visits of inspection to both district and approved audits being carried out at local authorities.

The other form of audit is called approved because the appointment of the auditor needs the Secretary of State's approval. The approved auditor must be a member of one of the designated accountancy bodies which, at present, are the three Institutes of Chartered Accountants (in England and Wales, Scotland and Ireland), the Association of Certified Accountants and the Chartered Institute of Public Finance and Accountancy, though other bodies of accountants in this country may at some future time be added to the list. The resolution appointing an accountant as the approved auditor of a local authority has no effect until the Secretary of State is satisfied that the appointee is a member of one of the above bodies and that he has enough experience and resources to hand to carry out an adequate and efficient audit. The criteria by which the firm's resources are measured against the standards set by the Department of the Environment include the numbers of staff of various grades involved and the time they will spend on the audit, the extent of the underlying support services, such as secretarial, specialist and ancillary staff, the need for an appreciable depth of knowledge of the law, finance, accountancy and administrative practice related to local authorities, and the terms of the contract to be entered into (for which a standard form is recommended). The Secretary of State must be dissatisfied with the firm's potential performance before he can proceed to refuse to give his approval. He can also withdraw his approval at any future time, should he consider that standards have not been maintained. The 1972 Act also deals with the termination of appointment, resignation, disqualification or death of an approved auditor — such matters are not relevant to the district audit which is a service with a perpetual existence, whilst accountancy firms are not allowed to become limited companies.

The financial year-end for local authorities is the 31st March, although the Secretary of State has the power to alter it to a different date for authorities in general or for individual cases. In the past, changes have usually arisen only when a body is ceasing to function or in situations where services are transferred — Parliament chooses some inconvenient dates for accountants in the public service to conform with, e.g. local authority gas undertakings passed on 30th April 1949, personal health services converted on 5th July 1948, lotteries operated from 1st May 1977 which was a Sunday. The external audit takes place as soon as practicable after the end of the year, bearing in mind that the accounts have to be completed on an income and expenditure basis and time is taken up in ascertaining debtors and creditors and calculating and transferring central administration charges and service departments' recharges. Some progress has been made towards current or continuous auditing (i.e. during the year) as, under the 1972 Act, the auditor has access to documents at all times, but the main audit work is of a completed nature (i.e. on the prepared accounts after the year-end). The procedures applicable to both types of audit, district and approved, are basically the same, though that for the approved audit is more circuitous — study of the legal provisions will indicate that their effect is to apply district audit to all local authorities whenever material irregularities occur in their financial transactions.

The duty of the auditor, whether district or approved, is to examine the accounts in order to satisfy himself that none of the legal requirements affecting expenditure and income has been disregarded and that the accounts have been prepared in accordance with acceptable accounting policies and comply with the statutes and regulations as to their contents and layout. He is assisted in his duty by the audit code of practice which explains what the Department of the Environment consider are matters for his concern and investigation during his examination of the accounts. Examples of areas to which he should direct his attention are the adequacy of the internal check, internal control and internal audit, the consistent application of accounting procedures, and instances of waste thrown up in the accounts, etc.. If he discovers any matter giving rise to concern on his part, he must consider whether it is in the public interest to report it to the council of the local authority or bring it to the attention of the public. The audit code in this instance also gives examples of cases which could call for reports. These include fraud, weak financial control, losses arising from waste or inefficiency, etc. Any report he decides to make to the local authority on the audit of its accounts must be sent not later than 14 days after the end of the audit (a copy goes to the Secretary of State), and the authority must give it early consideration.

The local authority being audited must provide the auditor with reasonable facilities to enable him to work, and he has the right of access at all times to such documents as he thinks are necessary to the audit. He can ask the authority's officers and others who hold or are accountable for documents which he thinks he needs for the audit to supply information and explanations. Furthermore he has the power, under threat of court action, to demand that they appear before him and produce the documents in question. This is a very wide power — to summon persons who are neither officers nor members of the authority to make an appearance — and is used sparingly and only in cases where the auditor is convinced there is no other alternative open to him. An anomaly appears to exist, however, in that, after the auditor has taken the matter to court, and the court has levied the punishment laid down in the Act, i.e. a fixed fine and a fine which continues for each day that the person wilfully fails to appear, there seems to be no machinery for actually making him come to the auditor. If the fines are paid, the person apparently need not make an appearance — a possible example of cost-benefit analysis on the part of the person involved, especially where the contents of the documents might be compromising.

Both kinds of auditor are not permitted to pass on information they have obtained during the audit other than for the purpose of carrying out their duties as auditors. The Local Government Act 1972 makes unauthorised use of information a criminal offence on the part of the approved auditor whilst the district audit staff is subject to the present Official Secrets Act. The regulations, however, state that the auditor (district and approved) must not give out any additional information about transactions than that contained in the documents and accounts deposited for inspection unless the authority permits him. This situation could cause a local authority some difficulties, as past law cases have had the effect of restricting the public's right of inspection of vouchers, etc. by excluding those which contain personal or confidential details about private individuals, e.g. claims for educational awards, rate rebates, etc. which give personal circumstances and income, whereas the auditor has the right of access to all documents he considers he needs to see for audit purposes.

The same scale of fees is laid down for both classes of audit, the local authority paying the Secretary of State for a district audit of its books, and the approved auditor directly for his audit. There is therefore no financial benefit in selecting either alternative.

The Procedure under District Audit

1. The first step in the procedure may be held to take place when the district auditor responsible for the area informs the local authority of the date on which the audit of the accounts will start. This date is usually that from which he can be questioned about the accounts and receive objections to items in them. (It is probable that this date has already been agreed informally towards the end of the previous audit). At least six weeks' notice is recommended to enable the authority to carry out the legal procedure.

2. The local authority advertises the date in the press, with at least 14 days' notice of where and when the accounts, documents, vouchers, etc. will be deposited for seven days immediately before the audit starts, so that persons interested may inspect them. Any such person (and the definition is undeniably wide in interpretation) can take copies and send an expert to act as his agent.

3. The auditor formally opens the audit on the date arranged, and whilst it is proceeding, any local government elector for the area (or his representative) may question the auditor about the accounts and object to any item or items contained in them. If an objector is aggrieved by a decision of the district auditor (possibly a rejection of the objection, after due consideration by the auditor), he may require the auditor to give him the reasons for his decision in writing. If the elector is still dissatisfied, he can appeal to the court.

4. If the auditor considers that an item in the accounts is contrary to law (and he not prevented from proceeding further with the matter by the action of the Secretary of State in giving his sanction to the item involved), he has the discretion (bearing in mind the amount of the item, the cost of the court proceedings, the strength of the evidence and the point of law at issue), to apply to the court to declare the item of account contrary to law. If the court makes the declaration, it may order that the accounts be corrected, and, if the item is expenditure, it may order the person or persons responsible to make repayment to the local authority. The court is required to take account of the motives and means of those held to be responsible. If a person believed that the expenditure was intra vires or otherwise acted in a reasonable manner, the court should not order repayment. In cases where repayment is considered, ability to pay must be considered and part repayment may be ordered. A serving councillor who is involved in responsibility for unlawful expenditure exceeding £2,000, can be disqualified by the court from membership of a local authority for a period stipulated by the court.

5. In circumstances where the auditor is satisfied that a person has not paid over money he is holding for the authority or has caused the authority to lose money by his wilful misconduct, the auditor must certify the sum involved as due from that person, and the local authority can recover it by court action. The Secretary of State can given his sanction where a person fails to pay in money but he cannot stop the district auditor acting in a case of wilful misconduct giving rise to a loss. Also, when the loss or deficit certified exceeds £2,000 and it arises from a councillor's wilful misconduct, there is an automatic disqualification from local authority membership for five years. A person from whom the auditor has certified a sum as being due, can, if he feels aggrieved, ask for the reasons for the decision in writing and then appeal to the court. Decisions in past cases make it appear that the persons subject to this procedure are councillors and members of staff, as, if the auditor were to certify sums as due from contractors, debtors, etc., this would mean that he had become a debt collector for the authority which should collect its own debts. Similarly, losses arising from negligence by employees in carrying out their duties are a matter for the local authority outside this procedure.

6. If the auditor finds matters of minor importance which are in error, he can agree to the accounts under audit being corrected. Many points arising

(not necessarily errors) are settled by discussions with the chief officers and the decisions reached evidenced by memoranda.

7. Throughout his examination of the systems and transactions, the auditor can always decide that a matter is of such importance that he must report on it to the authority or bring it to the attention of the public.

8. Nevertheless, most audits are not as dramatic as this exemplification indicates, and the auditor and his staff steadily fulfil their main duty to satisfy themselves that the accounts comply with the law and have been prepared in accordance with proper accounting practices.

9. At the close of the audit, the auditor must complete a certificate in prescribed form. An unqualified certificate states that he has completed the audit and considers there is no matter on which he should report, and there appear to be no sums he should certify as due in respect of income not brought to account and loss by wilful misconduct. If he has made or intends to make a report or has issued a certificate, he qualifies his audit certificate.

10. If the auditor makes a report to the local authority on the accounts, it must be sent not later than 14 days after the end of the audit. The authority must consider it as soon as practicable, and the report (and the agenda for the meeting at which it is to be considered) must be made available to the public. A copy of the report goes to the Secretary of State who must also be told if there is no report.

11. The audit fee is calculated on the authority's gross expenditure and income (with prescribed deductions), and is certified as correct by the auditor before it is paid.

12. Most local authorities are required to prepare an abstract of audited accounts in prescribed form which must carry the approval or the comments of the auditor.

N.B. The procedure for extra-ordinary district audit is dealt with after that for the approved audit because of the link between them. It must not be forgotten, however, that the Secretary of State can call for an extra-ordinary district audit at his discretion at any time in respect of the accounts of any local authority whatever its type of audit.

The Procedure under Approved Audit

1. The approved audit follows the same course as the district audit at the start, viz. the fixing of the starting date, arrangements for advertising the deposit of the accounts and the rights of inspection, the formal start of the audit and the questioning of the auditor about the accounts.

2. There is no provision for objection to the accounts at the audit, nor has the approved auditor the power to go to the court regarding items contrary to law. Instead, a local government elector (who presumably has failed to convince the approved auditor of the illegality of the item which was the subject of his questions) may apply direct to the Secretary of State for an extra-ordinary district audit to be held. The Secretary has complete discretion as to whether he complies or refuses.

3. Similarly, the approved auditor has no power to certify as due from the person responsible sums not brought to account or lost by wilful misconduct.

4. This absence of powers indicated in the previous two paragraphs, is balanced by requiring the approved auditor to report to the Secretary of State when such cases occur which call for the application of the missing powers. Thus on receiving the auditor's report, the Secretary can call for an extra-ordinary district audit or take other action as he decides. As with the district auditor, the approved auditor can always report to the authority or the public on matters which he considers important.

5. The closing stages of the approved audit are identical with those of the district audit, viz, correction of matters not giving rise to concern, by adjusting the accounts, memoranda, etc., satisfaction regarding the accuracy and legality of the accounts and their method of preparation, signing the certificate of completion of the audit, sending of any report he decides to make on the accounts to the local authority, agreement of the audit fee, and approving or commenting on the abstract of accounts.

Procedure under Extra-ordinary District Audit

The Secretary of State may call for the district auditor to hold an extra-ordinary district audit of any local authority's accounts if he considers it desirable, either on his own instance, from a report by either class of auditor, or from an application by an elector or the local authority involved.

The audit can be restricted in extent to the matters which have been queried, and where approved audit has applied, the more powerful district audit powers now become available.

1. The audit may be preceded by three days' notice to the local authority, and owing to the lack of time, there is no deposit of the accounts, no questioning of the district auditor, and it need not be advertised, unless the Secretary of State requires it.

2. The district auditor otherwise conducts this audit in exactly the same manner as in an ordinary audit. He can receive objections from an elector and decide to dismiss or uphold them. He can approach the court for a declaration regarding illegal items (always subject to the Secretary of State's power to sanction such sums). In addition, (again subject to the sanction) he can certify sums as due from persons in respect of amounts not brought into account or (in cases where the sanction is inapplicable) losses caused by wilful misconduct. The powers of the court and the rights of individuals are unchanged by the fact that the audit is extra-ordinary.

3. When the items and transactions under query have been thoroughly investigated and the necessary actions taken, the audit is closed in the normal way with a certificate and a report to the authority (if the auditor makes one) within the time allowed. The authority considers the report

under the usual conditions. The cost of an extra-ordinary audit is usually recouped from the local authority but the Secretary of State may bear the whole or part.

The Local Government Audit Code of Practice

Prior to the re-organisation of local government in 1974, borough councils were subject to district audit for certain of their accounts, and under a "municipal" audit for the rest. By local Act powers, some boroughs replaced the municipal audit by a "professional" audit (i.e. by a professional accountant). A few boroughs had decided to be wholly under district audit, as was the case with counties and their districts.

The municipal audit was described by one judge as ephemeral, while the professional auditors were few and isolated, and accused of being too commercial in their approach. The district audit was held to be too legalistic in outlook, concentrating on whether expenditure was strictly legal without regard to it being prudent or well-advised.

Under the Local Government Act, 1972, all local authorities were allowed to continue the tradition of non-district audit by choosing an approved auditor if they wished. (A freedom more apparent than real). To obtain the approval of the Department of the Environment, however, he must show the ability and resources to do a first class job of work. The opportunity was also taken to extend the duties of the district auditor in the direction of administrative efficiency and the control of waste in local affairs.

The higher level of competence expected from auditors of public funds was further emphasized by the issue of an audit code of practice drawn up by the Department of the Environment after consultation with the accountancy bodies. The code is to be observed by both district and approved auditors and amplifies the provisions of the Act and the Regulations by detailing the extra duties which the auditor of a local authority has to discharge in comparison with the auditor of a commercial undertaking.

There is little new about his first duty − to see that the accounts comply with legal requirements − which means that expenditure is legal, income is raised by lawful processes, and limits, etc. on the amounts of transactions are observed, and that the accounts agree with the underlying records.

The second duty is to ensure that proper accounting practices have been followed, and the observance of this duty has wider implications, such as whether different sections of the public have received unfair treatment in apportioning costs, whether internal control (including the internal audit) is adequate, whether the accounts show any appreciable loss caused by waste, extravagance, poor value for money, etc., and also how the auditor can help to improve and maintain integrity in the conduct of public affairs. One aspect of financial control is specially mentioned − whether the local authority has reached important financial decisions by considering irrelevancies, or by omitting relevant factors. In this area, the auditor needs to take care as he may be accused of interfering in the right of the council to decide policy.

The code also goes into some detail about matters which may call for report by the auditor. They include defects in dealing with tenders, in incentive bonus schemes, in the management of loans and surplus cash, in contract payment methods (which result in over-payment of contractors), as well as in circumstances mentioned in the two preceding paragraphs. As the decision to report is not lightly taken, the public, either directly or via the local authority should only be approached on matters of substance.

The Department of the Environment, via the Audit Inspectorate, is responsible for the maintenance and improvement of audit standards, and, in the code, mention is made of two measures which help in this direction. First, the auditor is required to play his part in arrangements for up-to-date information on law and practice to be circulated to all auditors. The law and practice notes will be prepared centrally from information from the Department and auditors, and then circulated. A charge is made for the service.

Second, co-operation and consultation between auditors – district and approved – and the Audit Inspectorate is envisaged at local and national levels. Information on matters of mutual interest, advice by the district auditors to approved auditors and to local authorities are forms which it can take.

Examples of Reports

Report of the Auditor on the Accounts of the Ingenting District Council

Office Address

To the Members of the Council,   Date,

Ladies and Gentlemen,

In compliance with Section 160, Local Government Act 1972, it is my duty to report to you that the audit of the authority's accounts for the year ended 31st March 19-3 has now been completed.

I wish, however, to draw to your attention the following matters which have arisen during the audit: –

1. *Stocks of Office Stationery*

It was observed that stocks of office stationery are being held in many departments in excess of foreseeable needs. I therefore recommend that there should be a review of current procedures for the ordering of such items.

2. *The Provision of Office Accommodation for Audit Staff*

When the audit was formally opened, it was found that suitable office space had not been earmarked for the use of the auditor and his staff so as to enable him to carry out his duties adequately. This oversight was corrected when a complaint was made but I would remind you that it is the responsibility of the authority to provide these facilities.

....
Auditor to the Council

N.B. This form of report would be for the consideration of the members of an authority whose accounts had been audited. The published report of the auditor which would appear in the abstract of accounts would probably be unqualified because the points the auditor raised with the Council were relatively minor. An unqualified report might be as follows: –

I have completed the audit of the accounts of the Ingenting District Council for the year ended 31 March 19-3 in accordance with all the relevant legal enactments and regulations.

I am also satisfied that I need take no action under the Local Government Act 1972, as required by: –

(a) Section 157 (viz. the making of a report to the Council).

(b) Section 161 (viz. the certifying of sums due from persons responsible).

Date

Office Address   Signature of the External Auditor.

The Advisory Committee on Local Government Audit

The Advisory Committee on Local Government Audit was formed by the Department of the Environment in response to a recommendation in the Layfield Committee report for the creation of a new independent investigatory body which would be concerned with, and report publicly on, such matters as the prevention of extravagance, the obtaining of value for money spent, and the efficiency of local administrations generally. At the time it was first formed, there was criticism of the Committee's powers and membership. It was suggested that the Government had failed to implement the full spirit of the Layfield recommendation, as the Committee's terms of reference comprise the consideration of the Chief Inspector of Audit's report each year and the making of suggestions to deal with any matters of concern to local and central government authorities, together with a duty to ask for details of, and to study and give advice on schemes designed to encourage the obtaining of value for money in services provided by government bodies.

The Committee has to date reported upon such matters as unacceptable delays in finalising and publishing local authority financial accounts, and the need for strengthening arrangements for computer audit, incentive bonus scheme operations, and contracts for building works. Approval has been expressed for the growing practice of exchanging information between organisations and producing figures which permit comparisons to be made between authorities in performing their services to the public. The Committee also recommends that there should be closer links between audits in the public sector and that public rights in relation to the inspection of deposited accounts should be extended.

Court Decisions in Auditing Cases

A number of law cases affecting local authority audits are given below as a matter of interest to students: –

1. Marginson v Tildsley, 1903 – the ex-chairman of the Finance Committee who was disqualified by bankruptcy and no longer resident in the area was, nevertheless, an "interested person" who was entitled to inspect the deposited accounts and documents.

2. R. v Bedwellty Urban District Council, 1934 – an interested person may employ an agent who is suitably qualified (e.g. an accountant) to inspect the accounts on his behalf.

3. Re Magrath, 1934 – Past consideration is no consideration, and a local authority must not pay for services rendered where there was no previous promise on its part to do so.

4. R v the Inhabitants of Chiddingstone, 1862 – the financial accounts cannot be re-opened and corrected once the district auditor has completed the audit. They are termed "res judicata" – "the matter has been judged".

5. Roberts v Hopwood, 1925 – an excess payment (in this case relating to wages) is ultra vires to the extent of the amount overpaid if the local authority has not exercised its power of discretion reasonably.

6. R v Roberts, 1908 – a local authority is not required to accept the lowest tender and is protected against action by the district auditor if it has given the matter proper consideration and heard the advice of its officers as to the best value for money, given there are no other grounds for concern.

7. R v Monmouthshire County Council ex parte Smith, 1935 – documents which contain details of the personal circumstances of members of the public (e.g. applications for education awards) are not available to interested persons when inspecting the deposited accounts and vouchers.

Questions

7.1 Describe briefly what a district auditor is.
7.2 What are the rights of a local government elector in connection with the audit of a local authority's accounts under District Audit?
7.3 Who can be described as an "interested person" under the Local Government Act 1972 and what are his or her rights?
7.4 Give a concise description of the system of approved audit applied to local authorities' accounts.
7.5 What is the meaning of "res judicata" and what significance does it have in local government audit?
7.6 Outline the relationship between the external and internal auditors of a local authority.
7.7 In what circumstances arising from the audit of accounts can a councillor be disqualified from holding this office?
7.8 Outline some matters over which an external auditor of a local authority must have concern in carrying out his audit.
7.9 Outline the legal requirements regarding the external audit of local authorites.

7.10 How is an extra-ordinary District Audit called for, and in what way does the procedure differ from an ordinary District Audit?

7.11 Discuss the power of the Secretary of State to sanction items of expenditure or amounts not brought into account in respect of the accounts of local authorities.

7.12 What factors might make a local authority choose Approved Audit instead of District Audit for its accounts?

Chapter 8

Internal Auditing in Local Authorities

The Accounts and Audit Regulations 1974 require each local authority to arrange for a current internal audit to be carried out upon its own financial transactions and that this audit must be under the control of the officer who has been made responsible for the local authority's finances. Internal audit is therefore statutory and is part of the duties of the treasurer or director of finance, and the internal audit staff have the right of access to such documents as they think are necessary to carry out their duties and can demand information and explanations for that purpose from any officer.

The Local Government Audit Code of Practice which the external auditors of local authorities are under a duty to observe, stipulates that one of the important matters to which they must pay attention is the adequacy of internal audit arrangements. This underlines the importance which is now attached by the central authorities to the maintenance of internal controls in local government.

There appears to be little record of when and how internal audit practices were introduced into local authorities. It is probable that the first arrangements were fairly informal, being in the form of a watching brief by the local J.P.s and parish officers — who were doubtless very familiar with the affairs and people of the locality — over the actions of those persons who were involved in the collection of the Poor Rate and the payment of assistance to the needy, together with the financing of such services as then existed. In the closed community of the parish of the time, shortcomings in standards of conduct by public officials would soon become common knowledge and a matter of gossip. Finally, allegations would reach the ears of authority. During the 19th century, however, the local authorities began to grow in the size of their areas and numbers of staff they employed, and consequently, more formal arrangements became necessary to control the actions of staff and the use of funds. Again, it is probable that the first attempts at internal auditing in a modern sense were made by senior members of the finance staff during office hours whenever they found time to spare from their main duties. The continued increase in the scale of operations in local government led to the next step when members of staff were specially appointed or seconded wholly to internal audit duties. Nevertheless, the level of internal audit coverage varied considerably throughout the country, partly because of the variations in the size and resources of the local authorities, and partly from the differences in the finance officers' powers of persuasion in getting their councils to appoint extra staff for internal auditing purposes. Difficulty was experienced most in the smaller authorities, such as the rural district councils, in providing an acceptable level of service in this respect, owing to lack of resources.

The bargaining position of the treasurer was, however, strengthened by a decision given in Attorney-General v De Winton 1906 (which is often referred to as "The Tenby Case"). This case involved the legality of certain transactions in the financial accounts of the Municipal Borough of Tenby and, among other matters, it was held that the treasurer was directly responsible to the ratepayers to take all reasonable steps to ensure that the funds entrusted to his control were applied in accordance with the law. Furthermore, he must not let any orders from the council over-ride his duties to the citizens. Thus, if the members refused him an internal audit staff whom he considered to be essential to enable him to do his work properly, his final line of action would be to resign. Although the case dealt with a borough, its effect was extended in due course to all classes of local authority, albeit, to varying degrees.

The next milestone in the development of the use of internal audit was reached in 1930. In that year, the Accounts Regulations (usually referred to as Memo/150) were issued by the Ministry of Health for application to accounts subject to district audit. The regulations laid down that one chief financial officer (i.e. not departmental finance officers acting separately within their own domains) should be responsible for the continuous supervision of all accounts and financial records covered by district audit within the whole local authority. Thereafter, this practice was extended by the municipal and county boroughs to those accounts which were not under district audit as a means of encouraging good internal procedures as well as their standardisation throughout the authority. The authority had to obey the regulations as regards the services under district audit, so, in the interests of simplicity, there was little choice but to extend them to all financial activities (Counties and districts were fully under district audit at the time).

In 1932, in answer to questions posed by a metropolitan borough council (in those days, the word "metropolitan" referred only to London), a King's Counsel, i.e. a leading barrister, expressed the opinion which may be summarised as follows: –

(a) it was an essential part of the borough treasurer's duties to maintain an internal audit of the accounts of the council on a continuous basis,

and

(b) his responsibility as to the accounts being correct and reliable could only be properly carried out through an internal audit undertaken by staff acting under his control.

Although the enquiry concerned a local authority which was completely under the district audit system of the time, the effect of the answer was to reinforce Memo/150 in extending the application of the chief financial officer's internal audit role to all the accounts of all local authorities.

The next development occurred over thirty years (and a war) later. The Local Government Act 1958 placed a duty upon every local authority to make safe and efficient arrangements for receiving and paying out money and to place them in the charge of the authority's finance officer. Most local authorities already had systems of financial regulations but the duty to conform with the Act called for a comprehensive code which had of necessity to cover the functions and scope of internal audit and its rights of access to documents and information where these matters were not already included. One unexpected aspect to the Act's provisions was a noticeable delay on the part of some treasurers in revising the regulations as they were reluctant to report to members on a matter which implied that the previous financial code (suggested or, at least, operated by the treasurer) was defective.

After 1958, the position regarding internal audit rights and duties remained unchanged until the passing of the Local Government Act 1972 when the internal audit became compulsory with effect from 1st April 1974.

The internal audit system now applied to local, water and passenger transport authorities might well serve as a pattern which Parliament can use as a base for future developments in the audit of public sector authorities generally. Present day economic problems call for a tightening of financial control and a high level of management of scarce funds and resources, and the strengthening of the internal audit powers appears to be a necessary factor in this. The argument that this puts too much power into the hands of the treasury can be countered by pointing to the system of corporate decision-taking which makes the financial viewpoint only one of several. The internal auditor, in the past, was almost solely concerned with the audit of financial records, statements and procedures. Now there is the opportunity to operate on a wider basis.

The internal auditor is first desirous of ensuring the reliability of the internal controls – not just the division of staff duties, but the whole set of rules and procedures which provide a sound, ordered basis to the routine work of the authority. He wishes to be satisfied that these controls are being complied with by the management who are receiving effective financial reports from the system and making efficient decisions in regard to future plans. This need for efficiency extends to the prevention of losses of assets as well as the best use of resources. The internal audit's role might thus be summed up as helping the departmental administrators (including those employed in the finance division) to carry out their duties more efficiently by ensuring that they receive up-to-date, accurate and complete information for managing and decision-making. One might say that all the auditor's efforts in analysing and appraising controls, compliance and records are directed to this end.

For instance, the internal auditor in auditing a contract would be interested in aspects other than the accuracy of the calculations and the legality and proper authorisation of the payment. He would enquire into the need for the contract, the method used in doing the work, the effectiveness of the result, the occurrence of avoidable delays, etc. and consider the availability of alternatives and improvements. He would then make recommendations aimed at improving the procedures and decision-taking processes for the future. Implicit in this wider approach, is the need to rely on the expertise of others.

The Organisation of the Internal Audit of a Local Authority

It is the usual practice to form the members of the internal audit staff into a section which is distinct from the remainder of the finance division. They occupy separate office accommodation but are backed up by the general ancillary services, such as secretarial, reprographic and computer facilities, provided by the division. There are various reasons given for this degree of segregation. There is the need on the part of the audit staff for single-mindedness and dedication in carrying out duties which may be said to be underrated or even resented by most of their colleagues in the authority's employ. Added to this, there is the need to acquire training in techniques and knowledge of a specialised nature, the necessity of guarding the confidentiality of documents, statements, reports and actions, and to set standards which assist the internal auditors to preserve a measure of reserve in their relations with other members of staff, especially those whose work they audit. (On the other hand, auditors have been known to issue from their base and strike up a closer acquaintanceship with staff in the pursuit of information on suspected irregularities). The maintenance of a separate unit also gives the chief internal auditor a degree of seniority and authority in dealing with other officers in the finance division and in other departments, and a higher level of independence in giving him direct access to the director of finance.

Various attempts have been made to depart from the custom of keeping audit staff separate. Before the re-organisation in 1974, some authorities operated on what was called a functional basis, whereby teams of staff of various categories (accountants, auditors, etc.) were given the task of carrying out all the financial duties appertaining to a service. Thus one team would deal with payments to creditors, salaries and wages, stores accounting and other such tasks which were carried out by its accountant members, whilst the auditor members would perform the audit function. There is little record of how well the system worked, but perhaps it is sufficient to say that it never seemed to spread. A less ambitious attempt has been made since re-organisation in sharing the audit function among the members of staff who are occupied with the related accountancy duties, so that one assistant may do both the accounting and audit functions for one service. It has been found in most cases that this combination of duties has been to the detriment of the auditing which has almost always fallen behind at times of pressure of work when the accountancy has been kept up to date in preference to the audit. Suggestions have also been made for the amalgamation of internal audit and management services in view of each being involved in systems work, the auditor criticising and reviewing the procedures planned and installed by the systems analyst. Whilst there appears to be scope for informal co-operation, the specialised and confidential nature of audit work seems to be a stumbling block to putting the sections together as one unit.

The chief internal auditor is responsible for the overall supervision and forward planning of the section. He is, of course, subordinate to the director of finance and reports to him on both routine and extra-ordinary matters. (For instance, periodical reports on the observance of accounting procedures in a particular department might be regarded as routine, whereas a report on the discovery and extent of a major fraud is, fairly obviously, extra-ordinary in nature.) An important aspect of his duties is to co-operate with the external auditor in getting the best use of resources in covering both types of audit, and to satisfy him as to the adequacy of the work of the internal audit staff. He should possess a strong, independent character, an objective approach to problem-solving, an ability to make decisions coolly, and should defend and support his subordinates as well as expect to be supported by the director in cases where correct actions or decisions are criticised.

The way in which the internal audit staff is deployed to do its work is decided by many inter-acting factors which are of two main classes, the first being the resources available for the tasks to be done, whilst the second is the volume and variety of the tasks themselves. Thus, the pattern of deployment depends, firstly, on the number of the staff, their abilities, qualifications and experience, together with the supporting services placed at their disposal. The second class of factors includes the duties allotted to internal audit by the standing orders (such as the "minimum financial audit", "value for money" audits and various types of non-audit work), the range of services administered by the authority, the volume and nature of the transactions, the requirements of the external auditor, and the general duty to contain the risk of error or fraud to a minimum.

The usual arrangement is to organise the internal audit staff into teams composed of different grades of personnel. Each team is headed by a senior fully-qualified auditor who allocates duties to his semi-qualified and unqualified assistants and clerical staff. Audits are often assigned to teams on a service basis. One team would thus deal with the audit of the education service, another with social welfare, and so on. Exceptions to the team approach to audit occur in the case of specialists, such as computer auditors, projects auditors (who specialise in examining the transactions contained in capital schemes), systems auditors, etc. who may be involved in specific aspects of all the services. Care must, however, be taken that the team system does not become inflexible and have a divisive effect on the staff, so that members of one team treat members of other teams with reserve, and the chief internal auditor must rotate duties and staff occasionally as well as bringing teams together for large-scale efforts when necessary.

In dividing the workload of the section among his teams, the chief internal auditor is basically trying to give maximum coverage against the risk that errors, losses and frauds might be escaping discovery despite the existence of internal control measures. The number of the staff in the internal audit section and the time they can spend on any aspect of the work are both limited and arguments can be made for directing their attention in two diametrically opposing directions. The first is to concentrate on those areas where error, wastage and fraud is most likely to occur, though relatively minor sums are involved, and the second is to give priority to the examination of those areas where financial loss from unauthorised actions may be rare but can involve quite large amounts of money. Besides these two extreme cases, there is a whole range of intermediary situations, and the chief internal auditor is usually constrained as to how he should deploy his forces by what has been judged as proper in the past, either in his own experience or, even, that of his predecessors in office. Certain tasks will have been traditionally carried out at specific times by a given number of his staff, and adjustments would be made to meet changing circumstances.

The chief internal auditor can, however, make a mentally fresh start by considering from first principles how he should allocate his resources. This situation could only occur in practice when a new authority is formed, a new service started or a newly-appointed auditor-in-chief takes up his office. (There is a passing resemblance to zero-based budgeting in this approach – each activity must qualify for inclusion in the audit coverage on its own merits). He may, therefore, draw up outline audit programmes for the routines which he considers should be included in the "minimum financial audit". Among such activities would be the maintenance of internal check, the security of cash collected, transferred, banked and finally paid out by the organisation, the safekeeping of those assets whose nature exposes them to the danger of theft or unauthorised use and the control of financial stationery, such as cheques, official order forms and receipt books. The amount of work involved in these programmes would be assessed and changes made, probably cuts, and made to fit within the total resources, whilst, at the same time, leaving room for the other aspects of auditing, such as "value for money" and specialised audits, including computer systems, projects and investigations into fraud.

However, to assist him in fashioning a fresh approach to the problem of allocating his resources, the use of risk indexes is now a growing feature in the planning of audits. A risk index is a device which is intended to give an objective indication of the relative importance of the various aspects of an audit, and thus it can be used to take the place of, or perhaps better, to reinforce the auditor's judgement. A risk index includes for each area, aspect or service such factors as the amount of cash receipts, credit income, stock-in-hand, payments by cash, cheque or bank transfer, sums of cash held in imprests, and assessments of the internal check, other controls, and the past history of fraud in the service. It can be seen that factors of this nature are of interest to an auditor in studying an assignment, and they are allotted weightings (i.e. multipliers) in proportion to their relative importance or vulnerability to error or fraud. Each service is thus entitled to the proportion of the total audit resources which its index number bears to the total of all the index numbers. Further work is needed in deciding just what those resources should be but inherent in the idea is that the audit effort should be seen to be cost-effective — the best results from the lowest cost — though the auditors's professional judgement still has a part to play here as elsewhere in the practice of auditing.

The division of the workload among the internal audit teams in the section has another dimension and that is the manner in which it is discharged over time. Internal audit is continuous and current by nature and the records to be audited are being produced non-stop without respite. Each audit task takes time to carry out and the auditor has to decide the frequency and depth of his checks so as to keep up to date with the flow of data, whilst using the time available to the best advantage. In addition to the daily or weekly check upon current transactions and compliance with standing orders which must be kept up to date, the audit staff must look beyond this at the adequacy or improvement of systems, the safekeeping of assets, and the avoidance of all forms of waste. It is therefore essential to have a plan which consists of a timetable of objectives to be reached which will give adequate coverage of the local authority's transactions, including the security of its assets, over a cycle of a number of months or even several years.

Such a timetable is usually envisaged as having two main stages. The first stage which is prepared consists of the long-term timings for jobs to be done over the base period which has been chosen to cover each important activity at least once. Considering that the plan covers a fairly long time, it must be flexible enough to take revisions where necessary. This plan is sectionalised, so that the work tasks for the next few months can be identified and prepared for as they come on line.

The other stage deals with those audits which are to be commenced immediately or in the next few days. It shows in greater detail than the longer-term plan, the assignments to be carried out, the tests to be done, the steps to be taken, the comparisons to be made, and the personnel who are allotted to do the work.

The need for flexibility must be emphasised at all times. In the longer-term, the local authority may be given the duty to run a new service under an Act of Parliament at some date in the future, whilst revisions of a more immediate nature may arise in the need to audit new projects or to carry out a special investigation of a newly-discovered large-scale fraud.

It is obvious that there must be arrangements to monitor that the plans of the above system are being fulfilled, and these include the keeping of accurate and detailed records by the audit staff of the tasks done and the time taken to do them. Senior staff must carry out constant reviews of progress, and make adjustments and improvements where the need for them is indicated.

Procedure for Carrying Out an Audit

The steps which an auditor takes in undertaking and completing an audit may be classified into the following stages: –

(a) Information collecting
(b) Planning
(c) Performance
(d) Review and Report

The approach adopted here is intended to cover aspects common to both the internal and external audit of local government services in regard to the procedures the auditor follows and the techniques he uses. In the interests of completeness, a *new* audit assignment has been assumed, but in real situations, some records and files would probably be available to the auditor from previous audits.

It is suggested, therefore, that, on being assigned to an audit under the short-term stage of the audit plan, an auditor should proceed as follows: –

(a) *Information Collecting*

He needs to inspect and makes notes of the contents, or obtain copies of documents dealing with the powers and duties of committees, the scope of responsibilities of departments, and legal provisions governing activities and methods of operation employed in the services. He also needs to read and copy extracts from committee minutes, deeds and contracts, standing orders and financial regulations, departmental memoranda on internal procedures, and any relevant correspondence files.

He requires the organisation chart applicable to the department with the names of officers and details of their duties, a complete list of accounting books and supporting records with the names of the persons responsible for keeping them, a fully-detailed explanation of the internal check system and other controls, and (if applicable), a copy of the latest audited accounts, auditor's report, and capital and revenue estimates.

The auditor must also investigate any sources of information outside the local authority. For instance, he should note items in the press, such as announcements, advertisements and news items which may supply data to support or contradict the evidence given by the books and other records kept within the authority. Similarly, the financial accounts of other local authorities may indicate such matters as the existence of undisclosed sources of income. Handbooks, reference books and Government pamphlets dealing with particular services may help the auditor to understand their background and aims.

Other information of interest to him are statistics relating to the volume of transactions, as shown by the number of invoices paid, the number of receipts issued, etc., the dates when his attendance is needed for the purposes of the audit, e.g. to observe the stock being counted at the year end, and the locations which he has to visit and the distances involved, as well as the best routes.

He opens up a system of files to hold the various documents and working papers which he accumulates during his examination. The two major components of the system are the permanent file which should contain the information which is of use from audit to audit, and the current file which holds the papers connected with the current audit and records its progress. The permanent file thus contains such documents as extracts from Acts of Parliament, scales of charges, standing orders, organisation charts, details of the accountancy system and procedures. The current file is composed of working papers showing tests carried out and the results obtained, figures re-calculated and compared, items queried and the answers given to the auditor, the use of ratios or other statistics, such as graphs of trends, etc.

(b) *Planning*

The auditor now undertakes a review of the information he has collected in order to arrive at an estimate of the size of the task in hand. He is particularly concerned as to how much time needs to be allotted to the examination of the internal control system by himself and his team, and how much to the transactions and entries in the accounts. The reason behind the auditor's interest in the internal control is that modern auditing practice leans towards the examination of systems and away from the traditional practice of checking every entry in the books in a mechanical manner. The argument is that a good system which is followed properly prevents or, at least, limits error and fraud, and thus the checking of transactions can be reduced in extent.

He therefore draws up programmes aimed, first, at ascertaining whether the internal control system in use is the same as the one which has been laid down officially in the documents he has been given, and secondly, at discovering any points of weakness in system design or operation. For these purposes, he can use internal control questionnaires, write descriptions of the procedures in narrative form, and draw up flowcharts which show such aspects of the system as information channels or document movement. Whilst he is recording the system, he considers whether it is logical in design, and whether duties are allocated properly for the observance of the principles of internal check.

Internal check is the division of the clerical and administrative work among the staff so that one employee, in carrying out his allotted duties in the normal manner, applies an automatic check upon the way other employees (usually employed at an earlier stage in the procedures) do their assigned tasks. The term is also applied, with somewhat less force, to describe the situation where an employee, usually in the capacity of a supervisor, carries out specific checks upon the work of others. The basic rule is that no employee should be allotted duties which enable him to control all the steps in a transaction as it passes through the organisation. In particular, the ideal is that no one person should be able to authorise or originate an action, have custody of any of the assets acquired by the action, and be in charge of the recording aspect, either in the books or in the preparation of documents, such as invoices. It is obvious that to divide the work in this way can prove difficult or well nigh impossible in small firms owing to the staff employed being few in number, and other measures may be needed to take its place, e.g. warning notices to customers to expect machine-issued receipts, the restriction of access to places where certain work is done, the use of ratios, trends, and other statistics on levels of such items as cash income, bad debts written off, etc..

Where the auditor's enquiries into the system reveal ways in which it can be improved in streamlining its logic or repairing weaknesses in internal check, he notifies the departmental or service head, and the matter is discussed and improvements or corrective action agreed. In view of the strength of the position of the auditor (both internal and external) in local government, well-founded criticism of a system is unlikely to be ignored by the staff under audit. This is somewhat different from commercial audits where an auditor's suggestions can, on occasion, be ignored or agreed reforms delayed, forcing him to refuse or qualify his report on the accounts. It must be realised that improvements to an internal control system operate from the date they are introduced and thus they do not apply to the period under audit when transactions have taken place under a defective system. The auditor has to decide how serious any past defects have been and this can result in him widening his tests of the individual transactions.

Assuming that the auditor has now satisfied himself as to the adequacy of the internal controls as officially laid down, he still has to make sure that the staff is actually complying with them in carrying out the work.

To do this, he prepares audit programmes to test that (a) the official system is the one in use, (b) the staff are complying with it to a degree which he finds satisfactory, and (c) the records of the transactions and the accounts produced by the system are complete, accurate and reliable.

The programme to ascertain that the official system is in use contains tests designed to corroborate this, being mainly by observation of the way the work is done, and documentary evidence consisting of prescribed initialling codings, etc. Replies to an I.C.Q. may assist the enquiry.

The second programme consists of compliance tests which are aimed at assessing the degree of obedience among the staff in carrying out the official system. The auditor is looking for examples of non-compliance, such as the omission of initials or signatures, failure to issue confirmatory orders for verbal contracts, and payments of excess amounts out of petty cash, where such actions or failure to act are contrary to the laid-down procedures. These two programmes are often amalgamated into one, as it is really only a matter of degree whether a failure to comply is a form of short-cut in the official procedure or is itself a different procedure, excepting, of course, examples of omission through laziness. In any case, the auditor must obtain results which he considers to be satisfactory from his examination of the evidence, as his approach to the third series of tests is profoundly affected by this. A sound system and a high degree of compliance enable him to reduce the extent of his examination there. A inadequate system or a high rate of non-compliance force him to carry out a complete check of the books, and even after a complete check he may still be unsatisfied as to their accuracy, particularly with regard to possible omissions. This is because he has no reliable basis for deducing the existence or amount of any transactions omitted from the records.

The programme designed to test the authenticity, correctness and completeness of the records and book entries and the reliability of the final accounts contains what are called transaction or substantive tests. They are aimed at ensuring that the transactions being audited are arithmetically correct, correctly treated in accordance with accountancy principles, authentic in nature by having actually taken place, and are all present without omission.

(c) *Performance*

In the planning stage, the auditor has prepared his programmes in which he has dealt with the locating of the sources of evidence which he thinks will be of service in his examination, and the various audit techniques which he can apply to them. His task is now to start working through the programmes, using the techniques appropriate to each class of transaction. A list of the major techniques available to him might read as follows: –

(i)   Vouching
(ii)   Verification
(iii)   Confirmation
(iv)   Recalculation or re-computation
(v)   Enquiry
(vi)   Scrutiny and correlation
(vii)   Knowledge after the event
(viii) Internal control questionnaires
(ix)   Audit programmes and check lists
(x)   Statistical sampling
(xi)   Surprise and unpredictability
(xii)   Analytical techniques.

(i) *Vouching*. This is the inspection of the documentary evidence relating to each transaction in the books. (Documents are often in the form of vouchers, hence vouching). The examination is intended to ensure that a transaction is authentic, correct in amount, properly approved and accurately recorded. Examples of documents which can be subjected to vouching are invoices from creditors, petty cash vouchers, copies of orders issued, committee minutes, contracts, bank pass sheets, receipt counterfoils, stock sheets, etc..

Vouching is not merely the mechanical comparison of the evidence and the book entry. It is more than just the agreeing of the value given by the document or voucher with the amount entered in the accounts. The auditor must keep on the alert for anything of a discordant or unusual nature. He therefore pays attention to such points as names, dates, the nature of the item or service involved and its relevance to the activities of the body being audited, initials and signatures as evidence of proper certification, the accuracy of prices and calculations, the correctness of the coding to capital or revenue, the addition of items in different typescript, etc.. He makes a note of missing vouchers which he requires to be produced − as copies, if necessary, and all vouchers should, if time and volume permit, be cancelled or marked in some way to prevent them being used again in any manner. In any case, it is a good policy to cancel petty cash vouchers.

A distinction is sometimes made between vouchers or documents created internally by the organisation being audited and those coming from outside. The external sources are regarded as supplying more reliable evidence of transactions than the internal ones which, it is argued, are more amenable to manipulation. Vouching may also be applied to the use of press reports, advertisements, etc. and minutes and reports of other organisations. For instance, a local organisation may advertise a meeting to be held at a local school and the auditor would make a note to check that a charge was made for the accommodation provided.

(ii) *Verification*. Vouching provides evidence of the genuineness of book entries, but where a transaction produces an asset, vouching cannot prove the existence or value of the asset at the time of the audit (assuming that it has not been disposed of by then). After vouching has been carried out, therefore, the auditor inspects the asset to satisfy himself that it exists. He also checks its identity where there is a danger that it may have been substituted by a similar item, and its condition where this may affect the valuation in the final accounts. Verification does not necessarily prove that the asset inspected is actually owned by the organisation, and the auditor may need to use a confirmation procedure. This is especially so, in relation to such items as investments when only a certificate can be produced as evidence and the body in which the investment is made is asked to confirm that it is authentic. Assets such as cash, stock-in-hand, and furniture and equipment can be counted, though it is advisable to verify all the assets of each class at the same time to prevent items being substituted for others. As has been said, one cannot verify an asset which has been disposed of, and one is then mainly restricted to vouching the terms as evidenced by the contract, the receipt of the sale proceeds, with the book entries.

Verification can be applied to the authentication of liabilities where, for instance, an asset which has not been paid for is inspected, but, otherwise, vouching, confirmation and the use of hindsight are usually the only techniques available for checking amounts owing to creditors.

(iii) *Confirmation*. This is the process of obtaining evidence from sources outside the organisation being audited as to the genuineness of transactions or the existence and value of assets and liabilities. The auditor makes a direct approach to the appropriate source which must be a firm or person of genuine nature and independent of the body under audit. (The auditor must check on this). In his approach, the auditor asks for confirmation in writing direct to himself that the facts as shown in the accounts are correct. When this technique is applied to debtors and creditors, it is referred to as 'circularising' and may be positive (when a reply is asked for to all requests) or negative (when an answer is only expected in case of a difference in records or a dispute). Confirmation can be used also for cash at bank, investments, and the certificate of a solicitor as to the legal effect of a deed.

(iv) *Re-calculation or re-computation.* The auditor needs to check calculations from their original sources, because correct arithmetic does not necessarily mean that the basic data was correct. Similarly, machine listings are not always totalled correctly – previous totals may not have been cleared or there may be other manipulations. Examples of re-calculation are wages computations, allocation of central administration charges, the pricing and evaluation of stock-in-hand.

A procedure encountered in small-scale audits is to carry out all the book-keeping entries again, using the prime documents and to compare the results obtained with the draft accounts prepared previously. There is usually an absence of internal check because of the lack of size of the organisation involved, and there is still the doubt about possible omissions from the records.

(v) *Enquiry.* This is the basic means available to the auditor for finding out facts about the accounts he is auditing. He should have the ability to ask a series of pertinent, searching questions whilst noting the replies. He must remind members of the staff, if necessary, of his rights of access to documents and to such information and explanations as he may require, and that he has the power to request persons to come to him with documents he wishes to see. The auditor often puts the same questions to different members of staff and cross-checks the various answers while, at the same time, using his own personal observations.

(vi) *Scrutiny and correlation.* These techniques are carried out by the auditor in systematically studying the records and accounts with the aim of discovering anything which is out of the ordinary and may indicate underlying error or fraud. For instance, an account based on the totals of monthly schedules should only contain twelve entries, not eleven or thirteen. The purchase or erection of a building should create running costs such as rates, repairs, insurance premiums, etc.. The auditor can use these techniques more widely than with the accounting records by "taking a walk round the yard" and "going beyond or behind the books" whereby he may see events and actions or overhear remarks which may give a lead to the discovery of error or fraud in the accounts.

(vii) *Knowledge after the event.* The auditor has the benefit of enjoying what is called hindsight or wisdom after the event in cases where a matter may be clarified by evidence arising between the event and the holding of the audit. For instance, the receipt of £100 after the year end from a person who is shown on the Balance Sheet as a debtor for £100 is good evidence that the debt existed and was collectible. The technique might be regarded as the vouching into a later period or up-to-date. It is obvious that its use to the internal auditor is restricted as he is mainly involved in current auditing.

(viii) *Internal control questionnaires.* These are lists of questions which are designed to bring out the features of systems of internal control. The questions are about such matters as the procedures followed by staff in doing their work, the records kept, and the persons responsible or involved, so as to enable the auditor to use the answers to evaluate the logic and effectiveness of the systems. The auditor must, of course, use other techniques, such as corroborative and compliance checks and observation, to verify that the answers he has received agree with the true situation. It is recommended that the auditor retains control of the I.C.Q. and asks each question in turn, filling in the replies from what the interviewee tells him. Prior knowledge of the questions still to be asked may affect answers to current questions. As with the technique of enquiry (of which this is perhaps a formalised version), the same questions are put to different persons whose replies are cross-checked. The drawing up of an I.C.Q. is no mean task and, furthermore, review may need to be continual if procedures tend to change in ways which improve their effectiveness.

There are rules to be observed in the way the questions are phrased. There should be no ambiguities in meaning (i.e. no questions which can be read in two ways). The words used must be familiar to the interviewee. Questions must be brief and never irrelevant. Answers should be yes, no, a name or a number, though occasionally, in answer to what is called a "key" question (e.g. Is there any way in which materials can be issued from the stores without a stores requisition note being issued?), the answer may be in narrative form, if the interviewee has a positive answer. Staff should not normally be asked for their personal opinions, as the auditor deals in facts. Attempts are made to standardise the questions in the I.C.Q.s in use for the various procedures, and the convention has grown up that a negative reply to a question indicates a weakness in the system.

I.C.Q.s can be linked to audit programmes — to some extent they are programmes on system evaluation converted to questions — and are also used in conjunction with flow diagrams and charts which can often reveal gaps and illogicalities not revealed by other means.

The advantages of using I.C.Q.s include the following — they make it easier for the auditor to concentrate on the system, they save time by highlighting faults and help the system of delegation to junior staff who also benefit by receiving useful training and extra responsibility. In addition, the auditor can be more confident about his assessment of the procedures and the degree of compliance by the staff, and is therefore better equipped to decide on the extent to which he should sample the transactions rather than making a complete check. Disadvantages arising from the use of I.C.Q.s include the effort required to draw up questionnaires in the first place, complete them from the staff's replies, and update them periodically. It is also argued that there is a loss of initiative on the part of the audit staff in going outside the area covered by the questions, especially as there may be an appearance of completeness in coverage which is misleading and thus dangerous.

In this connection, it might be useful to consider the reasons why an auditor decides to include certain questions in an I.C.Q.. For instance: —

(a) Is each remittance of cash, cheque, money or postal order recorded immediately it has been removed from its envelope and crossed "Account Payee" where appropriate?

This question is intended to make sure that a complete record of all incoming money is made before it can go astray within the organisation. In addition, the list of remittances provides a check of all later stages in their handling. Later questions will deal with the issuing of receipts by the cashier, the payment of the money into bank, the entries in the cash book and the debtors' personal accounts, so as to ensure that the list agrees with the later evidence and records, both in total and detail. The auditor will, of course, need to make compliance tests to be satisfied that the comparisons are duly made by the personnel responsible.

(b) Is the previously-issued receipt book taken back from a collector when he or she is issued with a new one?

This question is asked to ensure that no collector has the opportunity to retain a receipt book (possibly by saying it was lost) and to take money and issue receipts from it without accounting for the cash involved. In addition, the returned receipt books can be inspected for any unusual aspects as regards the condition of the counterfoils, correctness of additions, etc., and agreement with past payments into bank.

(ix) *Audit programmes and check lists.* These are detailed schedules of the checks, comparisons and other tasks to be carried out in undertaking an audit. The tests are usually listed in the order in which they are to be done and the person completing a step is required to sign or initial it, insert the date and "check it off" — this gives rise to the use of the term "check list" in this connection.

The auditor compiles these programmes in an attempt to cover all the important aspects of the work in the time available. To draw up an effective programme calls for a knowledge of the aims of the organisation, its chain of command, internal control measures, accounting methods and records, sources of income, types of expenditure, and relevant legal provisions governing its actions. (One might also claim that an auditor who draws up a programme from scratch is well on the way to possessing a wide knowledge of the organisation he is auditing, and, moreover, is acquiring it in a controlled and recorded manner).

It is argued that passing on a programme from audit to audit and from auditor to auditor leads to a loss of initiative on the part of the audit staff. The work becomes routine and mechanical, and any omissions and weaknesses are perpetuated, if the programme is not reviewed. The position can grow worse, if the procedures alter unnoticed. Furthermore, the staff whose records are being audited may, in due course, be able to forecast what the audit staff will check, and prepare accordingly. A final point is that the existence of a programme may mean that auditors concentrate on completing its tests and do not have the time left to pursue enquiries into discrepancies revealed.

Against this, it is contended that a programme provides a base from which to operate, and make improvements in the tests. It is particularly useful in introducing new staff to the work and assists in delegating areas of work to junior staff. A programme shows how far the work has progressed if there is a change of staff, and also shows who did the tests so that responsibility can be fixed where queries arise later. If an automatic periodical review is built into the programme, this reduces the chance of it becoming out of date, and encourages the audit staff to suggest improvements.

(x) *Statistical sampling.* Auditors have long used a technique called "test-checking" by which a relatively few documents, entries or other items are checked in a particular section of the records, and inferences are drawn from the conditions revealed by the sampled items as to the state ruling in the whole section. The reasons for adopting this procedure were twofold. The first was that the volume of transactions, the limits on audit staff, the existence of deadlines for reporting, the cost of the audit compared with the fee, and the need to move on as soon as possible to another audit, forced the auditor to reduce the load of work in order to be able to give more attention to those areas needing it. The second reason was the belief which accountants had acquired from reading about the work of statisticians that sampling could be relied upon to reflect the conditions existing in the population of data from which a sample is taken. The main trouble was that the auditors were often unaware of the conditions under which sampling should be operated in order to have the security of the theory of probability around it. The main requirement which the auditors failed to comply with was that of randomness in the choice of items. The meaning of random choice may be taken to be that each individual item in the collection of documents, etc. being sampled has an equal change of being chosen each time that an item is selected. The defect in test-checking was therefore that the choice of the items for inclusion in the sample was not random. Instead it was based on convenience, judgement or an attempt might be made at random choice by taking items in an haphazard manner. Where convenience ruled, the auditor took February for wages, as it is the shortest month, and, say, August for sales, because it was the quietest (unless the firm sold ice-cream). Besides this bias, the staff of the firm could foresee the choice being made. To make a judgement sample, the auditor chose a number of items which he thought represented the whole population of items, whilst haphazard choice consisted of taking those items which caught the eye during a run through documents or lists. Both these methods were subject to subconscious bias on the part of the person selecting the sample.

The old-style test-checking has now been superseded by statistical sampling which is carried out by accountants and auditors whose grounding in mathematics has been greatly improved in the last few years. The choice of items is now as nearly random as it is possible to make it in the particular circumstances of a sample, and meeting this condition means that any inferences which can be drawn from the sample results can be applied to the whole section of data within confidence limits which one can measure. For instance, the auditor can say that, from the results given by random sample, he is 95% confident that the true value of the stock-in-hand is between £500,000 and £525,000. Besides the need for randomness of choice, the size of the sample is also a factor in these measurements. The number of items chosen must be "adequate" so that there is room for the randomly chosen items to be representative of the whole, but a general rule is that the more items one has the time to test, the better.

Sampling is suitable for those classes of transactions which are of large volume but have small individual values, and are subject to the same internal control procedures. An example is sales invoices covering a large number of items of low value. Items which are of high value and unique in themselves should not be sampled but require a complete check. Examples are investments and the purchase of buildings. The characteristics of each of these items are peculiar to itself, and though they are all controlled by the internal procedures, they do not form a population of like nature as is the case with sales invoices. In addition, an error is more likely to be material in view of the larger amounts of money involved in each case. Even in cases where sampling appears appropriate, the internal control must be checked to ensure that it is adequate and being properly applied. (The reason for this is that sampling needs a population of similar items, and if the internal control is defective, then all the items have not been treated in an identical manner, and are thus not similar). Therefore, if the controls are inadequate or their observance is poor, then sampling should be avoided and a full check made (and even then the auditor may remain disatisfied with the completeness and accuracy of the records). Another instance where sampling is ineffective is in a case where the extent of a fraud needs to be ascertained — it is a good rule that sampling should be abandoned as soon as fraud is discovered in an area of the accounts. (Again, because the population is no longer made up of similar items — some are affected by fraud).

When the auditor desires to use statistical sampling, he can carry out the following procedure: —

(a) He defines the aspect of the data which he wishes to test, e.g. whether invoices bear the correct budget codes, whether the authorising officer's initials appear, whether an invoice is correctly calculated, etc. He tests the data for its suitability for sampling i.e. the volume is large, the individual values are small, and the financial control is adequate and in operation. He assures himself that he has the whole range of items accessible to him from which to select his sample.

(b) If each item has its own serial number, then random numbers can be chosen from a table or generated by a computer program, and those items whose numbers are the same as the random numbers are those checked. As many items are chosen as can be handled in the time available, or, where the auditor has laid down some pre-conditions about confidence limits, the required sample size can be obtained from tables or calculated.

If the items are not numbered, each nth item may be chosen, taking care that the number chosen for n does not coincide with some sort of cycle of repetition in the data.

There must be no substitution of a more accessible item (e.g. a filed invoice) for one that has been indicated but is hard to get at. Such actions ultimately could cause bias in the results given by the sample and make any conclusions drawn from them misleading.

(c) The items selected for inclusion in the sample are now tested in respect of the chosen aspect (or aspects, as a random sample may be used for different tests, usually as separate operations), and inferences about the whole of the data are drawn from the sample results. For instance, confidence limits for the rate of incorrect calculations in all sales invoices could be expressed in the following manner − "we are 95% confident that the error rate in sales invoices is between 0.1% to 1.9%.

As previously mentioned, a sample may be used for more than one purpose. A sample of documents may be drawn in order to test the adequacy of the compliance with standing orders and checked for the required initials which show that the staff have followed the procedure. The auditor may come across errors in calculations on the documents and thus may use the sample (plus more items randomly drawn, if the auditor wishes) to do a check of transactions to ascertain the occurrence of miscalculations.

On occasion, data may be divided into strata, especially where values are being estimated. In valuing stock by sampling, the items may be sampled at different levels according to their value. The most valuable stock items may be checked completely, the less valuable ones sampled to a decreasing extent as their values fall. This produces a definite figure for the most valuable stock and reduces the uncertainty in the final total value arrived at for the whole of the stock.

The commonest forms of sampling which are used by an auditor are discovery, estimation and attributes sampling.

Discovery sampling is of use when the auditor is prepared to accept a given unavoidable but fairly low rate of error, non-compliance with internal control procedures or even minor cases of fraud (e.g. private letters sent via the office post) but he wishes to be fairly confident that if the rate of occurrence rises, his sample, which he takes periodically, is large enough to contain at least one example of the error, non-compliance or fraud. For instance, an auditor can be 95% confident of finding at least one incorrect invoice where the error rate is 2% or more by taking a sample of 148 invoices. This method is thus a defence against things getting out of hand whilst an auditor remains unaware of the changes.

Estimation sampling is useful for testing whether figures, mainly in the nature of totals, such as stock-in-hand, debtors, creditors, purchases and sales, etc., are reasonably accurate. The sample result gives an indication of the range of values within which the book figure should fall. Taking an example where 10,000 different lines of stock are held, and assuming that the auditor takes a sample of 100 of the categories, and obtains a mean value per line or category of £50 and a standard deviation of £10, then he could be 95% confident that the total value of the whole stock should fall between roughly £480,000 and £520,000. If the book figure is £507,453, then it is acceptable according to this test.

Attributes sampling can be used to monitor the rate of error or other occurrence in a clerical procedure. A small number of instances is sampled at intervals of a day, week or month, and the results are charted. If the trend line for the number of errors, etc. starts to rise to show the rate of occurrence is increasing, the matter is investigated.

Mention might be made of the terms "directional sampling" and "alternative population" which relate to the technique of sampling from a set of documents which is more likely to be complete than the set actually under investigation. Thus, if the auditor wishes to sample sales invoices, he can sample instead from the stores issue notes (i.e. the alternative population) which "direct" him to the corresponding sales invoices. The advantage of this method for the auditor is that to select from the sales invoices might lead him to miss cases where there was a failure to prepare an invoice from the stores issue note.

A difficulty experienced in using statistics for auditing purposes is that, while one is recording an error as an event, there is no difference in treatment between 1p. or £1,000,000 so far as the theory is concerned. For this reason, in an attempt to quantify error in money terms, cumulative monetary unit sampling is being developed. The basic calculations are somewhat involved and assessments of the adequacy of internal control and estimates of materiality (i.e. the value at which an error in the accounts becomes too large to be acceptable to the auditor) are required.

(xi) *Surprise and unpredictability.* The use of surprise is an extremely useful technique, mainly, in cases involving failure to comply with internal control requirements or fraud, though the auditor must always try to be unpredictable in carrying out his tests and to keep to himself what he is actually checking and why. Visits to establishments may have to be arranged in advance and be at regular intervals but he can vary the order of calls now and again, and very occasionally retrace his steps. A surprise audit of a petty cash imprest an hour after the regular audit may reveal matters of interest, such as unauthorised I.O.U.s. It must also be emphasised that items to be included in a sample must not be revealed prematurely as they may receive special treatment before the auditor gets to them, and another confidential matter is the use of ticks and other marks, the different shapes and colours signifying what has been checked and for what aspect.

(xii) *Analytical methods.* Mention has already been made of the usefulness of organisation charts, index numbers, ratios, and sampling to the auditor in his work. In addition to these, there is a host of techniques available to him for analysing the figures he is auditing. There are flow diagrams and process charts for systems analysis, time graphs for cash flows, control charts for sample results, correlation and regression for forecasting, and a whole range of what are called significance tests which use mean values and measures of dispersion to indicate whether data has changed in nature.

Explanations of most of these techniques are best obtained from the study of textbooks on statistics but brief descriptions of two forms of representation – flow diagrams and process charts – are given below and in Appendix V.

Flow Diagrams
These are used to analyse procedures into logical sequences of actions so that a comprehensive guide is given for the successful completion of the procedure under all possible eventualities. These diagrams are often encountered in connection with computerisation as a means of introducing the logic needed by the machine.

There are two principal symbols,

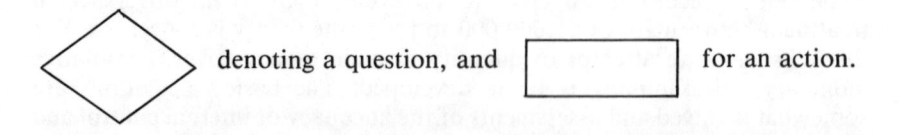

◇ denoting a question, and ▭ for an action.

It is also the convention to assume that the sequence proceeds downwards and to the right and only those lines which do not conform to this are given arrow-heads. In the example, however, most lines have been arrowed to show their direction.

Example
Procedure for the Re-imbursement of an Expense Voucher from a Petty Cash Imprest.

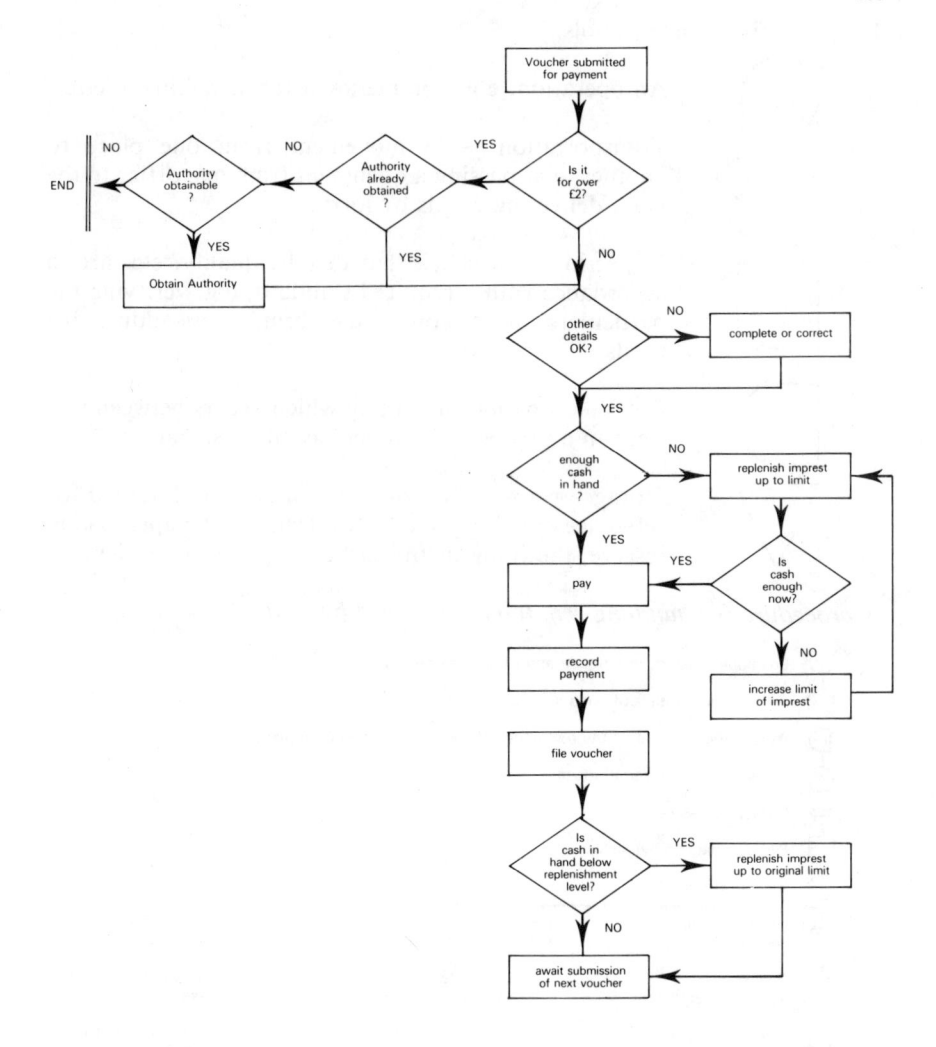

[Flowchart: Voucher payment process]

Process Charts

Another form of diagram which is used to show the various steps in a procedure is known as the process chart. It differentiates between types of activity (or non-activity) and originated in industrial process applications but can be adapted for office and clerical operations. The symbols used in this technique can be superimposed on a map or plan so as to show both the types of activity and the locale in which they take place.

The chart is normally one of two types: –

1. It can show the processes carried out in doing a certain job, or
2. the chain of activities of a person in doing a task.

There are five basic symbols: —

○ An operation, e.g. completing a form, writing a letter.

⇒ Transportation — a movement from one place to another, e.g. passing a document from one office to the next, delivering goods by lorry.

□ Inspection — a check that details, quality, etc. are in accordance with a required standard, e.g. verifying the particulars on a completed form, cross-adding list totals.

D Delay — a period of waiting which occurs between two steps in a process, e.g. letters awaiting signature.

▽ Storage — a wait in some store or file, until needed for reference or use e.g. a ream of headed notepaper held in reserve, the filing of the carbon copy of any order.

A procedure for handling remittances received by post.

○ Envelope opened, remittance and invoice extracted.
□ Amount and details of cheque, etc. checked.
D Awaits the opening of the remainder of the post (placed on a pile).
○ Listed with other remittances
⇒ Passed to cashier
□ Details checked by cashier
○ Receipt prepared

⇒ Receipt to postal section   D Remittance awaits close of business   D Carbon copy of the receipt awaits next day
○ Placed in addressed envelope   ⇒ Taken to bank with other sums   ○ Copy separated from others
D Awaits close of business   ○ Paid into bank or put in night safe   ○ Amount posted to credit of payer
⇒ Taken to post office   ▽ Carbon copy of the receipt filed
○ Envelope posted
▽ Receipt filed by payer

Computer Flowcharts

These are of various types and are used to show the steps in the processing of data through a computer. In many aspects they resemble the charts and diagrams applied to the logic of manual systems except for the employment of symbols representing computer processes and hardware.

Procedure for the Purchase and Allocation to Branches and Budget Codes of Library Books

1. The invoices from the suppliers for the purchases of library books for the past month are put through the certification procedure and coded to budget votes. They are sorted into creditor alphabetic order.

2. The certified invoices are batched, pre-listed total obtained, and converted to punched cards which are verified.

3. The cards are input and undergo a validation program. Any errors are corrected and re-input. The validated data is transcribed on to a magnetic tape.

4. The tape is processed by a program which produces a print-out of cheques, advices, totals for reconciliation, and exception reports, together with a reproduction of the input tape.

5. The data is now sorted into budget code order by a sort program which produces book stock intake (titles and numbers of copies), expenditure code listings, totals for reconciliation and exception reports.

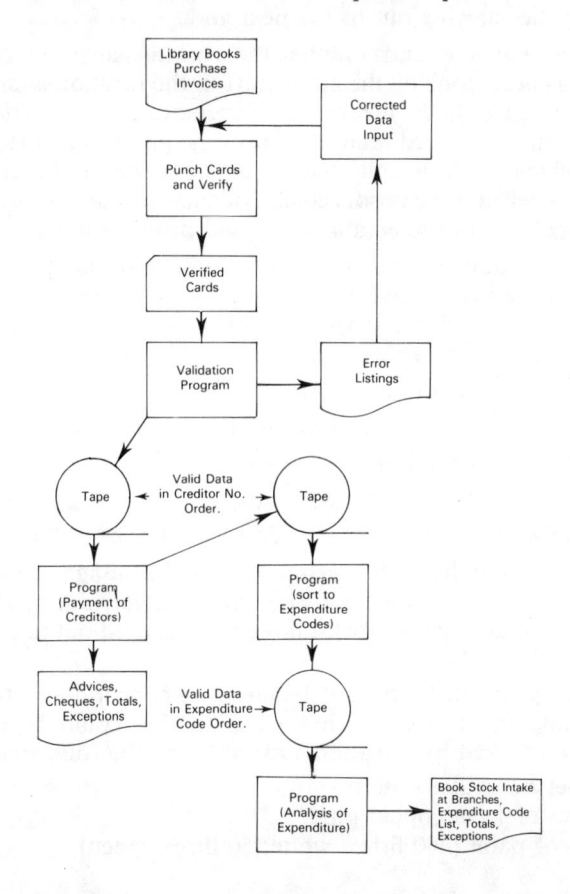

(d) *Review and report*

When the tests contained in the audit programmes have been carried out and their results recorded, the auditor proceeds to analyse the nature and value of any errors which have been discovered, whilst, at the same time considering the possible extent of any errors which have remained undiscovered. He is concerned as to the total effect of both types of error upon the financial figures, especially their reliability. Whilst the known mistakes have been corrected, the manner of their occurrence — by accident, by intentional alteration of figures, by the suppression of documents, by the confusion of capital and revenue, or other ways — and who made them — staff or management — may have implications which need to be mentioned in his report and borne in mind in future audits.

The auditor also reviews the way in which he has carried out the audit work. He considers whether he has used his resources to the best advantage in covering the various classes of risk, whether he has applied the correct techniques to the examination of the largest possible number of transactions as well as the internal control system, and what improvements he might introduce into the carrying out of the next audit.

The next task is to arrange and complete the working papers which show the work which has been done by the audit staff in the form of summaries and analyses of assets, liabilities, income and expenditure, tests carried out and their results, queries raised and the answers given, together with the information which has been collected about the service under audit. These papers may be needed to be produced as evidence in court in, say, a case of fraud, and should be in presentable form and properly indexed.

The auditor's final duty is to report on the results of the audit to the person (or persons) entitled to receive it. In the case of the internal audit, this would normally be the chief internal auditor or some other senior finance division officer or, more rarely, a departmental Head.

Example of an Internal Audit Report

Confidential

To: The Chief Internal Auditor					Date
From: The Group Leader for Housing Audits
Subject: *Deficiencies in Materials for Housing Repairs*

On receipt of a report from the costing section that usage of materials on the Town Centre housing estate had risen unexpectedly during the last few weeks, I requested an interim stock-taking to be carried out in the presence of members of the audit team.

This stock-taking revealed serious deficiencies of copper hot water cisterns, copper pipe and paint, for which no explanation could be given. The shortages were checked by the audit staff as being the following: —

    5 copper hot water cisterns
   100 metres of 1 cm copper pipe
   450 litres of paint (400 litres, white; 50 litres, green)

It is recommended that urgent consideration should be given to referring this matter to the police for their investigation.

I have discussed the circumstances with the responsible officers of the Housing Department, and arrangements for the storage and handling of materials have already been strengthened to my satisfaction.

Distribution of Report:
Copy 1   Chief Internal Auditor (for action)
Copy 2   via C.I.A. for Director of Finance (for information)
Copy 3   Housing Audit Current File
Copy 4   Enquiry File − for Police (if and when needed)

Computerised Systems

An electronic computer is a machine which processes data in accordance with instructions which it carries permanently, or which can be entered temporarily in its own memory. The processes are mathematical, and while a computer is said to be able to add, subtract, multiply and divide, basically it only adds and the other three calculations are obtained by various contrivances. The following examples try to convey an idea of how this is done though, in practice, the procedures are more refined and make use of "position" (i.e. 1 can be 1, 10, 100, etc. according to which column it is in).

For instance, if the maximum value that a computer can handle is 999,999 then to deduct a value, say, 45,000, the input reads "add 955,000" (which is 1,000,000 less 45,000, and is known as the complement). Multiplication is obtained by adding the value the required number of times, e.g. 45 × 3 becomes 45 + 45 + 45. Division is a little more complicated − the complement of the divisor is repeatedly added to the dividend until the answer is of the desired degree of accuracy, e.g. 45 ÷ 15 is obtained by 45 + 999,985 + 999,985 + 999,985 = 000,000 i.e. zero, and the answer is 3, being the number of repetitions needed.

The computer is called electronic because its internal workings (if one can call them that) are entirely electrical, with no moving parts. Mechanically-operated parts do occur, however, for instance, in the input and output units − paper tape is sprocket fed, line printers move the paper and the hammers.

There are five main elements in a computer, each of which carried out a phase of its operations.

1. The data, having been converted into a form that the machine can read, is INPUT via an INPUT DEVICE, such as a card or tape reader. The data may also be keyed via a key-board terminal direct into the computer without the need for conversion into machine-sensible form.

2. The data is placed in STORAGE in the MEMORY which can take the form of magnetic tapes, drums, discs, etc.. Tapes and exchangeable discs can be removed from the computer, stored and re-loaded when needed.

3. When the data is needed for processing, it is called from storage by the CONTROL UNIT which indicates what operations are to be performed upon it. This unit reads each instruction contained in the program in turn, and arranges for it to be carried out.

4. The operations are executed by the PROCESSOR, COMPUTING UNIT, or ARITHMETIC AND LOGIC UNIT which is designed to do the simple arithmetic involved in adding, subtracting, multiplying and dividing. As it can decide which of two values is the greater, the processor has the power to make decisions by choosing the greater or the lesser, whichever, is indicated by its instructions as the "better". Thus if stock held falls below the re-order level, the computer can ascertain this and re-order.

5. The processed data is now fed through an OUTPUT DEVICE which reproduces it in the form required by the program. There are a variety of media available, according to whether the output is to be read by human eyes or by machine, e.g. line printers, optical printers, visual display, microfilm, etc. for the former, magnetic or paper tape, punched cards, for the latter, and optical character recognition and interpreted punched cards for both. (An interpreted card has the characters which the holes represent, printed along its top edge).

The above five elements (input and output devices, storage, control unit and processor) along with the media (tapes, etc) are termed "hardware", while the expression "software" is used to describe the program of instructions which tells the computer what to do and in what order. Software can also include such items as tuition in programming skill and methods. Thus a magnetic tape is itself hardware, but if it contains a program, its contents are the physical manifestation of software.

The Organisation of the Computer Department

Because the use of a computer concentrates the processing of data into a few hands, the degree of internal check must be made as high as possible even though there is not the scope for dividing up the work which is found in manual methods. The electronic data processing department is usually divided into a number of sections – the control section, the data preparation section, the computer room, the tape or file library – under the control of an operations manager. Then, separately, there are the systems analysts and the programmers who may be in two sections, or may work in teams as one section, under a manager with a suitable title. Both these managers report to the computer manager who has overall responsibility for the efficient running of the department.

The Processing of the Data

The internal control system for the processing of the input into output allocates the procedures and duties to the various sections in the following way: –

1. The control section is the sole authorised channel between the computer department and the user departments whose data is to be processed. At the times laid down input documents are submitted to the control section by authorised personnel of the user department. These documents are batched, pre-listed, and pre-totalled (number of documents, total monetary or other unit values, and/or hash (or nonsense) totals, e.g. of the vouchers' serial numbers).

2. The batch or batches of vouchers are passed to the preparation staff who convert their contents into a machine readable form, e.g. punched card, paper tape, etc.. The input media are returned to the control where totals are agreed with those of the pre-lists, and then forwarded to the computer room for processing as required by the schedule of job-timings.

3. The computer room staff (the operators) process the data by subjecting the input to the program tapes which have been issued to them from the library (again in accordance with the job-timing schedule). The operators keep a logbook of jobs done, times, errors, corrective actions, operator on duty, etc.. The output is forwarded with the input media to the control section whilst the programs go back to the tape library.

4. The control section once again reconciles the output total with the pre-listed totals, and otherwise tests the output for accuracy before sending it to the persons in the user departments authorised to receive it. In financial applications, the user department staff authorised to submit input to the computer should ideally be different persons from the staff authorised to receive the resultant output, e.g. cheques to pay creditors.

Programming Arrangements

The designing of the programs (i.e. the tasks and procedures which are computerised) is carried out by systems analysts and programmers in collaboration. There are procedures for checking the programs for errors (i.e. de-bugging) to ensure that when they are brought into use they give the required results. There is also a variety of internal checks which can be incorporated into the program, e.g. the validation of codes as being on the official list. Programs can be kept on magnetic tape and read into the computer when needed for processing the data for a specific job. The tapes are passed for safekeeping to the library and only issued on proper authorisation. Amendments to the programs are strictly controlled to prevent errors and unauthorised alterations.

Other Aspects of Internal Control

1. The manual systems of the organisation, particularly in the departments handling data before input to the control section, and after data is output by the control section, must be in accordance with internal check principles of checks and controls in the division of duties.

2. Access to the computer department should be restricted to authorised personnel, and be via the control section which should be as far as most outsiders would penetrate. In addition, staff belonging to the sections of the

department should be controlled as to entry into other sections, e.g. programmers should not be permitted in the computer room during processing as they might interfere with operations — for instance, substitute a punched card in an input stack with a fraudulent one, and replace the correct one later. Out-of-hours access also needs to be controlled, doors and cabinets should be locked, etc..

3. Precautions must be taken against fire, damage, failure of the environment (temperature, air conditioning, etc.), and standby arrangements should exist if breakdown occurs from these or other causes such as power failure. Standby arrangements should cover the safety and confidentiality of the data besides the basic need to get the input processed on a compatible computer.

4. The vital importance of a high level of accuracy should be reflected in the insistence upon employing staff of ability. Recruitment and training procedures must exist to maintain or improve the calibre (quality) of the various classes of staff involved in preparing source documents. It must be remembered that an error in the input can affect many aspects of the output as the item in error can be used in several applications without the intermediate checks which would probably be found in a clerical system operating under internal check principles of dividing duties among members of the staff. An incorrect creditor's invoice could cause errors in the expenditure analysis to purchases, the creditor's personal account, the cost accounts and stores records (goods received), ratios of purchases/sales, the cheque and its accompanying advice note, all without any opportunity to query it at the time.

5. Any internal control system must incorporate provisions for automatic periodical reviews of the adequacy and degree of compliance with the laid-down orders (and their possible improvement).

Mini-computers, Micro-computers, and Terminals

The development of desk-top computers, terminals linked to main-frame computers, and accounting machines programmed to carry out specific computing tasks, means that the procedures whereby all processing is channelled through a computer department become impossible to enforce. The principles of control and internal check applicable to the computer areas now need widening to areas in the remainder of the organisation, viz. restricted access to the machines and terminals, the use of identifying keys and codes to input data or to obtain information, the inclusion of tests within the programs to query unusual items or instructions automatically (i.e. the computer being programmed to report attempts to mainpulate its actions or records).

The Audit of a Computerised System

An organisation which has a computer section for the processing of its financial data, may be divided into two parts for audit purposes. Firstly, there is the origin of the transactions and their preliminary recording in the executive departments which create the input to the computer, and then there is the handling in the executive departments of the output after leaving the computer section. These operations are governed by traditional methods of control and conventional audit techniques are applicable. No transaction must fail to reach the computer and no output must fail to arrive at its legitimate destination. The other part is the computer section where traditional methods of control and conventional audit techniques also play their part but a new dimension is introduced by need to check what goes on inside the machine.

The auditor starts the audit of a computer section or system in a similar way to that in which he would approach any other system. He reviews the adequacy of the internal check and other control procedures by means of I.C.Q.'s, his own observations and corroborative tests. Then he tests the degree of compliance with the approved system. As with any other administration, the internal control system defines the duties and regulates the actions and movements of the staff, protects hardware, files, media and documents from unauthorised interference, ensures correct processing of authentic input into accurate output, and anticipates breakdown or other stoppages.

Assuming that the auditor is satisfied with the internal controls, he now proceeds to vouch the transactions which requires him to ensure that the programs do exactly what they should, that all data is processed without omissions, all error reports have been dealt with correctly, and no unauthorised activities have occurred in connection with the processing.

To check that the programs have been properly de-bugged (i.e. contain no errors which would cause incorrect output), the auditor has two choices of action (or he could do both). He can audit "round" the computer or "through" the computer.

To audit round the computer, he checks the accuracy of the input and uses a "test pack" (a program designed to cover all possible variations and exceptions in the data) to obtain output which is checked against that given by the actual program, or he uses the "black box" technique, where some data is processed manually and again compared with what the computer prints out. He can also use "interrogation programs" which interrogate the memory banks by linking two or more aspects of the stored data to reveal unusual items for further study. The auditor needs to know nothing about computer programming to do these things but there is always the danger that he is missing something. The test packs may not cover all the possible eventualities, the items chosen for the black box method may not include those in error, and the interrogation programs may not ask the right questions.

On occasion, the auditor may need to require data to be printed out in order to obtain documentary evidence of the accurate processing of the source data. He may also use the computer to assist him in his audit work, for instance, by selecting random samples of items for his inspection. (It must be remembered that computer time is money and the auditor must adapt his call on computer time to the overall demands on the computer).

Auditing through the computer means that the auditor undertakes the study of computer programming, so that he is accomplished enough in systems design, flow charting, assembling programs, operating the console, etc. to decide whether programs are accurate and contain no unauthorised manipulations or illogicalities. He can supervise and assess any alterations suggested or found necessary in programmes as well as the error correction procedures undertaken by operators. Another important addition to his powers is the ability to suggest (and insist upon) the inclusion of program controls and checks, such as tape identification and control totals or record counts, validity checks on codings and results of calculations, access by password, audit trail to previous item of the same nature, etc..

Fraud in Local Government

In public authorities it is the responsibility of the members, either elected or appointed, to take care of the funds placed under their stewardship, and via the management, to take the responsibility for the prevention and detection of fraud within the organisation. The external auditor is not required to guarantee to find all cases of fraudulent activity in the accounts for the period he audits, nor, in fact, to search specifically for such cases unless he has received some indication of their presence. His duty is to plan his work and carry it out in a professionally competent manner which will ensure that he has a reasonable chance of finding any significant frauds, and when he becomes aware that something is not in order, he must investigate it thoroughly. (This is known as "being put on enquiry"). The internal auditor, unlike his external counterpart, is a member of the management but within the scope of the work allotted to him by management, his approach is essentially the same professionally, although he does not have the statutory responsibilities carried by the external auditor.

Fraud may be looked upon as occurring in three main ways, and for this purpose may be regarded as: —

(a) acts carried out by staff members with the intent to misappropriate or misuse assets or to obtain some unearned or unauthorised reward from their work whilst concealing the effects of the fraud by some deceitful means, such as the falsification or, even, the destruction of records. Fraud by employees of an organisation may be betrayed by the occurrence of out-of-the-ordinary entries or unauthorised transactions which may not be evidenced by documents, by continuing inadequate internal check (especially where complaints from the public are dealt with by one person), and by unexplained transfers in the accounts just before and just after the year end. The attitude of employees to questioning may also indicate areas for enquiries — for instance, flippant or non-committal answers, refusal, vagueness or reluctance to provide answers or documents.

(b) actions taken on the orders of top management which result in the production of financial statements (Revenue Accounts and Balance Sheets, etc.) which are meant to mislead the reader by distorting the view given of the state of the service, business, etc.. One example might be the overstatement of the value of the closing stock-in-hand to give a larger surplus or to reduce a deficit for the period of the accounts in question.

(c) information of an incorrect or misleading nature which has been given by members of the public with a view of obtaining for themselves some financial or other kind of advantage from an authority. This could include the giving of incorrect income details in order to obtain a rate rebate or the tenancy of a council dwelling by jumping the queue.

The question of dealing with cases of fraud discovered in accounts under audit by an internal auditor is extremely complex as each case is unique in itself. General rules are thus somewhat difficult to lay down and opinions differ on the methods undertaken and the ordering of events and actions in investigating any individual cases. For instance, there is the difficulty, in practice, of deciding exactly when the police should be brought in to a case of alleged fraud, though the theoretical answer is probably "the earlier, the better", because they prefer to obtain and bear witness to evidence which they have collected themselves, rather than use that of other persons. The following suggestions cover a hypothetical case and are provided with some hesitation because of the complex nature of such situations, but it is felt that they should be given for the sake of completeness and in order to make the student aware of the need for care and the obtaining of advice in handling investigations.

Where an internal auditor becomes aware that there are irregularities, either past or occurring, in the accounts, records or behaviour of the staff he is auditing, he must first ensure that his facts are correct by re-checking them exhaustively and then report them to his group or team leader who will then take charge of further investigations. (Where information has been supplied by an informant, the auditor should tell him that he might eventually be required to give evidence in court).

The auditor in charge now needs to obtain as much background and supporting information as he can before he takes further action. Such information includes the amount of recorded evidence and personal testimony and its degree of availability, reliability and legal acceptability, the possibility that the cause of the irregularities was not fraudulent acts but errors or inefficiency, perhaps occurring under stress, the extent to which specific individuals may be involved and their record of service to date, the existence of weaknesses in the internal control system which could give opportunities for fraud, and whether the present position discloses the full extent of any unauthorised operations or is only "the tip of the iceberg".

(The group auditor will have informed the chief internal auditor immediately the matter was raised and the chief internal auditor will have reported to the director of finance).

After the senior auditor has considered these points and had such further checks carried out as he considers necessary, he is eventually faced with the decision, given that he is still of the opinion that the matter must be proceeded with, to interview the person or persons involved. Before he does this, he will inform the chief internal auditor of his intention (and through him, the director of finance and the head of the department involved). It may be possible to hold an informal man-to-man interview in order to discuss the matter and give the officer the opportunity of explaining his actions where the matter is fairly trivial or unclear and the officer has an unblemished record of service over years. On the other hand, the auditor may decide to be formal and arrange for the sequestration of the records and vouchers containing the evidence of irregularity in order to prevent their disappearance, destruction or amendment.

One person is usually interviewed at a time and the interview must take place with at least two officers present besides the suspect (i.e. the auditor and a colleague, and, often, a representative of the department involved, and, perhaps, a policemen, where circumstances give rise to the need because the police are already involved from an earlier investigation). The auditor should on no occasion be left alone with the interviewee.

The interview must be planned to bring out the facts in an impartial manner by asking the suspect in a courteous but persistent manner for explanations of how the events took place and the entries were made in the books. There should be no threats, pressure or duress nor any offers of inducements to obtain answers. The auditor is required to have regard to the Judges' Rules which apply to the obtaining of evidence, and he should have studied these before the interview. Failure to observe the rules, may give rise to questioning of the way he carried out the interview when the case reaches court. In addition, as soon as the auditor becomes aware that he has reasonable grounds from the evidence and the answers, to suspect the interviewee of having committed a fraud, he must immediately give a caution before any more questions are asked. The required words are — "you need not say anything, but if you do, it may be taken down in writing and given in evidence". It is often recommended that the auditor should stop the interview immediately he becomes aware that he should caution the suspect, rather than continue and run the risk of transgressing the Judges' Rules and weakening his case in court. Where a policeman is present, he could, of course, take over if his opinion agrees with the auditor's. Care must be taken in dealing with a person who says he wishes to confess, and it is often recommended that he should make it to the police who should be asked to attend, if not already present. It is also recommended that notes should be taken of the questions and answers during the interview or immediately afterwards.

After the interview has finished, the auditor's next step is to consult his superiors (the chief auditor, the director of finance and legal staff are involved as well as the appropriate committee) and either inform the police himself or be contacted by them via his superiors, where further proceedings are called for.

Audit Committees

Audit committees were first formed in the United States of America (where they are now common) as a way of guarding an organisation against the danger of producing misleading financial accounts or related information. Such information could be deceiving, for instance, in the way it is presented or the assumption it carries that the underlying records and internal controls are adequate in effect upon the figures produced. As management is responsible for the reliability of all such matters, the committee is an instrument whereby board members and senior staff are involved directly with auditing policies and practice.

The main area of development of audit committees has been in limited companies (or corporations, as they are usually called in the U.S.A.) and whilst they have spread to other countries, their occurrence here has been to date somewhat rare. It is normal practice for the committee to consist of up to six persons chosen from among the directors and top managers. The committee reports to the main board on the matters referred to them, and the director members are often "non-executive" which means they are on the board because of their experience and knowledge of the business and can be impartial because they are detached from the actual running of the firm.

The committee's terms of reference often include such matters as the settlement of disputes between management and the external auditors, the encouragement of collaboration between internal and external auditors, the need to divert resources to the internal audit function where it has been neglected, the review of financial statements before they are finally issued and the education of staff on the need for good internal control and, especially, a high degree of compliance with standing orders.

The transplanting of the idea to public sector organisations has been suggested, arguing that there is a role for an audit committee made up of a small number of experienced members who would carry out specific duties laid down by financial regulations on similar lines to those ruling in commerce. The performance review sub-committee of the policy and resources committee of a local authority as suggested in the Bains Report is also mentioned as suitable to take on audit committee duties. It is argued that as it already investigates current methods of carrying out policies for ways of introducing internal economies, and is, on occasion, helped by internal audit, the added duties are a logical extension of its present ones and may well strengthen them.

Behavoural Auditing

This subject has several names and is in danger of meaning different things to different people. It is called "Human Aspects of Auditing", "Participative Auditing" and "Behavoural Approaches to Auditing" besides the title given here. It embodies a new attitude to audit work.

The idea behind the proposal to adopt behavioural auditing is for the auditor to discard his traditional, independent, somewhat inflexible and figure-oriented approach to audit and to adopt a more sociable attitude in carrying out this duties. By this, it is meant that the auditor should take part in a battle for the minds and hearts of men. He should take account of the thoughts and feelings of those whose work he audits and convert them from a possibly antagonistic, or at least, unhelpful or suspicious state of mind to a degree of participation and cooperation by representing, with conviction, the audit's success to be a necessary part of the overall success of the organisation.

Various suggested lines of action are available to the auditor: –

1. The auditor should lose his reputation as a "policeman" and try to make those whom he audits to regard him as someone they can consult and who will help them with problems in their work.

2. He should require procedures to be set up for enabling management to contribute to the audit. Managers and other staff can offer advice as to the areas needing improved control and attention from the auditor. This participation would be especially useful in auditing systems but the audit of individual transactions would have to remain impersonal as at present.

3. The discovery of errors in the records should no longer be counted as a victory for the auditor and a defeat for the audited. (Such an attitude is vehemently denied by auditors but it exists within the minds of the persons whose errors have been found, especially as there is no chance of retaliation, for who audits the auditor?). An error found should be looked upon as a means of showing where joint action can bring improvements in standards and any apportionment of blame should be resisted.

4. There should be informal meetings to consider audit reports before they are finalised and issued on such matters as system defects with the staff of the management services section who installed the systems being criticised. The same arrangements could apply with departmental matters, where the staff involved could put their point of view. Such reports might be amended in the light of the discussions and the further facts which come to hand, and staff attitudes significantly softened so far as the auditor is concerned.

Whilst the proposals for equipping the auditor with a "human face" are applicable to both sets of audit, it is usually felt that they have more relevance to the internal auditor than the external one.

Most debates upon the advantages and disadvantages of adopting these lines of action finish, however, with the acceptance that the auditor must retain the ultimate sanction of adopting his role of policeman and acting with reserve in cases where probity is in question, as opposed to error. There appears no way, in view of the frailty of human nature, in which the auditor can dis-arm himself completely if he wishes to do his work properly. While the majority of people are honest and would respond to treatment, there is a small but ever present minority who would turn the situation to their advantage.

Questions

8.1 Outline the legal requirements in connection with the internal audit arrangements of local authorities.

8.2 Describe some of the techniques which are available to an auditor in carrying out an audit.

8.3 Give a brief description of the steps involved in carrying through an audit.

8.4 To which points should an auditor direct his attention in reviewing the operation of a computer installation?

8.5 What are the main advantages and disadvantages of continuous auditing?

8.6 Why should an auditor use audit programmes and what drawbacks should he bear in mind in doing so?

8.7 Describe what is meant by a flowchart and discuss the pros and cons of using such a technique in administration.

8.8 Indicate what matters you would expect to be dealt with in financial regulations in regard to the banking of money received on behalf of a local or public authority.

8.9 What action should an auditor wish to see taken when a cheque sent by a local authority in payment of an account is reported as lost by the creditor concerned?

8.10 What advantages does the use of statistical sampling give to an auditor and what difficulties might he experience in employing the technique?

8.11 Draw up a flow chart for the essential steps in the procedure of a local authority for approving applications by persons buying dwellings, for loan advances under the Small Dwellings Acquisition Acts.

The conditions to be fulfilled are: –

a. The dwelling must be within the area of the local authority.

b. The valuation of the property concerned must exceed the loan asked for. If not, a reduced advance is offered to the applicant.

c. Personal particulars, e.g. income, employment record, character references must be satisfactory and assurances must be given by the would-be borrower as to residence in the dwelling.

8.12 Show, in the form of a process chart, the basic elements in a buying procedure and include the issue of a purchase order in quadruplicate and its subsequent employment.

8.13 What duties could be given to an Audit Committee in a local authority?

8.14 Outline what you understand by the term "Behavioural Aspects of Auditing".

Chapter 9

Water Authorities

Historical Summary

There is ample evidence to be found in archeological sites that water engineering was first introduced to this country by the Romans. During the centuries of their occupation they built fairly complex systems of waterworks, aqueducts and pipes to carry water to their villas and cities for public baths, fountains, lavatories and washing places, as well as to meet the basic need for water for drinking and cooking purposes. Remnants of their work can be seen in excavations in places such as Bath, Chester and York.

After the Roman armies withdrew from Britain, the incursions of the Angles, Saxons and Jutes, who were followed by the Danes and the Vikings, brought the so-called Dark Ages and the loss of much technology, including that of water supply. Thus, up to the 19th century − over a thousand years after the fall of Rome − the inhabitants of this country drew water mainly by hand from local springs, wells, rivers and lakes. This water was, of course, untreated, and, indeed, the people had little idea of sanitation, but as they lived for the most part in rural areas and were relatively thinly dispersed, there was not too much pollution from their own waste products. Nevertheless, there were epidemics of water-borne diseases, such as cholera, and these grew commoner and more serious as the small mediaeval settlements were turned by the Industrial Revolution into towns and cities which became more and more congested and industrialised.

Public water supplies via aqueducts and pipes began to be organised in some cities, but many people in the larger towns (and especially London) were still forced to use springs and wells which were obviously polluted by seepage from latrines, dung-heaps and rubbish tips. In the 1830's and 1840's, there were a series of grave cholera epidemics which killed thousands of people and resulted in Parliament passing the Public Health Act 1848. Under this Act, local Boards of Health were formed to provide pure water supplies and to ensure adequate draining facilities within their allotted areas. Water companies (i.e. privately-owned public utility limited companies) began to appear, together with municipal undertakings operated by the Boroughs, Urban and Rural Districts which were the successors of the local Boards of Health, and which provided the service under powers given by Private Acts or the Public Health code. This code was progressively refined by a series of Acts until it culminated in the Public Health Act 1936.

In tune with the call for the re-organisation of many public services after the second World War, the Water Act 1945 introduced provisions to be applied in a standardised manner nationally to water supply, although the local authorities still retained their powers as water suppliers.

The next step was taken under the Water Act 1973 which relieved the local authorities of their powers and set up separate bodies (regional water authorities) which could act in unison to provide a national service and make it possible for the nation's water resources to be developed as one operation.

The Legal Basis

The regional water authorities formed by the Water Act 1973 cover nine regions in England (Anglian, Northumbrian, North West, Severn-Trent, Southern, South West, Thames, Wessex, and Yorkshire) and the Welsh Water Development Authority covers the whole of Wales. The Act places duties of a supervisory nature upon the Department of the Environment in respect of water supply, sewage treatment and disposal, the prevention of river pollution and other related matters, and similar responsibilities upon the Ministry of Agriculture, Fisheries and Food in connection with such matters as the drainage of land and the operation of freshwater fisheries. Both the Ministries have the power to give directions to the regional water authorities or to make regulations with regard to their allotted functions. In addition, there is the National Water Council which advises the departments and the authorities on questions arising in the implementation of the national water policy and assists in a number of staffing matters, including arrangements for staff training.

The Council is also responsible for administering the staff pension fund for the whole of the public sector water supply industry and for salaries and wages negotiations with the trade unions involved. It consists of a chairman and ten persons (with experience of the industry) who are appointed by the Minister together with the chairmen of the R.W.A.s. Its running costs are charged upon the R.W.A.s. Other advisory bodies also exist − for example, the Water Research Centre, the Central Water Planning Unit, the Water Data Unit and the Water Space Amenity Commission.

The functions given to the R.W.A.s on the 1st April 1974 came from two main sources. The first set of functions came from the local authority sector and related to water supply and the collection, treatment and disposal of sewage. The second source was the river authorities (which were abolished by the Act) from whom came duties related to the drainage of land, the control of river pollution, and inland fisheries. These transferred duties have been extended and added to under the provisions of the Act as progress has been made towards the planned national water policy. The range of functions now carried out by the water authorities includes the prevention and control of pollution in rivers and streams, measures for land drainage, the use of water-gathering grounds and reservoirs for recreational purposes, the regulation of fresh water fisheries, and the sale of water fittings and appliances, besides the main task of supplying water (including wholesome water for domestic needs). The R.W.A.s also have a duty to conserve, re-distribute and increase water resources in accordance with nationally-decided policies, and can make bye-laws for the prevention of waste or pollution of water.

The majority of the members of an authority are appointed by the local authorities (counties, districts or boroughs) in the region, the chairman and the remainder being appointed by the two central departments involved. Only the chairman (and the chairmen of the regional and local land drainage committees) receives pay, although all members can claim allowances for expenses and losses arising from the carrying out of official approved duties.

Each R.W.A. is a separate legal entity. It has a distinct existence in the eyes of the law from its members and officers who act in its name. It is called a statutory or public corporation, and it has the power to do anything which it considers will facilitate the performance of its duties − which appears to permit the authority a very wide discretion in what it does, so long as the objective is relevant and not actually illegal, whilst undue extravagance is avoided. The R.W.A. can also appoint such officers as it thinks it needs for its functions to be properly carried out.

Except for the issuing of a precept (for land drainage costs) or the borrowing of money (and a few minor matters), the authority can arrange for the carrying out of its functions by a committee, a sub-committee or an officer, or, on an agency basis, by another R.W.A. Certain committees are required to be appointed by law, for instance, the land drainage committee which is statutory. Otherwise, as with the appointment of officers, the authority can form such committees as it wishes. These can include a policy and resources committee similar in powers and duties to those found in local government, and functional committees to deal with such matters as the use of water space by yachting clubs and others. Joint committees may be formed with other bodies on matters of common interest, and members of the public can be co-opted on to most committees up to a maximum of one-third of the total membership.

Because of the extensive area of operation of the regional water authorities, it has been found necessary to split the regions into divisions, and to share the various functions of management between the regional headquarters and the divisional offices. The headquarters staff is headed by the chief executive who leads a team of officers − the director of finance, director of operations, director of administration, director of resource planning, and such other officers as the authority considers necessary − to advise the members of the authority in the taking of decisions and to carry out such decisions and to co-ordinate the work of the divisions generally. Each division is controlled by a divisional manager who is in charge of a team of officials who are responsible for playing their part in the carrying out of the authority's functions as laid down by the authority in its scheme of divisional delegation.

A number of water companies which were formed in the early days of water supply development still operate under arrangements made between themselves and the regional water authorities within whose areas they are situated. Owing to their involvement in the present structure of the industry, these undertakings are subjected to a measure of control in matters of finance which goes well beyond that which is normally found in commercial and company law as applied to limited companies.

The water authority has a legal duty to provide a water supply for domestic purposes but can ask for a payment (called a "guarantee") to be made to it for a number of years in a case where it has had to provide a new main and the water charge from the supplies does not cover a reasonable portion of the cost. Water for commercial and industrial purposes must be supplied on terms which are not unreasonable. Such supplies may be refused, however, where they would over-tax the authority's water resources (especially where it would put at risk its power to supply water for domestic purposes). There are also obligations to provide water for public safety and public health purposes, such as hydrants for firefighting and supplies to public baths.

Local authorities were relieved of their power to supply water under the Water Act 1973, but they still possess duties related to the wholesomeness of water and the sanitary standards of dwellings. In addition, local authorities have the power to pay towards the above-mentioned "guarantees".

The role of the Secretary of State for the Environment under the Water Act 1973 is, as has already been said, to supervise the actions of the regional water authorities, jointly with the Minister of Agriculture, Fisheries and Food, in implementing a nationally-decided water policy. (He and the R.W.A.s are assisted in their operations by a number of advisory bodies.) Besides the Ministers being answerable to Parliament in respect of their actions in carrying out their allotted duties, they also possess a number of other powers and duties aimed at giving them the necessary degree of control. They have the right to appoint some members of the Authority (and the power of appointment brings with it the power of dismissal), the power to give directions on matters which are considered to be of such importance by the Government that the R.W.A.s must act in accordance with the wishes of the State, the power to issue regulations, and to approve (i.e. confirm) bye-laws governing water supply and other activities. Further areas of control include the approval of capital programmes and borrowings, the operation of external financing limits (often referred to as cash limits), and the agreement of targets, such as an annual rate of return on capital, and the use of performance measures and indicators, such as unit costs of manpower. In addition, the individual authorities must make Annual Reports to the Minister on their activities and finances, and must always supply him with any information he thinks he needs in order to carry out his statutory supervisory and co-ordinating duties.

The regional water authorities maintain systems of liaison for the purposes of joint action and the receipt of advice with local authorities and other organisations which represent the interests of industry, commerce, farming and the general public and consumers in their areas. One good example is found in the provision of amenities for recreation on and around reservoirs, for which there is a growing demand from persons with competing interests. In addition, there are internal arrangement for dealing with complaints and representations from consumers but such persons may also approach councillors of local authorities who are members of the Authority, and, if still dissatisfied, they may complain to the Local Ombudsman. This official is an independent Commissioner appointed under the Local Government Act 1974 with the power to enquire into matters of mal-administration. (R.W.A.s are only one of the public authorities subject to his enquiries and you are referred to the appropriate section of Chapter 4). The arrangements for the external audit of the financial accounts also give opportunities to local residents to make enquiries and representations, as the R.W.A.s are under the same audit as local authorities. Finally, matters can be brought to the notice of local Members of Parliament who may raise them on suitable occasions in the House of Commons or before a Select Committee (particularly, the Select Committee on Nationalised Industries).

Finance

Regional water authorities are required to make sure that, over a period of years, their income should be enough to meet their costs. For this purpose, costs are taken to include a proper provision for the depreciation or renewal of assets and sums taken to the reserve fund.

Their sources of current income include the water rate for unmeasured supplies (i.e. to houses and other property which has no meter), and for sewage collection (i.e. sewerage costs), treatment and disposal, charges for metered and bulk supplies (i.e. measured), charges for the treatment of trade effluent (i.e. industrial liquid waste discharged into the sewers), the sale of by-products, and a large variety of minor sources of income. Precepts are leviable by the R.W.A. in recovering the cost of land drainage from local authorities whose areas are involved. As with most public corporations and nationalised industries, the water authorities must not show undue discrimination in fixing their charges against any class of customer. The water rate (or to give it its official description, the water supply, sewerage and environmental services charges) is the major source of income and is very similar in character to the general rate levied by rating authorities. It is an amount per £ of the rateable value of the property which is levied for a period (usually a year). The rateable value comes from the same valuation list as that used by the rating authorities. Differences do occur, however, as, though the debtor can go to prison for non-payment if the R.W.A. follows the rating procedure via the magistrates, there is an alternative way of enforcing the debt via the county court which does not necessarily lead to imprisonment. Finally there is the power to cut off the supply under certain circumstances, which is not available in respect of the general rate.

The water and sewerage charge differs from the local authority rate in two other aspects. First, there is no automatic right to pay by instalments beyond the half-yearly sums laid down under the Act, though domestic consumers are offered the concession of paying in four instalments. Second, there is no provision for rebates for people in need, as exists for the general rate — this has caused criticism because the sewerage charge, especially, used to be part of the local authority rate.

The Government operates measures of control over water authorities' capital expenditure programmes and their borrowings to finance the schemes included. Loans may normally only be obtained from the National Loans Fund though there is limited access to temporary borrowing and to loans from overseas. There are, however, other sources of an internal nature which can be used to meet capital expenditure or to repay some of the existing debt. Firstly, there is the temporary use of internal funds. Secondly, there are revenue contributions to capital outlay whereby capital items are paid for out of current income. Thirdly, there is what is called the Internal Financing Reserve (which is also referred to as the Internal Capital Financing Provision) which is fed from two main sources. The first of these is the charging of supplementary depreciation on the fixed assets, so that the Revenue Account is charged with amounts in excess of what would be normally considered as adequate, and these are credited to the Reserve. The second source is the Central Interest Account. This is credited with the difference between the interest actually paid on loans and the interest which would have been paid if the current rate of interest had been paid on the written-down value of the authority's assets. This difference is held to be the cost of temporary finance provided by using the authority's internal resources and each activity is charged with its share of the benefit it has received. The credit balance on the Central Interest Account may be transferred completely to the Internal Financing Reserve or if only part is taken there, the rest is taken to one of the Reserves which form part of the working balance.

The idea of creating an Internal Financing Reserve was adopted as a way through the difficulties which each R.W.A. faced when it inherited the assets and liabilities of the former municipal water undertakings and sewerage and sewage disposal systems in 1974. The transferred services are capital intensive in nature, which means that expenditure on capital assets and works is heavy, and the local authorities had financed it in the past out of long-term loans. The new authorities were thus required to pay a large proportion of their income in the form of debt charges on this inherited debt. Furthermore, the 1973 Act required higher standards of service and allotted new duties which called for improvements in facilities, whilst the local authorities had tended to defer schemes of development as they became aware that the services were to be taken from them. The new water authorities were therefore faced with the need to borrow heavily, if they continued the former practice of the local authorities, and suffer a corresponding growth in the already heavy loan charges. In addition, there were limits to the sums which could be borrowed under the external cash limits system and the source of loans was restricted to the National Loans Fund.

The only way in which the R.W.A.s could hope to relieve the position was to finance as much capital expenditure as possible (and perhaps repay some of the crippling loan debt quickly) out of internally-generated funds. At the same time, internal funds were at a low ebb when they were handed over by the local authorities who had run down the level of working balances as the date of the transfer approached. There was little relief available there.

Soon after the transfer, the suggestion was made that as the R.W.A.s were to be run on commercial lines, they should discard the local authority approach of regarding debt repayment (i.e. the annual sinking fund contribution repaid to the Loans Fund) as equivalent to depreciation, adopt the commercial approach of calculating asset values and charge adequate depreciation against revenue. This idea was adopted and it resulted in the divorcing of capital payments from loans. Dealings in loans were thereafter treated merely as a means of regulating the cash flow. It might be of interest that the depreciation provision exceeded the former loan repayment instalments, as the assumed lives of the assets were shorter than the sanction periods.

The decision was then taken to charge supplementary depreciation over and above the basic provision, and the taking of this sum to an Internal Financing Reserve, as has already been indicated. It can be argued that this procedure and the Central Interest Account adjustment have assisted in an inordinate rise in water charges over the last few years, but against that it can be said that a rise was unavoidable in view of the need to carry out essential work (such as replacing the collapsing Victorian sewers in the large cities) and to build up working balances.

Criticism of the increases in water rate and other charges led to the formation of a central fund for the industry under the Water Charges Equalisation Act 1977 with the aim of introducing a measure of equality in levels of charges whereby those authorities and companies whose charges are below average are required to contribute via the fund to those whose charges are above average. Contributing authorities have reservations about the justice or financial good sense of this scheme.

The Water Act 1973 requires each R.W.A. to prepare a long-term view of the development of its region over the next 20 years and the central departments have called for medium-view plans covering five years to be used as the basis to the long-term plan and the annual estimates. This procedure fits in with the national economic plans embodied in the Public Expenditure Survey (or PESC) system mentioned in Chapter 15, as the water supply industry's figures are a component of the public sector payments and receipts.

Each regional water authority must prepare its accounts each year, and, after they have been audited, send a copy together with the auditor's report (as part of the statutory annual report) to the Secretaries of State who must present them to Parliament where they are the subject of further scrutiny and report.

The National Water Council is the administering body for the superannuation scheme for the various classes of employee of the regional water authorities, who act as employing authorities in arrangements akin to those applicable to local government (where the county administers the superannuation scheme for its own staff and those of the districts in its area). The similarity between the two stems from the fact that the majority of the employees were transferred from local authority funds in 1974. The salaries and wages of employees are also centrally negotiated by the N.W.C. but there are arrangements at regional and divisional level for consultations in which craftsmen, manual and non-manual personnel are represented.

The water companies operate their own superannuation scheme in regard to their employees and are also affected by any nationally-agreed revisions of staff conditions of service.

The Form of the Published Accounts

The financial accounts of the regional water authorities are prepared in a format which has been arrived at by agreement within the water supply industry, so that the financial performance of each region can be compared more effectively with the others.

The Revenue Account is made up of several separate sections, each dealing with an aspect of the service: –

Water Resources

Water Supply

Sewerage and Sewage Treatment and Disposal

Maintenance of Water Quality

Pollution Control

Provision of Recreation and Amenities

Fisheries

Land Drainage and Flood Protection.

The balances on these sectional Revenue Accounts are carried to a Summary Revenue and Appropriation Account, the balance of which appears on the Balance Sheet.

The Water Resources Revenue Account contains the costs of maintaining the reservoirs and gathering grounds, the transfer of raw water (i.e. untreated) between reservoirs, the monitoring of flows and the carrying out of research. It is credited with charges for abstracting water which are levied upon individuals, firms, and, as a matter of transfer to the water supply function, on the authority itself.

The Water Supply Revenue Account is charged with the abstraction charges already mentioned plus the cost of obtaining raw water from other sources.

It also bears the cost of treatment and the distribution of the now treated water to the consumers. The account is credited with the charges made upon the consumers for measured and unmeasured supplies (by meter, when the consumption is measured in litres or gallons, or by rate, when it is a number of pence in the £ on the rateable value, though there are special charges for some kinds of use).

The Sewerage, Sewage Treatment and Disposal Revenue Account contains the appropriate costs indicated in its title, and is credited with the proceeds of the sewerage rate and the charges for the treatment of trade effluent.

The Recreation and Amenities Revenue Account deals with the costs of facilities for fishing, boating, yachting, walking and other pastimes which are provided on and around the reservoirs and other properties owned by the authority. Charges are made to the people and associations which use these amenities, but this Account is normally in deficit.

The Land Drainage Revenue Account is charged with the maintenance costs of drainage works, sea defences and flood warning systems. It is credited with the proceeds of precepts on local authorities and grants-in-aid from the Government.

The contents of the other minor Revenue Accounts are indicated by their titles.

The Summary Revenue and Appropriation Account shows the operating surplus for the year for the authority as a whole. (It is supported by a statement showing the totals of the income and expenditure and the surplus or deficit on each activity). This operating surplus is added to the balance in hand brought forward from the previous year. The excess arising from the Central Interest Account is then added, and thereafter deductions are made in respect of appropriations to Reserves (General) and to the Internal Financing Reserve. The resultant balance carried forward to the next year appears on the Balance Sheet.

The Balance Sheet, like the Revenue Accounts, is in narrative Form, and shows the Fixed Assets analysed as to date of their acquisition — either pre-vesting or post-vesting. The Fixed Assets are then shown as financed out of Loans Outstanding, the General and other Reserves, any excess of Current liabilities over Current Assets, and the balance of the Summary Revenue and Appropriation Account.

The annual accounts are supported by a Statement of Source and Application of Funds, a Statement of Accounting Policies (which explains the treatment of certain of the items in the accounts), together with details of Fixed Assets and their costs, Depreciation Provisions, Loans Outstanding and Interest Paid, as well as a subjective analysis of revenue expenditure and income over all the authority's activities. (Subjective analysis is by Employee Costs, Running Costs, etc.) Comparative figures in respect of the previous year are also given where appropriate. A current cost Profit and Loss Account is also to be included in the published annual accounts.

Audit

The financial accounts of the National Water Council, the regional water authorities in England and the Welsh National Water Development Authority are all subject to the same external audit arrangements as those of local authorities. The bodies are free to choose either district or approved audit, and, at present, only two have selected district audit (Thames Water Authority and the Welsh National Water Development Authority), the remainder being under approved audit. As the authorities are required by the Water Act 1973 to prepare final accounts and to send them with the auditor's report to the Minister, there is no requirement, as there is with local authorities, to issue an abstract of accounts.

Internal audit arrangements are also similar to those applicable to local authorities in being statutory in character and employing the same practices and techniques. One aspect in the audit of the accounts of water authorities which is of interest is the need to examine the expenditure and income of district and borough councils on the sewerage system in their particular areas. This is because the local authorities have been made agents of the water authorities by Section 15 of the 1973 Act (although there is discretion about the terms of the agreement) and are entitled to be reimbursed their net expenditure on approved work. From the water authorities' point of view the task is a mammoth one as each authority is involved with scores of local authorities. In addition, there are four sets of auditors involved in the situation – two internal and two external – all of them statutory. Thus, whilst the internal audit of the arrangements is current in nature, the external audit of each body involved will tend to occur at a different date, especially in coming before or after that of the water authority. In at least one instance, this has led to a water authority's external auditor qualifying his report in respect of sums involved in uncompleted local authority audits.

Questions

9.1 What functions are carried out by the Regional Water Authorities?
9.2 For what services and on what bases do Regional Water Authorities make charges?
9.3 Outline the arrangements for the external audit arrangements in the water supply industry.
9.4 By what means can a Regional Water Authority prove responsive to public opinion?
9.5 What are the functions and constitution of the National Water Council?
9.6 In what ways can the central departments control the actions of the R.W.A.s?
9.7 Outline the manner in which the administration of a R.W.A. is carried out.
9.8 Describe the working of the Internal Financing Reserve of a R.W.A..
9.9 What are the powers of the Local Ombudsman in regard to a R.W.A.?
9.10 What power has a R.W.A. to appoint officers and committees?

Chapter 10

Passenger Transport Executives

Historical Summary

Primitive systems of transport existed in this country in mediaeval times in the form of coaches for the rich and waggons for goods and persons who could not afford their own carriages. The predominant method of travel was, nevertheless, by horse which was often the only means negotiating successfully the muddy tracks which served as highways at that period. The middle of the 17th century, however, saw the appearance of the stage-coaches which developed a network of routes which linked London with the larger towns in the provinces. These stage-coaches called at inns where passengers were taken up or set down, and as they only travelled during daylight, the journey from London to York took seven days, because of the shocking state of the roads.

Nevertheless, travel by stage-coach was for the relatively wealthy, and there were no facilities for the less affluent, other than to walk (or as the expression goes – "use Shanks's pony") unless they could beg a lift from a waggoner who was going their way. This was particularly the position in the towns, as town-dwellers could only travel from one part of the town to another on foot or by a conveyance that they owned or had hired themselves.

In 1829, an ex-coachman, a Mr. Shillibeer, started a service of horse-drawn omnibuses (the name given to buses at the start because they were "for everyone" to travel in). These supplied a service on a route from Paddington to the Bank of England through the central part of London. This venture proved successful and was the fore-runner of similar enterprises in other parts of London and elsewhere in the country. In 1855, a number of these London companies came together to form the London General Omnibus Company which ultimately came to serve practically all of the capital.

A few years later, tramways (sometimes called street railways) were introduced to this country. They, like buses, were drawn by horses at the start, but steam engines were used to some extent for a period, but, ultimately, the trams were powered by electricity supplied by means of overhead cables.

Whilst buses and trams were competing with each other in serving the built-up areas of the country, the railways had developed the old stage-coach system out of all recognition and were also competing to an increasing extent by linking the suburbs and centres of the larger cities.

To begin with, all these forms of transport were in private ownership but towards the close of the 1800's, the local authorities of the time (e.g. the county and municipal boroughs and the urban districts) were given the legal powers to run bus and tramway undertakings. One advantage of municipal involvement in passenger transport was that the local authorities tended to combine the two transport media within their areas. The tramcars usually followed a number of mainline routes to which they were restricted by the need for a permanent way consisting of rails set into the highway and overhead wires carried by poles, and the buses served the more out-of-the-way parts of the town or those which were unsuitable for trams by being, for instance, too hilly.

The early years of the 20th century saw the introduction of the bus powered by a petrol engine. The petrol-driven bus was victorious in a war which raged at that time between it and steam-driven and electric buses. The L.G.O.C. inaugurated its first horseless bus service from Hammersmith to Piccadilly in 1904 and the last horse-drawn bus was withdrawn from service in 1910 in the London area. The trams now began to feel the weight of the competition from the new type of bus. In spite of the cheapness with which trams could be run after the capital costs of the rails and wires had been met, they began to be gradually superseded. Other factors which brought about the triumph of the bus were its greater degree of comfort and quietness in running and its flexibility in following routes, as it needs no tracks. Nevertheless, the tram carried many more passengers than the bus — it was estimated that five trams took as many passengers as eight buses.

The final stages of the change-over to buses occurred after the cessation of hostilities in 1945 when almost all the trams left the roads of the towns and cities of the country. (Blackpool is an exception, as trams still operate there along the seafront and the "Golden Mile"). The removal or covering up of the rails gave room for more petrol-driven traffic and eliminated a source of street accidents, as the tracks used to become greasy and slippery, especially in wet weather. Just before the first World War, the bus undertakings began to bring competition to the railways by running outings into the country for town-dwellers at cheap fares, and by the later 1920's, long-distance coaches were taking further business from the railways, both as regular services and as excursions to the seaside and elsewhere.

As the 20th centry proceeded, the growth in traffic began to cause congestion on the roads, particularly in the London area, where the out-of-date roads, increased population and the building of dormitory towns made travelling difficulties greater. This problem applied, of course, to most of the larger provincial cities as well, but conditions in London, as the seat of government, are always more apparent to the politicians in power than difficulties elsewhere in the country. Consideration was therefore given to the means of improving the public transport facilities in the capital, and this resulted in the formation of the first public corporation to provide and co-ordinate such facilities in a conurbation in this country.

This corporation was the London Passenger Transport Board which was set up in 1933 to be responsible for operating the bus and underground railway services in London. However, in comparison with modern ideas and practices, the degree of integration was small, as the local authorities of the time were responsible for the building and maintenance of roads and for traffic matters, whilst the main railway system was owned and operated by privately-owned limited companies.

The outbreak of the 1939-45 war delayed any further experiments in the co-ordination of urban transport until the Transport Act 1947, as part of the programme of nationalisation, created the British Transport Commission which was given the task of organising an efficient system of public transport and port facilities for passengers and goods for the whole country. The Commission operated via Executives, and the L.P.T.B. was dissolved and the London Transport Executive of the B.T.C. took its place. In the event, the centralised nature of the Commission, the hugeness of its assignment, the varied nature of its activities, and the criticisms and opposition it met from many sources, resulted in its dissolution in 1963 after little had been done about improving road passenger services. So far as London was concerned, it once again became subject to a public corporation of its own — the London Transport Board.

The next attempt to solve the problems of public transport was aimed at the major cities. The necessary legal basis was contained in two statutes. The first was the Transport Act 1968 under which the Secretary of State designated four passenger transport areas. These areas were under the control of passenger transport authorities and operated by passenger transport executives and comprised the following conurbations (or metropolitan areas, as they now came to be called) — Merseyside, South East Lancashire and North East Cheshire (SELNEC), Tyneside, and West Midlands. The second Act was the Transport (London) Act 1969 which dissolved the London Transport Board and gave its functions to the London Transport Executive which was to be controlled by the Greater London Council, acting as passenger transport authority for its area. The final step to reach the present position relating to passenger transport was taken under the provisions of the Local Government Act 1972.

The Legal Basis

The 1972 Act brought the provincial conurbations into line with the arrangements under the 1969 Act in London and the change operated from the 1st April 1974 when local government in the areas outside Greater London was re-organised. The new metropolitan county councils were made into Passenger Transport Authorities, South Yorkshire and West Yorkshire having been added to the original four of the 1968 Act. Outside the metropolitan counties and Greater London, the shire (or non-metropolitan) county councils were given the duty of encouraging the formation of a co-ordinated and efficient passenger transport system, and all the operators of bus services in their areas (i.e. local authorities, private firms and the National Bus Company) were required to co-operate with the policies of the county council.

In the non-metropolitan county areas, district and borough councils often operate bus undertakings under national legislation or Local Act powers. Each is allotted an area of operation and is subject to the supervision of the local Traffic Commissioners whose approval is needed to all changes of fares and service facilities. The legal framework within which the local authorities work includes separate accounts, methods of treating surpluses and deficits, powers of acquiring assets such as vehicles, land and buildings, and the making of agreements with other operators for inter-operation and through running across boundaries. As already mentioned, each authority must co-operate with the county transportation plans.

The metropolitan county council usually acts through a transportation committee in its capacity as the passenger transport authority. The committee is made up of members of the county council and other local authorities in the area together with a number of persons appointed by the Minister of Transport. The P.T.A.'s duty is to lay down the general policy which the executive should follow in its efforts to run a properly integrated and efficient public transport system in the metropolitan county. To ensure that the executive obeys the authority, the executive cannot act in certain crucial matters without the authority's approval. Such matters include the completion of the annual estimates or budget, the decision to levy precepts upon rating authorities to meet deficits on the Revenue Account, the implementation of major capital schemes, the borrowing of money, the form in which the capital programme is submitted to the Department of Transport, major changes in services, the compulsory purchase of land or its sale, and the revision of fares and charges. The P.T.A. must hold an annual meeting and at least three others each year and these are to be chaired by a member who has been elected chairman by the remainder.

The passenger transport executive is made up of officers and other persons appointed by the authority to implement policy and to carry out the actual work of management of the transport undertaking. It can, subject to the consent of the authority in the cases mentioned above, do anything which is required for the purpose of the undertaking, such as acquiring land by agreement or compulsorily, buying other businesses, providing catering services, handling luggage, carrying goods, repairing and maintaining vehicles, etc. One of the duties of the P.T.E. is the integration of the various forms of passenger transport in the area. It was given the existing bus, ferry, and other companies owned by the local authorities and has power to acquire any privately-owned firms it considers it needs, but the railways remain under the control of the British Railways Board. The executive is therefore required to carry out a continuous review of the rail services available to people travelling to and fro up to a maximum of 25 miles beyond its boundaries. If British Rail is required to supply such services against its own wishes, the P.T.E. must meet any loss incurred. The Minister may direct the P.T.E. to review and enter such arrangements, and

Government grants may be paid towards the deficits met by the P.T.E. in such cases.

The executive is a corporation with a legal existence separate from the authority. Its signature is its common seal which is affixed to all important documents, contracts, precepts, etc. The members of the P.T.E. are mostly chief officers, e.g. the director-general, secretary, and directors of finance, operations, planning, industrial relations, etc. and other persons who have experience of public transport operations. Meetings are at least monthly and chaired by the director-general, and decisions are reached on a corporate management basis, which means that the officials act as a team. The Government department which is responsible for supervising the general policies concerning the nation's transport arrangements is the Department of Transport. The Minister of Transport has a number of statutory duties under the Transport Act 1968, such as the appointment of some members of the passenger transport authorities, the giving of directions to executives for them to make agreements with British Rail regarding commuter services, (directions can also be given on transport matters which the Government thinks must be carried out in the national interest), the approval of Transport Policies and Programmes submitted by the counties as passenger transport authorities, the giving of consent to borrowings and the application of the external financing (or cash) limits. Some duties which are usually allotted to the Minister or Secretary of State to enable him to control any particular class of public corporation, are, in this instance, given to the county council, as mentioned in the previous paragraph. The Minister of Transport also appoints Traffic Commissioners who form a tribunal in each Traffic Area for the control of standards of design, safety and performance levels of buses – the Commissioners license the vehicles, operators, drivers and conductors, ensure that the buses are in a proper, roadworthy condition to carry people, are managed in accordance with regulations, and are manned by reliable staff. They also consider applications for increases in fares and changes in the service supplied. The Transport Act 1980 has introduced a degree of relaxation of the conditions under which licences to operate are granted, together with the extension of the right of the public to take part in car-sharing schemes.

P.T.E.s are required to make arrangements by such means as joint consultative committees for discussions to take place and decisions to be reached on matters of staff conditions of service, such as salaries and wages, safety at work, etc. between the management and the representatives of the workforce.

There is machinery for dealing with complaints from the public on the level of service in the form of a section of the administration of the P.T.E. which makes internal investigations but, in many counties, there are advisory committees set up by the county council on a non-statutory basis with the duty of representing the users. The National Transport Consumers' Council (which was previously called the Central Transport Consultative Committee for Great Britain) and below it, a regional system of transport users' consultative committees deal with the standards of service provided by various forms of inland transport, including buses. These organisations may approach bus operators with suggestions and also make annual reports to the Ministry of Transport. Other ways in which public opinion may be expressed are by approaches to councillors of constituent local authorities who are members of the executive, via the external auditor in the annual audit procedure (i.e. inspection of the documents, questioning of the auditor and objections to items in the accounts), and perhaps to the police where platform staff are incivil to passengers — incivility is an offence under the Road Traffic Acts.

The staff of the passenger transport executive are members of the county superannuation fund (the county council is the P.T.A.) under arrangements as to deductions from pay and benefits receivable which are mentioned in Chapter 3.

Each passenger transport authority and its executive are required to produce and publish a joint annual report on their activities. It is normally combined with the audited financial accounts in brochure form.

Finance

The Transport Act 1968 lays down that the accumulated balance on the Revenue Account of the executive must always be a credit, i.e. an amount in hand. Thus, the income must be enough to exceed the expenditure over a period of years, though occasional annual deficits within the above condition appear acceptable. Expenditure is also defined as including a proper, adequate charge for the depreciation of fixed assets or their renewal, together with any amounts which the P.T.E. thinks are necessary to be paid into a Reserve Fund. The terms of this Act are narrower than those normally applied to a public corporation (these are usually to "break even over a period of years"), and this implies that the Government does not intend to carry out any rescue operations where a crisis is caused by an executive delaying decisions to increase fares or to introduce economies in its operations.

The executive includes the following among its sources of current income — fares paid by passengers, charges for the private hire and contract hire of coaches, charges for carrying parcels, income from advertisers (inside and on the outside of buses, on the backs of tickets, etc.), sales from catering, rents of kiosks and other properties, various grants from the P.T.A. or the Government in support of concessionary fares, bus or railway route costs, and rebates on fuel costs.

On the capital side, the P.T.E. has the power to borrow money for various purposes, such as the financing its capital expenditure on buildings, works, plant and vehicles, the provision of working capital, and the buying up of transport undertakings and businesses of a related nature. The amounts borrowed and the executive's capital programme (which indicates the future capital expenditure) both need the approval of the authority and the

Minister, and, in addition, the Minister supervises the operation of the system of cash limits (or, as they are often called, "external financing limits") as laid down by the Government. The executive is empowered to borrow money in ways similar to those available to local authorities generally, and this includes access to the facilities of the Public Works Loan Board. Over the last few years, in line with the rest of the public sector, there has been an increasing tendency to avoid capital expenditure and the problems of borrowing, depreciation or renewal provisions by leasing assets such as buses and other vehicles, plant and machinery, etc.. Internally generated funds are also used to finance capital schemes, and one such fund can be created by depreciating the assets on the basis of their replacement value instead of their historical cost, writing down the assets by the lower figure and earmarking the excess.

The Form of the Published Accounts

Each passenger transport executive is required by law to prepare annual accounts in a form which is laid down by its P.T.A. and must send a copy of the accounts and the auditor's report to the Minister of Transport and to its constituent councils in its area of operation. The accounts are in consolidated form because they include the operations of both the executive and its subsidiary companies, such as coach firms, property companies, etc..

The Consolidated Revenue Account is in narrative form and contains the transaction relating to passenger transport activities, analysed between road and rail services, and other activities, such as the carrying of freight. The Account shows the income and expenditure and the resultant surplus or deficit arising from each activity, together with items of income and expenditure of a general nature, such as income from investments.

The Consolidated Balance Sheet is also narrative in form and shows the fixed assets and net current assets from which are deducted the current liabilities, so as to leave a balance which is financed from loans and reserves of various classes. There are notes and schedules which show how the items on the Balance Sheet are made up and a Statement of Source and Application of Funds is also given.

Statistics are presented covering various aspects of the executive's transactions and operations, such as mileages run and numbers of passengers carried by bus or rail, numbers of the different classes of employee (i.e. drivers, conductors, inspectors, engineers, etc.), numbers of buses and other vehicles, and of bus depots and stations. Corresponding figures are given for the previous year in the financial accounts and in many of the statistical tables.

Audit

The arrangements for the external audit of the financial accounts of passenger transport executives are laid down by the Local Government Act 1972, and are thus, in essence, the same as those applicable to local authorities. Most P.T.A.s have chosen, on behalf of their executives, to take approved audit, instead of the district audit. The subsidiaries of an executive are subject to audit under the Companies Acts but the auditor for the P.T.E. reports on the consolidated accounts for the whole of the group. So far as the internal audit is concerned, this occupies a similar position to that of a local authority.

Questions

10.1 What is a Passenger Transport Authority, a Passenger Transport Executive, and the relationship between them?

10.2 Outline the sources of income to a Passenger Transport Executive.

10.3 What are the arrangements for the external audit of the accounts of Passenger Transport Executives?

10.4 Indicate the main legal requirements governing the financial accounts of a Passenger Transport Executive.

10.5 Outline the functions of the Traffic Commissioners.

10.6 What are some of the powers of the Minister of Transport in relation to Passenger Transport Authorities and Executives?

10.7 What difficulties led to the formation of the London Passenger Transport Board in 1933?

10.8 For what actions and decisions does a P.T.E. need the consent of the P.T.A.?

10.9 In what ways can a person complain about the standards of a publicly-owned bus service?

10.10 What legal rule applies to the Revenue Account balance of a P.T.E.?

Chapter 11

Development Corporations for New Towns

Historical Summary

Up to fairly recent times, the founding of a settlement and its later development into a town was influenced by many factors which interacted in a somewhat arbitrary manner. In the first place, the choice of the site was governed by a number of features, such as the availability of water, food and fuel, the presence of a hill or other geographical feature providing a defensive position, the occurrence of some natural resource, such as metal ore, and the nearness of a river ford, harbour or trade route. The changing importance of these and other factors decided the way in which the settlement grew or died out.

While it is true that instances can be quoted of towns being founded in a planned manner, especially by the Romans, the original grid-iron pattern of the Roman fort, if it survived the Saxon invasions, was soon hidden by a hotchpotch of rude dwellings occupied by people who lived there for reasons other than the military ones which caused the building of the fort originally.

After the close of the mediaeval period, the idea of creating planned communities which might be said to foreshadow the concept of New Towns, began with the building of model villages by land-owners with a progressive outlook for their tenants and estate workers, and the provision of "company towns" by industrialists of possibly like mind to house their workforce. Later, garden cities, as they were attractively named, were planned and erected by land developers for those who wished to escape from urban spread, and, in the thirties of the present century, local authorities built large-scale self-contained housing estates as suburbs to the larger cities. Wythenshawe in Manchester is an example of this approach.

The moving of large numbers of people into the countryside, by creating new communities there, was first conceived as part of the British nation's post-war policy to relieve congestion and overcrowding in the war-damaged and run-down centres of the country's larger cities, such as London, Liverpool and Birmingham. The laying out of new suburbs was at that time (and still is), to any great extent, out of the question, because of the existence of "green belts" around many urban areas where building of all kinds was restricted, if not completely prohibited. The green belts are designed to prevent neighbouring towns from merging, and are earmarked for agriculture, woodlands and recreational purposes. The sites for the first New Towns were thus in the open country.

The New Towns Act 1946 was enacted and the process began of forming development corporations which were each in turn given the task of establishing and developing a self-contained community in an area designated as suitable for the purpose by the Secretary of State for the Environment (to give the present title of the responsible Minister). Whilst the most common objective in designating a New Town is, as has been said, the reduction of over-population in the larger cities, some have goals which, though related to the main purpose, differ somewhat from it. For example, Newtown (a coincidence in names which must have given occasion to confusion) in the county of Powys in Wales was intended to bring to a halt and eventually to reverse a trend to depopulation in Mid-Wales, whilst Corby in Northamptonshire was designated in the hope of reducing that area's dependence upon the steel industry by diversifying local employment opportunities. As time passed, one can discern a change in approach to the selection of sites as the Government became aware of the extra costs and difficulties experienced in creating a community from nothing but open agricultural land in comparison with those faced when a New Town was sited where some basic services were already present.

It is thus possible to detect three possible stages in the evolution of New Towns. The first wave was designated between 1946 and 1950 when 14 New Towns were started in undeveloped country areas and were allocated target populations of some 100,000 people. The second stage occurred from 1961 to 1966 with the designation of eight sites which were mainly on the fringes of existing centres of population where some infrastructure (i.e. roads, sewers, water supply, local services generally) already existed. Their intended populations were between 80,000 to 180,000. The third development took place from 1967 to 1970 when seven New Towns were started. These tended to be larger in scale than those of the two previous generations, as their ultimate populations were to be between 200,000 and 250,000 in most cases, though Red Rose in Lancashire was to contain 430,000 people. The intention in the case of these New Towns was that they would link up numbers of small towns and villages. The town of Red Rose, which was the last to be designated, has not been proceeded with by the Government.

Approximately 30 New Towns have been designated so far, (of which 21 are in England and two in Wales), and the present climate of official opinion is that no further New Towns should be started in the foreseeable future, and that finance should be diverted to the regeneration of the run-down inner city areas. For this reason, emphasis is now being given to urban aid programmes, partnership schemes involving local and central government, and proposals to set up urban development corporations in the dock areas of London and Liverpool. Proposals have also been made for New Towns to sell off a significant proportion of their assets to bring in sums to the national Exchequer.

The Legal Basis

The law underlying the development of New Towns is contained in the New Towns Act 1965 (which consolidated the Acts of 1946 and 1959), the New Towns Act 1968 and the New Towns (Amendment) Act 1976 and the supporting regulations.

The process of forming a New Town begins with the selection of a suitable area and its designation as a site by the Minister who then appoints a number of suitable persons to be members of the development corporation. They comprise the chairman, deputy chairman and up to seven other members. The appointments are part-time and salaries are paid. The development corporation is a separate legal entity (i.e. a public or statutory corporation) and a seal is used to sign important documents on its behalf.

The administrative arrangements are under the control of a general manager who leads a team of specialist officers − planning, engineering, architecture, finance, legal matters, estate management, etc. − appointed by the corporation. The chief finance officer acts as accountant, collector and paymaster as well as adviser on the appraisal of the financial effects of future policies. He is also the officer who provides the Government departments with the estimates and forecasts of expenditure which they demand as part of the system of central control over the activities of the development corporation.

After all the members and staff have been appointed, the first task facing the development corporation is to draw up proposals for the development of the area. These proposals require the approval of the Secretary of State who must be satisfied that the rate of return on the capital to be invested is reasonable. If he is satisfied with the proposals, he give the necessary planning approval and gives authority for money to be advanced from Government funds to meet the costs of development as they are incurred. When the development corporation has in all important respects completed the New Town, it is dissolved and its assets and liabilities are dealt with in accordance with the law which, however, has changed from time to time as Government policy has altered. Under the original New Towns Act of 1946, the local authorities and statutory undertakers for the area took over the assets and liabilities of the dissolved corporation. Thus, housing, schools, gas, electricity and water installations, etc. went into the ownership of the appropriate public organisation. The New Towns Act 1959 altered this procedure as the Government had come to realise the revenue-earning potential of the New Towns in respect of rent income when they were complete. In response to the criticism that assets which had been paid for out of national funds, should not be given away in order to benefit localities, the Government, therefore, decreed that all housing and commercial or industrial estate property should be transferred to the Commission for the New Towns (a new public corporation), whilst the rest of the assets were dealt with in substantially the same manner as under the 1946 Act. This arrangement has been further amended by the New Towns (Amendment) Act 1976 which provides for the transfer of New Town housing property to the local housing authority under certain conditions. The Act provides that such transfers can be made where the Minister directs that consultations are acceptable and, either the Commission for New Towns already holds the houses, the New Town is already 15 years old or the New Town appears substantially complete. It is intended that neither profit nor loss should arise on the transfer and that the property transferred is accompanied by the debt outstanding on it.

The site chosen as suitable for a New Town may be completely rural, completely urban, or a mixture of town and country. Whatever the character of the original site, however, the intention is to make the community, when it is fully developed, complete and self-contained in respect of shopping facilities, employment opportunities, and amenities for a variety of sports and recreations, so that the New Town's inhabitants have every opportunity to develop a distinct civic consciousness akin to that possessed by people who live in longer-settled neighbourhoods. One characteristic which may, however, distinguish New Towns from older areas is that the proportion of young people tends to be greater in the New Towns.

The corporation has a duty to provide various classes of dwellings (for rent and for sale), factories, shops, officers and other buildings. It has the power to buy, sell or lease land, carry out building and other works on land, provide gas, electricity, roads, car parks and sewerage facilities. In effect, it can do anything necessary for the developing of a new community. It must be realised that the forming of a development corporation and the designating of an area as the site of a New Town do not remove any powers and duties from the existing local and other public authorities already serving the area. Thus, instances where duties overlap between the development corporation and the other authorities occur fairly often and the Government has found it necessary to lay down guidelines which suggest how the costs of providing services are to be shared.

The Secretary of State is responsible for supervising the activities of the development corporations and the Commission for the New Towns and has been given certain statutory duties in this respect. He is answerable to Parliament in regard to the manner in which he carries out these duties and the general effect is that he can be questioned on matters of general policy connected with the New Towns but the routine management is outside the ambit of his duties. This independence of the management from Government interference into routine affairs is one of the reasons for adopting the legal device of a public corporation to implement Parliament's wishes. Nevertheless, if a routine matter becomes important enough by, say, repetition or aggravation, the Minister may need to answer Parliamentary questions. The New Towns Acts do, however, give the Secretary of State the power to give directions to the corporations and the Commission as to the way in which they carry out their duties. Such directions are normally made in the national interest, such as conforming with the demands of national economic plans, for example, selling off assets. Examples of the Minister's powers and duties (including some mentioned elsewhere) include the appointment, dismissal and salaries of members, the appointment of the auditor (who has some duties owed directly to the Minister), the prescribing of the form of the accounts, the requiring of an annual report, approval of capital expenditure proposals, authorisation of sums advanced, the laying down of financial targets and the imposing of the system of cash limits (or, as they are now called, external financing limits).

Finance

The development of a New Town takes an appreciable number of years, and during the early years, the capital costs which do not produce revenue are at their greatest. At the start, land has to be acquired and roads built on it, gas, electricity, water and sewerage services must be laid as well, and all this is without any immediate return, and, what is more, these works are on a scale far beyond the current needs of the population until the provision of accommodation permits people to move in in large numbers. The first years thus show a growing deficit on revenue account. Revenue income begins to rise as the revenue-earning capital assets are created, such as housing, shops and stores, factories and offices. As these properties are completed and are tenanted or leased, rent income grows. The sale of developed land (i.e. land which has been provided with the various services, such as gas, electricity, water, roads, etc.) also brings in capital receipts, but it takes several years, even then, to reverse the trend from increasing deficits to reducing ones. With the completion of the Master Plan (as the approved proposals for the New Town are called), the annual deficit slowly changes to a surplus, but time is still needed for the accumulated losses to be paid off before the properties yield a profit. Ultimately, New Towns, as originally envisaged in the legislation, should be immensely profitable to the Government because although costs and interest they pay are affected by inflation, their property values are similarly inflated. If, on the other hand, many of the properties are sold off, short-term capital profits are made with the loss of long-term revenue profits.

Besides the rents received in respect of the various classes of property, other sources of revenue income consist of Government grants and subsidies in support of the cost of providing housing accommodation, and contributions from local and public authorities in respect of such services as sewerage and sewage disposal. Purely capital income arises from the sale of land, houses and other buildings, and the charging of premiums at the start of leases. Shortfalls in both classes of income against revenue and capital expenditure are met out of borrowings. These mainly comprise advances from the Department of the Environment which are repayable with interest over a period of 60 years. The total advanced is limited to the sum estimated previously by the development corporation as necessary for its revenue and capital needs and working capital. Development corporations may also go into overdraft at the bank for short periods or lend to one another. The leasing of assets has developed in recent years as a method of avoiding capital expenditure.

The Form of the Published Accounts

The financial accounts of a development corporation must be prepared each year in the form which is laid down by the Department of the Environment. The Revenue Account which is in narrative form, is in a number of sections, one for Housing, one for Other Property, and one for Ancillary Undertakings, and the annual balances on these three are transferred to the General Revenue Account which appears among the balances on the Balance Sheet. The Balance Sheet is also in narrative form and shows the cost of capital assets together with current assets less current liabilities, and how they are financed out of the loans, debt redeemed and reserves.

The Housing Revenue Account contains rent income and government subsidies, and the costs of providing the residential accommodation – administration repairs and maintenance, debt charges, etc.. The Other Property Revenue Account contains rent income from industrial and commercial buildings and the cost of their upkeep and debt charges. The Ancillary Undertaking Revenue Account deals with sewage disposal and sewerage costs against which charges for the treatment of effluent and contributions by local authorities are set. The General Revenue Account, as has already been stated, contains the balances of the other Revenue Account sections but also bears the cost of work of a general nature, such as debt charges and maintenance of roads, open spaces and parks, which do not fall into the other categories.

Corresponding figures for the previous year are required for the items in the Revenue Accounts and the Balance Sheet. The accounts are supported by analysed statements of capital expenditure, notes on accounting principles, and statistics on land and buildings owned by the corporation.

Audit

The Commission for the New Towns and the development corporations are subject to external audit in respect of their accounts by persons who are appointed annually by the Secretary of State for the Environment. These auditors must be members of one of the designated accountancy bodies which are qualified to audit accounts under the Companies Acts. The fee paid to the auditor and any variations in giving him extra duties must be agreed by the Minister but in all other respects the auditor and the corporation contract with each other. The auditor also has a number of responsibilities to the Minister, particularly in reporting excessive, unapproved and even unauthorised expenditure incurred by the corporation. As soon as the accounts have been audited, a copy of the audited accounts and the auditor's report must be sent to the Secretary of State as part of the corporation's statutory annual report on its activities and progress. The Secretary of State is required to prepare a statement of the advances made by his Department to the Commission and the corporations, and the sums he has received from them, and submit this statement, accompanied by the accounts and auditor's report for each of the bodies involved, to the Comptroller and Auditor General who lays them before Parliament with his report, after he has examined them.

The arrangements for the internal audit of financial transactions and procedures are the responsibility of the development corporation which is required by law to institute such controls as it thinks necessary for the proper carrying out of financial duties and the adequate protection of cash and other assets.

Questions

11.1 For what purposes are new towns built?

11.2 Outline the first steps in creating a new town?

11.3 Summarise the powers of a Development Corporation.

11.4 What are the main sources of income to a Development Corporation?

11.5 Indicate what actions may be taken when a new town is substantially complete.

11.6 What form does the external audit take in a Development Corporation?

11.7 Outline the advantages and disadvantages of siting a New Town in the open country as opposed to building it on the fringe of an existing community.

11.8 What arrangements can be made regarding housing properties under the New Towns (Amendment) Act 1976?

11.9 Discuss the pros and cons of selling off New Town assets.

11.10 Draw up an organisation chart for a Development Corporation.

Chapter 12

Health Authorities

Historical Summary

The present system of community health care in this country owes its origin to the charity of the medieval monks who provided hospitals attached to their monasteries for travellers, beggars and others, and to the existence of the church parish organisation by which the faithful took care of any of their fellow-parishioners who were ill or in need. The dissolution of the monasteries in 1536/9 by Henry VIII was a great set-back to the order of things, and though the Statute of Elizabeth 1601 placed a statutory duty upon the parishes to look after their sick poor, a number of centuries passed before the situation was recovered. During the 18th and 19th centuries, hospitals were founded in increasing numbers, often by wealthy men of good will. It was gradually realised that there was little value in providing poor people with food, clothing, etc. if they were always too ill to work and keep themselves, and that hospitals were an essential part of any system of rescuing people from poverty by reducing the ravages of disease upon their bodies. This was also accompanied by the use in hospitals of improvements in medical treatment and surgery which reinforced the arguments in their favour. Thus, in the second half of the 19th century, in addition to the introduction of many basic preventive measures for public health in respect of clean water, drainage, refuse removal and housing conditions, there was a wave of hospital building. Most hospitals were provided on the basis of endowments by the rich, voluntary contributions from the public and fees paid by patients for their treatment, but there were also Poor Law hospitals as part of the institutions of the Guardians of the Poor where the needy could be treated. Doctors, midwives, nurses, as well as other practitioners became involved in charity work in poorer areas. An indication of the close relationship seen between the two branches of Poor Law and Health was the creation of the Local Government Board to supervise both. (A further indication of the relationship occurred in 1919 when the Local Government Board became the Ministry of Health).

The early years of the present century saw the local authorities of the time develop various personal health services, such as maternity and child care, medical treatment of schoolchildren, clinics for the treatment of diseases, and the introduction of Lloyd George's National Insurance Scheme divided the doctors' practices between private and 'panel' patients. (The use of the term 'panel' meant that the doctor had an arrangement whereby he received a fee for each insured person on his list of patients). In 1929, the Poor Law hospitals were transferred to the local authorities who thus became involved in the provision and running of hospitals. During the 1939-45 war, the national needs meant the virtual take-over of the hospitals (both municipal and voluntary) by the Central Government. The degree of central control brought out the variations in the level of service throughout the country and indicated that, in any case, there should be an overall improvement in facilities after the war was over. It was further felt that local authorities would have insufficient resources to support the costs of applying new medical and surgical techniques arising from war-time research and experience, especially, in view of the unsatisfied demand for treatment which was making itself felt in the attitude of the people. Plans were thus drawn up for the nationalisation of the hospitals, and, under the National Health Service Act 1946, the decision was made to place the former municipal hospitals under specialised organisations distinct from the local authorities. These organisations were called Regional Hospital Boards and Hospital Management Committees. At the same time, the local authorities were made responsible for expanded services in the field of personal health, for instance, the provision of ambulances, health visitors, and home nurses and health centres from which G.P.s and other practitioners would operate. The relationship between the various practitioners and the State which underlay the 'panel' was extended to cover the whole population and brought up to date to meet modern conditions by the formation of Executive Councils, although with some misgivings on the part of many professional people who were jealous of their independence of action and judgement. It must be remembered that private medicine continued to exist, and hospital treatment, in particular, was obtainable in privately-owned hospitals or in private wards in NHS hospitals, for which the patients (often coming from overseas for treatment by specialists) paid fees. This is still the position today, though the number of private beds in the NHS has been reduced whilst private hospitals have proliferated.

As soon as the 1946 Act brought in the so-called 'tri-partite' system whereby community health functions were spread over three classes of organisation (Regional Hospital Boards, Counties and County Boroughs, and Executive Councils), criticisms were made that the general practitioner felt isolated and frustrated by having to pass patients to hospital specialists, the patient was often confused by the roles played by the three organisations, and liaison took up much staff time. Furthermore, the participating authorities were in competition for resources, and if treatment could be passed to another part of the service, the costs were also transferred, though the overall result might not be optimal in total resources used. For instance, the timing of a patient's discharge from hospital had an effect upon the need of the local authority to provide home nursing.

The next step forward was taken on the 1st April 1974, when a golden opportunity occurred to correct some of the short-comings of the 1946 Act arrangements, as the same day saw the reformation of the local government system and the creation of the Regional Water Authorities. The hospitals, personal health, and practitioners' services were brought together under the control of the Department of Health and Social Security. The new agencies for the integrated services were Regional and Area Health Authorities (and below the Areas, the Districts). It should be noticed that these are entitled "Health" and not "Hospital" as before, because they have much wider duties. Criticisms have again been made of the new system on various grounds, such as the present division of functions between the NHS and the local welfare authorities.

In July 1979, a Royal Commission made a report upon the working of the National Health Service. When it was given its terms of reference, the Commission was required to bear in mind the interests of the patients and the employees and to consider how best to employ the resources of the NHS in money and manpower. The Commission took up the first instruction to the full by emphasizing in its report that, in its opinion, the NHS was there to serve the patients and that their (and their families) interests were regarded as paramount over every other consideration, including those of the staff.

The report dealt with five major aspects of the service, as seen by the members of the Commission: —

(a) An overall review of the state of the nation's health and its health care services was given. The services, on the whole, received approval as to their standards, though one criticism was that there were too many tiers and administrators in the set-up.

(b) The services rendered by the NHS to the patients were then considered and it was recommended that there should be action on preventive medicine. For instance, there should be a hardening of attitude (supported by the use of the media) against smoking, alcohol, road accidents, and the encouragement of the fluoridisation of drinking water supplies. The report also called for the time spent waiting for hospital treatment to be reduced and for patients to be told more about what is happening to them whilst they are there.

(c) The industrial relations between the NHS and its staff were regarded as needing a more systematic basis, which could include the setting up of a national dispute procedure. The Commission also commented upon the roles and career structures for doctors, nurses and midwives.

(d) The report re-affirmed the need for close collaboration between the NHS and other organisations, such as the universities, private practice and, especially, the local authorities with social welfare and education functions. Mention is made of co-terminosity (i.e. common boundaries for health authorities and local education and welfare authorities), common membership of both types of body, joint consultation, joint financing schemes and the sharing of staff. The Commission remained unconvinced by the arguments that health and social welfare should be unified under one authority, and recommended no drastic changes in the present system.

(e) Various managerial and financial aspects of the service were then discussed and, in particular, the need for a high standard of hospital management as the lynchpin of the NHS. It was also felt that the RHBs and a form of District should replace the present system. The Regions should take over the detailed running of the service from the DHSS, as the Commission failed to see how the Permanent Secretary of the DHSS could be held responsible to his Minister (who answers to Parliament) for all the aspects of such a huge service as the NHS.

As regards resources, the Commission considered that the basis upon which they were allocated was sound although inequalities did exist over the U.K. Ways were also discussed in which the service could be financed but the Commission found little alternative to the use of Government funds.

The Government's answer to the Royal Commission's Report was to issue a consultation paper "Patients First" at the end of April 1980, and to place a Health Services Bill before Parliament. Although consideration is still being given to the restructuring of areas, the latest proposals are the abolition of the AHAs and the upgrading of Districts to be the tier below Region. In addition, the principle of co-terminosity of boundaries with local authorities has been waived, so far as future changes are concerned. The transfer of power downwards is reflected by an intention to strengthen hospital management. This last point is also dealt with in a recently-issued discussion paper of the DHSS entitled "The Future Pattern of Hospital Provision in England".

The Legal Basis of the National Health Service

The National Health Service was established as part of an overall system of welfare services and is aimed at making an all-embracing scheme of medical care available to the people living in this country without expense or for as low a charge as possible. No-one would need to forego treatment because of being unable to pay but all would pay towards the cost of the service by being taxed, mainly on their incomes. Visitors from abroad have also had the right to free treatment unless they have come in order to obtain treatment, but consideration is being given to restricting this right in future to those whose governments give similar rights to British visitors in their countries.

The law relating to the service is at present contained in the National Health Service Act 1977 under which the Department of Health and Social Security has the duty of taking steps to safeguard and improve the physical and mental health of the nation. The NHS was originally formed on the 5th July 1948 under the Act of 1946, it was re-organised under the NHS Re-organisation Act 1973 which laid down the present system whilst the 1977 Act introduced a few updatings and consolidated the law on the NHS into one Act.

The present arrangement thus combines into one set-up most of the professions whose members are involved in caring for the personal health of the people. The 1973 Act integrated three separate services which had been run in an unrelated manner by three organisation. The G.P.s and other practitioners had been supervised by the Executive Councils, the hospitals had been run by the Regional Hospital Boards and Hospital Management Committees, whilst the personal health services, such as maternity and child care (and the school health service) had been run by the Counties and County Boroughs, which disappeared themselves and were replaced by the new Counties and Districts. One area of possible dispute is the status of the staff employed in the local authority welfare services which could have been transferred with the personal health services. The Government's uncertainty as to the border lines between the NHS and the welfare services is shown by the insistence on close liaison between the authorities involved. Statutory requirements enforcing co-operation at both member and officer level are contained in the 1977 Act, and, in addition, the 1973 Act laid down that the boundaries of the new Regions and Areas of the NHS should coincide with those of the local welfare authorities. In other words, an AHA matches a non-metropolitan county, a metropolitan borough or a London borough, with few exceptions, according to its geographical location. Perhaps, at some future date, the appropriate welfare functions will be taken over by the NHS or a new comprehensive body, and the current collaboration measures rendered unnecessary. It is of interest that in Northern Ireland there are Area Health and Social Services Boards which are responsible for an integrated health and welfare service. It may be that the experience earned here may be applied to the rest of the country.

The making of the boundaries of the AHA co-terminous with those of the welfare authority has, however, given rise to criticisms that such boundaries do not necessarily give a viable health care unit, owing to characteristics found in the population or simply because the area is too small or too large for certain functions.

The bodies which took over the three services are the Regional and Area Health Authorities and they act as the agents of the Secretary of State for Social Services at the DHSS. The new integrated service was, however, intended to be locally-based, in that the Regions would be made up of Areas, but the Areas were envisaged as divisible into 'Districts' where this would lead to giving a better service. The basic operational unit is thus the District, which may be defined as a locality where the residents form a community with common aims, interests and characteristics, but are, nevertheless, of sufficient numbers to justify, at an economic cost, the provision of a full range of basic health services by deploying staff and other resources, such as G.P.s, midwives, ambulances, hospital beds, health centres, medical supplies, etc. The hope was that, in choosing such a unit of service, the residents would develop a friendly relationship with the doctors in practice, through whom they gain access to the rest of the NHS, and identify with the District health staff, so that both public and staff would feel a sense of belonging and pride in their local services.

The DHSS which is the topmost in the three tiers of the NHS, is headed by the Secretary of State for Social Services and is responsible for the national planning of the service and for monitoring the way in which the RHAs and AHAs carry out their duties. The Secretary of State has the power to decide what the duties of the two lower tiers should be and to alter them when necessary. The Department is also involved in a number of centralised functions, such as staff remuneration and conditions of service (which are negotiated on a national level) and some aspects of medical research. The DHSS finances the NHS out of Government money, capital and revenue expenditure being reimbursed in the same manner, and quantities of medical and non-medical supplies are also issued from central stores. Priorities in the use of resources – staff, supplies, accommodation, finance, etc. – are discussed between the DHSS and the next tier, the RHAs. The Secretary of State receives general advice on NHS matters from the Central Health Services Council which is made up of persons he appoints who come from a prescribed list of organisations. The CHSC has five Standing Advisory Committees – Medical, Dental, Nursing and Midwifery, Pharmaceutical, and Ophthalmic – to which the Council refers matters needing detailed consideration by experts. The Minister is also advised by the Health Advisory Service for England and Wales which is concerned with the standards of operation in hospitals and other branches of community care.

In Wales, the Welsh Office replaces the DHSS and carries out the determination of overall policy and planning, allocates resources and monitors their use by the AHAs. There are no RHAs in Wales. Instead, there is the Welsh Health Technical Services Organisation which is classified as a Special Health Authority and has duties connected with major capital schemes, supplies, and computer services in respect of the whole of Wales.

The Regional Health Authorities occupy the second tier of administration in the NHS. There are 14 of them and they are all in England. They have the status of Public Corporations but are subject to a greater degree of control than is the normal practice. They are composed of persons appointed by the Secretary of State – the Chairman and at least 15 others who are appointed after consultations with specified bodies and include at least two doctors, one nurse or midwife, a nominee from the Region's medical school or schools while one third of the total membership must be nominated by local authorities and the Trade Unions must be represented. All members serve on a part-time basis and the Chairman is paid a salary on that basis. The RHA decides the policies and plans which suit the character and needs of the Region. It receives Government funds from the DHSS and allocates them to the Areas. It also monitors the effectiveness of their use by the AHAs. The RHA is responsible for performing functions which require a relatively large service area for efficient operation, such as the carrying out of large-scale capital works the development of computerised systems, support to the teaching of medicine and medical research, and certain services such as blood transfusion, and in the conurbations, mass radiography and ambulances.

In conjunction with its function of providing computer facilities for the Region, the RHA operates a computerised system of transactions within a group of bank accounts set up by arrangement with the bank. There is a

Regional account which is credited with money advanced by the DHSS and debited with payments of routine nature made by the RHA, its AHAs and their Districts. In addition, however, the RHA, AHAs and Districts each have their own local bank accounts which they can use to advantage in financial matters at their own level. The Regional account and these local accounts are treated by the bank as an entity in that local overdrafts are set off against the credit balance on the central account. This provides an optimal employment of cash as the credit balance can be kept at a minimum by forecasting the cash flows of the various tiers involved, whilst each tier has the freedom to use initiative in the handling of its local accounts. The advantages of centralisation and decentralisation are therefore experienced.

The Chief Officers of the RHA include the Administrator, the Finance Officer or Treasurer, the Medical Officer, the Nursing Officer, and the Works Officer. They form the Regional Team of Officers and their duties are to run the departments, advise the members of the RHA, and see that their decisions are carried out. The formal line of command is from the RHA to the AHAs but, whilst Regional Officers have no power to give orders, except by agreement of the members, to their opposite numbers at the Area level, they can inform them of decisions taken by the RHA which affect their work. For instance, the Regional Finance Office has the duty of monitoring and co-ordinating the work carried out by the Area Finance Officers besides being responsible at Regional level for such matters as budget preparation and monitoring, resources allocation, payment of salaries and wages and other bills, costing, internal audit, project appraisal and collection of income.

The involvement of the members of staff from the various professions in policy-making at the Regional level is arranged for by the appointment of Professional Advisory Committees which are called, respectively, the Regional Medical, Dental, Nurses and Midwives, Pharmaceutical, Optical and Paramedical. These bodies have the right of being consulted on developments affecting the standards of service rendered by the staff within the particular disciplines and to give advice to the RHA and the RTO from the point of view of the professions they represent.

The Regions are divided into Areas controlled by Area Health Authorities which occupy the third administrative tier. There are, at the present, 90 AHAs in England – from four to 11 Areas per Region – and in Wales there are eight AHAs. The Authorities are Public Corporations with a separate legal existence but, like the RHAs, they are under a fairly strict degree of Parliamentary control via the DHSS. The AHAs undertake all those services in the NHS which are not carried out by the Regions. They employ most of the various grades of staff found in the NHS and make arrangements with the professions through the Area Family Practitioner Committees, which are the successors of the old Executive Councils formed under the 1946 Act.

Each Area has a FPC which acts as the contracting party with the general practitioners (i.e. doctors), dentists, pharmacists, ophthalmists, opticians, etc.. The FPC is responsible for the operations of the Family Practitioner Service in the Area, possesses a measure of control over the practitioners in such matters as complaints by patients regarding service, and advises the members of the AHA on subjects related to its functions. The Committee is made up of 30 members, half of whom are practitioners of the various professions, and the other half are appointees of the AHA or the local authorities in the Area. So far as finance is concerned, the FPC is virtually independent of the AHA, it receives funds from the DHSS and pays the practitioners the contracted sums. The reason for the existence of the FPC is that a similar system was introduced for the 'panel' patients in the early days of National Insurance, and the doctors, particularly, are jealous of their independence from the Government, and find any attempt to change the relationship unacceptable.

The membership of the AHA is composed of some 20 to 30 persons who all serve on a part-time basis. The Chairman is appointed by the Secretary of State and receives a salary. One-third of the ordinary members are nominated by the local authorities who serve the Area and the rest are appointed by the RHA after due consultation with various professional bodies. In detail, the membership must include two doctors, one nurse or midwife, and representatives from medical teaching and the AHA staff. Where an Area provides a sufficiently large amount of support to medical teaching and research, it can be designated as a 'Teaching Area' which gives it the right to appoint consultants and senior registrars and permits increased representation from the universities and teaching hospitals on the AHA, or rather, the AHA(T) as it is now called.

The AHA appoints an Area Administrator, Area Medical Officer, Area Finance Officer or Treasurer, and Area Nursing Office who form the Area Team of Officers with the duties of advising the members of the AHA, carrying out their decisions, and managing the various departments at Area level.

The Area Finance Officer has duties similar to those of the Regional Treasurer in regard to the Area Health Authority and the Family Practitioner Committee, and controls the work of the District Finance Officers in Multi-District Areas.

In a similar manner to the pattern at Regional level, there are Area Professional Advisory Committees which advise the AHA and the ATO on professional matters. One of these is the Area Medical (Advisory) Committee.

In passing the legislation for the new NHS, the Government was concerned about the degree of co-operation needed between the various official bodies involved in community health, firstly, to make the best overall use of resources, and secondly, to reduce the risk of people, in effect, falling between two stools, owing to the existence of gaps between the services given by different agencies. Besides needing hospital treatment or medical care at home, a person may require help with housework or meals during convalescence or over a long period, facilities to be provided or conversions carried out at home to ease physical difficulties, improvements or changes in accommodation, advice or assistance with money difficulties, and the looking after of pre-school and school aged children, and the education of the latter.

Joint Consultative Committees were formed under a duty to liaise contained in the 1973 Act. The AHA and the local and water authorities appoint numbers of their members and officials to these Committees in order to co-operate and plan together in the realm of personal and environmental health, housing, education and the school health service, water supply and social welfare. Operationally, this consultation results in the sharing of the services of staff and the adoption of policies of close working by officials. A boost to collaboration has been given by the introduction of joint financing of schemes by the NHS and a local authority. Such projects are of benefit to both. For instance, the provision of homes for old people should relieve pressure on hospital beds needed for long-stay cases. Financing usually takes the form of the NHS helping the welfare authority by contributing to the capital or running costs of a scheme for a period or permitting the use of NHS land or property. Although the revenue costs ultimately fall on the local authority, the arrangement means that the project is carried out a number of years earlier than would be the case without the joint financing. In times of financial stringency, such schemes might never be started, if unaided.

The next step down from the Area is to the District which, as has been mentioned, is the unit of service in which the nature and size of the population and the optimality of supplying the whole range of health services are balanced. The District, unlike the Area and the Region, has no distinct legal existence, being just an agency of the Area by which it chooses to provide its services to the public. Most AHAs have divided their Areas into a number of Districts (six is the most) and are known as Multi-District Areas (MDA), but some AHAs, mainly in the metropolitan counties, have chosen not to split their Areas, but to remain as Single-District Areas (SDA) because they consider their inhabitants form one natural community. Districts always include a general hospital and contain from 200,000 to 500,000 people, but, except in the case of SDAs, their boundaries do not necessarily coincide with those of any local authority.

It is at District level where the health needs of the community are identified and met, and it is from here that the information is obtained from which the plans and priorities underlying the Area, Regional and, ultimately, Central Departmental policies originate. The District is managed by a District Management Team which consists of an Administrator, Community Physician, Finance Officer, Nursing Officer, a consultant and a general practitioner (the last two members of the team being elected by the District Medical Committee). The day-to-day routine operation of the NHS is thus controlled at District level by multi-disciplinary teams which reach their decisions by consensus in an atmosphere of equality and co-operation. Each member makes a contribution from his expert knowledge of his own discipline to the solution of problems of management, and at the same time sees that adequate weight is given to the view and attitudes of the discipline or profession to which he belongs. The four District Officers named first as members of the DMT are, of course, employed by the AHA, but, while the consultant (who is a hospital specialist) is salaried, the G.P. member is an independent contractor. The maintenance of the professional independence of the medical profession is an underlying reason for the team's consensus approach, and the absence of a specific manager or other person in charge of the team. The position of the two members from the medical profession (sometimes referred to as "clinicians") is somewhat undefined, as they represent the views of their profession at team meetings, whilst the other members are in charge of staff and are running the departments which will carry out any decisions taken. Nevertheless, their expert knowledge is undoubtedly essential to proper decision-taking.

The relationships between corresponding officers at Area and District levels can give rise to problems in the way that duties are allocated and how they are monitored, but the usual procedure tends to be that each officer acts through his team in his approaches to his opposite number. In addition to this, informal methods of communication and collaboration undoubtedly exist, dependent on the compatibility of the officer's temperaments and local management practices. Because of the difficulties experienced between Area and District, especially in the case of an Area with several Districts, where the member of the various DMTs have direct access to the AHA, the optimal arrangement is argued to be the Single District Area. In the case of a SDA, the Area Team of Officers is augmented by the two representatives nominated by the Area Medical Committee (i.e. a hospital specialist and a G.P.) and acts as the Area Management Team. One can see that the work of the Area Administrator and the Area Finance Officer may be expedited by this arrangement but the Area Nursing Officer would now be directly responsible for a large number of staff, whilst the Area Medical Officer has duties as the Community Physician which call for working with local and water authorities in such matters as epidemics, besides his administrative obligations.

The District Finance Officer, besides giving financial advice and representing the financial point of view at meetings of the DMT, is also responsible for such matters as are allotted to him under the scheme of management supervised by the Area Finance Officer. His duties include the preparation of the budget at District level and the appraisal of projects and services with a view to their being run optimally, i.e. with the best use of resources.

There are a number of advisory bodies which operate at District level. These include the District Medical Committee (which provides a forum for all the local doctors and elects two members of the DMT in a MDA, the Local

Medical Committee (for G.P.s), the Hospital Medical Staff or Medical Executive Committees (for consultants). Multi-disciplinary teams may also be formed under the name of Health Care Planning Teams or, if other authorities outside the NHS are involved, Joint Care Planning Teams, which look after specific groups, such as the mentally-ill, or investigate individual problems arising in the District. The members of a team can be drawn from a range of professions and fields of work and be given the necessary funds and other support by the DMT to carry out their assignments.

The public and patients are represented by Community Health Councils which operate almost exclusively at the District level. The number of members is variable according to local circumstances, and runs from about 20 to close to 40 people, half of whom are appointed by local government and the others by the RHA from nominees of representative local groups. The CHC has certain statutory rights and duties. It must be consulted on matters affecting the level of service in the District. So far as the AHA is concerned, it can ask for information, visit hospitals, request mutual meetings and make representations on behalf of the people living in the community. Its expenses are met by the NHS and it is required to make a report each year on its activities. The role of the CHC is seen by some as being of a two-way nature, either negative or positive. The negative approach is to criticise the service and to take up complaints, even to contacting local M.P.s in the capacity of constituents. The positive approach is to make efforts to educate the public in the use of the service and the need for environmental health measures, vaccination, immunisation, and the prevention of disease generally, and also to give support by publicity or other means of pressure to projects which the AHA is attempting to obtain for the District against competition from elsewhere because of restricted funds.

Besides the Community Health Councils, reference must be made to the introduction under the 1973 Act of a new procedure for dealing with public dissatisfaction in the NHS by the appointment of officials called Health Service Commissioners, three in all, one each for England, Wales and Scotland. Their function is to investigate complaints made by members of the public that they have suffered hardship or injustice because of the failure of a health authority to provide a service or to administer it properly. Complaints should usually have already been made to the authority first before an approach is made to the Commissioner and there is a time limit of a year in which to bring the matter to him, but he has the power to ignore both these conditions if he thinks fit. Certain matters are excluded from the Commissioner's jurisdiction, and these are mainly those for which there are already legal procedures which can be followed in order to obtain satisfaction. Examples are — the querying of medical diagnosis and treatment, staff conditions of service, contract matters, and complaints against practitioners. When his enquiry is finished, the Commissioner reports to the complainant, the Health Authority, and other organisations involved. The Commissioners make annual reports to the Secretary of State who lays them before the House. A Health Service Commissioner may only be dismissed by the joint action of both Houses of Parliament but he must retire at the age of 65 years. At present, the three offices of Health Service Commissioner are administered by the Parliamentary Commissioner for Administration as an addition to his duties.

Another organisation which is active in the field of preventive medicine (i.e. the creation of conditions and the taking of steps to ward off disease) is the Health Education Council. This body also has duties connected with the education of the citizens in health matters so that they are enabled to apply standards of cleanliness and hygiene in their way of life and avoid or reduce the danger of infection or of self-inflicted illnesses. Though the Chairman and other members of the Council are all appointed by the Secretary of State and it receives its finance from Government funds, the Council is nevertheless a separate legal entity, being a limited company with complete freedom of action within its powers. Besides duties which have been given to it to advise the DHSS and other central Departments, RHAs and AHAs, on the best ways of carrying out health education, the Council has a wide range of powers to run publicity campaigns, such as anti-smoking, undertake research, and support the actions of other bodies, both official and voluntary, by means of advice or otherwise. The Council is also involved with local authorities, particularly those responsible for education in helping to make school children and older students aware of the need for a healthy way of life.

The broad classification of the range of services provided by the NHS is (a) community health (b) hospital and specialist (c) family practitioner and (d) miscellaneous.

The community health services include the care of mothers and young children, midwifery, home nursing, health visiting, prevention of illness, vaccination, immunisation, rehabilitation, provision of artificial limbs and other aids, medical and dental treatment of schoolchildren, health education, family planning, and the provision of health centres.

The hospital and specialist services include the treatment of in- and out-patients, accident and emergency cases, day patients, etc. in the various kinds of hospital – general, mental, isolation and other specialised – by doctors, surgeons, dental surgeons, etc.. Some hospitals also provide arrangements for the teaching of medical students.

The family practitioner service provides the public with general medical, pharmaceutical, dental and ophthalmic services by contracting with the various practitioners for their services. The basis of the system is for the person desiring treatment to choose a practitioner and for the practitioner to accept the person as a patient. Treatment under the NHS is obtained in the vast majority of cases via the patient's G.P..

The miscellaneous services contain such services as the provision of ambulances for carrying patients to and from the hospitals, the blood transfusion service which collects blood, places it in banks and issues it on need, and mass radiography for the detection of such diseases as tuberculosis and cancer. The mass radiography services is a function of the Region, whilst the other two services are carried out by the RHA in the metropolitan counties.

Finance

As the NHS is an integrated service subject to a fairly high degree of direction from the Central Government, the way in which particular services are divided between RHAs and AHAs is more a matter of Departmental orders than the requirements of any statute. Consideration is given to the optimal size of area suitable for specific activities and the rural or urban nature of the locality or localities involved, but a measure of discretion is allowed in the actual method of carrying out the functions. For instance, it may be of value, economically and administratively, for an AHA in a conurbation to act as agent to the RHA in respect of the repair and maintenance of ambulances and be reimbursed its expenditure by the RHA, possibly by a book entry.

The division of expenditure (and, also, of income) into capital and revenue applies in the NHS as in all accounting systems, especially those of public sector authorities, but both types of expenditure, in so far as they exceed income, are met from the same source – current taxation. There are in fact, four main sources of income, two are internal to the service while the others are external in nature. The first internal source consists of fees and other charges paid by users of the service, e.g. charges for dispensing prescriptions, supplying or repairing surgical, optical and dental appliances, the accommodation and treatment of private patients, and miscellaneous items, such as rents. The second internal class of income is capital in nature, being the proceeds of the sale of land and buildings usually no longer needed. The two external forms of income stem from the Government and are used to meet the net expenditure of the service. The first is made up of the part of the National Insurance deduction taken from the pay of every employed person which is earmarked as the NHS contribution. After this has been taken into account, the bulk of NHS net expenditure is left to be borne out of general taxation, mainly the income tax. Advances to the service are, of course, made as combined payments from taxation via the DHSS appropriations as granted by Parliament.

The financial budgeting system of the NHS (which includes the estimating of other needs for the various services, such as manpower) is organised on two levels. The current year's activities and the coming year's estimates are linked to (a) a short-term plan which covers the next three years, and (b) a long-term plan for 10 years ahead. The short-term operational plan is revised and rolled forward one year at a time, as the official planning cycle is carried out each year. The long-term strategical plan, on the other hand, is not a rolling programme. It is prepared at one time for the next 10 years and is reviewed less often than one year, and then only in the light of major changes in government policy, treatment methods or technology. It must be remembered that the short-term and long-term plans are closely related, but a long-term view is needed to assess the impact of capital schemes which need a fairly long time to come to fruition. For instance, the provision of a hospital from drawing board to full operation requires a time span of several years, and whilst the impact of the capital costs cannot be forgotten, the cost of running the facility once it is built must not be overlooked. The annual planning cycle during which the coming year's expenditure (and income from charges, etc.) is estimated has, perforce, to be done before the actual amount of cash available from Parliament is known, although indications are given. When the actual figure is ascertained and notified, then the plans have to be revised to fit the actual allocation. In addition, the DHSS applies cash limits to the advances it makes to the NHS although their stringency may be reduced by increasing charges, in accordance with present Government policy, for those services for which charges are permitted.

Another feature of the planning and budgeting system is the emphasis upon consultation at all levels with the various consultative and advisory bodies, categories of staff and their associations, local and other authorities whose services inter-relate with the NHS, especially where joint financing schemes are envisaged, and other Government agencies and Members of Parliament representing the locality.

The annual planning and estimating cycle adopted in the NHS may be said to start at the DHSS. In line with the Secretary of State's responsibility to Parliament to provide an adequate and comprehensive health service, the Department decides the objectives of the national strategical plan and considers the steps to be taken in the coming year or years to bring them nearer. In drawing up the programmes and priorities for each service, the DHSS uses the data supplied to date by the lower tiers of the NHS, consults with advisory and other bodies, and complies with current Government policies in regard to the health services. The considerations also include assumptions on the amount of resources available for the next few years as envisaged in the Public Expenditure Survey.

The Department now indicates to each RHA a number of general guidelines it should follow in settling programmes and priorities, and supplies an estimate of the share of the total NHS resources it should receive. The RHA in turn redrafts the guidelines to suit its own purposes and the conditions in the Region, and passes them together with an estimate of how it is sharing out resources to each Area. The AHAs, acting through the ATO, now give instructions to the DMTs who prepare the actual plans and estimates for the Districts. Where the Area is a SDA, the AMT carries out the work.

The various tiers of the NHS are affected wholly or individually by a number of factors in considering the best way to develop the service within the policies laid down by the tier or tiers above them. Such factors include prosperity or slump in the economy of the country and consequent changes in Government resources made available, changes in population and differences in age-grouping, advances in medical treatment or technology such as to make proposed capital projects obsolete, new attitudes to such matters as community care as opposed to institutional care, as small "nucleus" hospitals instead of large self-contained complexes, and as the joint financing of schemes with welfare authorities. Another point that a subordinate tier must consider is the requirements of its superiors for arrangements in compiling the budget which assist in the process of monitoring performance. For instance, authorisation procedures can be tightened and responsibility for expenditure fixed upon specific officers. Indications are also available to the members and officers as to likely priorities in treatment by comparing their authority's statistics with those prepared by the DHSS for the nation. Such data would include the average number of patients per G.P., death rates from various causes, average age at death, cases admitted to hospital, claimants for sickness and invalidity benefits, as well as unit costs of operating services.

Bearing such matters in mind with reference to their own District, the officers of the DMT prepare the plan for the next financial year, revise the short-term plan and roll it one year forward, and consider the relevancy and any need for the amendment of the long-term plan. They carry out the required degree of consultation with the local organisations, and pass the programmes and estimates to the AHA which passes them to the RHA which then passes them to the Ministry. As the plans proceed up the tiers, they are checked, discussed, revised, approved and consolidated at each stage, after due consultation has taken place. For instance, at Area, the estimates of the Districts are totalled and the Area's administrative and service costs are added. Similarly, at Region the estimates of the Areas are added together and the Region's administration expenses and costs of services and major capital schemes are added. Finally, the DHSS produce national figures for the whole of the NHS.

When Parliament has approved the national budget which contains the total amount of money to be spent on the NHS in the coming year, the DHSS has the duty of dividing it among the RHAs in as equitable manner as can be arranged. Each RHA then has the responsibility of financing its own services and dividing the balance among its AHAs. Each AHA uses its allocation to meet its own costs and the costs of its Districts. When the NHS was formed in 1946, standards of health care differed greatly throughout the country, and this was still the position at the re-organisation of the service in 1974. Accordingly, as a matter of social justice, the principle has been pursued that the methods used to allocate funds to Regions, Areas and Districts should be designed to bring about, in as short a time as possible, an equality of community care standards everywhere in the country. Thus, wherever one lives, one should have access to the same level of facilities. Furthermore, in pursuing equality of treatment, the NHS must not level down but must adopt new advances in techniques as soon as they become available.

Also basic to the idea of equal standards of health care to everyone is the acceptance that allocations must reflect the needs of each locality and the main factor here is felt to be the number of inhabitants and their characteristics, in particular, their age composition. Thus, after due consideration, the method adopted by the DHSS in allocating revenue resources calls for the calculation for each RHA of a "combined average population" which is based on a weighting of the various populations in the Region (e.g. children, elderly persons, etc. and their rates of sickness) benefited by the main NHS services. Capital resources are divided in a similar manner but with an additional refinement. This is an adjustment made each year with the aim of eventual equality of total capital expenditure per head throughout the Regions. This is because it was found that, in the past, some Regions have been favoured more than others in the provision of hospitals, etc. and the argument is that equal cumulative capital expenditure per head implies equal standards of facilities and thus of service. Although it is recognised that the RHAs and AHAs may encounter different problems from those faced by the DHSS, the two lower tiers adopt a similar approach to the division of resources.

The monitoring of the manner in which each tier of the NHS uses the resources allotted to it, is full of practical difficulties which arise mainly because the output of the service, viz. health, is itself not amenable to measurement. A certain degree of measurement is, however, possible by comparing actual results with the plan, and from the use of costs statements, principally of unit costs, related to suitable activities, such as ambulance operations and laundry facilities, which can be compared with the experience in other parts of the country. Research is also being carried out on the possible applications of cost-benefit analysis to alternative programmes to decide on courses of action, despite what has been said above as to the difficulties of identifying costs and benefits and evaluating them.

The Form of the Published Accounts

The Regional and Area Health Authorities are required to prepare accounts to 31st March each year in a form prescribed by the Secretary of State and to submit them to him after audit. The AHA is also required to include in its accounts, those of the Area Family Practitioner Committee (which has corporate status) and the Community Health Council or Councils in the Area. The DHSS is required to prepare complete accounts for the NHS and these are placed before Parliament where they are further scrutinised by the Public Accounts Committee and examined and reported upon by the Comptroller and Auditor General.

It is the practice to produce the accounts in a form which incorporates the figures relating to the transactions of the AHAs with those of the RHA, in order to supply totals for the whole Region.

There are accounts showing the details of the revenue expenditure on the various services of the RHA and each AHA. For the RHA, there is an account for administration costs, the blood transfusion service, the ambulance services in the conurbations, the mass radiography service, payments to non-NHS hospitals for treatment of NHS patients, and research and development costs. For the AHA, examples of accounts are administrative costs (there is also an analysis of aggregated running costs of the Districts in the Region), the ambulance services in the shire counties, hospitals, community health services, joint financing schemes' costs, and the expenses of the Community Health Council and the Family Practitioner Service (which is analysed into General Medical, Pharmaceutical, General Dental, and General Ophthalmic Services).

Revenue income is gathered together in one account — charges to patients for treatment, appliances supplied, prescriptions filled, and miscellaneous items, such as rents. Revenue expenditure and income for the whole Region is carried to a summary account.

Capital expenditure on buildings, vehicles, etc. and capital income from sales of land and buildings, etc. are shown in a separate account analysed over services and authorities.

Details of the transactions of each Trust or Endowment Fund are given in an Income and Expenditure Account, a Capital Fund and an Accumulated Income Account. As the Trusts are distinct from the NHS funds, each also has a Balance Sheet. Revenue income is from property and investments, while revenue expenditure is upon welfare and the provision of amenities for patients and staff, as well as research grants. It is a general rule that Trust money should not be used for purposes which should be met out of NHS official funds. Arrangements for dealing with Trust and other non-Exchequer Funds are usually laid down in Standing Orders. The Finance Officer has responsibility for these funds and is to be consulted before any money or other form of gift is accepted on behalf of the Authority by any officer for the purposes of research and other health purposes. It is normally required that details of the investments of each fund are entered into a register and all documents of title should be deposited at the Authority's bank.

While the DHSS, as is the practice with most Central Departments, keeps its accounts on a cash basis, the RHAs and the AHAs are required to operate an income and expenditure accounting system. The two systems are reconciled in a "Department of Health and Social Security Account" for the RHA and each AHA, accompanied by individual "Statements of Balances" consisting of the year-end debtors, creditors, stocks-in-hand, cash-in-hand or overdrawn, and the balance over- or under-paid by the DHSS.

Memorandum Trading Accounts and Statements of Unit Costs and other supporting statements are produced but no Balance Sheet as such, though cumulative capital expenditure figures are given from the inception of the service. Corresponding figures are also given relating to the previous financial year where they are appropriate and assist the reader.

Audit

The RHAs, AHAs, Family Practitioner Service, Community Health Councils and other organisations within the NHS are required to subject their accounts to audit by NHS audit staff who are appointed by the DHSS and form the Audit Service within that Department. These auditors follow instructions issued by the Department as to the scope of their duties and the methods of carrying them out. This procedure differs from that ruling in local government where the external auditors operate under Regulations issued under the Local Government Act 1972.

In addition, as the NHS is the responsibility of a Central Department (the DHSS) and its agencies, the Comptroller and Auditor General who audits the activities of such bodies, is also empowered to carry out an audit of the accounts. He reports on them to the House of Commons via the Public Accounts Committee.

The internal audit function is carried out by the Treasurer or Finance Officer of the particular organisation as part of his duties allocated by management arrangements. He is given the power by Standing Orders or Instructions to conduct such examinations of the financial and other operations as he considers necessary to carry out his duties adequately. For this purpose, he is equipped with the right of access to any assets and records, and can require such explanations as he thinks he needs in order to satisfy himself as to the correctness of any matter.

List of Abbreviations used in the National Health Service

The National Health Service has been a fruitful field of abbreviations by the use of initials for the various organisations and officers involved instead of their full titles. This undoubtedly saves space and paper, and, once the reader has become accustomed to it, helps understanding. To assist in overcoming the first hurdle — that of knowing what the initials mean — the following list is offered.

AHA	Area Health Authority
AHA(T)	AHA (Teaching)
AMAC or AMC	Area Medical (Advisory) Committee
AMT	Area Management Team
ATO	Area Team of Officers
CHC	Community Health Council
DHSS	Department of Health and Social Security
DMC	District Medical Committee
DMT	District Management Team
FPC	Family Practitioner Committee
GP	General Practitioner (Doctor in Medical Practice)
JCC	Joint Consultative Committee

MDA	Multi District Area
NHS	National Health Service
RHA	Regional Health Authority
RMO	Regional Medical Officer
RTO	Regional Team of Officers
SDA	Single District Area
WHTSO	Welsh Health Technical Services Organisation

Questions

12.1 Describe briefly the structure of the National Health Service.

12.2 List the various main services rendered by the National Health Service.

12.3 What arrangements exist for collaboration between health and other authorities?

12.4 Outline the external audit arrangements in the National Health Service.

12.5 What are the duties of the Health Service Commissioner?

12.6 Describe the system by which estimates are prepared for the NHS.

12.7 Who are the members of the DMT and how do they consider matters and arrive at decisions?

12.8 Endowment Trust Funds are a feature of the NHS. What rules exist regarding their operation?

12.9 Describe the composition of a CHC and its main functions.

12.10 What is the role of the Health Education Council?

Chapter 13

The Gas Supply Industry

Historical Summary

The main types of gas which have been supplied through the mains and pipes of gas undertakings in this country for heating, lighting, cooking and other purposes are called town gas and natural gas. Town gas is, in effect, a mixture of various gases, such as hydrogen, methane and carbon monoxide, which is driven out of coal heated in furnaces, and purified by a number of processes. The production of town gas is accompanied by the manufacture of by-products, including coke, tars, sulphur compounds and ammonia, and most of these are quite valuable. Natural gas is found in underground deposits, in many cases in association with oil, and contains hydrocarbons, such as methane, ethane, and other gases. The natural gas actually supplied to the consumer is made up of some of the above constituents, duly purified. Gas supplies in this country were, by tradition, town gas, because of the presence of extensive coal deposits which were (and still are) easily accessible. The present widespread use of natural gas, which has virtually taken over the role of town gas, has only come about since the discovery of the undersea fields between Britain and Scandinavia, and the development of the technology which was needed to exploit them.

The demand for fuel for the processes of the Industrial Revolution gave rise to the opening of coal mines on a large scale and the increased use of coal, and an interest in the purposes to which its by-products could be put. Experiments began to take place in connection with the supply of coal gas for lighting and, in the late 18th and early 19th century, some success was experienced in the lighting by gas of public offices, factories and streets. About that time, the first companies were formed to supply town gas, mainly for lighting purposes, but other applications soon followed. The industry developed steadily and demand rose as inventions such as the incandescent gas mantle, gas stoves and heaters, industrial furnaces, etc. were introduced, and it withstood the introduction of other fuels and power sources, especially electricity. By 1949, the industry was a mixture of local authority-owned undertakings and privately-financed limited companies. Its turn in the programme of nationalisation in the post-war years came on the 1st May 1949, when it was placed under State ownership by the Gas Act 1948. This Act transferred the assets and liabilities of the existing producers to twelve area boards which were created as separate, independent and autonomous (i.e. self-ruling) legal entities. Each was thus a public or statutory corporation but their actions were subject to some measure of co-ordination by a central body, called the Gas Council. This, like the boards, was a new organisation and its duties were to give advice to the Minister responsible for the industry, promote the efficient operation of the boards, and provide the capital finance which they needed. The area boards were chosen as the operating units because, at that period, the industry was tied to supplying localities from gasworks, and up till then, there was no technique available for sending large quantities of gas from one part of the country to another.

The discovery and exploitation of North Sea gas in the period from 1965 radically changed the nature and structure of the gas industry. It turned from the making of town gas and the sale of coal by-products (which still continue, however, at a much reduced level) to the supplying of natural gas via country-wide systems of pipelines. A massive conversion programme took place so that consumers' appliances could use the new gas. The widening of the optimal area of operation from a locality to a possibly national level demanded a more centralised structure than formerly. At first, the powers of the Gas Council were increased by the Gas Act 1965, but this strengthening proved to be insufficient, and complete centralisation was achieved under the Gas Act 1972.

Under this Act, the British Gas Corporation was formed to replace the Gas Council, whilst the area boards lost their separate legal existence and became twelve regions of the new Corporation. (The regions are – Eastern, East Midlands, Northern, North Eastern, North Thames, North Western, Scottish, South Eastern, Southern, South Western, Wales, and West Midlands).

The Legal Basis

From the 1st January 1973, the British Gas Corporation is responsible under the Gas Act 1972 for the carrying on and developing of an efficient nationally-planned service for the production and distribution of gas (and its products) for domestic and other uses, together with the provision of gas appliances and fittings. It is also empowered to explore for gas and to exploit any gas and oil discovered. (Consideration is now being given to divesting the Corporation of its involvement in oil wells). The Department of Energy oversees the activities of the Corporation and consultations take place on matters of policy and how it is to be implemented. In a similar way, the Corporation holds discussions with its regions on more detailed aspects of policy and administration.

The Corporation is made up of the Chairman and at least ten and at most twenty other persons. All are appointed by the Secretary of State for Energy and the Deputy Chairman is usually designated from among the members.

The Secretary of State for Energy has the responsibility for supervising the operations of the British Gas Corporation under the Gas Acts and also has specific duties allotted to him by those Acts. As with the pattern for most public corporations, the Minister is answerable to Parliament for the way in which he carries out his statutory duties and this generally means that he can be questioned in the House on matters of general policy but the routine operations of the Corporation are not his responsibility. However, because of the dangers to the public inherent in the supply of gas (especially from explosion and suffocation), the gas industry has always been subject to a greater degree of central control than most other nationalised undertakings.

Examples of the Minister's duties are the approval of capital investment programmes and of the resultant borrowings, the setting and enforcement of external financing limits (or, as they were formerly called, cash limits), and the agreement with the Corporation of a target rate of return upon net capital. His consent is needed to transactions involving the Reserve Fund and to the use of revenue surpluses, and he must be consulted as to revisions of charges made to consumers. He appoints, dismisses and decides the salaries of members of the Board and can issue regulations under the Gas Acts and give directions to the Corporation to take action in accordance with the national interest. Such action may be on a matter of an economic nature and could, for instance, be the postponement of price increases or their implementation. Another instance of the use of the power of direction may occur when the Minister decides a dispute in the favour of a consumers' council against the Board and considers that his decision must be carried out. The Minister must ensure that the Corporation submits its annual report together with a copy of its accounts and auditor's report. He must prepare his own report on the gas industry and lay it and the other items before the House of Common where they go to the Comptroller and Auditor General and the Select Committee for Nationalised Industries for further examination and report.

The system of consumer representation under the legislation applicable to the supply of gas includes a National Gas Consumers' Council and twelve regional gas consumers' councils. Each of these bodies consists of the chairman and from 20 to 30 members who are all appointed by the Minister. The members are chosen from associations which represent local interests in industry, commerce, agriculture, etc. as well as the general body of the gas users. The regional councils are entitled to be kept informed by the Corporation of developments occurring in the gas supply industry and their recommendations and reports to the Corporation must be given due consideration. The regional bodies must also be in a position whereby they can receive complaints from users and have the right to approach both the Corporation and then the Minister, if necessary, in order to obtain satisfaction.

Finance

The British Gas Corporation must ensure that its income is enough to meet its outgoings, taking one year with another. Thus, over a period of years, there should be a no profit/no loss situation. The outgoings should include all the items which should be properly debited to the Revenue Account and include adequate depreciation of fixed assets and any necessary amounts taken to reserve. The sources of income include the sales of gas and by-products (for example, coke, tars, ammonia, etc.), the rent and sales of appliances and fittings, and income from rechargeable work carried out for consumers on installations, etc..

The widespread nature of the area served by the Corporation and the scale of its operations combined with the variety of its activities call for well-designed, integrated budgeting and management accounting systems which should provide a sound basis for the control of expenditure, the monitoring of current operations and the planning of future policies in developing the service. The main instrument of budgetary control is in the form of the Corporate Plan which is drawn up each year and covers the coming five years. This plan is based on forecasts prepared by the staff at headquarters for its centrally-operated services and by the regional staffs for their individual services, and these forecasts are all consolidated and submitted to the Secretary of State for Energy. After discussions and possible amendments to make it comply with national economic policies, the Corporate Plan is duly approved and put into operation.

Within the scope of the Corporate Plan, there are overall investment programmes for the whole of the gas supply industry which are agreed between the Department of Energy and the British Gas Corporation, and then the headquarters allocates the amounts approved between itself (for its own projects which are usually major in nature) and its regions (for their projects which are normally fairly minor). The Corporation has the power to meet its capital expenditure within the external financing limits, provide for working capital, and to repay loans out of monies borrowed from the Department of Energy, from other lenders, and from the proceeds of the issue of British Gas Stock.

The five year budget is linked with a long-term development plan for the industry which must, of necessity, be less detailed, and includes expenditure on possible lines of research foreseeable in the next decade and beyond. There is also a short-term budget based on the five year Corporate Plan. This also is prepared annually and covers the coming year in complete detail and the year after that in more general terms. The short-term estimates are drawn up by the managers at headquarters and the regions and each manager is aware of his responsibilities in realising the targets laid down in the plan as approved by the Board of the Gas Corporation. A thorough system of reports, monitoring and analysis of the financial figures by comparing actual expenditure and income with the budget is carried out continuously. There is a high degree of standardisation of records, procedures, account keeping, etc..

The British Gas Corporation has the duty of satisfying reasonable demands for gas and to supply it to the owner or tenant of a property situated within 25 yards of a gas distribution main which is in use, subject to the applicant conforming with such conditions as the Corporation is permitted to lay down. For instance, a charge may be made for the cost of the supply pipe in excess of 10 yards, as well as for the work done on and in the property. A deposit or security may be required in advance of doing the work, and if the charge for connection is, in any case, not paid, the supply may be disconnected after seven days' notice. There is power to refuse to supply when it is not for domestic use or for lighting unless the Corporation is protected against loss in laying the pipe or enlarging an existing pipe by requiring the applicant to agree to pay a minimum charge for a minimum period of use or to make a deposit or other kind of security.

The consumer has a choice between a meter which registers the consumption for which quarterly accounts are rendered, or a prepayment meter by which gas is paid for as it is used. If the consumer with an ordinary meter (i.e. one for which he receives a quarterly account) fails to pay an outstanding bill within 28 days, the Corporation has the power to cut off the supply, in any way it thinks fit, after seven days' notice in writing. This power, so far as domestic bills are concerned, is operated in accordance with the Code of Practice for the payment of domestic gas and electricity accounts, which has been agreed jointly by the two industries. (This code was produced to avoid or reduce hardship in cases where people find difficulty in meeting their home fuel bills. Such people are offered advice as to reducing their use of gas by proper operation of the appliances and fittings, the payment of arrears by instalments and the budgeting of present bills. A prepayment meter may be installed where safe and practical, and the debtors referred to the possibility of assistance from central and local authority social services. Only in cases where the consumer refuses to cooperate and is shown to be in no need of assistance is the supply disconnected).

In the case where a prepayment meter is fixed, the money belongs to the Gas Corporation, as the gas has been supplied, and if the meter is broken open and the money taken, the consumer may be held liable to pay again, if he is shown to have been negligent in looking after the meter and the cash.

A Gas Corporation official may enter premises without a warrant or the permission of the occupier if there is an emergency or he needs to check any fittings or pipes considered dangerous as to their actual state. Normally, a warrant from a justice of the peace is needed before entry can be obtained if the occupier will not give his consent after reasonable notice. Where entry is made forceably with a warrant, in the absence of any occupier, the property must be left as secure as it was previously. As little damage as possible should be done when any entry is made, and a claim for repairs may lie against the Corporation.

Disputes as to whether meters are reading incorrectly can be settled by reference to meter testing stations. Where the meter is proved incorrect, the Corporation bears the costs of removing, testing and replacing it. Where the user has complained that the meter is inaccurate and it is shown to be in order, the user has to pay the costs.

Where gas is supplied by meter and paid for by quarterly accounts, the consumer must inform the Corporation at least 24 hours before he leaves the premises, otherwise he may be charged with the gas used up to the next meter reading. Similarly, if a new occupier has made proper arrangements with the Corporation to take a gas supply, he is not affected by the existence of arrears owed by the previous consumer (unless he has agreed to pay them).

The Form of the Published Accounts

The accounts of the British Gas Corporation are prepared in consolidated form as they deal with the activities of the Corporation and of a number of its subsidiary companies, such as Gas Council (Exploration) Limited (which was, of course, set up during the period that the Gas Council was the central body).

There is a Trading and Profit and Loss Account which gives an analysis of transactions and operating results for three categories of activity — gas and oil, installation and contracting, and the marketing of appliances. The balance on the Account is carried into a Profit and Loss Account which bears general financing charges, such as interest and taxation, and shows the accumulated reserves carried forward on the Balance Sheet. Further analyses of such items as the turnover and the emoluments of members and senior staff are given in Notes to the Accounts.

The Balance Sheet, which like the previously-mentioned Accounts, is in narrative format, shows figures for the Corporation and for the consolidation (the difference being the amounts applicable to those subsidiaries which are included in the Accounts). The items on the Balance Sheet are supported by analysed schedules of assets and liabilities. These include Fixed Assets, Net Current Assets (e.g. stocks, work in progress, cash, etc.).

There is a Statement of Source and Application of Funds, and an explanation of the accounting policies adopted in preparing the accounts. Corresponding figures are given in respect of all appropriate items for the previous year. Current costs are to be incorporated in the annual accounts in a form such as a current cost Profit and Loss Account.

Audit

Under the provisions of the Gas Act 1972, the Secretary of State appoints the external auditors of the accounts of the British Gas Corporation and they must be members of one of the accountancy bodies recognised as qualified to undertake the audit of limited companies. The audited accounts and a copy of the audit report is sent to the Secretary of State each year and he presents them to Parliament.

Internal audit is primarily carried out by audit managers at the regions who report to their directors of finance and also to the Controller of Audit and Investigations at headquarters. The Controller is responsible for co-ordinating the operations of the internal auditors and the advising of the Corporation on policy matters. Close liaison exists between the external and internal auditors which makes it possible to prevent overlapping of audit work.

Questions
13.1 Outline the structure of the gas supply industry.
13.2 What changes occurred in the gas industry with the discovery and exploitation of North Sea gas?
13.3 Describe the external audit arrangements in the British Gas Corporation?
13.4 Give a brief description of the budgeting systems used in the gas industry.
13.5 What arrangements exist for the representation of users of gas?
13.6 In what ways can the Minister control the activities of the British Gas Corporation?
13.7 Explain the procedure under which a consumer may query the accuracy of his gas meter.
13.8 Outline the powers of entry of a gas official on to premises which are supplied by gas.
13.9 Under what conditions can an owner or occupier of a property require a gas supply to be provided?
13.10 What duties were given to the British Gas Corporation under the Gas Act 1972?

Chapter 14

The Electricity Supply Industry

Historical Summary

As with so many modern inventions, Britain pioneered the development of electricity for lighting and industrial purposes. The electricity supply industry had its beginnings in the late 19th century in the setting up of small power stations which were operated mainly by limited companies. These companies were independent of one another and served areas of a restricted nature around their stations by both generating and distributing electricity for lighting houses, shops, factories, streets, etc.. It was soon realised that there were economies to be had in large-scale operations and stations quickly grew in size and local authorities entered the field by forming their own undertakings. For many years, the industry was fragmented into a mixture of different sizes of units − a large number of small ones and a few relatively large ones − run by companies or local authorities without any co-ordination. Voltages and frequencies varied from undertaking to undertaking as well as the price per unit. Furthermore, the piecemeal development resulted in the towns being supplied with electricity whilst the rural areas were mainly ignored because of the cost of providing the cable, poles, etc. to cover the distances involved in reaching isolated farms, etc. Although the industry at the start was intended to compete with gas in providing lighting, new uses were found for electricity and these new uses increased as appliances operated by electric motors began to be manufactured in growing numbers. The shortcomings of the system of localised independent producers with their limited output of varying standards finally became too apparent under the demands put upon it by the first World War of 1914-18 but it was not until 1926 that the first real move towards unification took place and this was on the generation side of the industry. In that year, the Central Electricity Board was formed to construct a national power grid and to buy the output of a few chosen power stations (which were of a major size) so as to feed this into the grid for sale to the undertakings which distributed the electricity to the public and industry. The undertakings themselves had no change of status. They bought power from the grid but they also still produced electricity to meet some of their needs if they so wished. The building of the national grid brought electric power into the rural areas, though the sight of the pylons marching across the country brought protests from preservationists and the burying of some cables. In addition to the farms being supplied with electricity, industry too could move more easily into newer areas. From 1926 onwards, steps were taken to regulate electricity supplies and bring them to a national standard so that appliances could be used anywhere in the country. Though there were occasional difficulties and disagreements between the Central Electricity Board, the Electricity Commissioners (whose task it was to supervise the industry on behalf of the Government) and the undertakings, it can be said that the system stood the test of the second World War of 1939-45 with the, at times, incredible demands this must have made on resources.

The Labour Government which was elected to power in 1945 included in its proposals the taking into public ownership (i.e. nationalisation) of the fuel and power industries, and in 1947, the Electricity Act was passed to nationalise the whole of the electricity supply industry – both generation and distribution. The British Electricity Authority (in 1955 it became the Central Electricity Authority) was created, and from the 1st April 1948 it took over all the generation functions whilst Regional Electricity Boards were formed to become responsible for the distribution side of the industry. To start with there were 14 Boards in the area covered by the 1947 Act – twelve in England and Wales and two in South Scotland. North Scotland was outside the ambit of the Act because the North of Scotland Hydro-Electric Board had been formed some five years before, and remained on its own, producing its own electricity by water power and distributing it over its own area. South Scotland also followed the North into separate operation later. The two Boards already mentioned were amalgamated into the South of Scotland Electricity Board which became responsible for generating electricity as well as distributing it within its area. The Boards in England and Wales are – Eastern, East Midlands, London, Merseyside and North Wales, Midlands, North Eastern, North Western, South Eastern, Southern, South Wales, South Western, and Yorkshire.

The arrangement under the 1947 Act lasted until the 1st January 1958, when, for a number of reasons, including the accusation of control of the industry being over-centralised and a lack of clear rules on the delegation of functions which led to unnecessary overlapping, the Electricity Act 1957 was passed. This Act dissolved the Central Electricity Authority and replaced it by the Electricity Council and the Central Electricity Generating Board. Scotland, as already explained was unaffected by this Act and the twelve Boards which were now called Area Electricity Boards continued their functions of distributing electricity, selling appliances, and carrying out other work for customers. They had already been made separate legal entities under the 1947 Act and this was continued but now they were given greater freedom of action in reply to the charge that the previous arrangement was over-centralised.

The Legal Basis

The Electricity Council is the central body which supervises the industry under the overall control given by Parliament to the Secretary of State for Energy. It advises the Secretary of State on matters of general policy, helps the CEGB and the Area Boards to develop, maintain and improve the service, and carries out a number of functions which the Government have decided should be centralised, such as research planning and its carrying out, matters connected with the conditions of service of the staff, e.g. wage negotiations, pension fund, etc. and the provision of funds for capital financing of schemes carried out by the CEGB and the Boards. The members of the Electricity Council include six persons appointed by the Secretary of State (who include the Council's Chairman and Deputy Chairmen), the twelve Chairmen of the Area Boards, and the Chairman of the CEGB together with two other members of the CEGB.

The Central Electricity Generating Board is responsible for the running of the power stations and the maintenance of the grid lines and thus generates and transmits supplies in bulk to the twelve Area Boards. The CEGB also has arrangements with the British Railways Board to supply electric power to run the railway system. The CEGB is also responsible for planning and building new power stations and transmission (i.e. grid) lines. Stations are of various types. There are so-called conventional steam-generating stations fueled by coal or oil (sometimes mixed), steam-generating nuclear powered stations and a number of reactors which though not owned by the CEGB generate power for the grid, gas turbine plant, and hydro-electric stations which include the pumped-storage idea whereby water is pumped up to a high level reservoir in off-peak periods and then falls during peak demand periods so as to produce electricity. It is envisaged that natural gas will join oil and coal as a fuel for future power stations.

The members of the CEGB are all appointed by the Secretary of State. They consist of the Chairman, Deputy Chairman, four full-time members and up to four part-time members. Within and below the full Board, the Chairman and the full-time members form a body called the Executive which gives preliminary consideration to matters which are to be put in front of the whole Board and is thus in a position to make recommendations to the Board. The Executive also ensures that the Board's decisions are duly carried out properly and without undue delay and allocates to its members the responsibility for each of them concerning him or herself in particular functions or aspects of the work of the CEGB. The Board and the Executive are served by a number of Chief Officers who are in charge of the Headquarter's departments which include Finance, Research, Legal, Personnel, Management Services, Nuclear Health and Safety, Engineering, Planning and Secretary (for administration). The territory of the CEGB is divided into five Regions – Midlands, North Eastern, North Western, South Eastern and South Western. Each Region is under the control of a Director-General who is responsible for both generation and transmission matters in his Region. There are two Development and Construction Divisions headed by Directors-General which carry out generation and transmission projects of a large size in any of the Regions.

The Area Electricity Boards are responsible for dealings with the public and, more particularly, those persons and organisations using electric power. They provide the cables which distribute the electricity from the CEGB's transmission lines to the consumers' premises and make charges for the amount of power consumed. They sell or hire out appliances which are worked by electricity from their showrooms and also carry out contract work of various kinds, such as repairs to household appliances, re-wiring of premises, etc. The Boards are composed of persons appointed by the Secretary of State and these are the Chairman, the Deputy Chairman, four to six other members and the Chairman of the Electricity Consultative Council for the Area (who is actually appointed to the Council, and is a member of the Board by virtue of his office, or "ex officio" as the Latin phrase has it). There are four Chief Officers at Area Board Headquarters — the Secretary, the Chief Accountant, the Chief Commercial Officer and the Chief Engineer — who act under the instructions of the Board and have a duty to report to it in respect of the activities for which they are responsible. The titles of three of these officers explain their duties but the Chief Commercial Officer is in charge of sales and contracting arrangements with the Board's customers, and is especially interested in customer satisfaction with the quality of service and goods sold. The Boards' territories (i.e. Areas) are sub-divided into a further single or double tier according to what is thought to be more convenient for local circumstances. The original arrangement was to divide the Area into Sub-Areas, and then divide the Sub-Areas into Districts, but some Boards have dispensed with Sub-Areas whilst others have gone farther and use other designations, such as Groups for Sub-Areas. Such sub-divisions of the Area, whatever they are called, are controlled by managers who are assisted by engineering, clerical and finance staffs.

The role of the Secretary of State for Energy is to control the actions of the Electricity Council, the CEGB and the Area Boards in accordance with the duties placed upon him by the Electricity Acts and to be answerable to Parliament as regards the manner in which he carries out these statutory duties. His area of responsibility has more to do with questions of general policy as matters of day-to-day management are left to the bodies concerned. He is, however, the main channel of communication between Parliament and the industry. Examples of his statutory duties are the appointment, dismissal and also the fixing of salaries of members of the Boards and Council, the approval of capital investment schemes, advancing of loans, the operation of cash limits and the agreement of rates of return on capital. His consent is also needed to the creation of Reserve Funds and the sums transferred to and from them. Contributions to such Reserve Funds are regarded as properly chargeable revenue expenditure along with depreciation in arriving at the balance on the Revenue Account, and if this is in surplus, the Minister's consent is again needed for the surplus to be used for any purpose. He is consulted in respect of proposed changes in tariffs and charges for electricity. He has the power to issue regulations under the Electricity Acts on administrative, legal and technical aspects of the electricity supply industry, and, in addition, has the further power (which is used fairly infrequently) of giving orders or directions, as they are called, to the various organisations in the industry to act in the national economic interest in such ways as delaying increases in charges, rescheduling capital investment schemes, etc.. Each organisation is required to make an annual report to the Minister together with copies of its accounts and auditor's report, and he must make his own report and lay all these documents before Parliament where they go through a process of scrutiny and report.

In each Area there is an Electricity Consultative Council which has the duty of looking after the interests of the consumers. This Council is made up of a Chairman and up to 30 members, some of whom are nominated by local authority associations and others by local organisations representing commerce, industry, farming, etc., as well as the general body of consumers. The Secretary of State must take account of these nominations in making his appointments to the Consultative Council. The Area Board (of which, as has already been mentioned, the Chairman is a member) has a duty to keep the Consultative Council informed on future plans and to receive any suggestions it may make. It is assumed that the Chairman will be in a position to give his Council members information on such matters which have been discussed by the Board, besides the formal channels of communication between the two bodies. The Council must consider such matters as alterations in scales of charges, in level of service, and in any arrangements affecting consumers, and it must appoint representatives or committees to receive complaints and generally to look after the interests of the inhabitants of the various localities in their Area. All reports by the Council, including those in respect of matters which it has been asked to consider by the Board, are made to the Board, and where disputes arise between the Council and the Board there is machinery for them to be settled by the Electricity Council. Representation of the consumers also exists at the national level via the Electricity Consumers' Council.

If the tenant or owner of a property which is not supplied with electricity asks in the required manner for a supply to the property, and the premises are within 50 yards of an existing live electricity main, the Area Board is required to provide it, subject to the following conditions. Where the connecting cable is more than 20 yards long, a charge can be made for the cost of the excess over the 20 yards, and the Board also charges for the work done on the private land and in the building. The Board has power to demand an advance deposit or other form of security in respect of the charges, or require an agreement to be paid a minimum charge for at least two years. If the connection is made but the charge on the applicant in respect of providing the supply is not paid, the supply can be cut off.

There is usually a choice available to the customer as to whether a prepayment meter is fixed so that he pays as he uses the current or an ordinary meter is supplied which is read quarterly and for which an account is rendered. If a user fails to pay the quarterly account, the Area Board has the power to disconnect the supply, and as no requirement is made as to notice, this means that the supply can be cut off without notice. Recently, however, this power is only used when the "Code of Practice" proves to be inapplicable. This Code of Practice was drawn up by the electricity and gas supply industries jointly with the intention of avoiding hardship to domestic users who find difficulty in paying their bills. The code includes the giving of advice on how to use electrical and gas appliances economically, arrangements for regular payments on account, the installation of prepayment meters where they are safe and practicable, and assistance from social security authorities. Only in extreme circumstances and after all avenues have been explored will a domestic supply be disconnected. Similar considerations do not, of course, apply to non-domestic supplies.

An additional scheme of aid introduced by the Boards is the Government Discount Scheme under which persons receiving Supplementary Benefit and families in receipt of Family Income Supplement are entitled to a 25% reduction on the account for one winter quarter.

Money inside a prepayment meter belongs to the Board because electricity has been given for it, except in the case of meters fixed by a landlord to sell electricity to lodgers, tenants and visitors. He is allowed to make a prescribed maximum charge which gives him a relatively small surplus to meet expenses when he has paid for the total consumption registered on his master meter. In the case of prepayment meters directly linked with the supply, however, the consumer may be liable if the meter is robbed and the money taken, if he can be shown to have been negligent in looking after it. In that case, he may have to pay twice.

An employee of the Electricity Board can normally obtain entry to premises with the agreement of the occupier or owner after a reasonable period of notice. Where entry is refused and the reasons for wishing to go on to the property are sound, a warrant can be obtained from a J.P. which allows entry without the need for consent. If force is needed to enter with the warrant, and the occupier is absent or the place is vacant, the property must be left as secure as it was before. Where damage is done in forcing an entry in this way, it should be kept as small as possible and a claim for the cost of re-instalment may be brought against the Board.

In cases of emergency, however, where life or property is in danger, an official may go on to the premises without consent or warrant.

A consumer must give 24 hours' notice to the Board when he is moving from the premises so that the meter can be read and an account rendered. If he fails to do this, he is liable to pay for the electricity used up to the next reading. There is no right of recovery against a new tenant in respect of an outgoing tenant's arrears, unless they have arranged between themselves that the incoming tenant will pay the arrears. Any queries as to the accuracy of meters can be referred to official meter examiners.

Finance

Under the Electricity Act 1947, each Electricity Board must ensure that its income is enough to meet its properly chargeable expenses, taking one year with another. Furthermore, tariffs should be simplified and standardised so that the costs of supplying the four principal classes of customers (industrial, commercial, domestic and agricultural) should be recovered from each class. Revenue income thus comprises the sale of electricity, sale of appliances and profit on contract work with a small contribution from rentals of meters, etc..

The capital programme of the industry is drawn up by the Electricity Council from three sources. The first is its estimates of what it needs to develop its own functions, the second consists of the forecasts of the CEGB in respect of developments in new power stations, transmission lines, etc. and the last component comes from the Area Boards which lay out their schemes for expansion and improvement of distribution. The combined investment programme is approved by the Secretary of State after being tailored in accordance with the national budget allocations.

Capital expenditure is financed in various ways. The Secretary of State makes advances of long-term nature. The Electricity Council borrows from outside sources for the whole industry. Internal funds are also used to meet capital expenditure, e.g. superannuation funds and profits. There is also power to borrow short-term money.

In recent years, the Government has introduced measures for the economical management of national funds, such as the use of cash limits (now called external financing limits) and the setting of performance targets for the various public corporations. Cash limits are applied to capital monies advanced to the Electricity Council by restricting them to the original sum fixed in the estimates plus an acceptable rate of inflation. If the rate of inflation exceeds that assumed originally, then expenditure must be cut back to keep within the cash limit. With regard to the performance of the industry, the Government agrees a rate of return on net assets which it is expected should be realised.

The Form of the Published Accounts

The Electricity Council produces a statutory annual report on its activities which is published in conjunction with the annual accounts for the whole industry. The form of the accounts is laid down under the Electricity Acts 1947 and 1957. There is a Consolidated Revenue Account and Balance Sheet (in narrative form) for the Council, the CEGB and the twelve Area Boards. These are supported by statements covering the whole industry in respect of such matters as the sale of electricity and appliances, the analysis of revenue expenditure according to activity, details of the various classes of fixed assets, provisions for depreciation of fixed assets, contributions to the Central Guarantee Fund, the nature, cost and value of the various investments held, the source and value of current borrowings. (The Central Guarantee Fund was set up under the 1957 Act to provide money to meet any failure by an electricity authority to pay interest due or to repay a loan, or to reimburse the Treasury any sums it has had to pay as guarantor on behalf of the authorities).

The Electricity Council prepares its own final accounts separately from the consolidated figures described above. They consist of an Income and Expenditure Account and Balance Sheet which are both in narrative form. In the Income and Expenditure Account, the expenditure is analysed over headings such as administration, consumer services, research, etc. and the income (of which the major item is rent received) is deducted to give a net deficit which is met out of contributions from the CEGB and the Area Boards. The Income and Expenditure Account thus balances each year. The Balance Sheet contains as assets, any balances owed by the CEGB and the Area Boards in respect of contributions to the above-mentioned deficit and advances for capital purposes, fixed assets, current assets from which current liabilities are shown as a deduction, and investments held. The total of these items is then shown as financed out of issues of British Electricity Stock, loans from the Government, overseas borrowings, and the balance in hand to date of the Central Guarantee Fund already mentioned.

The CEGB's annual accounts together with its statutory annual report made to Parliament on its activities are published in the same brochure as the report and accounts of the Electricity Council. The CEGB has a Revenue Account and Balance Sheet. The Revenue Account is laid out in narrative form and shows the income arising from the sales of electricity and steam, less expenditure analysed into activities such as the cost of generation, transmission, administration, depreciation of fixed assets, additional provision for the replacement of fixed assets, etc.. This gives an operating profit figure from which interest paid is deducted to give the profit for the year and this is transferred to the Balance Sheet. (The additional provision for asset replacement is based on 40% of the depreciation figure on historical cost and is designed to meet inflationary rises in capital expenditure). The Revenue Account is supplemented by a number of detailed statements which analyse the various expenditure headings. The Balance Sheet is narrative in form and shows the fixed assets – property, plant and equipment, the initial cost of nuclear fuel, etc. plus current assets and less current liabilities. The net total is then shown as financed out of loans from the Electricity Council and the CEGB's own reserves. There is also a Statement of Source and Application of Funds.

The annual accounts of each Area Board are produced and published separately together with the Board's required annual report. There are aggregated figures for the Boards' financial transactions within the consolidated accounts given in the accounts produced by the Electricity Council but their details must be looked for in the Boards' published accounts. The accounts consist of a Revenue Account and Balance Sheet in narrative form. The Revenue Account contains the income from the sale of electricity to the consumers from which the cost of purchasing the power from the CEGB is deducted to give a net figure from which the costs of distribution, consumer service, administration, account collection, depreciation of fixed assets, supplementary depreciation towards the cost of replacement of fixed assets, etc. are subtracted. After a final deduction of interest and financing expenses, the balance on the Revenue Account is carried to the Reserve on the Balance Sheet. The Balance Sheet shows the fixed assets less depreciation, together with current assets less current liabilities, and these are financed out of loans from the Electricity Council and Reserves i.e. the transfers from the Revenue Account to the Area Reserve together with the supplementary depreciation already mentioned (the Area Boards operate the same policy in this respect as the CEGB). There are statements analysing the various items in the Revenue Account and Balance Sheet, together with a Statement of Source and Application of Funds. All the sets of accounts contain accounting policy statements with notes and comparative figures for the previous year. A current cost Profit and Loss Account is also to be included in the annual accounts when published.

Audit

The Electricity Act 1957 requires the Secretary of State to appoint external auditors who must be members of a recognised body of accountants. The bodies audited are the Electricity Council, the Central Electricity Generating Board and the twelve Area Electricity Boards. The auditors report to the body audited but a copy of the report and the accounts to which it refers is sent to the Secretary of State who lays them before Parliament.

Internal audit is similarly based on the above bodies. In the case of the Boards, a typical set-up is the establishment of an Internal Audit Division which audits the activities of each tier in the organisation in accordance with powers allotted by standing instructions. Close liaison exists between the internal and external auditors, with the exchange of information in both directions and the use by the external audit staff of reports issued by the Internal Audit Division.

Questions

14.1 Describe briefly the organisation of the electricity supply industry.
14.2 Outline the external audit arrangements in the electricity supply industry.
14.3 What are the functions of an Electricity Consultative Council?
14.4 Describe the electricity grid system.
14.5 Under what conditions is the owner or occupier of a property entitled to require an electricity supply?
14.6 What powers has an electricity official to enter premises which are supplied with electricity?
14.7 Outline the legal powers of the Minister to control the actions of the electricity supply industry.
14.8 What statutory requirements govern the revenue operations of an Area Electricity Board?
14.9 What are the functions of the Electricity Council?
14.10 In what circumstances does the industry operate the Code of Practice in respect of domestic supplies?

Chapter 15

The Central Departments of the State

The Legal Basis

Until the U.K. became a member of the European Community, usually called the Common Market, the law-making process in this country involved three institutions – the Crown (personified in Her Majesty the Queen), the House of Lords, and the House of Commons. Their roles in the legislative procedure, however, so far as the effectiveness of their powers is concerned, are in the reverse order to that in which they have just been named. The House of Commons has the final say in what will become law, and whilst the House of Lords provides useful debates on occasion, it cannot prevent any Bill eventually becoming law if the Commons so insist. The Queen's role, in this instance, is merely to give her assent (i.e. agreement) to the Bills becoming Acts, and this is never refused nowadays.

The government in power at any one time is formed from the political party (or coalition of parties) which enjoys the support of the majority of the members of the House of Commons. It operates under the leadership of the Prime Minister who is appointed by the Queen. The Prime Minister, who is also the leader of the party, chooses a Cabinet of Ministers (and other Ministers and office holders who are members of the government, but not of the Cabinet) from the party members in both Houses. The Parliamentary programme of laws is planned and timed by the Cabinet which draws up government policies in accordance, as far as possible, with the party's election promises or manifesto, and sees that they are carried out. Cabinet decisions are traditionally presented as unanimous under the doctrine of collective responsibility whereby Cabinet Ministers do not make public any disagreement which they may feel with an aspect of current policy.

Under the European Communities Act 1972, the laws made by the European Community (made up of the European Economic Community, the European Coal and Steel Community and the European Atomic Energy Community) are binding upon this country. The laws are usually in the form of directives and regulations and over-ride national legislation but there is a measure of discretion in the way they are implemented because each member country has different legal institutions.

The Cabinet controls the presentation of Bills to Parliament, and after they have passed through the procedures in both Houses and received the Royal Assent, the new Acts are handed down to the government departments to be brought into operation. These departments are staffed by civil servants but are headed by politicians – Ministers or Secretaries of State – who may be in the Cabinet or not, but, in any case, are governed by the duty to ensure that their departments carry out official policies. The nature of the services called for by a particular law may require the departmental staff to implement it themselves or to act through other organisations such as public and local authorities. In the latter case, it is usual for current legislation to give the central departments a measure of control over the actions of the other authorities.

It is important to appreciate that the government departments can only do those things which Parliament has given them power to do, and this is particularly so in regard to their supervisory role over other bodies. The departments can only order an authority to take a certain line of action if they have the statutory power to do so. Occasions when a Minister has overstepped the limits of his power under an Act, are by no means rare, but they have usually arisen because the interpretation of the Act's provisions by his departmental advisers has differed from that ultimately given by the law courts. Nevertheless, the departments can influence decisions taken by the local bodies by giving them advice, either informally, in discussions and letters between officials, or formally, by sending out circular letters containing guidelines and useful information.

Originally, the Departments of State or Ministeries, as they are sometimes called, were part of the monarch's household. Secretaries or officials were responsible for dealing with such basic functions as the treasury, home and foreign affairs under the direct supervision of the sovereign. With the passing of the Middle Ages and the development of the economic and social order of the country, the administrative duties of the members of the royal court were transferred to bodies such as "commissions" which evolved into departments.

These departments, at the start, were few in number, but some 150 years ago, the growth in the range and detail of government action and regulation of activities began. Since then, the government departments and other agencies, such as advisory councils (which form part of the so-called QUANGOS – quasi-autonomous non-governmental organisations) have increased enormously both in number and size. Public corporations and nationalised industries have also proliferated. The requirements of the tasks given to the Ministers under the law have a direct effect upon the structure of their departments. Some departments of state are centralised in London, whereas others which have duties which call for a local presence or direct contact with the public, have established offices and branches throughout the country. There have also been efforts to move staff out of London. The Treasury may be taken as an example of centralisation, the Department of Health and Social Security and the Department of Employment have many local offices, whilst the Department of the Environment may be regarded as somewhat in the middle, as it has several regional offices and organisations to facilitate the carrying out of its functions.

Whilst, as has already been said, the central departments are usually under the control of the political head – the Minister – who is responsible to

Parliament to see that government policies are carried out, he is supported by the Permanent Secretary, the chief civil servant in the department, whose professional duty is to run the department on behalf of the Minister and to assist him in carrying out his duties in the House of Commons and in the Cabinet, if he is a Cabinet Minister. Below the Permanent Secretary and the departmental office staff, the department is divided into divisions, branches, offices, commissions, etc. according to the nature of the department and its work.

The personnel of most of the departments is organised in a fairly standard manner, consisting of various grades of administrators from permanent secretary (the departmental head) downwards, with finance officers, economists, statisticians, legal officers, personnel officers, information officers and general clerical staff. One factor in the encouragement of a uniform structure is that central control over staff recruitment, training, promotion, retirement and service conditions generally, is carried out by the Civil Service Department. The administrative, specialist, scientific and clerical staff are often called non-industrial civil servants, and there are also many categories of industrial civil servants who carry out various manual and miscellaneous duties in the Ministries and their installations.

The Ministries thus provide such services as the maintenance of order, internal security and defence, employment services, industrial development and trade, foreign and commonwealth relations, health and social security, inland revenue, customs and excise, and national economic planning, and they oversee local authorities in such matters as education, environmental health, and social services, and other public organisations or nationalised undertakings in respect of the particular service (or services) which they render.

No account of the development of the Civil Service and, indeed, the central departments in recent years can be regarded as complete without a reference to the Fulton Report. The Fulton Committee (which was so-called because its Chairman was Lord Fulton) was given the task in 1966 of examining the way in which the Civil Service was organised and the extent to which it was rendered inadequate for its role in government because of this. Besides the structure of the Service, there was particular reference to the methods by which staff were recruited and trained. For some time previous to the formation of the Committee, there had been widespread criticism of civil servants, alleging that they had failed to change with the times and were working in an old-fashioned, inadequate manner. In the event, the Fulton Committee in its Report in 1968 gave as its opinion that there was a lack of professionalism in the Service generally. According to the Committee, this defect arose from the preference for "generalists", e.g. arts graduates, over "specialists", e.g. accountants, in the recruiting and promotion of administrators. (The attitude to specialists might be summed up in the phrase – the expert should be on tap and not on top). Another ground for criticism was the lack of a satisfactory level of in-service training in modern management skills to the existing staff.

The Report proceeded to make a number of recommendations for curing the defects and for providing a sound basis for the Service's future development.

1. The creation of a classless Civil Service on the basis of "the best man for the job", whatever his or her career pattern and discipline. The needs of a particular position should decide the qualifications, experience and abilities of the occupant who should be appointed because he or she is the most suited to do the work well. There would be administrators of various classes, and specialists, such as economists, accountants, mathematicians, engineers, scientists, etc. but these should be drawn into occupational groups which could be contained in some score of grades. There should also be encouragement of late entrants into the Service to widen the common pool of experience. It was suggested also that the Minister should be in a position to appoint advisers from outside the Civil Service in order to give a new dimension to the advice he receives from the civil servants. A more radical recommendation was that there should be a Chief Policy Advisor for each Department who would rank equally with the present Head and whose purview would be to advise the Minister on planning whilst the present Head would continue to run the Department and advise on current matters.

2. Recruitment and other staffing matters should be centralised in a separate Civil Service Department headed by the Head of the Civil Service under the supervision of the Prime Minister. This Department should review in-training arrangements throughout the central departments, and Civil Service Colleges should also be set up to supply training in management.

3. There was a lack of contact between the Civil Service and the general public and a tendency on the part of the staff to secrecy, possibly as a protection against the questioning of advice given and decisions taken. Consideration should therefore be given to the opening up of governmental processes.

4. Civil servants should lose the protection of anonymity and become liable for their decisions and actions in managing Government projects and activities. In addition, the Civil Service should release suitable activities to distinct agencies or to newly-created public corporations. This would reduce the involvement of the Government in trading activities or, at least, make their profitability, or otherwise, easier to ascertain, and the responsibility allotted.

There has been considerable argument about how far these recommendations have been adopted to date. It is admitted that most of them have been introduced but it is alleged that they have been in a form which agreed with the letter of the Fulton Report and not with its spirit.

Nevertheless, the major changes which have taken place since 1968 include: –

1. The old class divisions were dispensed with and occupational groups were formed. These groups consist of various categories of staff, such as administration, professional and science, with a common standard for gradings and pay. It has been accepted that the most suitable candidate for a post should be appointed without regard to his past involvement in the Service.

2. Advisors are appointed by a Minister from outside the Civil Service where he considers it desirable but no progress has been made on the appointing of Policy Advisors in the Service who would hold equal status to the Permanent Secretary.

3. The recommendation to form a Civil Service Department has been fully implemented and methods of appointment and training have been amended. The Civil Service Colleges are also a reality.

4. The opening up of governmental processes has been under consideration without (according to critics) a great deal of progress. The Central Office of Information and Her Majesty's Stationery Office publish information on proposed and current government action but access to many areas of information are restricted in the national interest by the Official Secrets Act (which applies to civil servants particularly). Attempts have been made to amend this Act, but without success, despite the Franks Report in 1972, a White Paper and a Committee on the subject.

5. The Civil Service is still protected against being made publicly responsible for its actions in managing Government activities and advising Ministers upon policy matters, but there have been moves to hive off sections of the work, mainly of a trading nature, to separate governmental agencies or to public corporations. There has been some progress on introducing modern management techniques of budgeting in some departments. Among the new agencies are the Property Services Agency (run by the Department of the Environment), the Manpower Services Commission (accountable to the Department of Employment), the Equal Opportunities Commission and the Commission for Racial Equality. There are many examples of public corporations which have been created since 1968 – the Post Office in 1969, the British Gas Corporation in 1973, the British National Oil Corporation in 1976, and the National Enterprise Board in 1975, are some of the activities moved out of central government to corporations. This hiving off is at present being taken forward with proposals for the public, as individuals, to invest in one form or another in the nationalised industries and statutory corporations.

A brief survey is now given of the structure and functions of those central departments which have a relatively high degree of involvement in the activities of local and public authorities. For ease of reference, they are in alphabetical order which has little correlation with their importance to local bodies.

The Ministry of Agriculture, Fisheries and Food

The main functions of this department are self-evident from its title. It is concerned with implementing governmental policy in regard to the maintenance and development of the agricultural, horticultural, fishing and food processing industries. Specifically, this includes the prevention of diseases in animals and plants, and the control of the purity, packaging, labelling and handling of food. The department has duties concerning sea and inland fisheries, and, in, particular, those which are inland involve it with the water supply industry.

There are also relationships with international organisations, such as the European Economic Community in respect of the Common Agricultural Policy and the Common Fisheries Policy, and the Food and Agriculture Organisation of the United Nations.

The department is headed by the Minister of Agriculture, Fisheries and Food who is a Cabinet Minister and is assisted by two Ministers of State.

The Department of Education and Science

The Secretary of State for Education and Science (a Cabinet Minister) directs this department which is responsible for the application and maintenance of educational standards, the allocation of teaching staff and the distribution of building resources to the various levels of the education system (i.e. nursery, primary, secondary, further and higher). The department works with and through local education authorities, except in the case of the universities where it collaborates with the University Grants Committee (which advises on the allocation of monies to the universities). Schools and other establishments are subject to review by inspectors appointed by the department.

A Minister of State assists the Secretary of State. There are also functions connected with the encouragement of non-military scientific research. (The Chancellor of the Duchy of Lancaster is currently charged with the carrying out of Government policies in respect of the Arts, including the providing of financial assistance to art galleries, libraries and museums).

The Department of Energy

This department implements the policies of the Government under the direction of the Secretary of State for Energy in respect of the development, use and conservation of the various energy sources at present available, e.g. gas (manufactured and natural), electricity, oil, coal and smokeless fuels, and atomic energy. This means maintaining close relations with such bodies as the British Gas Corporation, the Electricity Council, the National Coal Board, the British National Oil Corporation (and the oil companies) and British Nuclear Fuels Ltd..

There is also a duty to promote the development of alternative resources, such as tidal, wave, wind, solar and geothermal power.

The Secretary of State sits in the Cabinet and has a Minister of State to help in running the department.

The Department of the Environment

The Secretary of State for the Environment directs this department which is responsible for many functions connected with the maintenance and improvement of the living conditions and physical environment of the people. This means involvement in such areas as local government, housing, new towns, urban renewal, planning and land use, environmental pollution control, water resources and supply, sewage disposal, sports and recreation, and the preservation of the countryside and historical buildings.

The department has regional offices in various chief towns, and is responsible for the operation of the Property Services Agency, which undertakes the provision of office accommodation and related services to all the Ministries. It is involved in motorway and trunk road enquiries and in aspects of road research.

The Secretary of State who is a member of the Cabinet, is assisted by two Ministers of State, one for Local Government and Environmental Services, and the other for Housing and Construction.

The Department of Health and Social Security

The Secretary of State for Social Services heads this department which supervises the social welfare and National Health services. The social services are administered from local offices of the department (e.g. pensions of various kinds, supplementary benefits, family income supplement, etc.) or by local authorities (e.g. facilities and services for the elderly, children, mentally and physically handicapped persons, and deprived persons). The National Health Service operates via Regional and Area Health Authorities which provide hospital, community health and family practitioner services, including blood transfusion and ambulances.

The department has two Ministers of State, one for Health and the other for Social Security. The Secretary of State for Social Services is a member of the Cabinet.

The Home Office

This department is under the control of the Secretary of State for the Home Department (almost always referred to as the Home Secretary) who is a Cabinet Minister and is assisted by two Ministers of State. The department is responsible for the management of the internal affairs of the country. Among its functions are the maintenance of public order, matters connected with the police, fire and civil defence services, the administration of the criminal law and the supervision of the courts, prisons and probation of offenders services. (The supervision of the courts is, however, shared with the Lord Chancellor who is a member of the Cabinet, presides over the House of Lords, and takes part in judicial proceedings in the Lords when it acts as the highest court in the land). The Home Secretary is in direct control of the Metropolitan Police Force because of the unique circumstances in the capital. Elsewhere the police forces are controlled locally, but the Home Office can supervise them by appointing inspectors and issuing regulations. Inspectors review the fire brigades in a similar manner.

The Home Office also deals with questions of nationality, community and immigration affairs, the confirmation of bye-laws, the control of lotteries and other forms of betting, the licensing of public entertainments, poisons and fire-arms, and the arrangements for national and local elections.

The Home Secretary has a unique position in the State because he acts as the channel of communication between the monarch and the citizens, and is the "keeper of the King's conscience" – he accepts petitions addressed to the Queen and exercises her prerogative of mercy in the granting of pardons. The Home Office, because it is probably the oldest and because all the other departments derived their duties from it, carries out any duties which are not specifically given to other Ministeries. This supplies a valuable flexibility in the face of unexpected developments.

The Department of Industry

The Secretary of State for Industry and two Ministers of State direct the government's policies for the promotion of industry, including the encouragement of research and design improvement, and the provision of supporting technical services. The department has specific responsibilities for steel (the British Steel Corporation), shipbuilding (British Shipbuilders), aerospace (British Aerospace) and postal and communication services (The Post Office – Royal Mail and Telecommunications). The Secretary of State occupies a seat in the Cabinet.

The Department of Transport

This department is controlled by the Minister of Transport who is not a Cabinet Minister. It carries out the official policy on matters connected with inland passenger and freight transport, e.g. buses, lorries, railways, ferries, canals, ports. It provides the motorways and trunk roads, and supervises the actions of the local authorities who are highway authorities for the other classes of roads. Vehicle and driver licensing are also a responsibility of this department. The Minister nominates the members of the nationalised transport bodies, such as British Rail and the British Waterways Board.

The Treasury

The Treasury is responsible for the planning and regulation of the national economic and financial strategies. It controls the expenditure in the public sector in various ways, oversees the collection of revenue from taxation and provides funds to run the services out of the money collected. It operates counter-inflationary policies such as the management of the money supply, control of credit, taxation levels and public sector borrowing allocations. It is responsible also for matters affecting foreign exchange, currency reserves and the balance of payments.

The department is headed by the Chancellor of the Exchequer (a member of the Cabinet), though the Prime Minister is the First Lord of the Treasury (which shows how important the Treasury is considered). There are also five Lords Commissioners who are M.P.s who act as Whips in the Commons, for the government naturally. The Chief Secretary to the Treasury, who is in the Cabinet, and the Financial Secretary and two Ministers of State, who are not, assist in the running of the department, and again, by their existence underline the importance of the Treasury in policy-making and implementation.

The Government receives advice from many sources, but one body which is chaired by the Prime Minister is the National Economic Development Council (NEDC, or "Neddy" for short). This is made up of representatives of central departments, management and trade unions, and acts as an advisor to the Government on many aspects of social and economic policy. It operates through a number of working parties which deal with specific questions referred to them and report their recommendations to the main Council. For this purpose, there is a supporting office organisation (NEDO). A matter being currently considered, is the reform of apprenticeship arrangements within industry, which requires the agreement of the Government, the employers and the trade unions before any changes can be made.

Remarks upon the Membership of the Cabinet

One of the powers enjoyed by the Prime Minister is that of appointing members of the Government, and among them, the Ministers who form the Cabinet. This power to appoint includes, of course, the right to dismiss. The Prime Minister's choice of Ministers is governed by two main factors — the character, experience and qualifications of the individual and his or her relationship with the P.M. comprise the first factor, while the second point is the current political importance of the department which he or she is to control. The Minister of certain departments are always in the Cabinet but others may be moved in or out of the Cabinet as the Government runs its course and policies develop and change.

In addition, the titles of departments and Ministers change in accordance with the functions allotted by Parliament, though a change of Government in consequence of an election result does not, of itself, change the functions, organisation or civil service staffing of the departments. This point is often made as a contrast to the practice in the United States of America, where important members of the civil service may be removed from office when there is a change of party in government.

The Cabinet may, for example, contain the following (not in exact order of precedence.

> Prime Minister and First Lord of the Treasury
> Home Secretary
> Lord Chancellor
> Foreign Secretary
> Chancellor of the Exchequer
> Chief Secretary to the Treasury
> Lord President of the Council and Leader of the House of Lords
> Lord Privy Seal
> Chancellor of the Duchy of Lancaster
> Paymaster General
> Secretaries of State for – Industry, Defence, Employment, the Environment, Scotland, Wales, Northern Ireland, Social Services, Trade, Energy, Education and Science
> Minister of Agriculture, Fisheries and Food.

Finance

It is a matter of interest and perhaps surprise to learn that, unlike local and public authorities, which are required by Parliament to keep their accounts on an income and expenditure basis, the central departments operate in the majority of cases on a cash basis. This means that the departmental estimates are divided into votes, each of which is earmarked for a specific purpose (called its ambit), and only when an invoice is paid, is it charged against the appropriate vote. No entries are made when the order is issued, or the goods and services received, and thus, if a vote is underspent, the sum underspent is lost to the department for that year and the actual payment falls against the following year's vote. A similar procedure is applied to receipts (which are called "appropriations-in-aid") where the cash is credited as it comes to hand.

This system has a number of advantages. It is speedy to operate and simple to understand. It saves staff time and, nowadays, can be linked by its very nature to the system of cash limits which the government operates to counteract the effects of inflation. The point is also made that many votes are merely transfers of cash from one part of the public sector to another, such as grant payments to local authorities which are paid on statements certified by auditors.

Its disadvantages are, however, many. There is, first of all, the difficulty of estimating the coming year's cash requirements when payments in that year may apply to transactions in previous years. In addition, flexibility is minimal because virement (i.e. the movement of an amount from an unneeded vote to one which needs it) is only permitted by the Treasury in special circumstances, and this discourages initiative on the part of accounting officers to try to optimise the use of their resources. There is no evaluation of debtors, creditors, expenses outstanding, income due, stock-in-hand, work-in-progress, nor any division between revenue and capital as regards assets — matters which are essential in an income and expenditure system. Any accountancy text book will explain the reasons why income and expenditure is preferred to receipts and payments as a book-keeping system, but briefly put, under receipts and payments, there is no basis for estimating the true cost of the services rendered or the goods produced in any one year, and no way of using that figure (as a unit cost, perhaps) to enquire into how far there has been "value for money spent".

However, notwithstanding what has been said about the majority of the central departments' accounting systems, there are exceptions. Some departments, and the Ministry of Defence comes to mind as an example, have introduced double entry, income and expenditure, and costing methods into appropriate areas of activity where a unit of output can be identified, performance assessed and a unit cost obtained. Memorandum accounts (i.e. accounts which are not an integral part of the system and, perhaps, by nature inadequately reconciled with its figures) are also to be found in administrative departments in respect of minor trading activities or those services for which charges are made to the public.

The annual procedure for providing for the spending needs of the departments begins in the spring or early summer with the officials of the Treasury and the other departments working together in compiling the Public Expenditure Survey. This contains the forecast cost of the various services for the five year starting the following April, under existing policies, and with evaluations of possible alternative courses of action. The forecasts are in respect of the revenue and capital expenditure of the central government and local authorities, government grants and loans, capital investment in the nationalised industries, capital expenditure of the public corporations, interest on the National Debt, and a contingency reserve to cover a measure of inflation above the price level assumed in the forecasts at the time they were made. The whole process is supervised by the Public Expenditure Survey Committee (or PESC), helped by the Programme Analysis and Review Committee (PARC, for short) which makes sure that the policy decisions called for in the forecasts are duly made, as it is little use voting money without a plan for its use. The Ministers are thus enabled to consider the total sum involved and take an overall view of the costs of current intentions together with the financial effect of available alternatives, if adopted. The Survey is published as a White Paper as soon as possible after the Cabinet has made its decision on it.

In the meantime, and taking into account the forecasts prepared for the coming year which are incorporated in the Survey, the various central departments prepare their estimates of their requirements for the next year and pass them to the Treasury in December. After being scrutinised by the Treasury officials, the estimates are placed before the Cabinet for their consideration and approval.

Approximately fifty per cent of the total of the estimated expenditure of the Departments is linked with the system of cash limits (or, as they have now come to be called in relation to the nationalised industries and trading public corporations, external financing limits). The other half which is free from cash limits contains such items as social security benefit payments, the amount of which is decided by the public in claiming them as of right, and is thus not amenable to control. The cash limit on any one vote, simply put, is the original estimate (which is probably on a cash basis, anyway) increased by the inflation rate envisaged in the contingency provision. These limits were introduced to reinforce the control of expenditure under conditions of high or increasing inflation, by warning the public bodies and their suppliers that unacceptable price rises mean a cut-back in expenditure in order to remain within the cash limits. The central departments disburse funds on their own services, and as advances, grants, etc. to public and local authorities. Thus they are subjected to cash limits themselves by the Treasury, and also apply them to the other bodies by controlling the payments made.

The use of cash paid as the basis for both estimate votes and the cash limits has encouraged some reorganisation and rationalisation of vote headings to be carried out, so that, for example, the responsibility for overspending on a specific vote by exceeding its cash limit falls on one officer or body. This process of matching estimates and cash limits is being continually developed.

After the Cabinet has considered and, after any revisions, approved the departmental estimates, they are placed before the House of Commons, so that Members of Parliament may debate the nature of the proposals and the sums of money involved. The estimates (now referred to as the Supply Estimates or Appropriations) are discussed during the 29 Supply Days which are earmarked for this purpose from February until early August when they are finally approved and incorporated in the annual Consolidated Fund (Appropriation) Act.

The estimates consist of two main classes of payment. The first category is called the Consolidated Fund Charges and these are such items as the interest payable on the National Debt, the salaries of judges and the Comptroller and Auditor General, the Civil List, etc.. The government is regarded as already committed to pay these, as they recur each year once the original approval has been given. Such items do, however, receive a measure of re-consideration in Parliament when their amounts are periodically reviewed in relation to the effect of inflation upon costs. The second class is called the Annual Supply Charges which are, obviously, the subject of the annual debate during the 29 Supply Days allotted by the government for this purpose. As it is a practical impossibility for the whole House of Commons to go into matters deeply because of the range of topics and the magnitude of the items, and because the Supply Days are sometimes used to make political points rather than discuss the estimates, detailed consideration is referred, when thought necessary, to the Committee of

Expenditure. This is a Select Committee of the Commons which investigates the various sets of estimates via its various sub-committees, whilst, at the same time, it considers methods of carrying out the policies embodied in the votes in more effective, possibly cheaper ways. This committee has the power to call senior civil servants of the various departments to appear before it in order to answer questions and produce documents which the committee desires to see.

The process of providing the funds which will be needed to meet the Supply estimates or appropriations approved by the House of Commons via the Committee of Supply, starts usually, in April with the presentation of the Budget to the Commons by the Chancellor of the Exchequer. The Budget takes several months to prepare in the Treasury and the Chancellor in his speech gives a review of the past year's events and trends in the national economic sphere, continues with an account of the estimates for the year just starting, and then presents his proposals for raising the money needed to meet the estimated expenditure. The final part of his speech dealing with changes in taxes is timed to take place after the close of the Stock Exchange for the day. This is intended to prevent last minute attempts to profit from such changes.

The Budget proposals (in the form of Ways and Means resolutions) are considered by the House and finally approved and authorised in the Finance Act in August. Thus, in the case of the central government, the estimates of expenditure and income are not finalised until well into the current fiscal year but arrangements exist for the continuous financing of the country, and as Parliament is sovereign in this area, there are no practical difficulties.

All the money received by the government from taxes of various kinds and miscellaneous charges is paid into the Consolidated Fund at the Bank of England. (Loans borrowed and repaid go through the National Loans Fund and foreign currency matters are dealt with in the Exchange Equalisaiton Account). All the central departments obtain their authorised needs from the Consolidated Fund under supervision by the Treasury. In addition to the duties of the Treasury in this connection, the Comptroller and Auditor General (carrying out the Comptroller part of his title) checks the correctness and completeness of the sums (e.g. tax proceeds) paid into the Consolidated Fund, the adequacy of the balance in the Fund for future calls, and that payments out of the Fund are made only in respect of approved estimates.

The Permanent Secretary of each department (i.e. the civil servant who heads the department on behalf of the Minister or Secretary of State) is usually given the responsibility of acting as an Accounting Officer. This means that he is answerable to his Minister for the legality of the payments made out of the department's appropriations, and for keeping within them (unless he has been given authority to overspend). He is also responsible to the Comptroller and Auditor General for the payments made being the correct amounts. There is some argument as to the degree to which one official who is not necessarily versed in or inclined towards accountancy and financial management can control such a wide area of expenditure as is contained in the activities of a Department of State. The answer lies perhaps in the formation of management teams to whom the task of controlling expenditure should be delegated.

The Form of the Published Accounts

The Appropriation Accounts (as they are called) for each department follow the form of the Estimates in that expenditure and income are analysed to the same sub-heads. In most cases, expenditure and income are payments and receipts, and these are compared with the Estimates item by item, so that differences, i.e. under- and over-spendings, are shown. Reasons for the differences are given in the form of notes. Where there is an overall underspending, the amount underspent is shown as surrendered. An overspending, if material, would probably be the subject of a report by the Comptroller and Auditor General to Parliament as regards its financing.

Audit

The accounts of the departments are audited by the staff of the Exchequer and Audit Department which is under the control and direction of the Comptroller and Auditor General (who is thus carrying out the second part of his title). This official possesses a high degree of independence in the way in which he carries out his duties. He is appointed for life by the Crown and his salary is an automatic charge on the Consolidated Fund. He is answerable only to Parliament in respect of his work and can only be dismissed by the joint action of the Lords and Commons. He is not a civil servant, and has usually held responsible public posts and has a thorough knowledge of governmental systems. He is, however, not necessarily previously trained in auditing, though he is in charge of a staff of skilled auditors and their ancillary workers, numbering in total nearly 600 civil servants.

The staff is organised into teams or sections which operate within larger groups or divisions. Each division is allocated a sphere of operation among the departments and accounts to be audited, and deploys its teams in the appropriate way according to the nature of the work. Where necessary, the general auditors are assisted by specialists, such as computer and systems auditors.

This system of audit incorporates characteristics of both external and internal audit, in having a completely independent chief auditor but a staff which is part of the establishment but seconded to the work. It was introduced under the Exchequer and Audit Act 1866 and applied to all the central departments, but various forms of audit applicable to individual departments had existed before the Act was passed. The objectives of the audit include the establishment of the accuracy of the accounts and the proper observance of any legal requirements as to the nature and purpose of the items and the way in which they are recorded and presented. The auditors must be satisfied that the sums appropriated have been actually approved by Parliament and have been spent in accordance with internal control systems which are adequate in design and applied in an efficient manner. They must also satisfy themselves that the procedures followed in the preparation of the forecasts result in appropriations which are realistic in amount, and they must consider whether value has been received for the money which has been spent. The audit staff have the right of access to the books and records kept by the central departments, the National Health Service Authorities, a few minor public corporations, such as the Civil Aviation Board, and by arrangement, the Universities and other non-governmental institutions which rely heavily on funds from Parliament.

The system has been criticised for lack of independence, because the staff of the Exchequer and Audit Department are civil servants who are recruited by the Civil Service Department which handles some aspects of their personnel management. Also, though encouragement is given to the auditors to enquire into "value for money" aspects of the expenditure audited, the main interest is in negative facets such as the prevention of illegality and the reduction of waste or extravagance, rather than positive matters such as good planning and use of departmental monies. The suggestion has also been made that one strong audit should cover all bodies whose main financing comes from government funds. Consideration is being given to passing legislation to strengthen the powers and independence of the present audit and to widen its scope by bringing the District Audit Service into the Exchequer and Audit Department or otherwise creating a single comprehensive service for all public expenditure met out of State funds.

The Comptroller and Auditor General's duty is to make a report on each set of audited accounts to the House of Commons, which refers them to the Public Accounts Committee (a Select Committee which has the duty to consider the report and the issues arising from them). These reports call attention specifically to instances of waste, extravegence, non-compliance with legal requirements, etc., and the Committee reviews the evidence, interviews the departmental officers and makes recommendations for correcting the matter, such as improvements in procedures, to the departments involved. The Committee makes periodical reports to Parliament and the press sometimes gives publicity to the more newsworthy examples of government inefficiency. As with all audits, however, minor matters are normally settled by discussions between the auditor and the officials of the department under audit, and recorded by memoranda, so that the audit report is unqualified. Where an audit reveals an overspending in the past year, the Public Accounts Committee must first report to the House of Commons on the circumstances under which the overspending happened, before sanction is given for it to be met in the current year out of a supplementary vote.

There are arrangements within the various departments for the internal audit of transactions (and to a lesser extent, systems and procedures) by members of their own staff under the direction of senior officials who have financial duties. It is apparent that auditing standards vary between departments, and that these can be improved in many cases. Mention is often made of the success of the Ministry of Defence's Directorate of Internal Audit in this direction. It is suggested that the status of the internal audit should be raised in order to improve its overall position in the central departments, by higher grading of the staff, the recruitment of more accountants, the secondment of members of staff with wide experience of the work of the department, greater emphasis on systems audits, and the inclusion of a spell in internal audit in the career plan of all prospective senior staff. The adequacy of the internal audit arrangements in any department may be investigated by the staff of the Comptroller and Auditor General, and both sets of auditors can work together by sharing their duties to avoid overlap, particularly where the internal audit is proved to be satisfactory in the opinion of the Audit and Exchequer Department.

Questions
15.1 List the central departments mostly involved with local government functions.
15.2 What are the duties of the Comptroller and Auditor General?
15.3 Outline the way in which Parliament budgets for central departmental expenditure.
15.4 What are the functions of (a) the Committee on Expenditure, and (b) the Public Accounts Committee?
15.5 What matters does the Chancellor of the Exchequer deal with in his Budget speech?
15.6 Outline the internal organisation of a typical central department.
15.7 How does the Treasury operate control over government finances?
15.8 What was the assignment given to the Fulton Committee in 1966?
15.9 Give an outline of the functions of the Property Services Agency.
15.10 What were the main recommendations contained in the Fulton Report?
15.11 Outline the nature and functions of the National Economic Development Council.
15.12 What does the Programme Analysis and Review Committee do?

Chapter 16

Public Corporations

The foregoing chapters in this book have dealt almost exclusively with services in the public sector which at one time or another have been part of the sphere of operation of local government, though, under present policies, some of these services are carried out by bodies other than local authorities. This chapter, on the other hand, is intended to deal with a number of public corporations and nationalised industries which have not been through the process of "municipalisation" but have each followed a separate path of development with its own particular pattern. Before the selected bodies are described, there is an attempt to lay down some general ground rules applicable to publc sector organisation and their control by the Government.

The variety which is found in the services and industries represented by these publicly-owned bodies stems to a great extent from the mixture of motives which led to their being taken into the public sector or to their being chosen as candidates for public financing when they were first created. Some are included in the public sector because it is felt that they should be protected against political pressure which might be exerted upon them and their activities, others because monopoly powers should be subject to control to prevent those powers being abused, some require large-scale planning and finance for efficient operation whilst needing to render uneconomic services which their other services must subsidise, and, in the case of some older industries, nationalisation has been a form of rescue operation by providing public money for reconstruction, and sometimes the maintenance of employment, either nationally or in the regions, has been a factor.

Despite all the differences, however, in the nature and origin of the various corporations, certain characteristics and principles of control and accountability of a common nature can be seen in the Acts of Parliament under which these organisations have formed or developed. A summary of many of these points may be expressed in the following manner: —

1. Public corporations are not Government departments (which are gathered together as "the Crown"), but are separate distinct legal beings over and above the human beings (acting as members or officers) who act for them. They are subject to the doctrine of Ultra Vires as they are creatures of statute and can only do those acts which the law has given them the power to do. One aspect of their independent status from the Government as a legal entity is that their employees are not civil servants, and there are cases where the workforce's status has changed where a

central department has become a corporation. (Another effect of altering the status of employees has been to make the statistics of Civil Service manpower somewhat confusing as staff are passed to and fro as changes occur).

2. Each public corporation is placed by Parliament under the control of a Secretary of State or a Minister who acts as the main channel of communication between the Government, the House of Commons and the managers of the corporation. The Minister is given a number of supervisory powers and duties in respect of the operations of the corporation and the actions of the managers, and he is answerable to Parliament for the manner in which he applies those powers or carries out those duties. This means that the Board which manages the corporation has some discretion as regard its internal arrangements and a degree of independence in areas of activity and decision-taking to which the Minister's powers do not reach.

The general rule has developed in Parliamentary usage that the Minister should be required to reply to questions of public importance or which are related to overall policy — pricing, investment in capital assets, borrowing to finance investment, forward planning, etc. — for which he has a measure of responsibility. He is not to be questioned (or may refuse to answer) on points of trifling detail to do with the routine management of the corporation. This ruling differs from that applied to questions in the House dealing with the affairs of a Government department. In this case, the Minister, as its political head, is accountable for and must answer in respect of all aspects of his department's work, even a most routine matter (A particularly bizarre example of this is the responsibility of the Secretary of State for Social Services for the detailed running of the National Health Service, notwithstanding that the RHAs and AHAs are legally public corporations). Specific examples of a Minister's powers and duties are to be found in the paragraphs which follow, but one power which is essential to him in carrying out his supervision of the public corporation's actions is that of calling for such information as he considers necessary from the Board to enable him to carry out his duties. This power can be exercised for general policy matters or for a routine affair which may develop from small beginnings to a matter of great public concern and be the subject of questions in the House.

3. The Minister has the power to appoint the members of the Board which manages the public corporation. He must hold consultations before appointments are made and choose persons who have experience or expertise in the service or industry involved. He appoints the Chairman and Deputy Chairman (or Chairmen) as such. These are full-time, normally, whilst the other members of the Board may be full- or part-time. The size of the membership of the Board varies in accordance with the particular organisation and salaries are paid in accordance with scales approved by Parliament. The power to appoint members to the Board also means that the Minister can dismiss them, and it is argued that this can be a potent

factor in the attitude of the Board towards the carrying out of the wishes of the Government where the wellbeing of the corporation may need to be subordinated to the economic benefit of the nation as a whole.

4. Public corporations have a general duty by law to meet all reasonable demands at the lowest cost which is compatible with the providing of an efficient service. There is usually an additional requirement to ensure that, over a number of years (which has come to be taken as four or five), income should be enough to cover the running costs (i.e. charges to revenue, including an adequate provision for depreciation of fixed assets and necessary contributions to reserves). In conjunction with this, the use of surpluses and transfers to and out of reserves usually require the Minister's consent.

In recent years, the Government has agreed with each public corporation on a rate of return on net assets as a target figure for its performance. In drawing up this target, allowance is made for any losses incurred by the public corporation in providing uneconomic services in the national interest or in foregoing price rises. There is normally a provision in the law giving the Minister the power to give directions to the Board to act as the Government desires in matters which affect the national economic interests. These directions are issued after the matter has been discussed between the Minister and the Board, and, as has been said, they are usually connected with the economy, such as making pricing policies conform with national priorities, the timing of investment policies, the provision of services which do not pay for themselves but which give social benefit, etc..

The Government has also introduced performance indicators, such as the cost per man-hour of services, which are intended to be used to measure the level of performance of public corporations where comparisons can be made, for instance, for different parts of the country.

5. The Acts which create the public corporations contain provisions for reports to be made regarding the progress of the bodies and their financial state. There must be an annual report to the responsible Minister which sets out the principal points of interest in the year's operations. The corporation is also required to prepare a set of annual accounts from properly kept records and to have them audited by a professionally qualified accountant appointed each year by the Minister. The audited accounts and the auditor's report upon them are sent to the Minister as soon as possible after the audit, and he lays these documents, together with the corporation's report and one from himself on the industry, before the House of Commons. There, they are considered, by the Select Committee within whose ambit they fall (usually the Select Committee on Nationalised Industries or S.C.N.I. for short), and usually become the subject of a committee report to the House in due course. It is required in many cases that the accounts follow the best commercial practice and it is also usual for the Minister to be able to lay down rules as to their form of presentation and contents.

6. The expenditure by the public corporations on capital schemes and the ways in which they finance it, particularly when the costs are not borne by internally-generated funds, are subject to a number of legal and financial controls. The investment plans of the corporations are prepared in consultation with the various responsible Ministers and their financing needs are a component in the Public Expenditure Survey (i.e. the PESC system) which is produced annually to cover the next five years. Power to borrow money up to permitted limits from the Government or other body or person is given by law and such loans can be for short or long periods. Borrowings from the Government can be out of the National Loans Fund or in the form of Public Dividend Capital on which a dividend is paid by the corporation to the Exchequer. So far as loans from outside sources are concerned, the Treasury has the power to guarantee the payment of interest or the repayment of principal, and can thus help any corporation in a time of difficulty. At present, most loans are from Government sources, so this power is little used.

One aspect in which public sector undertakings have to date tended to differ from private sector companies is that investors (some public authorities can issue stock) are unable to exert any influence upon the policies carried out by the management. The recent proposals by the Government to encourage investment by individuals in public corporations and nationalised industries may affect this principle but investment will probably not carry voting powers.

Recent years have seen the introduction of a system of cash limits which is applied to spending in the public sector, including the need for capital financing for the public corporations. Each corporation is thus required to keep its spending within the limit allotted to it by, where necessary, reducing the rate of payments combined with changing the timing and priorities of schemes. In practice, the cash limits tend to over-ride the legal limits laid down for borrowing entitlements and also supersede the figures included in PESC, as the cash limits are usually produced later and are more stringent.

7. It is usual to include a system of user or consumer councils in the legal arrangements for public services and nationalised industries. These bodies are intended to fill the need of the individual to feel that he can have some effect upon the actions of large-scale organisations which often approach virtual monopolies, especially where he perceives waste or experiences inefficiency. The Minister controlling the particular public corporation appoints the members of the council (who usually number 20 to 30 persons) from representatives of the various classes of users or consumers. Candidates are usually nominated by organisations representing the various interests and pressure groups. The council has the right to be kept informed of developments in services, changes in charges, etc. and can make recommendations about them and any other matters which might be referred to it. It also has a duty to receive and take up complaints from the public and to pass on to the Board any evidence of waste or inefficiency

which comes to its notice. The council meets a number of times in the year and normally receives support in respect of administration, accommodation and staffing costs from public funds.

Another matter which is of a nature akin to consumer representation is the requirement placed upon the public corporations to set up systems for joint consultation and negotiation on the terms and conditions of employment of their various classes of employees. Such matters as salaries and wages, pensions, uniform and other allowances together with measures for welfare, health and safety at work are within the ambit of the system and agreements made with other bodies (e.g. trade unions) are usually to be forwarded to the Minister.

8. Besides the general duty of controlling the actions of the public corporation, a Minister may be given certain detailed functions under the relevant legislation. Thus, in addition to the duties which have already been mentioned in the preceding paragraphs of this chapter, he may be made responsible for negotiations regarding wages and other staff conditions and for the management of the pension fund for the employees of the Board. He may also approve staff training arrangements and research programmes into areas of interest to the industry. He may also have the final say on matters put forward by the consumer council as needing action. The Minister can also exert influence on the Board and its decisions without actually using his legal powers, and, perhaps, in ways beyond the scope of these powers. Decisions can be reached in principle at informal meetings between the Chairman and the Minister or between their respective staffs. The Minister may persuade the Board to agree to a line of action without issuing a direction in return for a protective attitude to the corporation against Parliamentary interference in routine management. On the other hand, a Minister may tend to impose his will upon the Board by the implied threat of using his legal power of dismissal. It must not be forgotten, however, that chairmen and members of corporations may decide to submit their resignations when they disagree with official policy. Such occasions often prove embarrassing to the Government by giving the Opposition and the press an opportunity to criticise the Government's actions.

9. In addition to the Minister's duty to reply to questions in the House of Commons on matters relating to a public corporation which have been made his responsibility, there are other ways by which Members of Parliament are able to become informed about the operations of any corporation. Her Majesty's Opposition has the privilege of choosing the topics to be debated on the Supply days and these can include matters relating to nationalised undertakings and corporations. Similarly, debates can be arranged from the Government side to discuss the current state and future policies of various public sector bodies. Such debates are often based on White Papers or discussion documents and the Minister responsible for a particular industry may make statements. Another source of information arises from the publication of the deliberations and reports of the Select Committees of the House of Commons, especially that on Nationalised

Industries (S.C.N.I.) which scrutinises the annual reports and accounts of most public corporations. The Public Accounts Committee and the Committee on Expenditure (which are also Select Committees) are also involved on occasion in examining matters related to finance and administration of those corporations which are outside the ambit of the S.C.N.I., though overlapping can occur, for instance, when the whole public sector is considered by them.

Finally, the role of the Treasury must be mentioned. It has the right to be involved and consulted in all matters which have to do with finance – capital investment plans, pricing policies, use of funds, salary scales, efficiency of performance, etc. – as it is charged with the mechanics of maintaining the national economy and is reluctant to advance public money for wasteful or inefficient purposes. Each Ministry thus works in co-operation with the Treasury in controlling the individual public corporations allotted to it.

The following pages contain descriptions of the role, constitution and financial arrangements of a number of public corporations and nationalised industries but to avoid repetition, mention is restricted in some aspects to variations in pattern from the normal arrangements which have been summarised in the preceding paragraphs of this chapter.

The public corporations are listed as follows in alphabetical order: –

> British Aerospace
> British Airways
> British Broadcasting Corporation
> British National Oil Corporation
> British Rail
> British Steel Corporation
> National Coal Board
> National Enterprise Board
> Post Office (Royal Mail and British Telecommunications)

British Aerospace

British Aerospace is a public corporation which was formed under the Aircraft and Shipbuilding Industries Act 1977 out of a number of organisations in the aviation industry, such as the British Aircraft Corporation, Hawker Siddeley (Aviation and Dynamics), Scottish Aviation, etc. and their subsidiary companies. Its functions are to carry out research in connection with problems of flight and to design, repair, make and sell aircraft (for war or civil purposes), including rockets, missiles and space flight vehicles, together with their related operational and supporting systems. In carrying out its operations, the corporation has a duty to pay regard to the needs of national defence, and it has wide powers of acquiring firms and interests in firms and partnerships in pursuit of its objectives. It can have its duties changed or added to by order of the Secretary of State for Industry who is the Minister charged by Parliament with the responsibility of supervising the corporation's activities. The 1977 Act requires British Aerospace to encourage "industrial democracy" – the participation of the work force in policy decisions – within the corporation and its subsidiaries. In addition, the Act empowers the Secretary of State to give the corporation orders as to its financial duties, such as a requirement to give a minimum return on the capital invested, say, 20%. There is a maximum to the amount that the corporation can borrow but the Minister has power to increase the maximum within a given figure.

British Aerospace is managed by a Board whose members are appointed by the Minister. They comprise the Chairman, Deputy Chairman, and from seven to 20 other members. Some of these other members have functions allotted to them, e.g. Chief Executive (and his Deputy) for the Aircraft Group, Chief Executive for the Dynamics Group, Director of Finance, Director of Corporate Strategy, Technical Director and Industrial Director. At present, there are nine full-time members already mentioned and two part-timers. The chief officers who act under the instructions of the Board include the Secretary and Legal Adviser, the Treasurer and the Financial Controller.

The corporation must maintain proper accounting records from which accounts can be produced to give a true and fair view of the financial state of the whole organisation. The year end is the 31st December. The accounts contain the auditor's report, the accounting policies, a Consolidated Profit and Loss Account and Balance Sheet (which include the figures for the various subsidiary companies in the aviation field), a Consolidated Source and Application of Funds Statement, a Value Added Statement which shows the sources of the value added to the product and how it is shared among the employees (as wages), the providers of the capital (as interest), the government (as taxation) and the organisation (as retained provisions for depreciation, etc.), and details of the pay of members of the Board and employees in bands of gross salary. Comparative figures for the previous year are also given.

Auditing arrangements are similar to those applied in most nationalised undertakings. The Secretary of State appoints an external auditor who must be a member of a recognised accountancy body, i.e. one whose members are empowered to audit limited company accounts under the Companies Act, the appointment running annually. On the completion of the audit, the accounts and the auditor's report are sent by the Board to the Minister who places them before Parliament. The corporation also prepares an annual report on its activities and this is incorporated with the accounts and submitted to the Minister.

Under the provisions of the British Aerospace Act 1980, the Secretary of State has the power to decide when to carry out changes in structure and to make any financial arrangements needed to convert British Aerospace into a limited company which would be subject to the Companies Acts.

British Airways
The carriage of passengers and freight by air has never been completely nationalised in this country. The industry began under private enterprise during the 1920's and, though Government airlines occupy the major position in the market today, private operators are still entitled to share in the available traffic. State participation in air transport started by subsidising two important companies, Imperial Airways and British Airways, during the inter-war period. Imperial Airways linked the Commonwealth and Empire whilst British Airways provided routes in Europe (including the British Isles). The Government took a further step by merging these two companies into the British Overseas Airways Corporation under an Act of that name in 1939 but the commencement of the second World War in that year effectively stopped any developments for the following six years. In 1946, the Civil Aviation Act was passed which kept B.O.A.C. in being but restricted its area of operation by forming two other public corporations – British European Airways and British South American Airways – to serve the parts of the world given in their titles. Experimentation proceeded further. In 1949, the Air Corporations Act moved B.S.A.A. back into B.O.A.C., and thereafter the Civil Aviation Act 1971 merged B.O.A.C. and B.E.A. into the British Airways Board. To start with, the three corporations continued to exist together but this arrangement proved difficult and the Air Corporations (Dissolution) Order 1973 dissolved B.O.A.C. and B.E.A. and transferred all their assets and liabilities to British Airways (as it is now called). The two dissolved corporations became divisions of the main body. During the years of operation, various subsidiary companies have been acquired or started and these also form part of the group. This means that, besides its main duty of providing air transport for passenger and freight, the Board also has interests in holiday tour firms, helicopter operation, telecommunications and technical services, etc.. The Minister may also allow the corporation to make engines and parts of aircraft, e.g. frames.

British Airways is managed by a Board which contains from eight to 15 members – the Chairman, one or more Deputy Chairmen, and the other members are all appointed by the Secretary of State for Trade. The Board has a duty to ensure that its income is enough to meet its outgoings over a period of years and, in addition, it is required to agree with the Minister on a rate of return which should be earned on its net assets. The Minister also has the power to direct the Board, after he has consulted it, to carry out actions and make decisions in the national interest. These are usually to do with economic matters – revisions of tariffs, etc.. The Government may lend money to the Board for capital investments or allow it to borrow from other persons, home or overseas, but there is a limit set by Parliament as well as the current system of cash limits which restrict the corporation's actions. A portion of the money owed to the Government is called "Public Dividend Capital" and the Government receives income from this in the form of dividend.

The financial year ends on the 31st March and the Board is required to produce annual accounts in a form laid down by the Minister. The accounts contain the auditor's report, a statement of accounting policies, Profit and Loss Account and Balance Sheet for both the Group and the Board, Group Current Cost Statement and Statement of Source and Application of Funds and details of various items in the final accounts. These accounts are audited by a suitably qualified accountant appointed annually by the Secretary of State and, after the audit is finished, a copy of the accounts and the auditor's report go to the Minister and he lays them before Parliament. The Board is also required to make an annual report to the Minister and this also goes to Parliament along with the Minister's own report.

At present, the Government is planning to alter the financial structure of the corporation by offering a minority interest in the capital to the public in the form of shares so as to encourage more public participation whilst reducing an area of State intervention into industry and commerce.

The Civil Aviation Act 1971 also formed the Civil Aviation Authority which is a public corporation with the duty of issuing licences for the operation of airlines, the enforcement of safety regulations and the giving of aid and information regarding air safety, etc.. The Authority is also required to make certain that British airlines can cope with reasonable demands for air travel and that there is no discrimination against private airline operators in the getting of business.

The Secretary of State for Trade appoints the members of the Authority — six to 12 persons, including the Chairman and up to two Deputy Chairmen — and he has the power to give them advice in regard to their duties.

The Authority has a duty to ensure that income covers expenditure over the years. It has limited borrowing powers and its charges are subject to the approval of the Minister. Annual accounts must be prepared and these are audited by the Comptroller and Auditor General who places them before Parliament together with his report. The Minister also makes a report on his financial dealings with the Authority and this is examined by the C. & A.G.. The Authority's annual report and that of the Minister are similarly put before the House.

British Broadcasting Corporation

The B.B.C. is a corporation which was granted a Royal Charter in 1926 under which it was given the power to provide radio and television services to the nation. To this end, the Corporation can provide programmes, equipment, stations, studios, installations, vehicles, etc.. The B.B.C. is controlled by a Board whose members are appointed by the Queen and comprise a Chairman, Vice-Chairman, Governors for Wales, Scotland and Northern Ireland, respectively, and seven other persons. The Board considers matters of broad policy and uses committees for more detailed discussion of such matters as Programme Policy; Finance, Property and

Building; and Advisory Bodies. Persons from outside the Corporation are co-opted on to these committees where their special knowledge is of use. The members also form Groups to consider specific matters.

The Board receives advice from the General Advisory Council and a number of more specialised advisory panels on such matters as the effect of the B.B.C.'s activities upon the social order, religion, commerce, industry, agriculture, education, music, regional affairs, etc. Again, the members of these bodies are persons of experience and knowledge in the areas involved.

The chief officers appointed by the Corporation form the Board of Management. This Board includes the Director General (who is the chief executive), the Managing Directors of T.V., Radio, External Broadcasting, Finance, Public Affairs, Personnel, News and Current Affairs, and Engineering. They advise the members and carry out their orders.

The Minister who is responsible to Parliament in respect of the general operations and policies of the B.B.C. is the Home Secretary. He has power under the Wireless Telegraphy Acts to give orders to the B.B.C. on matters of national importance.

The capital and revenue expenditure of the Corporation is met, so far as Home Services are concerned out of the licence fees charged in respect of television sets, whilst the External Service is mainly financed out of government grant because the monitoring of foreign broadcasts and the teaching of English as well as the overseas news service in foreign languages are involved. So far as the Home Services are concerned, there is also a minor source of income from the sale of publications, discs, cassettes etc..

The financial year ends on the 31st March and the annual accounts are issued in conjunction with the Corporation's General Report which it is required to make under its Charter. The Home Services are dealt with in Income and Expenditure form, the income, as already mentioned, comes from TV licences and sales of literature, etc., but the expenditure is analysed between TV and Radio and divided between operating and capital. Income and expenditure on providing Open University broadcasts is kept separate. The External Service shows its revenue and capital expenditure allocated against the grant from the government. The Balance Sheet is in narrative form and shows how Fixed and Current Assets less Current Liabilities are financed by a Capital Account and other balances which include a provision for future pensions. There are a number of supporting statements giving details of accounting policies, distribution of licence fee income, analysis of Fixed Assets, etc.. Figures for the previous year are also given.

The Charter provides that the accounts of the B.B.C. should be audited each year by an auditor who must be duly qualified to carry out the audit of limited companies. The Corporation makes the appointment but the approval of the Home Secretary is required (the Postmaster General was originally the supervising Minister but after the last war the functions were passed to the Home Office).

British National Oil Corporation

The British National Oil Corporation was formed under the Petroleum and Submarine Pipelines Act 1975 and given the role from the 1st January 1976 of acting as a partner to the oil companies in exploring the continental shelf area belonging to the U.K. and developing the North Sea fields. The Corporation was given the duty of advising the Government on oil policy matters and looking after the national interest. (The role of advisor has now been withdrawn). It is involved in acquiring and re-selling much of the output of the oilwells, and it has all the foreseeable powers it needs to take part in the exploitation of the fields. It can carry out exploration, production, transporting, refining, storing, as well as the buying and selling of oil. It also has the power of providing research and staff training facilities and of acquiring subsidiary companies when it is desirable for the objectives of the Corporation. Its main subsidiaries are B.N.O.C. (Exploration) Ltd., B.N.O.C. (Development) Ltd., B.N.O.C. (Trading) Ltd., and B.N.O.C. (Ventures) Ltd., and there are a number of associated companies.

The B.N.O.C. is a statutory or public corporation and is controlled by a Board whose members are all appointed by the Secretary of State for Energy from persons with experience in the industry. The Board comprises the Chairman and Chief Executive, the Deputy Chairman (both of whom are appointed as such) and from eight to 20 other members of whom two are civil servants who act as "official members".

The Corporation is supervised by the Secretary of State for Energy who is responsible to Parliament for its broad policy but not matters of daily routine. He can given directions which the Board must obey in the national economic interest and has power to demand such information as he needs to carry out his supervisory duties. The Minister applies the system of external financing limits in respect of borrowings which he can advance out of the National Oil Account which his Department controls. (All the income from oil sales and licence charges are paid into this account, borrowings to the B.N.O.C. and its subsidiaries are passed through it, and their expenditure is met out of it. The Comptroller and Auditor General makes an annual report upon its state.) The Corporation is also under a duty to co-ordinate its actions with those of British Gas.

Although discussions have taken place at Government level about the sale of some of the Corporation's assets, the decision appears to be that there should be no sales at the present time, but ways of introducing capital from the public (as individuals acting as investors) are under consideration.

The financial year ends on the 31st December, and the annual accounts are in narrative form and are consolidated because of the need to include the subsidiary companies' activities. The Corporation must keep reliable records upon which the accounts must be based and show the profit or loss for the year in question. The accounts contain the auditor's report and accounting policies and are supported by notes. Corresponding figures are given for the preceding year's accounts. The Consolidated Profit and Loss Account contains figures relating to the sale of the Corporation's own oil and that purchased and re-sold, depreciation of general exploration costs, and provisions for site restoration. The Consolidated Balance Sheet shows the Net Capital Employed in the form of Net Fixed Assets, Site Restoration Expenditure and Net Current Assets, and its financing out of the National Oil Account and Advance Oil Sale Proceeds. (This last item is in respect of money received in advance of deliveries of oil). A Balance Sheet is also provided for the B.N.O.C. separately and there is a Statement of Source and Application of Funds, whilst there is a note in the report on the estimated effect of inflation upon the Profit and Loss Account.

The Secretary of State of Energy has the duty of appointing annually a member of a recognised body of accountants to audit the financial accounts of the Corporation. After the close of the audit, the Board is required to send copies of its annual report, its accounts and the report made by the auditor to the Secretary of State who must place these statements before the House of Commons together with his own report.

British Rail

Britain was the country which first invented and developed railways. During the 19th century, hundreds of small companies were formed in what was called a "Railway Boom". Many of these ventures failed but the surviving lines began a process of merging which culminated in the 1920's in the formation of four major companies – Great Western (GWR), London Midland and Scottish (LMS), London North Eastern (LNER), and Southern (SR). Despite these amalgamations, the railways had had difficulty in paying their way for many years and, finally, their equipment and rolling stock were run down in supporting the war effort between 1939 and 1945. Thus at the close of the second World War, the financial state of the railways which needed capital renewal and investment on a large scale (such as could only be supplied by the Government) together with the then current vogue to nationalisation led to their being transferred to public ownership.

The method adopted by the Transport Act 1947 was to form the British Transport Commission, an omnibus body, which took over the various classes of transport undertakings and acted via a number of Executives, each related to one form of transport. The cost of running the railways proved to be the major burden upon the Transport Commission and various attempts were made during the 1950's and at the start of the 1960's to alleviate the situation, including the replacement of the Railway Executive by Area Boards and the carrying out of the "Beeching Plan" aimed at reshaping or, perhaps as a better description, streamlining the railway system. The Government also relieved the railways of some of its liability for debt. Nevertheless, it was felt that the British Transport Commission was unable to integrate the various activities for which it was responsible and such criticisms and disappointment with results led to the passing of the

Transport Act 1962. This Act dissolved the BTC and the British Railways Board was set up as one of a number of public corporations with the duty of operating freight and passenger railway services in a safe, efficient and economic manner. The Board also runs related services via various subsidiary organisations, such as ferries, hovercraft services, hotels, catering, railway engineering, property and industrial estate management, transport consultancy, advertising, express freight services, harbours, etc.. Plans are afoot to offer minority interests in shareholdings in a number of these subsidiaries to the investing public so as to raise money which can be used for the expansion of British Rail and to allow management to concentrate on their main task of running railways. Nevertheless, it is intended that British Rail will retain minority interests, and besides selling shares to the public the Board may be able to bring in partners. The subsidiaries covered by the proposals include Sealink, B.R. Hovercraft, B.R. Property and British Transport Hotels. It is thus intended to denationalise the ferries (ships and hovercraft), the hotels (including Gleneagles), the docks at Cardiff, Grimsby, Hull, King's Lynn, Newport, Southampton and Swansea, and surplus goods yards and industrial estates built on British Rail land.

The Secretary of State for Transport appoints the members of the Board which contains from 12 to 19 members who include the Chairman, one or two Deputy Chairmen and other members, some of whom are part-time. There are five Regional Advisory Boards – Eastern, Midland and North West, Scottish, Southern, and Western – which have as Chairmen the Regional General Managers, and whose function is to advise the British Rail Board on matters to do with public and user relations. The Advisory Boards are drawn from representatives of industry and public authorities. There is also the British Rail Council composed of a joint membership of representatives of the British Rail Board and the Trade Unions involved in the industry.

The Minister has the usual powers of supervision of the industry, such as the power to give directions to the B.R. Board, the control of borrowing, the operation of the cash limits (called the external financing limits nowadays), and the duty to receive the Board's annual report and audited accounts (with the auditor's report) and to lay them together with his own report before Parliament. There they are subject to the scrutiny of the Select Committee on Nationalised Industries.

The British Rail Board must keep proper records and prepare annual accounts in a form laid down by the Secretary of State and is required to ensure that, year by year, income is not less than running costs. Running costs are to include any necessary provisions for the depreciation or renewal of assets and payments to reserves of a general nature.

The published accounts contain the auditor's report, Accounting Policies, the Consolidated Profit and Loss Account and Balance Sheet, Source and Application of Funds Statement and various Performance Indicators. There are also Statements of Reserves, Capital Expenditure, Loans, etc.

and a Current Cost Accounting Statement. Included in the detailed statements is one in regard to Government Grants received by British Rail to support the provision of uneconomic public services, standardisation, etc.. The year end is the 31st December and figures are given for the previous year.

The accounts are audited by a person appointed by the Secretary of State from members of any of the accountancy bodies recognised as auditors of limited companies under the Companies Acts.

The public and other users of the railways services are represented by the Central Transport Consultative Committee and for Wales, Scotland and various areas of England there are Transport Users' Consultative Committees. Unlike most consumer protection bodies, these committees have restricted duties as they are involved mainly in reporting to the Minister on suggested line closures and their effect on areas and individuals.

British Steel Corporation

Iron and steel production has a long history in this country where a significant contribution has been made to the technologicial advances which have led to the modern industry with its large-scale continuously operated plants producing high grade products. During the Industrial Revolution and the expansion of commerce and industry in the 19th and early part of the 20th centuries, the iron and steel industry experienced a greatly increased demand for its products, especially steel, but after the first World War, difficulty began to be experienced because of the depressed nature of the economy and a falling off in technological invention and progress. Difficulty also arose in finding funds to support the cost of modernising plant, such as furnaces and mills. The Government introduced a measure of protection against cheap imports and encouraged collective action by the industry but the advent of the second World War meant that Government control of such a vital industry was essential, and, indeed, the demand for its output was so great that rationing had to be introduced. The private ownership and management of the companies continued, of course.

The industry was one of those listed for nationalisation by the Labour Government after the end of the war but proved more difficult than the majority of industries involved because of its spread of products, processes, and undertakings over several regions of the country. The Iron and Steel Act 1949 came into operation in 1951 by forming the Iron and Steel Corporation which began to bring the various companies into public ownership. Within the year, however, the Government changed from Labour to Conservative and the Corporation was stopped from taking any further action in the direction of nationalisation. The Iron and Steel Act 1953 abolished the Corporation and the process of selling off the firms which it had already acquired was begun. The sale of these firms was a slow process and had not been completed before a later Labour administration renationalised the industry on the grounds of it needing more investment in capital assets and greater collective action. The British Steel Corporation was created under the Iron and Steel Act 1967 which nationalised a number of leading iron and steel companies, such as Colvilles, Richard Thomas and Baldwins, and British Steel and Tube, together with their subsidiary companies. The Corporation thus provides the major part (some 80/90%) of the country's output of crude iron and steel for industrial purposes, in addition to a range of items made from iron and steel and also chemicals produced by the subsidiaries.

The Act gives the Corporation the main duty of making and selling (both in home markets and overseas) enough iron and steel to meet reasonable demands but it must not practise discrimination against any class of customer. Customers are of two main classes — suppliers who hold stocks of iron and steel in the manner of wholesalers, and users who incorporate the raw metal into their product. The B.S.C. must also encourage the carrying out of research into the nature, manufacture and uses of iron and steel.

The Corporation is under the control of the Board which is composed of persons appointed by the Secretary of State for Industry. The Board includes the Chairman, two Deputy Chairmen (one of whom acts as the Chief Executive), and seven to 20 other members. The Chairman and his Deputies are designated as such by the Minister. The members of the Board must have wide experience of the industry and the Chairman must be consulted before a new member is appointed.

The current arrangement is for steel to be produced in five manufacturing divisions which agree roughly with the main steelmaking areas of the country. They are, namely, Scottish, Scunthorpe, Sheffield, Teesside and Welsh. The Corporation has a number of subsidiaries which include Redpath Dorman Long Limited, B.S.C. Chemicals, and B.S.C. Holdings (which is decentralised into Tinplate, Stainless, Forges and Foundries, Cumbria and Light Products).

The Corporation has a duty to make sure that its total income from all activities must be enough to cover its costs, taking one year with another. This means that each year is not to be regarded separately but taken in the context of a period of, say, five years, when surpluses and deficits ought to balance one another. Costs chargeable against income are taken as inclusive of adequate depreciation or renewal provision of assets. The B.S.C. should also maintain a General Reserve (which need not always be in hand, however).

Proper records must be kept to serve as a basis to reliable accounts which must be prepared in prescribed form. Loans may be borrowed for short or long periods with the consent of the Secretary of State who operates the external financing limits (or, otherwise called, cash limits) and has the power to make directions to the Corporation to take specific financial actions in the national interest.

An annual report and a copy of the audited annual accounts together with the auditor's report are sent to the Minister who places them before the

House of Commons with his own report. These statements are thereafter subject to investigation by the Select Committee for Nationalised Industries.

The published accounts consist of a Consolidated Profit and Loss Account and Balance Sheets for the B.S.C. alone and for the Corporation and its subsidiaries. The Balance Sheets contain Fixed Assets, Investments, Interests in Subsidiary Companies, and Current Assets less Current Liabilities. The Total Net Assets are shown as met by Capital Employed, i.e. Capital, Long-term Debt, the General Reserve, etc.. There are supporting statistics on financial and operating matters, a Statement of Source and Application of Funds, and a Current Cost Statement for the year. The accounts contain Accounting Policies and Notes, and details of items, such as Government and foreign loans, investments, etc.. The year end falls on the nearest Saturday to the 31st March, and thus a year contains either 52 or 53 weeks. Figures are supplied for the preceding year for purposes of comparison.

At present, the fall in the worldwide demand for iron and steel products coupled with increased competition from overseas has meant that the Corporation is implementing plans to reduce its productive capacity, both in plant and labour force, and deferring and cancelling capital schemes.

When B.S.C. was formed, an appreciable number of firms were left in the private sector, partly because the variety of their activities and products made it difficult to classify them for inclusion in a nationalisation statute. These companies are mainly involved in producing special forms of steel and alloys. Most of them are members of the British Independent Steel Producers' Association.

National Coal Board

The NCB was formed under the Coal Industry Nationalisation Act 1946 to take over the coal-mining industry from private enterprise. The Board had power to carry on searches for coal, preparing it for sale and selling it, as well as to manufacture and sell coal products, smokeless fuels, etc. and provide training and research facilities in the industry. Later Acts have extended the Board's powers to include the mining or production of minerals other than coal, e.g. oil. The NCB possesses subsidiary companies which deals with such activities as the marketing of smokeless fuels – unlike the mining of coal, the distribution of coal is not nationalised.

The members of the Board comprise the Chairman, Deputy Chairman and 11 other members (of whom five are part-timers) and are all appointed by the Secretary of State for Energy who is answerable to Parliament on questions of the Board's broad policy and has the power to give orders (i.e. directions) of a financial nature to the Board in the national interest, as well as to supervise the application of the external financing limits.

Two Coal Consumers' Councils (Industrial and Domestic) look after the interests of the coal users and those persons involved in the supply and sale of coal. The members of both Councils are appointed by the Minister and the number of appointees is a matter for his decision.

The Board has a duty to provide that its income is enough to meet its expenses taking one year with another and there are a number of grants under the Coal Industry Acts from the government which assist the Board in a variety of ways to meet the costs of implementing decisions of social or political nature. It has power to borrow up to a limit permitted by Parliament, temporarily or long-term, from the Secretary of State or from elsewhere. It must keep proper financial records and prepare accounts which accord with the best commercial standards and distinguish between coalmining and each ancillary industry. The accounts are audited by persons appointed by the Minister each year (the 1946 Act makes no mention of any qualifications being needed) and a copy of the accounts and the auditor's report must be sent to the Minister who has the duty of laying them before Parliament.

The annual accounts contain a statement of accounting policies, and the Profit and Loss Account and Balance Sheet are consolidated because the figures include the NCB's subsidiaries, though a separate Balance Sheet is also provided for the NCB alone. Supporting statements are supplied – Source and Application of Funds, details of Fixed Assets, Depreciation Provisions, Investments, Loans, etc.. There is also a Current Cost Profit and Loss Account. The financial year end is arranged to occur around the 31st March, so that a year's accounts may contain either 52 or 53 weeks. Comparative figures for the previous year are included where this assists the reader.

National Enterprise Board

The participation of the State in industry as a shareholder originally arose more by the accident of history than by any intention of setting a pattern by which the level of economic activity in this country might be raised or maintained. One example which comes to mind is the purchase of the shareholding of the Khedive of Egypt in the Suez Canal, which made the British Government a shareholder in the Company and secured the route to India for generations. Examples were, however, rare in the years up to the start of the second World War in 1939, but after that war was over, discussion of the question of nationalisation began to include methods of obtaining control of privately-owned industries by the purchase of shares by the Government, possibly by investing State pension funds. In addition, post-war Governments were involved more than previously in attempts to control the economy, especially the level of employment, and thus the performance of British industry became a matter of concern in this respect.

In 1966, the Industrial Reorganisation Corporation was formed under the Act of that name. Its function was to encourage efficiency in industry by internal changes, such as the merging of firms, and could offer short-term loans to such firms. It also had the power to buy shares in companies, though this was to be used more as a means of injecting capital for a short period than as a way of obtaining a measure of control − the shares would have to be sold in due course when the need had passed, and not held permanently. Tactics changed, however, when a further Act (the Industrial Expansion Act 1968) was passed by Parliament. This gave the Government the power to acquire shares in any company by negotiation and agreement. This development was short-lived, as the following Conservative Government abolished the I.R.C. and repealed the two Acts, because it believed in assisting industry by loans and grants rather than by becoming involved in the operation and policy-making processes of firms. It was felt that such actions were the speciality of businessmen, and not of civil servants and politicians.

Aid was therefore continued by these methods under the control of the appropriate Minister (Departmental responsibilities and titles changed from time to time). He was advised by the Industrial Development Advisory Board which was formed under the Industry Act 1972, as to where in industry the application of Government finance would have the best effect. Only in extreme circumstances, was the State permitted to buy shares in an ailing company, and even then, this was subject to certain limits as to the sum paid and the percentage holding acquired in the firm.

Ultimately, on another change of Government, the Industry Act 1975 created the National Enterprise Board which was given extremely wide powers to help to make British industry efficient and able to meet foreign competition, both at home and overseas, and to save and create jobs in the various sectors in which it involved itself. To enable it to carry out its allotted functions, the Board has the power to invest money in existing firms with a view to improving their productivity, to start up new manufacturing ventures, or to take control of companies by negotiation and agreement where their record of performance and their future prospects give rise to concern. The N.E.B. is also able to place its resources of expertise in financial matters at the disposal of any firm which finds itself in need of advice and approaches the Board.

The National Enterprise Board acts as a holding company for the State investments in private industry, and, following the directions of the Secretary of State as to its financial duties, it acts as guardian of the national interest in the firms in which the investments have been made. In addition to its current holdings, it has the power to become involved in any area of industry which it feels would benefit from its intervention, with the exception, however, of commercial television broadcasting and publishing (although it is allowed to issue its own staff journals and similar internal publications). The ban on activities connected with what is called the media appears to be intended to prevent accusations being made that a Government agency is in a position to influence news and programme content. Up to the present time, holdings are mainly in firms involved in large-scale manufacturing and advanced technology, such as British Leyland, Ferranti Limited, International Computers Limited, Fairey Holdings, as well as a selection of smaller concerns. To assist the N.E.B. in carrying out its duties, the Secretary of State has the power to demand information from companies in regard to such matters as the numbers of employees, capital expenditure incurred, the volume of sales, etc..

The Secretary of State for Industry appoints the Board which consists of the Chairman, one or more Deputy Chairmen (all of whom are full-time) and from eight to 16 other members (who are part-timers). The Chairman and his Deputy or Deputies are chosen by the Minister from among those he has appointed. The Northern and North West Regions are covered by Regional Boards which are composed of persons appointed by the N.E.B. and have the power to carry out projects costing up to £500,000 and play an advisory role for larger schemes in their Regions.

The Board is financed out of the National Loans Fund, but part of the money advanced to it by the Government is separately provided as "Public Dividend Capital" upon which the Government receives dividends. (The National Loans Fund advances bear interest).

Besides laying down the Board's duties, the Secretary of State agrees a target rate of return on capital, operates limits to borrowings, and can give directions to which the Board must conform in the national economic interest.

The N.E.B. is required by law to prepare proper annual accounts based on reliably-kept records. These accounts should be in prescribed form and follow the highest commercial standards of preparation and presentation. A copy of the Board's annual report, audited accounts and auditor's report must be sent to the Minister who must place them before the Commons with his own report.

The auditor is appointed by the Board after consulting the Department of Industry and he must be a member of one of the accountancy bodies qualified to audit the accounts of limited companies.

The published accounts contain the auditor's report, a Statement of Accounting Policies, the Consolidated Profit and Loss Account, Balance Sheet and Statement of Source and Application of Funds for the NEB and its subsidiaries, the Income and Expenditure Account and Balance Sheet for the Board on its own, and Profit and Loss Accounts and Balance Sheets for the major subsidiary companies. The accounts also provide details of shareholdings, fixed assets, minority interests, etc.. The financial year end is the 31st December, and corresponding figures are supplied in respect of the previous year's accounts.

Currently, the Government is reviewing the future role of the National Enterprise Board, though to date practical responsibility for British Leyland and Ferranti has been taken from the Board and the interests in Ferranti and Fairey have been sold off. It now appears that the Board will be faced with a restricted scope of operations in which it will take on no new responsibilities but look after the remainder of its current holdings which are mainly in companies in the fields of office equipment, electronics and computers.

The Post Office
Letter and message carrying services have a long history which extends into antiquity but the development of the present range of services (of which letter carrying is only one) given by the Post Office originated in the call for more and speedier methods of communication which were found necessary during the Industrial Revolution and are even more necessary today. As with so many enterprises, the embryo postal services in this country were set up under private ownership, and when the Government became aware of the revenue accruing from charging cheap and fixed postal rates on a high volume of letters and packets, it took over the service as a State monopoly. Nowadays, it is the letter handling services which run at a loss, being supported by profit earned by the telephone and allied services. Dissatisfaction with this situation, coupled with a report of the Monopolies and Mergers Commission on the unsatisfactory state of the postal services in London, has led to suggestions that the Post Office's monopoly should be breached by bringing in private competition. Current proposals for the reform of the Post Office are contained in the British Telecommunications Bill which is at present before Parliament. Under this Bill, it is intended to form two public corporations — the Royal Mail (the suggested title for the truncated Post Office) for postal services and the Girobank, and the British Telecommunications Corporation for telephones and telecommunications generally. On the telecommunications side, private firms would be allowed to operate in areas of technology, such as data processing and private branch exchanges, and to sell additional telephones to existing subscribers. On the postal side, charities would be allowed to deliver Christmas Cards, and private firms to offer services for the exchange of documents, the bulk handling ot items for eventual posting via the Royal Mail, and express deliveries. Postal deliveries in cities may also be open to private enterprise.

The Post Office was originally a Government Department — one of the oldest — and it was manned by civil servants under the control of the Postmaster-General as the responsible Minister. It has acquired new duties and lost others during its long history from its formation in the 17th century and its status and organisation have also varied, especially in the current century. A major step was taken when it became a public corporation under the Post Office Act 1969 and was, at first, controlled by a Minister of Posts and Telecommunications who took the place of the P.M.G. (and was also in charge of broadcasting). This Ministry was abolished later and the responsibility for the Post Office was given to the Secretary of State for Industry. (The Home Office took over much of broadcasting). The Act of 1969 took the employees out of the civil service, as is usual with public corporations.

The Secretary of State for Industry appoints the members of the Post Office Board which manages the corporation. He chooses the Chairman and consults him in the appointment of the others who number from six to 12 persons and may be full- or part-time.

The Post Office has an overall duty to provide postal and telephone services sufficient to meet all reasonable demands as efficiently as possible and not to discriminate against any class of customer to an undue extent. The range of services is wide – the carriage and delivery of various classes of letter, package, etc., the sale of stamps for postage and other purposes, the issue of various types of licence, the payment of pensions and other allowances, the provision of facilities for the remittance of money, National Bank and Giro services, public and private telephones, telegraph services, news and information (Prestel), data transmission (Datel) and teleprinter (Telex) networks via the telephone wires. Experiments and developments in the service are taking place continually. The various counter services are provided to different degrees in three classes of establishment – Head Post Offices, Crown Sub-Post Offices and Scale Payment Sub-Post Offices – and the telephone service is administered from its own premises and head quarters.

To carry out its work, the Post Office is organised into 11 Regions – London Postal, London Telecommunications, Eastern, Midland, North Eastern, North Western, South Eastern, South Western, Wales and the Marches, Scotland, and Northern Ireland.

Independent bodies which have the duty to look after the interests of the public are provided for in the law relating to the Post Office. There is the Post Office Users' National Council which covers the whole country and three separate P.O. Users' Councils for Wales, Scotland and Northern Ireland. The Secretary of State for Industry appoints all the members of the four bodies, nominating each Chairman as such. In the case of the National Council, the Minister selects three persons by his own decision but the rest of the membership consists of persons representing various interests among the users who are chosen after the Minister has gone through a process of consultation. The maximum number of persons in the Council is 30. The members of the Councils for Wales, Scotland and Northern Ireland are all chosen after consultation and each body numbers up to 25 persons.

The Post Office is required to ensure that its income is enough to meet its costs (including depreciation and contributions to General Reserve) over a period of years. The system of cash limits or external financing limits is applied to the Post Office and, within this system, it has the power to borrow for capital expenditure, payment of debt, the acquiring of other related businesses and the provision of working capital. The Minister may advance loans and the Treasury can guarantee the interest and capital payments on any loans. Financial targets are agreed with the Government on the costs of the various services which should not rise faster than the general level of prices, as a general rule.

There is a duty to keep proper records to facilitate the production of reliable accounts which must be prepared each year in a prescribed form and in accordance with the best commercial standards.

The Secretary of State appoints the auditor of the accounts from persons who are members of one or other of the accountancy bodies which are recognised for the audit of company accounts. A copy of the audited accounts and of the audit report thereon must be sent without delay to the Minister who is required to place them before Parliament together with his own report.

The annual accounts of the Post Office are in narrative form and comprise a Profit and Loss Account, a General Reserve Account, a Balance Sheet and a Statement of Source and Application of Funds for the whole of the activities of the Post Office in consolidated form, and then for each of the component parts – Telecommunications, Postal Services, National Girobank, and Postal Orders. The year end is the 31st March.

The General Reserve in each case is built up from provisions for supplementary depreciation of Fixed Assets based on replacement cost. There is, of course, the normal depreciation based on historical cost figures.

The Balance Sheets contain the Fixed Assets, Investments and Current Assets, less Current Liabilities, and show how these are all financed from Long-term Government Loans, Public-dividend Capital, Foreign Loans and the General Reserve.

There are supporting statements – Accounting Policies and Notes on the accounts, details of assets, loans, depreciation provisions, and corresponding figures for the previous year are supplied where appropriate.

Questions

16.1 Outline the characteristics of a Public Corporation.

16.2 Why is a Public Corporation referred to as a creature of statute?

16.3 In what ways are Public Corporations controlled by Parliament?

16.4 Describe briefly the rights and duties of a Minister who is made responsible for a nationalised industry.

16.5 What are the functions of the Civil Aviation Authority?

16.6 Outline the system of user representation in the Post Office.

16.7 Give various grounds for the occurrence of State ownership in industry.

16.8 What services are rendered by the Telecommunications section of the Post Office?

16.9 What is the S.C.N.I. and what does it do?

16.10 Outline the types of income received by the B.B.C. and how they are utilised.

Appendix I

Examples of Internal Control Procedures: –
(a) Income
(b) Payment of salaries and wages
(c) Petty cash imprests
(d) Payment of creditors' accounts
(e) Inspection of documents by councillors
(f) Outbreak of fire in the office
(g) Inventories of furniture, plant and equipment
(h) Conditions under which advances are made for house purchase

Standing Orders and Financial Regulations lay down procedures which the members and staff are required to observe in carrying out their duties in connection with the authority's business.

(a) *Income*

Every employee who receives money on the authority's behalf shall immediately give an acknowledgment of it to the payer, unless the payer places it in a locked box to which the employee has access only when accompanied by a witness. The above acknowledgement may be in the guise of a manually or machine issued receipt, ticket, token, towel wrapper or other form approved by the Finance Director. The employee shall keep the money safe at all times, and shall check the sum collected (which shall be countersigned by the witness to the unlocking of a box), immediately prepare such records as are prescribed by the Finance Director, and pay the sum intact to the chief cashier or direct to the authority's bankers without delay. The receipt books or other records, duly balanced, shall be delivered to the cashier when the money is paid in to him, or where the sum has been directly banked, the counterfoil of the bank paying-in-slip shall be delivered instead. Each employee who banks money shall give enough information on the paying-in slip, its duplicate and each cheque, to link the cheque with the payment of a specific debt. All transfers of the authority's money between employees shall be evidenced by the receiving officer's signature.

All forms of acknowledgment of money – receipts, tickets, etc. shall be controlled by the Finance Director who shall arrange for them to be ordered, pre-numbered, securely stocked and issued on signature to collecting officers.

Each departmental Head shall maintain arrangements approved as adequate by the Finance Director for the prompt recording and collection of all items of income due.

Each departmental Head shall inform the Finance Director without delay of all agreements, contracts, leases, etc. requiring the receipt of money by the authority, and the Finance Director shall have the right to inspect the relevant documents.

Each committee of the authority shall review its scales of charges for services and amenities within its terms of reference at least once a year, and the departmental Head involved may report to the committee thereon, after consulting the Administration (Legal) and Finance Directors.

(b) *Payment of Salaries and Wages*

The Finance Director shall approve and control all arrangements for the payment of all salaries, wages and other emoluments to all the authority's employees. He shall be notified by each departmental Head of all events affecting such payments – appointments, dismissals, absences, promotions, suspensions, etc. arising from committee decisions or otherwise. Such notifications shall be in a form required by the Finance Director and certified by the departmental Head or other authorised officer.

(c) *Petty Cash Imprests*

All advances for petty cash purposes shall be made by the Finance Director, and shall be in the form of imprests of amounts deemed necessary for the purposes for which they are made. The Finance Director shall review the amount of each imprest periodically, and shall lay down the nature and maximum of the items of expenditure which may be paid out of petty cash. The imprestholder shall obtain receipts where possible for payments and in all other cases must prepare a voucher giving details of the item. He shall also produce his records at any time on request by the internal audit, and shall repay the imprest to the Finance Director on ceasing to hold the imprest for whatever reason.

(d) *Payment of Creditors' Accounts*

Each departmental Head shall be responsible for all orders issued by his department for works, goods, services, materials, etc. unless there is a contract in existence for the matter. Where verbal orders are given, a confirmatory order must be issued as soon as possible. The Finance Director shall approve the form of the official orders, which shall be signed by the departmental Head or an authorised officer of his department, and shall also control the arrangements for the issue of order books.

Each departmental Head shall arrange that creditors' accounts, when received, shall be agreed with the order (which shall be marked off), quotation, contract terms, minute, etc. and certified as to receipt and satisfactory condition of goods, services, etc. and the correctness of prices and extensions. Such details shall be evidenced by the signatures of the various employees who have carried out the steps, on a certification grid stamped on the account.

The Finance Director shall receive the invoices scheduled in monthly batches in alphabetical order and shall make such further checks and enquiries as he considers necessary. The accounts and schedules shall be passed to the appropriate committee for approval for payment by the Finance Director by bank cheque or via Giro.

(e) *Inspection of Documents by Councillors*

A councillor may apply to the Director of Administration, for the purpose of his duty as a councillor and not otherwise, to inspect any document which has been the subject of consideration by the Council or one or more of its Committees. He or she shall also be entitled to be supplied with a copy of any such document upon request.

He or she must not intentionally ask for or inspect any document concerning any matter in which he or she is interested professionally or has a pecuniary interest (either direct or indirect) according to the Local Government Act 1972, and the Director of Administration may refuse to produce for inspection any document which would be protected by privilege in court proceedings or the inspection of which would be against the interests of the local authority as a whole.

Any officer in the employ of the Council who supplies any information in writing to a councillor must at once forward a copy of such information to the Chairman of the Committee involved.

All council or committee minutes shall be open to the inspection of councillors during the hours when the offices are open for business.

(f) *Procedure on the Discovery of an Outbreak of Fire in the Office*

1. By the officer in charge of the office: –
   a. He or she must arrange for the notices entitled "Fire Regulations" to be displayed in prominent places in the area under his or her control, and ensure that the staff are aware of and understand their content.
   b. There must be a practice fire drill periodically without warning.
2. By the member of staff who discovers an outbreak of fire: –
   a. He or she must immediately set off the nearest fire alarm.
   b. He or she must then ring the office telephone switchboard operator to give details of the location and other essential details of the fire.
   c. He or she should fight the fire with the nearest equipment of a suitable nature, if this can be done without bodily danger, until the firemen arrive.
   d. He or she should, in any case, leave the building as soon as practicable.

3. By the office telephone switchboard operator: −
   a. On hearing the word "fire", he or she must dial 999 and ask for the Fire Brigade, and listen and take note of the message details which the member of the staff discovering the fire will give direct to the Fire Brigade.
   b. He or she will immediately inform the building supervisor.
   c. He or she will leave the building, if necessary for safety.
4. By all other members of staff: −
   a. They must leave the building by the exit nearest to their place of work.
   b. On no account must they get into a lift but use the stairs if on upper floors.
   c. They must gather at the assembly point indicated on the fire regulation notices in order to be counted.
   d. No one must go back into the building for any reason whatsoever until instructions are received that it is safe to do so.

(g) *Inventories of Furniture, Plant and Equipment*
1. The Head of each Department is required to keep an inventory of all furniture, plant and equipment under his control. He must arrange for this inventory to show the nature of each item and its location together with any identifying numbers, etc.. The lists must be kept up to date.
2. The contents of the inventories should consist of items such as furniture, equipment, instruments, utensils, and vehicles. Permanent and immovable fittings and assets should be excluded from inventories but shown on terriers.
3. Each Departmental Head must ensure that the lists are checked against the actual items by members of his staff who are not involved in the keeping of inventories. These checks must be carried out periodically and a record made of this on the inventory form.
4. Arrangements must exist and be observed for the monthly reconciliation of items bought or disposed of between the accountancy assistants responsible for the Department's accounts and the person in control of inventories.
5. A newly-appointed Head of Department must take responsibility for the inventory by signing for it when he takes up his appointment, after an opportunity to employ his staff on such checks as he desires before signing.
6. The inventories and access to the assets contained therein must be available at all times to the Internal Audit staff in order to enable them to carry out their duties. Similarly, the inventories must be available for use in valuing assets for insurance purposes.
7. The Director of Finance is empowered to prescribe the form of inventory records to be kept by Departmental Heads.

(h) *Conditions under which Advances are made for House Purchase*
1. The advance will be secured by a legal mortgage and the title deeds will be deposited with the Authority.
2. All amounts due for principal, interest, insurance premiums, etc. must be paid on the date they are due to the Director of Finance.
3. The borrower must live in the dwelling for a period of three years from the date the advance is made or the house completed, or must move into it within six months from the date the advance is made.
4. The borrower must take out property insurance cover for the full value of the house in the joint names of himself (or herself) and the Authority, and this will be done through the Authority and the borrower will be responsible for paying the premiums.
5. The dwelling must be kept in a sanitary condition and in good repair, so that it is fit for human occupation at all times.
6. The standard of the construction and other work which is the subject of an advance must be to the satisfaction of the Director of Works.
7. The house must not be used in a way to cause a nuisance to adjacent occupiers or owners, and must not be used for the sale of intoxicants.
8. An authorised officer of the Authority may enter the house at all reasonable times in order to make sure that the above-mentioned conditions are being observed.

Appendix II

Examples of Costing Methods applicable to Public Authorities: –
(a) Job costing
(b) Contract costing
(c) Output costing
(d) Operation costing
(e) Simple process costing
(f) Break-even analysis
(g) Standard costing

(a) *Example of Job Costing*

The direct works department (or direct labour organisation) of a public authority has been occupied with two jobs during a period of operation. The following cost figures have been drawn up for the period in question.

		£			£
Job 1.	Direct Wages	500	Job 2. Direct Wages		100
	Direct Materials	300		Direct Materials	200
	Direct Expenses	100		Direct Expenses	100
		900			400

Machinery and Plant		Works Costs		Administrative Costs	
	£		£		£
Wages	200	Wages	130	Wages	70
Materials	50	Materials	70	Materials	50
Expenses	170	Expenses	90	Expenses	420
	420		290		540

Machinery and Plant used by Job 1. 50 hours
Machinery and Plant used by Job 2. 20 hours

Oncost Rates have been decided in advance on the basis of a budget.

Machinery and Plant   £6 per hour of usage
Works Costs   50% of Direct Wages
Administrative Costs 40% of Prime Cost

The entries in the cost accounting system will be as follows: –

Dr.	Machinery and Plant Expenses Account		Cr.
	£		£
Expenditure –		Allocation to –	
Wages	200	Job 1 (50 hours @ £6)	300
Materials	50	Job 2 (20 hours @ £6)	120
Expenses	170		
	420		420

Works Expenses Account

Expenditure –	£	Allocation to –	£
Wages	130	Job 1 (50% of £500)	250
Materials	70	Job 2 (50% of £100)	50
Expenses	90		
Balance c/f (over-recovered)	10		
	300		300
		Balance b/f	10

Administration Expenses Account

Expenditure –	£	Allocation to –	£
Wages	70	Job 1 (40% of £900)	360
Materials	50	Job 2 (40% of £400)	160
Expenses	420	Balance c/f (under-recovered)	20
	540		540
Balance b/f	20		

Dr.   Job 1   Cr.

	£		£
Direct Wages	500	Recharged to Service	1,810
Direct Materials	300		
Direct Expenses	100		
Prime Cost	900		
Machinery and Plant Usage Oncost, 50 hours @ £6	300		
Works Oncost, 50% of £500	250		
Administration Oncost, 40% of £900	360		
Total Cost	1,810		1,810

Job 2

	£		£
Direct Wages	100	Recharged to Service	730
Direct Materials	200		
Direct Expenses	100		
Prime Cost	400		
Machinery and Plant Usage Oncost, 20 hours @ £6	120		
Works Oncost, 50% of £100	50		
Administration Oncost, 40% of £400	160		
Total Cost	730		730

(b) *Example of Contract Costing*

In local authorities, contracts are often carried out by direct works departments and the custom is to recharge the cost of the work to the spending committee for which it has been done. The procedure is thus akin to that used for job costing except that the scale of operation is larger.

Details of Contract 1234	£
Direct Materials issued to the Contract	120,000
Direct Wages incurred on the Contract	48,000
Direct Expenses incurred on the Contract	17,000
Charges for Plant and Machinery used	15,000
Central Administrative and Departmental Charges allocated	6,000
Materials in hand at the end of the Contract	10,000
Materials transferred to another Contract	5,000

Contract Account

Dr.

	£	£	£
Direct Wages			48,000
Direct Expenses			17,000
Direct Materials		120,000	
less Materials in hand	10,000		
Materials transferred	5,000	15,000	105,000
Plant and Machinery			15,000
Central Administrative and Departmental Charges			6,000
			£191,000

Cr.

Recharge of Total Cost to Spending Department		£191,000

(c) *Example of Output Costing*

Metropolitan Borough Council of Z.
Unit Costs of School Dinners for 19-2/3.

	Expenditure		Cost per Dinner	
Personnel –	£	£	p	p
Administrators and Clerks	700,000		3.50	
Meals Supervisors	1,200,000		6.00	
Kitchen and other Staff	5,300,000	7,200,000	26.50	36.00
Buildings –				
Maintenance and Repairs	170,000		0.85	
Fuel, etc.	400,000		2.00	
Cleaning	70,000		0.35	
Equipment and Furniture	30,000		0.15	
Rent, Rates, etc.	200,000	870,000	1.00	4.35
Running Expenses –				
Crockery, Utensils, etc.	320,000		1.60	
Laundering	50,000		0.25	
Overalls, etc.	20,000		0.10	
Provisions	4,500,000	4,890,000	22.50	24.45
Haulage		210,000		1.05
Central Establishment Charges		270,000		1.35
		£13,440,000		67.20p

Number of dinners served 20,000,000
Number of Days 195

(d) *Example of Operation Costing*
Z Public Authority
Transport Costs for the Year ended 31st March 19-3

	Expenditure £	£	Cost per 100 miles £	£
Personnel –				
Administration	52,000		1.300	
Drivers	1,304,000		32.600	
Mechanics	325,000	1,681,000	8.125	42.025
Buildings –				
Maintenance	5,000		0.125	
Heating, Lighting, etc.	9,000		0.225	
Rates, etc.	17,000	31,000	0.425	0.775
Equipment –				
Tools, etc.	12,000		0.300	
Overalls, etc.	2,000	14,000	0.050	0.350
Running Costs –				
Fuel, Tyres, etc.	123,000		3.075	
Vehicle Parts	247,000	370,000	6.175	9.250
Administration –				
Office Expenses	8,000		0.200	
Central Establishment	75,000	83,000	1.875	2.075
Other Expenses		3,000		0.075
Loan Charges		153,000		3.825
		£2,335,000		£58.375

Number of vehicle miles 4,000,000
Cost Unit: – 100 vehicle/miles

(e) *Example of Simple Process Costing*

A product is manufactured by two processes, the output of process 1 is the input of process 2. Process 2 produces the finished goods.

The input of resources to process 1 comprises labour £5,000, materials £3,000 and overheads £2,000, and the planned output is 550 units but the actual output proves to be 530, there being 20 units lost by normal processing operations. There is no work in progress carried forward within this process.

The 530 units are input to process 2, and further resources applied to them, i.e. labour £12,000, materials £6,000, and overheads £2,120. The output of finished product is 480, there is a loss of 10 units which is within the process tolerances, and 40 units are only half processed by the end of the period. The 10 units are sold as scrap for £12 each.

Process 1

	Units	£		Units	£
Labour	–	5,000	Normal Wastage	20	–
Materials	–	3,000	Output to Process 2	530	10,000
Overheads	–	2,000			
	550	10,000		550	10,000

Process 2

	Units	£		Units	£
Input from Process 1	530	10,000	Sale of Normal Wastage	10	120
Labour	–	12,000	Finished Goods	480	28,800
Materials	–	6,000	Work in Progress c/f	40	1,200
Overheads	–	2,120			
	530	30,120		530	30,120
Work in Progress b/f	40	1,200			

(f) *Example of Break-even Analysis*

The following estimates apply to a proposed children's community home. The items have been divided into fixed and variable costs, the fixed being incurred when no children are accommodated. The variable costs vary pro rata to the number of children in residence, and are based here upon the maximum who can be accommodated – 30 children. The authority calculates that the acceptable charge for a child-week is £100 and wishes to know at what number of children the charges would equal total costs.

Expenditure	Fixed £	Variable £	Total £
Personnel	6,000	45,000	51,000
Buildings			
Upkeep	500	2,000	2,500
Heating, etc.	800	5,700	6,500
Rates, etc.	4,500	–	4,500
Furniture	200	2,800	3,000
Running Expenses			
Utensils	100	900	1,000
Provisions	900	20,600	21,500
Clothing	200	1,800	2,000
Pocket Money, etc.	–	5,000	5,000
Other	100	1,400	1,500
Travelling Expenses	400	3,100	3,500
Central Establishment	6,300	7,500	13,800
Loan Charges	25,000	–	25,000
	45,000	95,800	140,800
Income			
Accommodation Charges to Staff	1,000	5,800	6,800
	44,000	90,000	134,000

Solution:

The variable cost per child per annum is £90,000 ÷ 30 = £3,000, and if the required number of children to break even is x, then the total costs are £3,000x + £44,000 (i.e. the pro rata variable cost plus fixed cost).

Using x again, the total charge for children will be £5,200x (i.e. x children @ £100 for 52 weeks).

The two expressions are equal at the break-even point: –

$$3,000x + 44,000 = 5,200x$$

and this solves to x = 20.

Thus, if the authority accommodate a minimum of twenty children, the costs of the home would be recovered on the above basis.

The problem may also be solved by graphical means: –

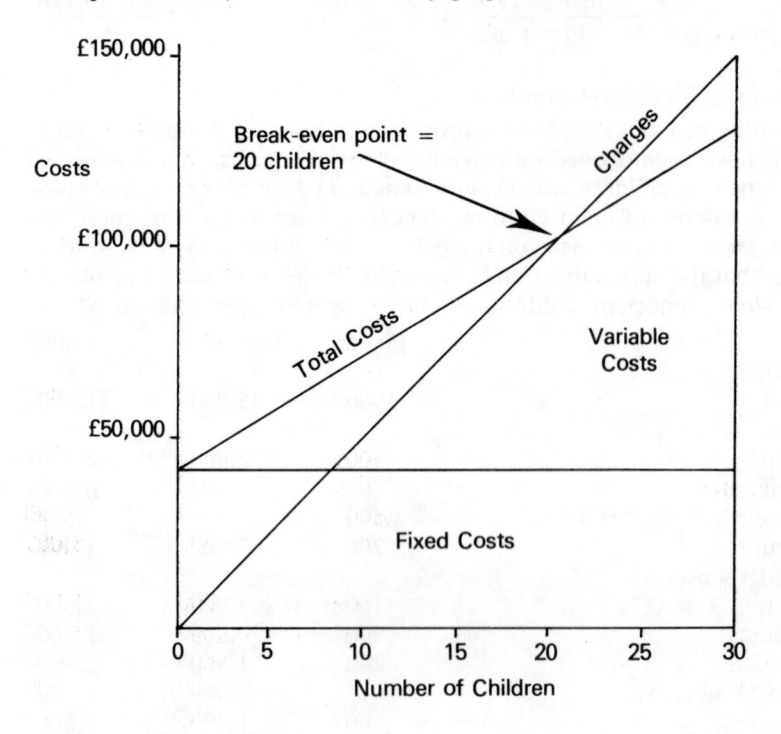

(g) *Example of Standard Costing*

A works department is allotted the job of constructing a watchman's hut for the highways department.

The standard costs for the job are: –

Carpenter's Wages – £5 per hour for 40 hours.
Materials –   Wood, 300 units @ £1 per unit.
                    Nails, Iron Fittings, 50 lbs. @ 50p per lb.

The actual costs per the records proved to be: —
Carpenter's Wages — £5.20 per hour for 44 hours.
Materials — Wood, 310 units @ 90p per unit.
Nails, Iron Fittings, 55 lbs. @ 70p per lb.

	Standard £	Actual £	Variances		£	£
Wages —	200.00	228.80	Efficieny £5 (40 − 44)	=	− 20.00	
			Rate 44 (£5 − £5.20)	=	− 8.80	− 28.80
Wood —	300.00	279.00	Usage £1 (300 − 310)	=	− 10.00	
			Price 310 (£1 − 90p)	=	+ 31.00	+ 21.00
Nails, etc. —	25.00	38.50	Usage 50p (50 − 55)	=	− 2.50	
			Price 55 (50p − 70p)	=	− 11.00	− 13.50
	525.00	546.30				− 21.30

Appendix III

Examples of Audit Programmes applicable to Public Authorities: –
(a) Income from the General Rate
(b) Investment by the public in local authority bonds
(c) Cemetery and crematorium fees and charges
(d) Income from games in the parks
(e) Rents of Authority-owned dwellings
(f) Checking of a contractor's final account
(g) Charges for water supplied by meter
(h) Charges and licences for the abstraction of water
(i) Pensioners' free travel passes
(j) Property left on buses
(k) Charges for emergency treatment in hospital under the Road Traffic Act 1972
(l) Trust fund (endowment)
(m) Transfer of New Town housing to a local authority
(n) Quarterly accounts for electricity or gas supplied by meter
(o) Income from the sale of electricity for roadlighting
(p) Advances of grant in support of expenditure on a local authority service
(q) Computerised weekly payroll.

(a) *Income from General Rate*
1. Update the permanent file in respect of events which have occurred since the last audit – minutes, copy of latest rate demand notice, copy of any new regulations, etc.
2. Prepare or revise an internal control questionnaire to check that the internal check is adequate and that the set procedures are followed in levying and collecting the general rate.
3. Check the arrears brought forward from the previous period in total and by sampling for individual items. Payments in advance should be similarly verified.
4. Ensure that the total rate due agrees with the total rateable value per the valuation list and that the amount levied is at the correct rate in the £. The rate income should be checked in total and single items randomly sampled to see they are correctly calculated. The possibility of new properties being overlooked should be tested by using completion certificates for new council dwellings, the electoral roll, press advertisements regarding new houses for sale, etc.. In such cases, the omissions should be notified to the Inland Revenue for their action. Test that the correct rate in the £ is levied on residential, mixed and other classes of property, and that exempted properties still qualify

(e.g. a lighthouse has not been converted into a dwelling). A check must be made of rate charges levied on empty properties — that they are in accord with the resolution and calculated correctly, and relief is given on proper grounds.

5. Check the total cash received from the receipt records into the summaries and the bank. Test individual items for accuracy. Ensure that no delay exists in banking receipts to avoid the danger of teeming and lading. Amounts received must be compared with the instalment arrangements, in regard to value and timings.

   Check any discount for early payment is correct per the resolution and is calculated properly, is in respect of a payment by the required date, and relates to the eligible class of property.

6. Check the accuracy of the owners' allowances (compounding) and compare them with agreements and resolutions to ensure conditions are applied correctly and the percentages are correct.

7. Check the empty periods by inspecting correspondence, claims, etc. and recalculate individual items.

   The system of dealing with rate rebates must be reviewed for adequacy and satisfaction obtained as to degree of compliance by the staff, especially as to division of duties of assessment, authorisation and recording. Sample individual applications as to accuracy of calculations, make comparisons with other sources, such as rent rebate or allowance claims and previous year's claim. Check in total, using trends and ratios, and vouch calculation and receipt of the government grant.

8. Irrecoverable amounts (write-offs) are also checked to correspondence, excusal for poverty or by the justices, committal to prison records, and to the minutes and lists approved by the committee for writing-off. Ensure that the statutory recovery procedure has been carried out before the amount was written off.

9. Check all refunds are correct and are paid to the person who overpaid. Inspect correspondence, application forms, cheques, etc..

10. Check that the arrears carried forward are correct in total and detail, and that collection procedure is being followed. Observation can be extended to receipts during the new rating year and individual debtors can be approached for confirmation. Payments in advance should be similarly checked and the reason for their occurrence ascertained.

11. Review the audit just undertaken and makes notes in the permanent file regarding improvements in the next audit.

(b) *Investment by the Public in Local Authority Bonds*
1. Up date the permanent audit file by adding any minutes, correspondence, latest terms of issue (interest rates and periods, etc.). Note any matters outstanding from the previous audit.

2. Review the internal control system relating to bonds for adequacy. If any weakness is discovered, it should be discussed and remedied. An internal control questionnaire may be compiled and used to test the detail and logic of the system and whether it is being adequately complied with by the staff. In using an I.C.Q., the auditor asks the questions one by one from the various members of the staff. (If they are given the questionnaire, they can read all the questions, and tailor each answer according to what is asked later). The auditor checks the accuracy of the answers he has received and noted on the I.C.Q. by observing the relevant activities and cross-checking the replies given by different persons.

3. Check that the application forms for new bonds agree in amount with the receipts issued by the cashier and the bank paying-in slips. The forms details must agree with those in the bond register — name and address of investor, amount, interest rate, period of loan, etc.

4. Check the issue of the temporary receipt and its details, and its return duly acknowledging the receipt of the bond certificate. Check the issue of the certificate through the system of control. Ensure all certificates are controlled as to printing, checking, pre-numbering, storing, issue, completion, being signed and despatched.

5. Where bonds have fallen due for repayment since the last audit, check the notifications sent out and the options for renewal or repayment duly received. Renewals — check that the register details agree with the option form. Repayments — examine the cancelled discharged bond, check the details of the payment voucher and the cheque, and ensure the register amended.

6. Where bonds have been transferred, check the details of the transfer form, the cancelled bond and the issue of the new one. Ensure the register is amended. Other amendments, such as change of name when a woman marries, are merely endorsed on the bond and recorded in the register.

7. Check the correctness of the periodical interest payment — gross and net. This can be checked in total and sample checked in detail, as also the payees and the returned cheques (for erasures, etc.).

8. Review the audit programme and make any notes or suggestions which might improve the next audit. Such notes are entered in the permanent audit file.

(c) *Cemetery and Crematorium Fees and Charges*

1. Bring the permanent file up to date by adding minutes, correspondence, revised scales of charges, alterations to cemetery plan, etc.. The law requires the keeping up to date of burial and cremation registers, and scales of charges must be available to the public.

2. Review the system of internal control and internal check for its adequacy. Discuss and require the correction of any weaknesses found.

Use an internal control questionnaire to ascertain the system and the degree to which the staff comply with it.

3. On arrival at the department's office, check the cash held against the receipts issued that day, and check the petty cash imprest. (Subsequently, check the payment into bank).
4. Check that the correct fees have been charged for each entry in the burial and cremation registers. Check the plan and new graves, etc. for burial fees and sales of grave spaces having been received. Also compare the entries in the death announcements in the press.
5. Verify all charges for grave maintenance are per the scale. Check their completeness by comparing with the burial register, the sales of grave spaces register, and the time records of the maintenance staff. Note all graves which appear to be maintained in case the income is being diverted.
6. Similarly check other sources of income – sale of cremation urns, coffins, book of remembrance entries, monument fees, etc..
7. Check the ministers' fees paid by the cemetery and crematorium are per the scale and have been recharged on the undertaker. Inspect the lists to test authenticity of ministers' signatures.
8. Enquire regarding the disposal of gold, silver, etc. (from jewellery, rings, etc.) found in the ashes.
9. Review the audit procedure with a view to its improvement. Also give consideration to the "value for money" aspects.

(d) *Income from Games in Parks*
1. Obtain copy of scale of charges, hours of play, duties of staff and their names, and the location of the tennis courts, bowling greens, boating lakes, putting greens, etc.
2. Check the system of control of tickets – the method of ordering, checking, pre-numbering, storage, registration and issue (and recall at the end of the season). Issue should be on signature.
3. Ascertain from the register the numbers and values of the tickets in the attendant's possession at the time of the visit by the audit staff.
4. Check that cash is present for all tickets issued, re-add all listings and re-calculate total value of the issued tickets.
5. Examine remainder of tickets to ensure they are intact (none removed from the middle of the roll).
6. Ensure all players have correct tickets, both in number (e.g. one each or one for a party), and in sequence (not old tickets re-issued). The tickets must also be official.
7. Trace cash via the cashier's records and paying-in slip into the bank. Verify the analysis of takings is to correct budget codes in the ledger.
8. Use graphical methods to measure fluctuations and trends in the level of receipts, noting the weather conditions daily.

9. Check return of unused tickets at the end of the season.
10. Observations can be made of the numbers of players using the amenities during a shift and compared with the records of tickets issued and receipts paid in. (Collusion may exist between the employee issuing the tickets and the one who tears or cancels them).
11. Review audit and internal control procedures with a view to suggesting improvements. Consider whether the level of charges is adequate and the use of resources is optimal in the rendering of the service.

(e) *Rent Income from Authority-owned Dwellings*
1. Bring the permanent file up to date by adding minutes, correspondence, revisions of rent scales, etc. since the previous audit. Note any matters outstanding from them.
2. Review the rent collection and recording system for adequacy of control. If weaknesses are discovered, indicate their presence immediately and discuss remedies with the responsible departmental officers. Draw up or revise an internal control questionnaire which, along with tests and observation (to corroborate the truth of answers), is used to ensure that the system is actually being complied with.
3. Ascertain the accuracy of the total weekly debit: –
   Check that the actual rent debit per dwelling agrees with the approved scale for its class. The existence of new dwellings can be checked from the completion certificates, public utilities accounts, observation of contracts in progress, etc.. The sales of houses, etc. can be checked from contracts, minutes, etc.. The total weekly debit can be compared with the figure obtained at the last audit, suitably updated.
4. Ascertain that charges have been made for occupied dwellings: –
   The rent of each dwellinghouse should be a standard debit each week (or fortnight). The start of letting of new houses should be linked to the date of the completion certificate plus a reasonable delay. The cancellation of the rent charged for dwellings sold should be in line with the contract of sale.
5. Check the collection of the rent by the various ways available, e.g. cash at the head office, district offices, paid to collectors, direct debits, Giro, etc.).
   Ensure by observation that internal check operates in respect of cash handling, recording transactions in the office, and authorising allowances. Sample rent books or cards, collection slips, etc. are added correctly, contain no erasures, alterations of suspicious nature. Similarly with paying-in slips where the date and time may reveal teeming and lading. Ensure all receipt forms, slips, etc. are pre-numbered and controlled on issue.

6. Check the arrears position.

    Ensure that arrears beyond the limit acceptable for the normal collection arrangements are followed up without delay by central office staff who have no access to office records or the issuing of rent cards. The arrears should be aged and stratified by amount and the oldest and largest traced through to date, and correspondence, etc. inspected. Smaller more recent cases may be sampled to see if the procedure is being followed. A check must be made upon the collection of arrears owed by tenants who have left before they are considered for writing-off.

7. Check cases of prepayment

    Trace cases of prepayment as they are carried forward. Try to ascertain reasons – tenants may overpay before their holidays so that no payment is needed when they are away. Check rent cards, slips and collection records, etc. Check any refunds of prepayments which should arise only if tenant leaves unexpectedly.

8. Ascertain the accuracy and authenticity of rebates and allowances.

    Sample rebate applications should be compared with the approved scheme and with previous year's from the same tenant. Ensure that internal check prevents one person calculating, recording, collecting, etc.. Check any arrangements with the D.H.S.S..

    Allowances should arise in cases of arrears written off after due attempts to collect. All documents, correspondence and evidence of court action, etc. plus committee minutes (authorising the writing-off) must be inspected.

9. Other points of importance

    Calculate ratios and trends which may reveal hidden effects, and compare with those previously calculated. Check the division of the gross rent into rent, rates and water charges and its treatment in the books and accounts. Carry out a review of the audit just undertaken and leave suggestions for improved audit action in the permanent file for the next audit.

(f) *Checking of a Contractor's Final Account*
1. Study the contract document, materials specifications, bills of quantities, price lists, rise and fall (or fluctuations) clause items, variation orders, minutes, correspondence and the final account submitted by the contractor.
2. Check all the calculations and additions in the final account and agree them with those in the contract where applicable.
3. Total all the previous payments made on account and ensure they are deducted in the final account.
4. Vouch the allocation of costs to the contract – wages, materials, expenses – from the contractor's invoices and books of account.

5. Inspect the site of the works, compare actual materials, etc. with the records. Re-measure parts of the work such as volume of concrete used and compare with amount provided in quantities.
6. Adjust the contract price for various factors: −
   (a) provisional and prime cost sums − the actual cost replaces the estimate,
   (b) rises and falls in the prices of items listed in the fluctuations clause,
   (c) additional or reduced costs arising from variation orders,
   (d) ex gratia payments made to the contractor (for costs outside his control for which he should not be liable),
   (e) penalties due from the contractor (for delays, etc.),
   (f) retention money which is retained until the maintenance period is ended in case the contractor fails to correct any defects arising in the period.

   Amend the account in cases where the above items are incorrect, or if they are unreasonable, consult with the contractor, engineer or architect.
7. Enquire regarding the compliance of the contractor with the conditions of the contract, e.g. fair wages paid to employees, the application of British Standards to materials, etc..
8. Vouch all the extra costs (administration, etc.) charged to the project.
9. Check the contract is part of an authorised scheme which is included in the estimates − probably capital.
10. Ascertain that finance is available to meet the cost − borrowing, revenue, special fund or recharge to another organisation − and, if supplementary estimates are needed because of overspending, report on this.
11. Consider finally any methods of improving the contract and audit procedures, and of obtaining better value for money in respect of future contracts of like nature.

(g) *Charges for Water supplied by Meter*
1. Enquire into the authority's policy as to the installation of metered water supplies in premises used for business or trade, hospitals, schools, hotels, and other circumstances where requirements are above normal domestic, shop or office levels. (There is power, ultimately, to place all supplies on meters).
2. Obtain a copy of the scale of charges, minimum charge and unit charge for water consumed.
3. Enquire into the adequacy of the procedures for reading meters periodically, rendering the accounts and the recovery of the sums due or their ultimate writing off. Report on any weaknesses revealed.

4. Obtain list of new meter agreements and check that size of meter and charges are correct. Test against stock of meters, i.e. purchases, issues and held in stock. Enquire regarding new premises which should be supplied by meter. Check terminations of supply are authentic. Test check sample of present supplies to ensure charges agree with agreements.
5. Reconcile total number of supplies up to date, using agreements and other records, e.g. meter readers' cards.
6. Sample a number of cards chosen randomly to verify correctness of readings and calculations, leading to the invoiced charge. A block of cards may be taken and checked and balanced with the total charge for the area involved.
7. Watch for low readings (meter out of order), high readings (bursts) and consider reasonableness of actions of staff in estimating charges for such events.
8. Investigate that all amounts written off are only authorised after the recovery procedure has been completely carried out.
9. Apply statistical checks to the total gallonage supplied and the charges made, e.g. compare with the previous period after any necessary adjustments. Check that ledger and final accounts agree with summarised meter rental figures.

(h) *Charges and Licences for the Abstraction of Water*
1. Ascertain the licence-holders from correspondence, applications, minutes, invoices, observation of new river-side factories, etc..
2. Check security of licence forms – printing orders, storage, pre-numbering, issues and entries in register of licences.
3. Enquire as to the procedure for charging for water abstracted, its adequacy, (i.e. internal check), degree of compliance, etc.
4. Check that amounts taken are in accordance with the formula laid down by the authority, that each licence-holder is billed and the recovery procedure is fully followed in all cases of arrears. Investigate all items written off and enquire regarding withdrawal of licence.
5. Enquire as to relationship between water sources being tapped and the abstraction rate.

(i) *Pensioners' Free Travel Passes*
1. Obtain a copy of the resolution of the Executive and the detailed scheme, showing the conditions of issue and use and the qualifications needed by passholders. Obtain the set of procedures under which passes are issued.
2. Study the procedures for adequacy and report on any weaknesses revealed.

3. Draw up and arrange for completion of an internal control questionnaire to test that the official system is the one actually being operated.
4. Proceed to check degree of compliance with the system by observation and inspection of records as to completeness of evidence of internal check.
5. Pay particular attention to the procedure and records connected with the ordering, printing, pre-numbering, storage and registering, and issue of blank passes. All blanks must be accounted for — either evidenced by an application form by a retained cancelled (spoilt) blank or held as stock.
6. Inspect a sample of applications to ensure that passes are only issued to qualified persons. Attempt to satisfy yourself as to existence of applicant and correctness of details supplied — electoral roll and D.H.S.S. local office may assist this. Ensure that at least two officials are involved in the actual issue.
7. Observe the procedure as it is applied to a number of applications as they pass through the system and be present at the time of issue.
8. If a charge is made for new passes or replacement of those lost, vouch that the correct amount (the number issued times the charge) is receipted and the cash paid into the bank and the correct entries made in the income (nominal) account.
9. Inspect any returned passes for evidence of non-compliance with the procedures of issue, lack of authenticity, etc..
10. Ensure that conductors are properly instructed how to check passes when they are presented and observe the degree of compliance whenever you ride on a bus (on occasion, paying the fare instead of presenting your pass).

(j) *Property Left on Buses*
1. Read the statutory regulations in force governing the procedures in regard to items left on buses. Note the scale of charges payable by the claimants, amounts due to the conductors who have handed articles in, and the content of the records to be kept.
2. Obtain a copy of the Executive's rules and test them for adequacy.
3. Acquire copies of all register folios, forms, receipts, etc. and inspect them for completeness of detail and adequacy of design. Ensure all these are controlled as to ordering, pre-numbering, entry in register of stock, storage and security, and issue to the office staff. Such forms could include lost property register sheets, receipts given to conductors for items, receipts given to claimants in respect of cash received for charges, forms for listing items sent to public auction.
4. Visit the lost property department and check the completeness of all pre-numbered documents shown as held. Check the cash and trace it to bank in due course.

5. Check the completeness of the numbering of all entries made since the last visit. Check all additions, balancing cash received with the bank records for the period. Ensure correctly coded per budget vote.
6. Compare a sample of entries in the lost property register with the corresponding receipts issued to conductors. Take a sample of the counterfoils of the receipts and compare with the register.
7   Check the disposal of a number of randomly selected items.
   (a) If claimed, then check correctness of charge, receipt of cash, trace cash to bank, check accuracy of conductor's reward and trace it to his wages record.
   (b) If sold at auction, then test that statutory period has passed for retention, check auction list and vouch receipt of money from the auctioneer into the bank via his certificate of sales.
   (c) If still held, inspect a number of items to ensure they are there, especially those held for a long time and of attractive nature in a monetary sense. Use commonsense in cases where items are written off because they proved to be of perishable nature and had to be disposed of as valueless.
8. Check that all notices to the public are properly shown in the lost property office and, if present on a bus when an item is handed to a conductor, enquire later as to whether it was handed in. Satisfy yourself that platform staff are aware of their duties in this respect.

(k) *Charges for Emergency Treatment in Hospital under the Road Traffic Act 1972*

1. Obtain a copy of the relevant legislation in force. This is the latest Road Traffic Act and its supporting regulations which provide that a hospital can charge the user of a motor vehicle at the time of an accident for emergency treatment to any injured person involved, at a prescribed rate.
2. Examine the records of admissions and emergency treatment over the period under review, and note the cases where motor vehicles were involved.
3. Enquire about the system of recording details of such cases and the adequacy of the system − that the staff understand their duties, that forms used are clear, that necessary signatures and details of persons chargeable are obtained. Suggest improvements where necessary.
4. Check the details extracted from the records against the invoices prepared in respect of claims and verify the correct charge made. Reconcile the total charge for the period.
5. Enquire into the collection procedure and any cases which are unpaid after a fairly long period to ensure that recovery procedures are being properly applied. Investigate all charges which have been written off, by inspecting correspondence, minutes, etc..

6. Trace the cash received into the bank account by checking receipts, paying-in slips (cheques should be linked to the invoices they paid), and bank statements.
7. Compare the total income obtained in the audit with the ledger figure and that in the final accounts.

(l) *Trust Fund (Endowment)*
1. Obtain a copy of the Health Authority's Standing Instructions regarding the operation of non-exchequer funds. These will include such matters as: –
    (a) The purposes for which gifts may be accepted (i.e. health services or research).
    (b) Such funds will be held in the name of the authority and all financial transactions must be controlled by the Finance Officer.
    (c) All investments shall be entered in a register and all certificates deposited in the authority's bank.
    (d) The Finance Officer must act in investment matters in consultation with the local advisory committee (which contains members with financial knowledge – bankers, stockbrokers, etc.).
2. Peruse the legal documents – deed, will, etc. under whose condition the fund was formed. Note any requirements in respect of investments, use of monies, etc. and check that they have been observed in practice.
3. Enquire as to internal check procedures by which the day-to-day transactions are carried out, and their adequacy and the degree of compliance with them. Obtain list of books, records, etc. and officers responsible for them.
4. Vouch the cash account – receipts and payments – from invoices, correspondence, receipt duplicates, paying-in slips, minutes, brokers' notes, etc. and trace to bank statement. Obtain certificate of bank balance and check the bank reconciliation. Ensure tax deductions recovered, if claimable.
5. Ensure cash items correctly allocated between capital and revenue. Vouch revenue items and test accrual of debtors and creditors, confirming the balances. Vouch and verify the capital items – usually the purchase and sale of investments. Check the investment register is up to date and inspect certificates, ensuring they are kept securely. Confirm holdings with the registrars involved.
6. In the case of sales of investments, check calculations and ensure entry in investment register is endorsed.
7. Consider correctness of use of fund monies – that they are not used for purposes which should be paid for out of public funds.
8. Consider investment policy in regard to possible yield and the use of the Trustee Investments Act 1961. Consider the use of surplus cash.

(m) *Transfer of New Town Housing to a Local Authority*
1. Read the New Towns (Amendment) Act 1976, a copy of the direction of the Secretary of State to commence local consultations, correspondence with Department of the Environment and the local authority, minutes, etc..
2. Obtain a copy of the approved transfer scheme agreed between the Development Corporation and the District Council, containing the terms of the transfer and lists of the properties transferred.
3. Compare the lists of properties with the map of the site of the New Town to obtain some impression of the shape of the area involved for the effect upon administration of its removal from New Town control.
4. Verify the transfer of the properties by observation and checking of rent books, the District Council's abstract of accounts, and the entries in the Development Corporation's accounts.
5. Re-calculate the financial adjustments required by the transfer scheme, comprising the notional loan debt outstanding on the assets taken over and the annual payments by the District of principal and interest for the agreed period.
6. Check the entries in the Periodic Income Register and vouch the actual receipt of the loan debt charges, tracing them to the bank.
7. Verify that the correct New Town grants and Housing Subsidies have been terminated for the transferred properties (houses). Comparison with the accounts of the District which should now contain corresponding items, should be made.
8. Consider the effect of the reduction of the burden of the transfer on staffing needs (i.e. collectors) and on administration generally.

(n) *Quarterly Accounts for Electricity or Gas supplied by Meter*
1. Using an internal control questionnaire, enquire into the procedures for the periodical reading of meters, the preparation and rendering of the accounts and the recovery of the charges. Test the degree of compliance with the system is adequate from inspection of the forms and records.
2. Check that the new supplies which have been applied for since the previous audit have been arranged. Test whether new buildings, etc. in the area have been connected. Check that a sample of disconnections is correct by inspection of state of premises involved, etc..
3. Enquire into accuracy of older supplies by checking a sample of the records.
4. Balance total of supplies at the time of the audit.
5. Check the arrears brought forward from the previous quarter and the carrying out of the recovery procedure under the code of conduct.
6. Check a sample of meter reading cards against rental. Re-calculate charge against tariff. Test the readings of a number of meters and compare them with the records.

7. Vouch a sample of the charges into the rental, compare with previous charges. Carry out all additions to check the total of the rental charges and agree this with the ledger and the final accounts.
8. Sample the receipt of money, tracing it to bank and to the correct personal account. Carry out total checks on the cash received.
9. Vouch all items written off for authenticity, accuracy and proper approval after the full recovery procedure has been operated.
10. Check the meter stock records and compare with new and disconnected supply records.
11. Keep charts, ratios, etc. to watch trends in the various figures.
12. Review the system audited and the method of carrying out the audit for possible improvements.

(o) *Income from the Sale of Electricity for Roadlighting*
1. Obtain copies of the statutory provisions applicable to public supplies, the approved scales of charges, agreements with Highways Authorities (i.e. the County Council, though it may be with the District on occasion), correspondence and minutes, etc..
2. Examine the procedures laid down for connecting new street lamps and lighted traffic signs, etc., for disconnecting those withdrawn from use, for charging per the scales laid down, and consider their adequacy and logicality.
3. Use an internal control questionnaire and observation of actions and records to decide that the degree of compliance with the system is satisfactory. The laid-down procedures and those actually operated must be reconciled to give the optimal approach.
4. Check the accuracy of the records of new connections of lamps, etc. in the period since the last audit for numbers and charge. Carry out a total check of the current numbers charged and the charges made, allowing for disconnections. Inspect a sample of new, older and terminated supplies by visiting sites.
5. Enquire regarding any omissions by vouching new connections from records of new roads, estates, etc.. Maps and street directories may be of use in this work.
6. Check the invoices rendered during the period are correct for numbers of connections and charges made. Their total should balance with that already obtained from the previous audit steps. Ensure that the correct local authority is invoiced for its street lamps, etc. in its area, and that the income is coded to the correct budget code and correctly shown in the final accounts (Income from Public Lighting in the Revenue Account).
7. Review the system of cash collection, trace cash to bank in a sample of cases and in total for the period, test paying-in slips for evidence of teeming and lading, such as putting cheques in the place of cash.

8. Enquire about arrears still unpaid, consider amount and age of each debt and ensure recovery procedure being fully followed. Check any amendments made by the Highways Authority to the invoices when remitting.
9. If any debt written off, ensure that the allowance is authentic, properly authorised and recorded in the minutes and in the accounts. If any cash is received in respect of an item previously written off, ensure that it is correctly treated (usually as cash income, but noted on the written-off copy invoice in the file) and enquire as to possible weakness in the collection system which needs removal.
10. Consider the procedures for their efficiency and costs and whether other methods would give greater value for money. Review the audit programme for improvements to be introduced at the next audit.

(p) *Advances of Grant in support of Expenditure on a Local Authority Service*
1. Obtain the statutory provisions relating to the service and its eligibility for grant aid, e.g. extracts from the relevant Acts, regulations, circulars, directions, etc..
2. Obtain a copy of the procedure for making advances, including forms, any coding lists, flowcharts, etc..
3. Examine system for compliance with the legal requirements and for adequacy of control and internal check.
4. Carry out checks on compliance with the laid-down system. Using an internal control questionnaire and observation, ensure authorisation of payments, calculation of amount and preparation and payment or transfer of grant sum are carried out by different employees.
5. Sample a number of local authority claims and trace them through the procedure from start to finish. In each case examine previous year's finalised claim and District Auditor's report or certificate and ensure final instalment of grant is correct by vouching the creation of the voucher and its payment during the current year. Vouch the current year's advances via the vouchers and the estimate for grant submitted by the local authority, making sure that the calculations, e.g. 90% on account, are correct and instalments have been made on the correct dates.
6. Carry out a total check by ensuring that all local authorities are listed with the amounts available for each of them, and compare with estimate made by the Department which is included in the authorised appropriations. Check that advances are charged to the correct vote code number.
7. Test that payments to date agree with the amount in the vote pro rata to the portion of the year already passed. Report if under- or over-spending appears to be indicated.

8. Consider whether any improvements can be made in the payment procedure and in the audit procedure just carried out, especially with regard to the efficient use of resources and the obtaining of value for money.

(q) *Computerised Weekly Payroll*
Employing Department
1. Examine the internal check and other controls for adequacy in respect of the completion of time sheets, and their authorisation, batching, pre-totalling and transfer as source documents to the control section of the computer department.
2. Ensure that the total numbers and grades of employees conform with the authorised establishment, that new appointments and promotions are duly approved, while resignations, dismissals and retirement are properly dealt with as to date, per the minutes, personal record sheets, etc..
3. Ascertain that the staff comply with the internal control system in a satisfactory manner by sampling time sheets to make certain that the hours worked, hourly rates, various allowances and bonuses, signatures of employee and foreman, job codings, deductions for national insurance and superannuation are correctly entered. Comparisons are made with the national insurance and income tax records. Starters and finishers are completely checked.

Computer Department
1. Examine the internal control system in the computer department for adequacy and compliance by the staff.
2. Ensure that the input (i.e. the time sheets duly batched and pre-totalled) is authorised, valid, complete and from authorised sources.
3. Ensure that programs give accurate results, that no data are lost in processing and that the operators' actions are controlled. To do this, flowcharts are prepared, programs reviewed, program checks incorporated, and tests carried out by test packs, interrogation programs and the obtaining of print-outs at strategic points in the processing.
4. Check that the output is complete and agrees with the pre-totals of the input, and that it goes to those authorised to receive it. Output takes the form of wage advices, cash analysis schedules, bank credit sheets, job costings, expenditure analysis, national insurance and income tax tabulations, etc..

Wages Department
1. Carry out tests upon the output documents in total and by sampling individual wage calculations back to source documents. Trace the income tax, superannuation and insurance contributions to the bank.

2. Examine the system for obtaining the cash and making up the wage packets, their transporting to pay stations, their payment to employees and the return and disposal of unpaid wages.
3. Check compliance with the system from observation and documentary evidence. Pay special attention to security of cash, returned wages and witnessing of payments.
4. Check the accuracy of budget codes − actual expenditure against estimate, and whether value is being received for money in the system being operated.
5. Review the audit procedure with emphasis upon future improvements.

Appendix IV

Examples of Internal Control Questionnaires: –
(a) Remittances received by post
(b) Control of receipt books
(c) Certification of invoices
(d) Ascertainment of sundry creditors at the balance sheet date
(e) Control of presigned cheques
(f) Control of petrol or motor fuel issues
(g) Fares from bus passengers
(h) Patients' property

I.C.Q.s are usually laid out in columnar form: –
i.e. column 1   serial numbers of the questions
    column 2   the question
    column 3   YES/NO replies
    column 4   Comments

It is a convention for a YES reply to a question to indicate that the particular procedure is adequate in this respect, whereas a NO reply implies that a weakness exists at this point.

The comments column is intended to contain answers such as names, numbers, and explanations, including errors discovered in the answers. The initials of the questioner are also entered here on occasion.

(a) *Remittances received by Post*
1. Is the incoming post protected against unauthorised interference before it reaches the officers who are authorised to open it?
2. If so, how does this occur?
3. Is the post opening location secure against unauthorised intrusion?
4. Is the post opened by at least two authorised officers who are present all the time?
5. Neither or none of the officers is involved in later handling of the cash or receipts or in recording book entries?
6. Is cash enclosed in an envelope counted and recorded as soon as the envelope is opened?
7. Is each open cheque, postal or money order crossed "a/c Payee" immediately it is removed from the envelope?
8. Is each cheque, postal or money order then immediately recorded?
9. Are all the envelopes opened at each delivery?
10. Is each envelope checked as being empty of contents at the end of each opening session?

11. Does the remittance register show –
    (a) the remitter or payer
    (b) the nature of the debt
    (c) the amount
    (d) whether cash, cheque, P.O., or M.O.
    (e) receipt number (to be entered by the cashier when the receipt is issued)
    (f) identification of cheques for which no receipt is issued per the Cheques Act?
12. Is the remittance register checked and initialled by both officers after the post has been opened and the remittances recorded?
13. Does the cashier sign for the remittances when they and the register are passed to him?
14. Does he immediately issue the receipts?
15. Does he enter the receipt numbers in the column on the register denoted by 11(e)?
16. After completing the register, does the cashier pass it to the internal audit?
17. Are all receipts passed to the post desk for despatch?
18. Does the internal auditor check that the register details and receipts are correct?
19. Does he trace the cash to the bank?
20. Does he check that the procedure for identifying cheques with specific receipts has been followed?
21. Is there a laid-down procedure for dealing with post-dated cheques, incorrectly completed cheques, etc.?
22. If so, give details.
23. Is there a procedure for remittances which are receivable by departments other than the treasury?
24. If so, give details.
25. Are complaints about missing payments investigated by the internal audit?
26. Does the internal audit attend and observe the above procedures without warning?

(b) *Receipt Books*
1. Is the ordering of receipt books restricted to one authorised officer?
2. If so, his/her name and position.
3. Are local printing firms warned only to accept orders for receipt books from this officer in official form?
4. Are the serial numbers of receipts checked on arrival from the printer?
5. If there are any printer's copies, are these destroyed?

6. Are the receipt books stored in a secure place?
7. Are they entered in a register immediately?
8. Are they issued only on signature to authorised officers?
9. Is the previously-issued receipt book taken back when a new one is issued?
10. Are measures taken to inform the public that only official receipts should be accepted?
11. If so, what are they?
12. Is there provision in the system for checking the stock in hand periodically?
13. If so, who is responsible for carrying out the check?

(c) *Certification of Invoices*
1. Is the invoice an actual invoice and not a statement, advice note or order form?
2. Does the invoice contain the name, address, telephone number, VAT number, style of business and other particulars of the originating firm or person which can be checked for authenticity?
3. Is it addressed to the public authority?
4. Is its date compatible with the current period and the date it was received? is it marked "copy"? Has it already been paid?
5. Are the goods or services rendered "intra vires" in nature, i.e. of a kind within the ambit of the authority's operations?
6. Is there an outstanding order, minute, periodical payment folio, statement, advice note or contract related to the payment?
7. Are the prices charged correct per the scale, price list or contract?
8. Have all the entitlements, such as discounts, credit notes for returned items been given?
9. Have any standing instructions or orders been observed regarding the procedure for dealing with items of the type and the amount of the invoice?
10. Have all the stages of receipt of goods or service, prices and calculations checking, coding to budget vote, certification by the chief departmental officer been completed and evidenced by signatures, initials, etc. and with due regard to the division of duties under internal check?
11. Have the subsidiary records been completed, e.g. stores records, inventory, entry in the periodical payments register, marking-off the order?
12. Can the items purchased or the effect of the service rendered be inspected?
13. Are there any other invoices from the same supplier with which this invoice can be incorporated into one payment?

(d) *Ascertainment of Sundry Creditors at the Balance Sheet Date*
1. Is there a list of sundry creditors extracted from the ledgers and certified as correct and complete by a senior officer?
2. Is the list added correctly and does it agree in total with the draft Balance Sheet?
3. Have the unpaid orders been examined and compared with the records of goods received, invoices, statements and correspondence?
4. Have accruals been made to annual payments, insurance premiums, ground rents, etc. to make them conform with the financial year?
5. Have the invoices received since the year end been examined to ensure that they do not refer to the previous year?
6. Are any estimated items included in the creditors?
7. If so, have these estimates been re-calculated and found to be reasonable?
8. Are any sums due to creditors in the list brought forward from the previous year?
9. If so, have these sums been tested for present authenticity?
10. Have correspondence, minutes, contracts, etc. been inspected to discover any amounts owing to creditors for which no order has been issued?
11. Have all creditors who appeared on last year's list and do not appear on the present list been the subject of enquiry as to any sums due to them?

(e) *Control of Presigned Cheques*
1. Is the printing of cheques only ordered on the signature of the Director of Finance or his authorised deputy?
2. Are the printing firms aware of this rule of the authority?
3. Are they asked to notify the authority if approached?
4. After printing, are the cheques securely controlled, viz. are printer's copies destroyed, serial numbers complete, numbers balanced?
5. Is the principal stock of cheques held at the authority's bank in a strongroom?
6. Are issues only made at a specific time each week of an estimated number of cheques certified by the chief payments officer as needed for the following week's payments?
7. Are these issues made only to an authorised internal auditor who identifies himself?
8. Are the cheques transported from the bank to the office of the authority by secure means?
9. Are the transported cheques immediately re-checked for serial numbers and total, any discrepancies investigated, and recorded in the register of cheques?
10. Are the cheques stored securely until called for?

11. Are issues only on authority signed by the Chief Accountant and made to an authorised officer of the computer section on signature?
12. Is he accompanied to computer section by another member of the staff?
13. Are the cheques kept under observation the whole time they are being processed in the computer section?
14. Are the numbers (serial and total) of the processed cheques verified after they have been printed by the computer section by the chief payments officer who signs for them and removes them to his own section accompanied by another member of staff?
15. Are frequent surprise checks made by the internal audit staff upon the procedures carried out to ensure compliance and accuracy of the records?

(f) *Control of Petrol or Motor Fuel Issues*
1. Has the authority its own pumps and tank installations?
2. Is all petrol and fuel delivered to these tanks?
3. Are the pumps and tanks only unlocked when in use and always attended then?
4. Is there a storekeeper/attendant who holds the keys and is responsible for storage, receipts and issues?
5. Is there an official order showing the quantity of fuel ordered and to be delivered? Does the storekeeper have a copy?
6. Does the storekeeper supervise the deliveries and check the quantity by dipping?
7. Does he fill out a stores received note (with date and quantity) and pass it to the cost office?
8. Is this stores received note compared with the order, invoice and petrol issues records in the cost office?
9. Does the storekeeper record the daily state of the pump registers?
10. Is there a daily mileage and fuel sheet (updated at each issue) for each vehicle which obtains its petrol at the pumps?
11. Are the issues per the pump registers reconciled with the mileage and fuel sheets by the cost office staff?
12. Are only authorised vehicles supplied with petrol?
13. Does the driver record the day's or shift's distances driven upon the mileage and fuel sheet?
14. Is this sheet handed in at the end of the duty, countersigned by the inspector and passed to the cost office?
15. Is the stock taken and reconciled periodically and any material differences investigated?
16. Do internal auditors attend at the installation to make checks and observations periodically and by surprise visits? Do they check the records in the cost office?

17. Are the figures of mileage and usage of fuel for each vehicle reviewed constantly and reported on periodically by the cost office?

(g) Fares from Bus Passengers
1. Is each conductor issued with a numbered TIM on signature when he starts a tour of duty?
2. Are all TIMs controlled and accounted for at all times?
3. Is each conductor given a pre-numbered way-bill when he starts duty?
4. Does the way-bill show the date, the route, the bus number, the conductor's name and contain spaces for opening and closing ticket numbers, cash collected, etc.?
5. Is the conductor instructed to enter the starting number recorded on the TIM at the start of each journey?
6. Is the cash collected entered on the way-bill together with the closing ticket number at the end of the duty?
7. Are the cash, the way-bill, and TIM handed in by the conductor to the cash office at the end of his duty?
8. Is the cash, the way-bill details and the TIM reading checked in the presence of the conductor and a witness by the cash staff?
9. Is the agreed procedure regarding "overs" and "shorts" always followed?
10. Do inspectors board buses on occasion and check that each passenger has a ticket of the right amount?
11. Do these inspectors check the conductors' way-bill details?
12. Is the cash paid into bank frequently and with as little delay as possible?
13. Are all the way-bills summarised for financial and costing record purposes?
14. Are copies of the bank paying-in slips passed to the chief cashier's office to form the basis of cash book entries?
15. Are statistics kept up to date for the levels of fares taken on the various routes with details of weather conditions, etc.?

(h) Patients' Property
1. Are all patients informed on arrival or as soon as practicable thereafter that the Authority would accept no responsibility for their valuables and personal property unless they handed them in for safekeeping in return for an official receipt?
2. If a patient is unconscious or otherwise incapacitated, are there arrangements to keep his property safe until he recovers enough to be informed of the rules? Are there arrangements for nights and weekends?
3. Is an explanation given of the nature of the items involved – cash, bank books, documents, valuables, clothes, etc.?

4. Are the items listed by the ward staff on the prescribed form, and the list and items reconciled with each other in the presence of the patient?
5. Is the form and the receipt portion signed by the Secretary who takes the items into safe keeping?
6. Does the person bringing the items from the ward counter-sign as witness?
7. Is the patient given the receipt portion as an acknowledgment of the items taken?
8. Are the items entered in the register by the Secretary and put into a secure place?
9. Do arrangements exist for the transfer of property when a patient is moved to another hospital?
10. Can items be handed in after the patient has been in hospital some time (e.g. gifts received by the patient)?
11. Is there a procedure for the return of property when the patient leaves the hospital? Is there a form for the patient to sign?
12. Are discrepancies investigated if patient complains of missing items?
13. Do arrangements exist for identifying persons entitled to claim the property of deceased patients?
14. Is there a procedure for the disposal of items where no claimant appears for the property of such patients?
15. Do the audit staff carry out periodic and surprise checks upon the degree of compliance with the procedures and the safety of the patients' property?

Appendix V

Examples of Flow Charts of Internal Control Procedures: –
(a) The ordering, receipt and payment for purchases on credit (manual)
(b) Credit sales procedure (manual)
(c) Admission to a course of study (manual)
(d) Applications for loans (manual)
(e) Sales invoicing and debtors' balances (computer)
(f) Updating stock-in-hand and allocating material costs to jobs (computer)

(a) *Procedure for Ordering, Receiving and Paying for Purchases*
1. The storekeeper issues a Requisition Note for goods needed. There are three copies, one to the buyer, one to the accounts department and one for the file.
2. The buyer prepares a Purchase Order for the goods. There are four copies, one to the supplier, one to the stores, one to the accounts office and the last for the file.
3. The goods arrive at the stores accompanied by a Delivery Note.
4. The storekeeper examines the goods for quantity and quality. He, if satisfied, prepares a Goods Received Note in three copies, one for the buyer, one for the accounts department and the third for use in the stores and the file.
5. The invoice is received from the supplier. The buyer checks it against his Purchase Order and the Goods Received Note, and passes it to the accounts department. Here it is checked arithmetically, compared with the documents held there and certified.
6. The accounts department arranges for the cheque to be drawn and sent to the supplier.

312

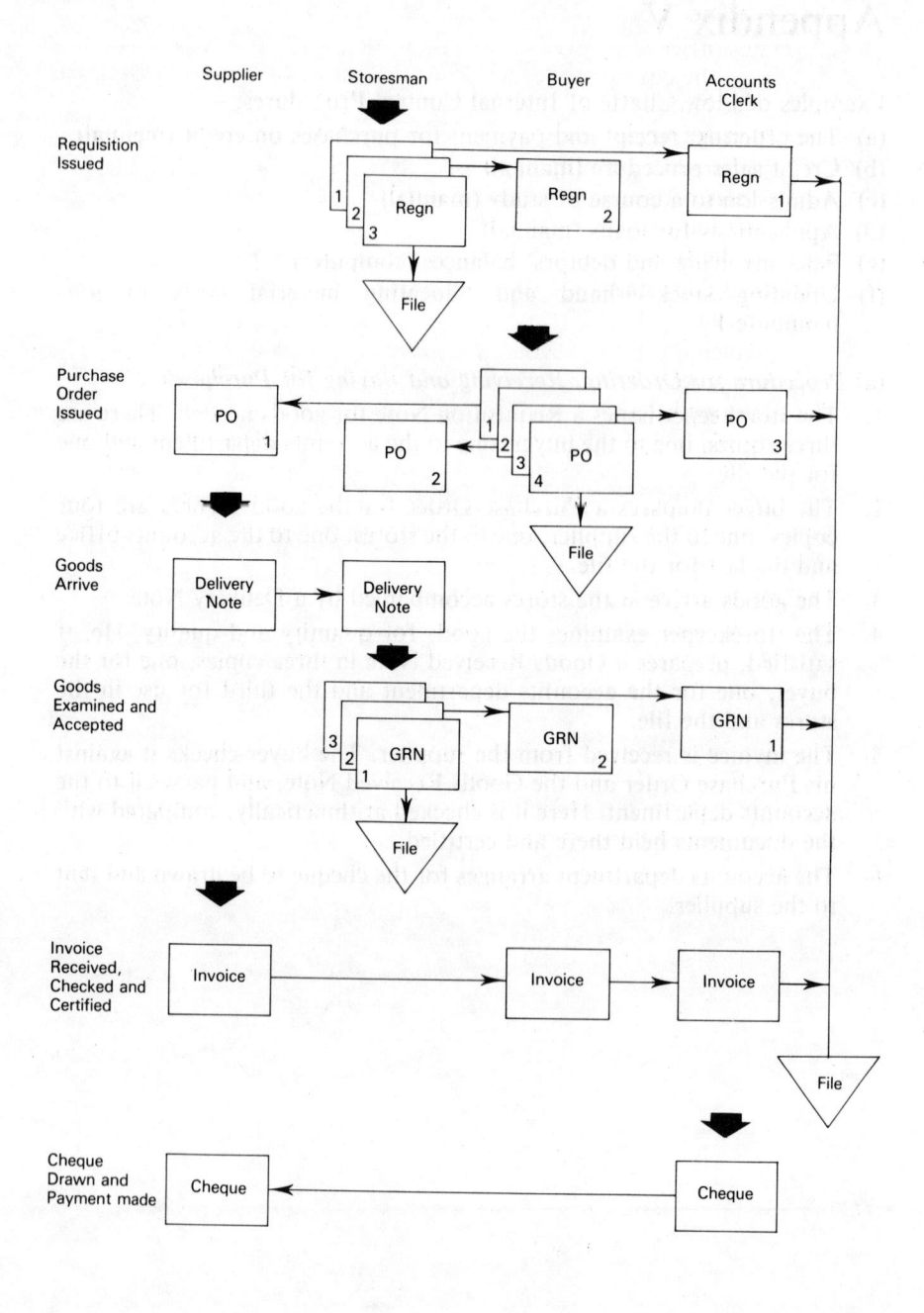

	Supplier	Storesman	Buyer	Accounts Clerk
Requisition Issued		Regn 1, 2, 3 → File	Regn 2	Regn 1
Purchase Order Issued	PO 1	PO 2	PO 1, 2, 3, 4 → File	PO 3
Goods Arrive	Delivery Note	Delivery Note		
Goods Examined and Accepted		GRN 1, 2, 3 → File	GRN 2	GRN 1
Invoice Received, Checked and Certified	Invoice	Invoice	Invoice	→ File
Cheque Drawn and Payment made	Cheque			Cheque

(b) *Procedure for Credit Sales*
1. The customer's order is received and passed to the sales office.
2. The sales office clerk prepares a Sales Order with four copies from the details on the customer's order. The first copy goes to the customer as an Advice Note and confirmation of the order, the second to the credit controller for approval.
3. After the credit controller has approved the Sales Order and returned it to the sales office, the third and fourth copies are sent to Despatch as authorisation to release the goods and send them. The approved copy goes on the file.
4. The third copy accompanies the goods as a Delivery Note, while the fourth is passed to Invoicing.
5. The invoicing clerk prepares the Invoice. There are three copies. The top copy goes to the customer, the second to the accounts clerk for collection and the third is filed with the copy of the Sales Order.
6. The cheque is remitted by the customer to the accounts office.

314

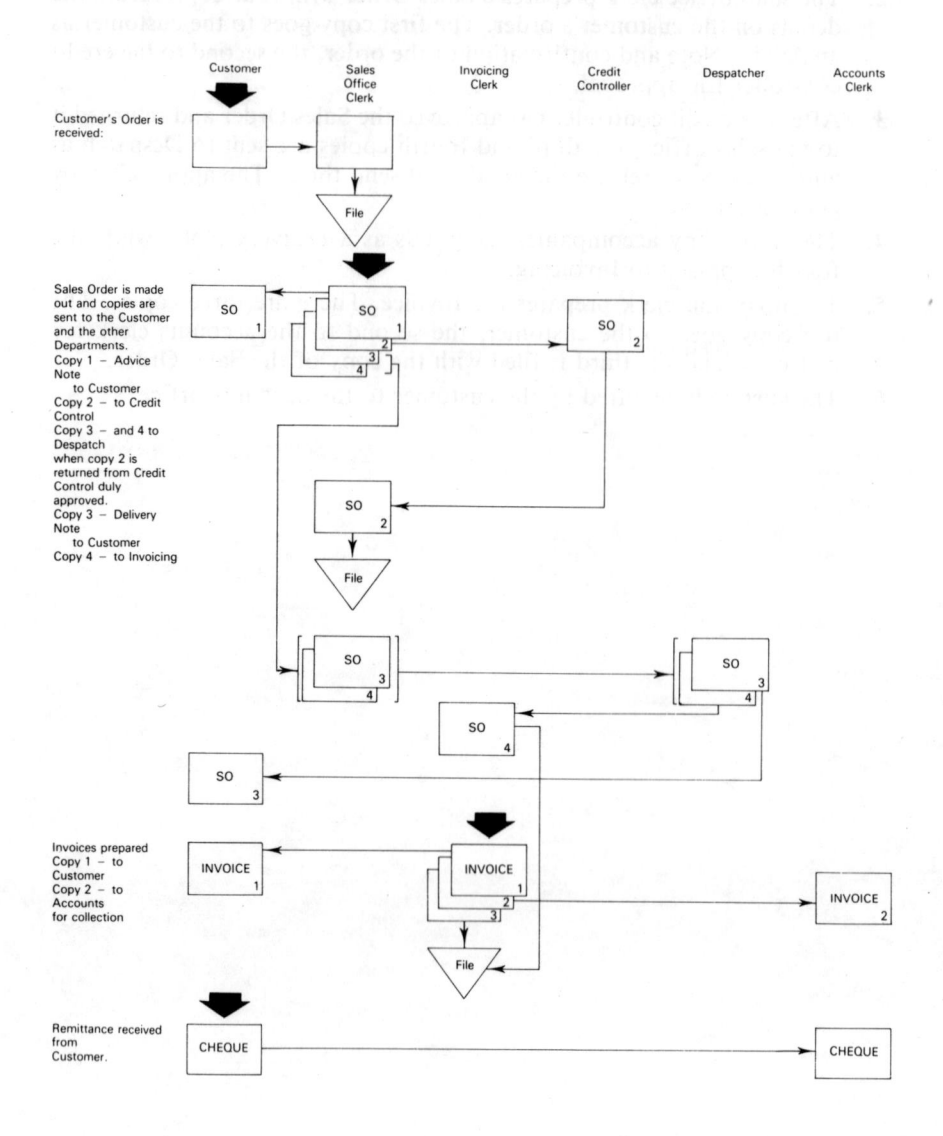

	Customer	Sales Office Clerk	Invoicing Clerk	Credit Controller	Despatcher	Accounts Clerk

Customer's Order is received:

⬇ → ☐ → ▽ File

Sales Order is made out and copies are sent to the Customer and the other Departments.
Copy 1 – Advice Note
   to Customer
Copy 2 – to Credit Control
Copy 3 – and 4 to Despatch when copy 2 is returned from Credit Control duly approved.
Copy 3 – Delivery Note
   to Customer
Copy 4 – to Invoicing

SO 1 ← SO 1,2,3,4 → SO 2

SO 2 → ▽ File

SO 3,4 → SO 3,4

SO 4

SO 3

Invoices prepared
Copy 1 – to Customer
Copy 2 – to Accounts for collection

INVOICE 1 ← INVOICE 1,2,3 → INVOICE 2

▽ File

Remittance received from Customer.

⬇ CHEQUE → CHEQUE

(c) Procedure for Admissions to Course of Study

1. The Application Form is first registered by Administration.
2. The form is checked for completeness of detail. If it is incomplete it is returned to the Applicant for the missing details to be inserted.
3. If the Applicant has the necessary qualifications for entry to the Course, a letter offering a place is sent.
4. If the Applicant has not got the necessary entry qualifications and no prospect of getting them before the course starts, a rejection letter is sent.
5. If the Applicant has a good prospect of obtaining the necessary entry qualifications before the course starts, a conditional offer of a place is made, dependent on success.
6. Otherwise, the Applicant is asked to re-apply after receiving a successful result in obtaining the necessary qualifications.

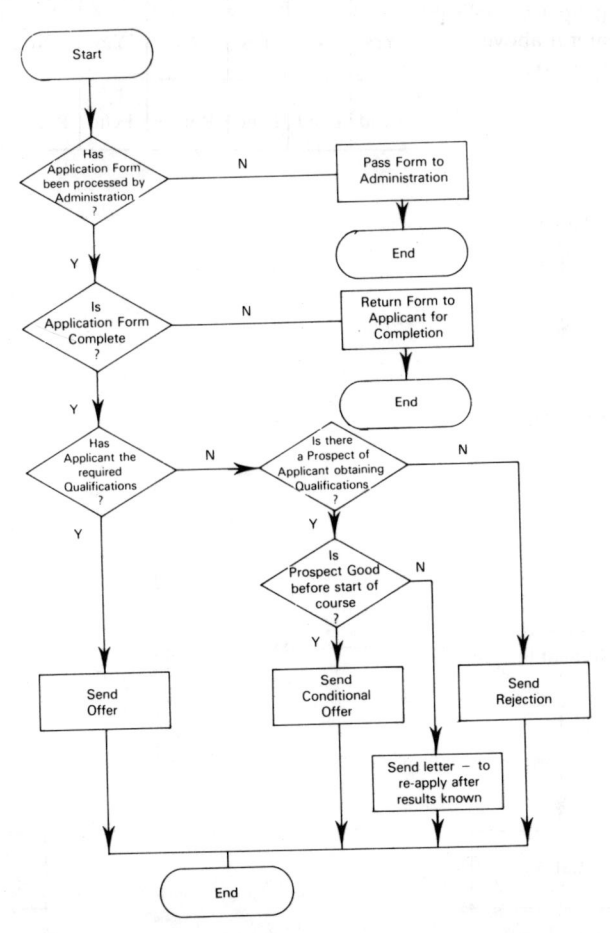

(d) *Applications for Loans*

A Housing Association has a scheme for making loans to residents. This requires the fulfilling of one, two or three conditions as regards the resident's status. The following decision table represents a guide to the officer who vets the applications: –

Applicant –   Combinations of Conditions

	1	2	3	4	5	6	7	8
1. Earns above limit laid down for amount of loan	Yes	Yes	Yes	Yes	No	No	No	No
2. Offers a guarantee from an acceptable person	Yes	Yes	No	No	Yes	Yes	No	No
3. Owns property applicable as collateral above amount of loan	Yes	No	Yes	No	Yes	No	Yes	No
	Lend	Lend	Lend	Refuse	Lend	Refuse	Lend	Refuse

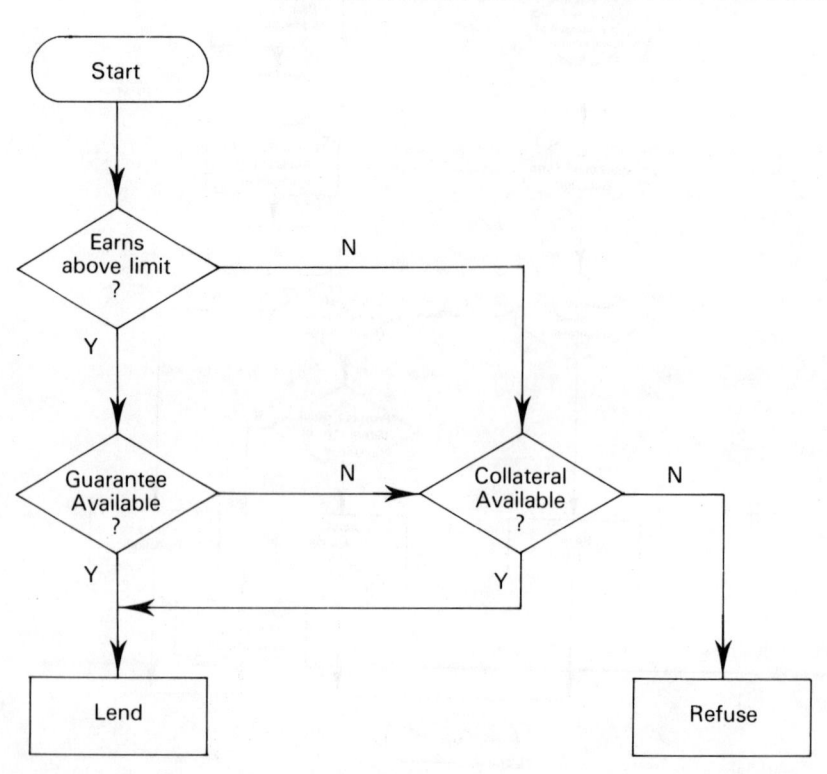

(e) *Procedure for Sales Invoicing and Debtors' Balances*
1. The prime documents for the period are batched – the sales notes, credit notes, items written off, cash receipt counterfoils, and discounts allowed – and converted to punched cards which are then verified.
2. The punched cards are input to the computer and subjected to a data validation (or datavet) program. Any errors are corrected and re-input.
3. The validated data are now output in the form of a magnetic tape file and thereafter sorted by a sort program into debtor number order in order to form the transaction file. (The debtors' balances brought forward file is already in debtor number order).
4. The transaction file is merged with the balances brought forward file by a sales invoicing and debtors' balances program.
5. This program produces the updated debtors' balances carried forward tape file and prints out sales invoices, total sales analysed and exception or error reports.

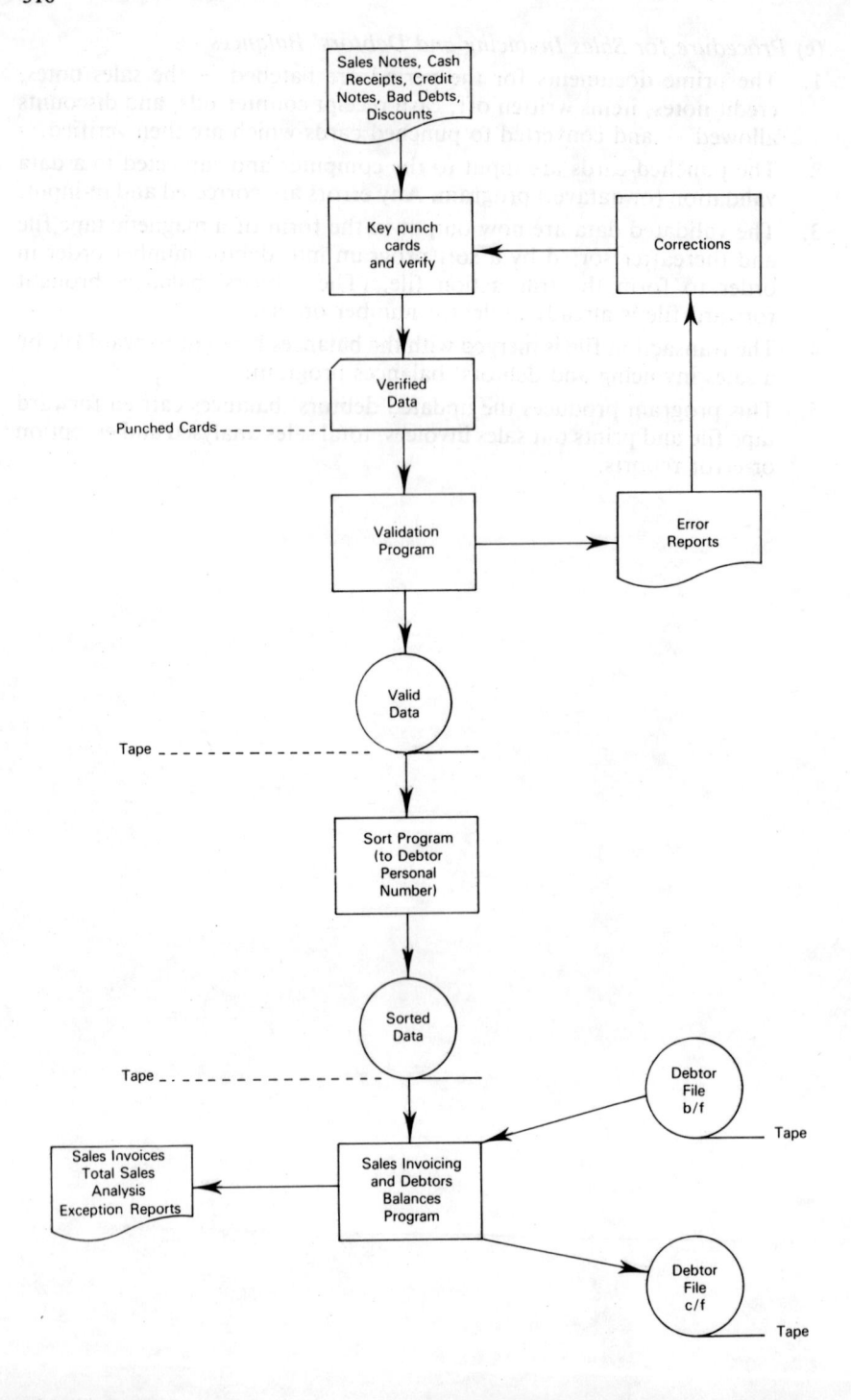

```
                    ┌──────────────┐
                    │ Sales Notes, │
                    │ Cash Receipts,│
                    │ Credit Notes,│
                    │ Bad Debts,   │
                    │ Discounts    │
                    └──────┬───────┘
                           │
                    ┌──────▼───────┐        ┌──────────────┐
                    │  Key punch   │        │              │
                    │    cards     │◄───────┤ Corrections  │
                    │  and verify  │        │              │
                    └──────┬───────┘        └──────────────┘
                           │
                    ┌──────▼───────┐
                    │   Verified   │
                    │     Data     │
Punched Cards ─────── └──────┬───────┘
                           │
                    ┌──────▼───────┐        ┌──────────────┐
                    │  Validation  │───────►│    Error     │
                    │   Program    │        │   Reports    │
                    └──────┬───────┘        └──────────────┘
                           │
                       ╭───▼───╮
                       │ Valid │
                       │ Data  │
Tape ─────────────────── ╰───┬───╯
                           │
                    ┌──────▼───────┐
                    │ Sort Program │
                    │  (to Debtor  │
                    │   Personal   │
                    │   Number)    │
                    └──────┬───────┘
                           │
                       ╭───▼───╮
                       │Sorted │
                       │ Data  │
Tape ─────────────────── ╰───┬───╯         ╭──────────╮
                           │               │  Debtor  │
                           │       ┌───────┤  File    │─── Tape
                           │       │       │   b/f    │
                           │       │       ╰──────────╯
┌──────────────┐    ┌──────▼───────▼┐
│Sales Invoices│    │ Sales Invoicing│
│ Total Sales  │◄───┤  and Debtors   │
│  Analysis    │    │   Balances     │
│Exception Reports│ │   Program      │
└──────────────┘    └──────┬─────────┘
                           │
                           │       ╭──────────╮
                           └──────►│  Debtor  │
                                   │   File   │─── Tape
                                   │   c/f    │
                                   ╰──────────╯
```

(f) *Procedure for Updating Stock-in-Hand and Allocating Material Costs to Jobs.*

1. The materials received notes, materials issued notes, materials transferred notes and materials returned notes for the period are batched and converted into punched cards which are verified.
2. The punched cards are input to the computer and subjected to a data validation program and any errors are corrected and re-input.
3. The validated data is output as a magnetic tape and this is sorted by a sort program into materials code number sequence.
4. The sorted transaction tape is merged with the stock-in-hand brought forward tape by an updating program which produces the stock-in-hand carried forward tape, the materials issued tape and prints out quantities and values for materials received, materials issued, stock-in-hand, and exception reports.
5. The materials issued tape is then re-sorted to job number sequence, and subjected to a program which prints out a tabulation showing material costs chargeable to jobs.

320

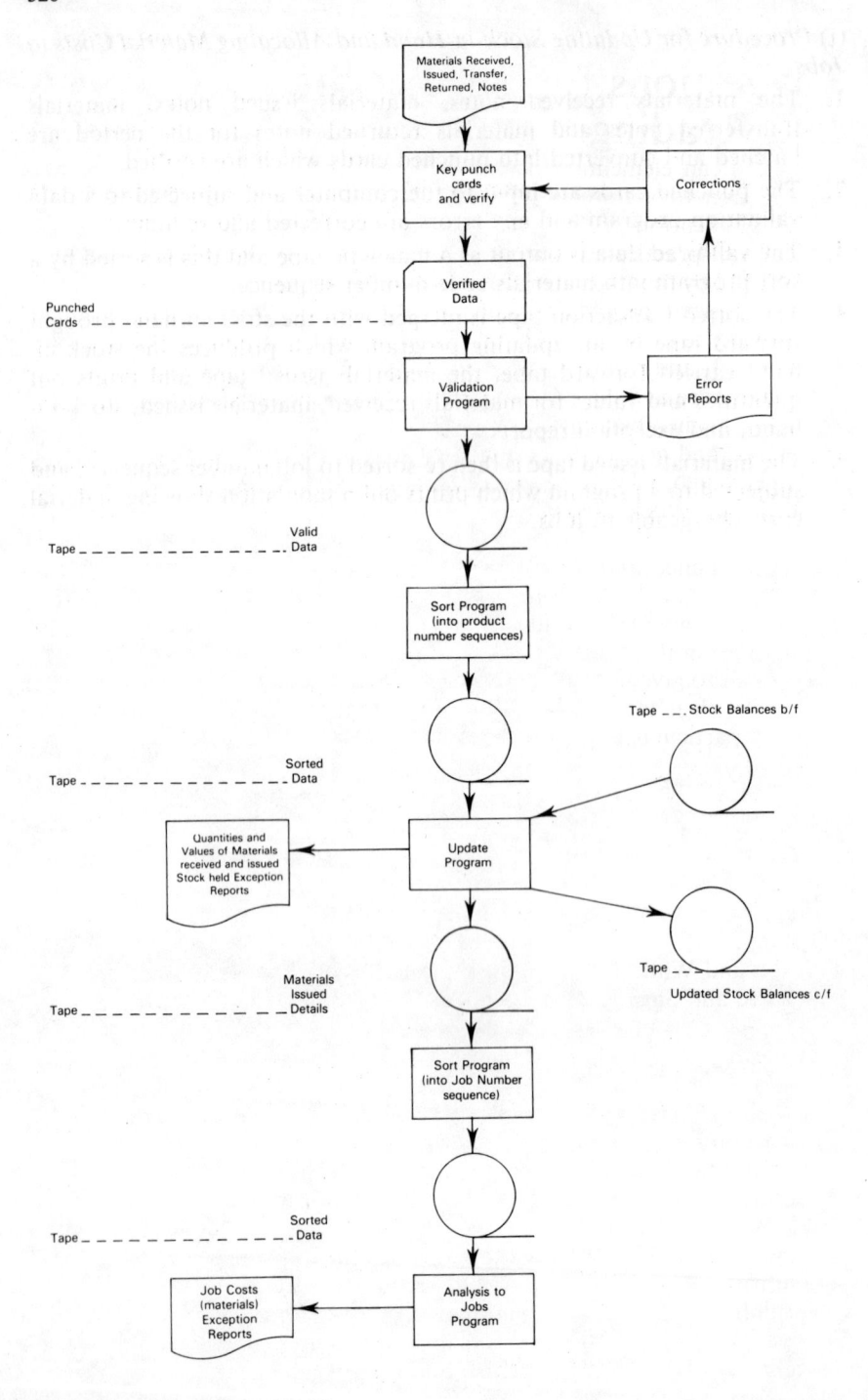

```
                    ┌──────────────┐
                    │ Materials Received,│
                    │ Issued, Transfer,  │
                    │ Returned, Notes    │
                    └──────┬───────┘
                           ▼
                    ┌──────────────┐      ┌──────────────┐
                    │  Key punch   │◀─────│  Corrections │
                    │   cards      │      │              │
                    │  and verify  │      └──────▲───────┘
                    └──────┬───────┘             │
                           ▼                     │
                    ┌──────────────┐             │
                    │   Verified   │             │
                    │    Data      │             │
                    └──────┬───────┘             │
                           ▼                     │
Punched                                          │
Cards  ─ ─ ─ ─ ─ ─ ─ ─ ─                         │
                    ┌──────────────┐      ┌──────────────┐
                    │  Validation  │─────▶│    Error     │
                    │   Program    │      │   Reports    │
                    └──────┬───────┘      └──────────────┘
                           ▼
                         ( ○ )
                           │
                                           Valid
Tape ─ ─ ─ ─ ─ ─ ─ ─ ─ ─ ─ ─ Data
                           ▼
                    ┌──────────────┐
                    │ Sort Program │
                    │ (into product│
                    │  number      │
                    │  sequences)  │
                    └──────┬───────┘
                           ▼
                         ( ○ )                  Tape ─ ─ ─ Stock Balances b/f
                                                      ( ○ )
                                Sorted
Tape ─ ─ ─ ─ ─ ─ ─ ─ ─ ─ ─ ─ ─ ─ Data
                           ▼                          │
    ┌──────────────┐   ┌──────────────┐◀──────────────┘
    │ Quantities and│  │              │
    │ Values of    │◀──│   Update     │
    │ Materials    │   │   Program    │
    │ received and │   │              │──────▶( ○ )
    │ issued Stock │   └──────┬───────┘
    │ held Exception│          │               Tape ─ ─ ─
    │ Reports      │          │               Updated Stock Balances c/f
    └──────────────┘          ▼
                         ( ○ )
                                           Materials
                                           Issued
Tape ─ ─ ─ ─ ─ ─ ─ ─ ─ ─ ─ ─ ─ ─ Details
                           ▼
                    ┌──────────────┐
                    │ Sort Program │
                    │ (into Job    │
                    │  Number      │
                    │  sequence)   │
                    └──────┬───────┘
                           ▼
                         ( ○ )
                                           Sorted
Tape ─ ─ ─ ─ ─ ─ ─ ─ ─ ─ ─ ─ ─ ─ Data
                           ▼
    ┌──────────────┐   ┌──────────────┐
    │ Job Costs    │◀──│  Analysis to │
    │ (materials)  │   │  Jobs        │
    │ Exception    │   │  Program     │
    │ Reports      │   └──────────────┘
    └──────────────┘
```

Suggestions for Further Study and Reading

A work of an elementary nature such as this which is intended to be an introduction to a fairly wide span of subjects may be criticised for the failure to mention professional accountancy matters, such as the various accounting practice standards which have been drawn up and are encouraged by the leading bodies of accountants with the aim of developing sound financial procedures and statements. For this reason, I take the opportunity to draw the attention of the reader to the eminent role played in the study of, and research into, public finance by the Chartered Institute of Public Finance and Accountancy, duly supported by the subscriptions and efforts of its members, over many years. This is especially so, since its areas of interest and activity were increased by the granting of a Royal Charter some years ago, when it relinquished its former more restrictive title of the Institute of Municipal Treasurers and Accountants. The reader is recommended to peruse the Chartered Institute's monthly magazine "Public Finance and Accountancy" and the numerous publications on many aspects of public sector finance which flow from CIPFA, which, in my opinion, go far beyond any other source in helping the student and practitioner in this field.

I also wish to give a list of books for recommended reading but would like to make it clear that the omission of a title from this list in no way means that any particular book is not recommended.

Abernethy	Internal Audit in Local Authorities and Hospitals
Barber	Local Government
Barber	Public Administration
Baugh	Introduction to Social Services
Cross	Principles of Local Government Law
Golding	Local Government
Hanson and Walles	Governing Britain
Hardacre and Sage	Local Authority Capital Finance
Hart	Local Government and Administration
Hepworth	Finance of Local Government
Jacques	Health Services
Marshall	Financial Management in Local Government
Normanton	Accountability and Audit of Governments
Redcliffe-Maud and Wood	English Local Government Reformed
Richards	Reformed Local Government System
Rockley	Accounting for Local and Public Authorities
Seeley	Local Government Explained
Stonefrost	Capital Accounts of Local Authorities
Thornhill	Nationalised Industries
Tivey	Nationalised Industries since 1960
Wright	British Social Services

Index

Abstract of Accounts 116
Accounting Entries 98
Accounting Procedures 97
Accounting Rate of Return 126
Accounts Regulations 1930 144
Additional Sources of Income to Local
    Authorities 75
Advisory Committee on Local
    Government Audit 140
Agriculture, Fisheries and Food,
    Department of 243
AG v De Winton 144
Allotments 43
Alternative Population 161
Analytical Techniques 162
Annual Supply Charges 249
Appropriation Accounts 251
Area Electricity Boards 230, 231
Area Gas Boards 222
Area Health Authorities 205, 207, 209
Art Galleries 27
Assigned Revenues 59, 76
Attributes Sampling 161
Audit Arrangements
    – Central Departments 251
    – Development Corporations 201
    – Electricity Supply Industry 237
    – Gas Supply Industry 227
    – Health Authorities 220
    – Local Authorities 131, 143
    – Passenger Transport Executives
        195
    – Public Corporations 256, 260, 262,
        263, 265, 267, 270, 272, 275
    – Water Authorities 187
Audit Code of Practice 138
Audit Committees 175
Auditing Cases 141
Audit Procedure 150
Audit Programmes 152, 157, 288
Audit Reports 139
Audit Techniques 153

Bains Report 50, 92
Banking Arrangements 104
Bank Overdraft 83
Batch Costing 121
Behavioural Auditing 175
Bill Discounting 83
Block Grant 75, 76
Break-even Analysis 285
British Aerospace 259
British Airways 261

British Broadcasting Corporation 262
British Electricity Authority 230
British Gas Corporation 223
British Independent Steel Producers'
    Association 269
British National Oil Corporation 264
British Rail 265
British Steel Corporation 267
British Telecom 273
British Transport Commission 190
Budgetary Control Systems 95
Budget Speech 250
Bye-laws 22

Cabinet Membership 246
Capital Accounts 110
Capital Budget 96
Capital Fund 44
Cash Book 98
Cash Flow Budget 97
Cash Limits System 249, 257
CEGB 230, 231
Cemeteries 27
Central Administration Charges 109
Central Departments 238
Central Electricity Authority 230
Central Electricity Board 229
Central Electricity Generating Board
    230, 231
Central Interest Account 183
Central Transport Consultative
    Committee 267
Chartered Institute of Public Finance
    and Accountancy 116, 321
Chief Internal Auditor 147
CIPFA 116, 321
Circularising 154
Civic Entertainments 43
Civil Aviation Authority 262
Civil Defence 28
Civil Service Colleges 241
Civil Service Department 240
Coal Consumers' Councils 269
Code of Practice – Gas and Electricity
    226, 233
Commission for Racial Equality 242
Commission for the New Towns 198
Committee of Expenditure 250
Committee Procedure 51
Committees 49
Communities 26
Community Health Councils 213
Community Health Services 214

Community Land 29
Comptroller and Auditor General 250
Compulsory Purchase of Land 21
Computer Audit 170
Computer Departmental Organisation 168
Computer Flow Charts 165
Computerised Systems 167
Confirmation 154
Consolidated Fund 250
Contract Costing 121, 283
Conversion to North Sea Gas 223
Corporation of the City of London 24
Costing Methods 119, 281
Co-terminosity of Boundaries (Health and Local Authorities) 206
Councillors – Powers and Duties 54
Council Proceedings 49
Countryside and Parks 42
Crematoria 27
Customer Protection 30

Departmental Finance Officers 93
Department of Education and Science 243
Department of Energy 243
Department of Health and Social Security 205, 244
Department of Industry 245
Department of the Environment 244
Department of Transport 245
Development Corporations 196
DHSS 205, 244
Directional Sampling 161
Director of Finance 91
Discounted Cash Flow 126
Discovery Sampling 160
District Audit 131
Districts (NHS) 206

Education 30
Education and Science, Department of 243
Elections 22
Electricity Authorities 233
Electricity – Code of Practice 233
Electricity Commissioners 230
Electricity Consultative Councils 233
Electricity Consumers' Council 233
Electricity Council 230
Electricity Supply Industry 229
Energy, Department of 223, 230, 233, 243
Enquiry 155
Environment, Department of the 244
Environmental Health 32
Equal Opportunities Commission 242

Estimation Sampling 161
Evaluation of Capital Projects 123
Exchequer and Audit Department 251
Executive Councils (NHS) 204
Expenditure Accounts 105
Extra-ordinary District Audit 137

Family Practitioner Committee 210, 211
Family Practitioner Services 214
Finance Director 91
Finance Division 92
Finance Sub-committee 91
Financial Control 90
Financing Budget 97
Fire Services 33
Flow Charts and Diagrams 162, 311
Food and Drugs 30
Foreign Loans 82
Form of Accounts
 – Central Departments 251
 – Development Corporations 201
 – Electricity Supply Industry 235
 – Gas Supply Industry 227
 – Health Authorities 218
 – Local Authorities 117
 – Passenger Transport Executives 194
 – Public Corporations 256, 260, 262, 263, 264, 266, 269, 270, 272, 275
 – Water Authorities 185
Fraud Investigation 172
Fulton Report 240

Gas – Code of Practice 226
Gas – Conditions of Supply 225
Gas – Corporate Plan 225
Gas Council 222
Gas Supply Industry 222
General Improvement Areas 35
General Rate 68
Government Grants 59, 75
Grants
 – Block 59, 75, 76
 – Percentage 59
 – Rate Support Grant 76, 87
 – Specific 59, 78
 – Transport Supplementary Grant 78
 – Unit 59
Greater London Council 24

Health and Social Services, Department of 205, 244
Health Authorities 203
Health Care Planning Teams 213
Health Education Council 214
Health Service Commissioners 213

Highways 33
Hindsight 155
Holding Accounts 109
Home Office 244
Hospital and Specialist Services 214
Hospital Management Committees 204
Housing 34
Housing Action Areas 35
Housing Revenue Account 36

ICQs 156
Income Accounts 106
Industrial Reorganisation Corporation 267
Industry, Department of 245
Insurance Fund 44
Insurance Risks 46
Internal and External Audit Relationships 7
Internal Audit 6, 143, 145, 166
Internal Capital Financing Provision 183
Internal Check 151
Internal Control Procedures 276
Internal Control Questionnaires 156, 304
Internal Financing Reserve 183
Iron and Steel Corporation 267

Job Costing 119, 281
Joint Care Planning Teams (Health) 213
Joint Consultative Committees (Health) 211
Justices of the Peace 13

Land Drainage Committees 180
Legal Decisions in Auditing Cases 141
Libraries 37
Loans Fund Operation 83
Local Authorites 49, 131, 134
Local Government Elections 22
Local Government History 13
Local Government Services 18, 20
Local Government System in England and Wales 23
Local Lotteries 38
London Boroughs 24
London City Corporation 24
London General Omnibus Company 189
London Passenger Transport Board 190
London Transport Board 190
London Transport Executive 190

Management Services 123
Management Teams 55
Manpower Budget 96
Manpower Services Commission 242
Marginal Costing 122
Master Plan for New Town 200
Methods of Borrowing 80
Metropolitan Counties 25
Metropolitan Districts or Boroughs 25
Mini-computers (Micro-computers) 170
Ministry of Agriculture, Fisheries and Food 243
Miscellaneous Health Services 214
Money Bills 83
Mortgages, PWLB and other 80
Museums 27

National Coal Board 269
National Economic Development Council 246
National Enterprise Board 270
National Gas Consumers' Council 224
Nationalised Industries, Select Committee for 258
National Loans and Investment Office 80
National Water Council 179
Natural Gas 222
Net Present Value 125
New Towns 196, 198, 199
New Towns Master Plans 200
NHS Audit Arrangements 220
NHS Finance and Budgeting 215
NHS Form of Accounts 218
Non-metropolitan Counties and Districts 26
North of Scotland Hydro-Electricity Board 230

Ombudsman 63, 213
Operating or Operation Costing 121, 284
Output Costing 121, 283

Parks 42
Parishes 26
Passenger Transport Authorities 190
Passenger Transport Executives 188, 190, 193
"Patients First" 206
Payback Period 124
Personal Accounts 107
Personnel Matters 54
Petty Cash Imprests 100
Planning 39
Police Service 40
Post Office 273

Press and Public Relations 63
Process Charts 163
Process Costing 121
Professional Audit (L.G.A. 1972) 132
Programme Analysis and Review Committee 248
Promotion of Industry and Commerce 40
Property Services Agency 242
Public Corporations – General Remarks 2, 254
Public Expenditure Survey (PESC) 248
Public Sector Accounting 9, 97
Public Sector Costing 10, 119, 281
Public Works Loan Board 80

Quangos 239

Rate Making and Collection 70
Rate Support Grant 87
Regional Advisory Boards (Railways) 266
Regional Electricity Boards 230
Regional Health Authorities 205, 207, 208
Regional Hospital Boards 204
Regional Water Authorities 178
Renewal and Repairs Fund 44
Report Writing 52, 166
Return on Investment 124
Revenue Accounts 110
Revenue Budget 96
Risk Indexes 148
Royal Mail 273

Sale of Council Dwellings 36
Sampling Methods 158
Scrutiny 155
Select Committee for Nationalised Industries 258
Shire Counties and Districts 26
Short-term Loans 82
Small Dwellings Acquisition Acts Advances 36
Smallholdings 43
Social Welfare 41
Specific Grants 78
Sport and Recreation 42
Staffing 54
Standard Costing 122, 286
Standing Orders and Financial Regulations 56, 95
Statistical Sampling 158
Stock Issues 81
Superannuation Funds 45, 56
Supply Days 249

Surprise and Unpredictability in Auditing 161
Suspense Accounts 109

Temporary Loans 82
Tenby Case 144
Terminals (Computer) 170
Testchecking 158
The "Free Twopence" 44
The "State" 1
Town Gas 222
Traffic Commissioners 191
Transport, Department of 245
Transport Functions of Counties 190
Transport Policies and Programmes 192
Transport Supplementary Grant 78
Transport Users' Consultative Committees 267
Treasury, The 245
Twopence Rate for Local Purposes 44

Ultra Vires Doctrine 20

Valuation for Rating 73
Verification 154
Voluntary Code of Borrowing 85
Vouching 153

Water Companies 181
Water Supply – Authorities' Duties 181
Ways and Means Resolutions 250
Weights and Measures 30